My Girl

Adriane Yamin's Memories about her four years dating
Ayrton Senna da Silva

ADRIANE YAMIN

DEDICATION

This book is dedicated to Ayrton (in memorian). It was with him that I learned what love is. That kind of love that simply "IS", that will never end, that is never forgotten or replaced. I am grateful to him for helping me discover, and revalidate over time, my real value as an individual – from that time, when I barely knew who I was, to the present day! During all these years after he was gone, much was revealed, which continuously reaffirmed the legitimacy of the feeling experienced between us, which was, is and will always be an indelible mark that I will carry with me forever. For what we lived and for what we could not live...

ACKNOWLEDGEMENTS

First of all, I thank God for accompanying me throughout my journey;

I thank my parents Amilcar and Marilene, for giving me life, good education, security and love;

I thank my whole family: grandparents, uncles and cousins, for so many examples of simplicity, joy and complicity; family is also where many learnings for life reside;

I thank my children, Rafaela and Pedro. Without them, today, my life would have no meaning and only with their understanding and authorization, I allowed myself to share this story once and for all.

In the course of life, there are also those soul sisters, who choose each other for inexplicable reasons, and this kind of brotherhood made it possible to carry out and complete this beautiful and pure love story. I can actually call these sisters my guardian angels.

My first guardian angel is my great friend and co-author of this book, Anna Osta, to whom I will never be able to repay such affection, compassion and generosity. She was the one who suggested it to me and held out her hands so that we could write my story together; she also helped me revisit these painful memories, which I certainly could not have done on my own. Thanks to her sensitivity and her grand heart, she realized my unresolved anguishes until my adult life and helped me to have the courage to revisit the past, as well as, later, finish the novel when I decided to publish it. It was hard work! No one but her could help me bring such a respectful and loving result.

My second guardian angel is a friend from high school, who lived with me when I still dated Ayrton and was with us on many occasions. She was the one who welcomed me in her family's house to comfort me and support me when I could not show my family members how suffering the break up was. We met again, many years later, when we had both started a family, and then again she gave me emotional support and went beyond: She offered me legal, financial, administrative support. Knowing the whole story, she saw the need to disclose it and believed in its potential. Even though she had her business, her children and her husband to manage, she happily managed to find the time and energy to help me publish this book. Her name is Rôsangela Martinelli.

I also thank each and every one who collaborated and helped enrich this novel with their memories.

"In memorian" I thank my eternal brother-in-law, Eduardo Abdelnur, who was very present in this story and still is, through the loving participation of his friends and family, thus helping me to tell in full what happened.

Forever grateful to Mrs. Neyde and Mr. Milton, Ayrton's parents, for having raised such a special and loving son, and also for accepting me into his family, for the respect and affection I have always received.

CONSIDERATIONS

I think it is important to show my overview concisely about the challenges faced by Ayrton at the beginning of his career, which I watched closely in the period we dated, year after year, so that these professional impressions do not get lost in the midst of these memories.

In 1984, Ayrton raced for Toleman, a second-level team. There, he had not a chance to show his brilliance in the face of the most powerful and perfected cars of the top teams — with the exception of Monaco, where the heavy rain leveled the disparate power among the cars. In this race, he showed his talent, exhibited his strength and scared many consecrated drivers and leaders of F1. The race was interrupted on the 32nd lap, with a red flag, with the allegation of lack of safety for drivers under the torrential rain; by "coincidence", the rookie in the team of latecomers was already in the second position in the race and approached dangerously the leader, Frenchman Prost, who was racing for McLaren at that time. The President of F1, also a Frenchman, decided to finish the race. But the rookie surprised and caught everyone's attention in F1 and outside it, welcoming Lotus the following year.

In 1985, debuting with a top F1 team, he did not have the best car, but he was in a position to join the fight for a place on the podium. The best cars during the years we were together were Williams and McLaren's, followed by Ferrari, Lotus and Benetton; the other teams were the so-called second tier. Ferrari, Lotus and Benetton surprised in some races, alternated in the best performance, but they could not keep pace throughout the championship, like Williams and McLaren.

That year, Ayrton suffered the consequences of being the second driver: His car had no priority in the team, and in the event of a dispute between the drivers, he was instructed to give preference to the first driver. That is, give way to his teammate and first driver of Lotus, Elio de Angelis. A real nightmare for a guy who wanted to win since forever!

Despite this, he started calmly, deciding to adopt a good neighborhood policy and adapt to the team and the car.

In 1985, he had already become the focus of the Brazilian press and was suffering from the harassment of famous people, which he also had to learn how to deal with, so as not to harm his work. After all, he was not there for fun.

As soon as the championship got heated up, he saw possibilities to improve; he wanted the car in perfect condition and made it clear on the tracks that he would not pave the way for Elio de Angelis. That was against his nature, he wanted to impose his competence at all costs. However... a ghost roamed his mind... some car adjustments, partially computerized, were controlled from the pits, especially the fuel. He was terrified that his car would be sabotaged, to force the second driver's preference. Which in fact did not happen!

This year consolidated his confidence as a driver, with two victories, seven pole positions and several podiums. It was also an important year for learning self-control. Ayrton learned from more experienced drivers that it was not enough to know how to drive faster than others, he had to have a strategic planning, know the strengths and weaknesses of both his and other cars, as well as the weaknesses of his rivals. His weakness was impatience and he would have to tame his temper. Another aspect of that year was psychological wars to which he was subjected by the consecrated drivers — obviously, because they were annoyed with that newcomer. Unfortunately for them, it did not intimidate him, it just made him stronger and more determined.

It is worth mentioning that Elio de Angelis was a teammate who did not directly cause Ayrton any problems; their dispute was for power within the team more than on the tracks. I do not recall Ayrton complaining about him at all!

In 1986, Ayrton no longer had the concerns he had the previous year in the team. He became the first driver and was even able to give his opinion when choosing the second driver of the team. But on the tracks, the year ended up like the previous one: competing against cars with more efficient engines.

Ayrton was studied that year by McLaren; however, some requirements of Mr. Prost, first driver of that team, displeased him and he preferred to stay in Lotus, making necessary changes, such as the engine. He was the pivot of the Lotus-Honda merger.

In 1987, Ayrton was more confident, with a new engine that had already proven its superiority and efficiency over the others, in addition to the electronic suspension that other cars were already using. He felt at home in Lotus team, full of hope in pursuit of his first title. There, he had formed a coalition of partnership and loyalty. But in the first half of that championship, he had already realized that he would not be the champion on that team in the short term and resumed his talk with McLaren. It was a hard fight between him and Prost before McLaren, which would last a few months until they reached a final consensus. During the season, Ayrton did his best, although his car was letting him down in several races. He took advantage of the moment to improve himself as a driver and his knowledge on cars and their adjustments. Satoru Nakagima, his teammate that year, a little clumsy, was an attraction by himself.

One of his greatest rivals, in and outside the tracks, lost strength after a serious accident at "Tamburelo"; that one, who could not stand to keep his mouth shut, throwing shade at his fellow countryman and at whoever bothered him (but unfortunately, his favorite target was Ayrton, who although very young, shone and became more and more beloved by fans around the world). In short, that was the end of that evil man's career, who lost his competitiveness as a driver. Maybe he had crashed the car when, inadvertently, he lost his mind by biting his own tongue full of poison.

Ayrton, also in 1987, had already stabilized the differences with the other more competitive drivers, who complained a lot about his audacity when driving, as well as the audacity of some more imprudent ones, such as Nigel Mansell, who had his hardships told to me by Ayrton, angry; but at that time, Ayrton was already enjoying himself in a way that he sympathized with the English man. On the other hand, Prost increased the pressure against him.

In the new McLaren team, Ayrton started 1988 rocking it! He believed he had to be the champion that year! Now more experienced, more professionally structured and with a car with maximum power, technology and constancy... He was sure to be the champion that year! That was definitely the most painful and tense year that I witnessed at his side; he did not accept failures, neither from himself nor from the team. His greatest rival was his teammate: Cold, constant and schemer, who had a car on equal terms and did not accept to have an inferior performance. The strategy during the races was individual: When in the pits, what the best tire for each track and weather condition was, among many others. Many variables could make you win a race, and they were of responsibility and total decision of each driver. Many say that that McLaren car, from 1988, was the best race car of all time, to this day! "Named as MP4/4, it brought fifteen out of sixteen grand prix, the last single-seat McLaren equipped with this propellant, Senna won his first title in Formula 1 with three points of difference to Prost; never in the history of the category has such a strong team been seen" (source: Area H). A single mistake, however, could ruin everything, as it was in Monaco race that year, where Ayrton crashed his car against the guard rail while in the lead and a few laps from victory, caused by a distraction of milliseconds. Think of the level of concentration, focus, determination, self- control and tension that Ayrton had undergone, leaving him in a high degree of stress.

Of course, it was so for all drivers, but Ayrton, because of his temper, did not accept losing the title that year! Under no circumstances! He himself had decreed a lot of expectation for himself as to his performance.

Figuratively, I can say that until then he had shown his claws to his rivals; that year, he reveled the lion's roar to lead the troop.

Prologue

Here I bring some reflections on this love story that I experienced and that took place in Brazil, between São Paulo and Rio de Janeiro.

I would like this story to be received as impartially as possible, as nothing is absolute – mainly due to the nature of human beings to believe what suits them better and due to the sudden change in the cultural perception in our society since that time. To do so, I think it is important to remove the masks, eliminate prejudices, whatever they may be, go back in time and open the heart. I make this invitation: Put yourself in the shoes of the real characters in this book, no idealizations! And thus experience the emotions, feelings and reasons of each one to act as they did, agreeing or not with their motivations!

This story, as it is being told now, is no longer just mine and Ayrton's, but it is also yours. Therefore, I reinforce the invitation to reflect on what really matters.

For me, it was a great life lesson, although very painful, which to this day continues to show me why certain events happened the way they did thirty years ago. While writing this book, I opened my "Pandora's box" so that I could go on with life more lightly.

Despite the experience brought by adult life, I limited myself to narrating the facts lived under the eyes of the girl I was. A painful dive into the past to honor my decision to report, without censorship, the period of our relationship and thus publicly make known the human being Ayrton was, as well as his genius and limitations.

Also, do not be fooled by the lifestyle we both led. Nothing is taken from this life besides the indelible mark of pure love in our hearts. Therefore, I hope our lifestyle to be seen only as a background for this love story. This is a plot about a man who already belonged to the world, with a conservative family education, with a girl who was starting her adolescent phase, in a protected, partially reclusive and absolutely unprepared way for adult life. And how to make that work? The positive aspect is that we were both raised based on similar principles, valued by our families, with parents who cultivated love for the family, according to the good customs of the time.

This narrative will show the great effort we made as a couple to stay together; the sacrifices and concessions often made against our will; as well as the tenacity to keep our feet on the ground so as not to succumb to loneliness; the fame and harassment; and the natural demands of each one's life. Because, in the end, we were just two human beings hoping to overcome obstacles, fighting for what we believed to be an important part of our dreams, to be happy in the long term.

I heard a little while ago people saying that "to be a great driver, one cannot stick to the past, nor plan for the future, but live only the present!", which made me understand more clearly what happened. I believe that the characteristic that distinguished Ayrton from the others and that made him an exceptional driver was to follow his positioning to the letter in every aspect of his life. Somehow, this made our history of love unfeasible. By the day of his death, setting up a family was not his goal and his personal life was not the priority.

However, and precisely because of this, the internal conflicts persisted even after our breakup and, in parallel, each of us sought, in vain, that same pure feeling in more "convenient" or "suitable" companies for the life we chose to lead. Nonetheless, things of love are not subject to "power and control", as the heart does not follow orders.

Enjoy this opportunity to experience a story with extreme and almost unbelievable situations, even for me!

Chapter I

To start this story, I shall first tell a small summary of my life until the day Ayrton and I met. I believe it is an essential preamble to elucidate the environment in which he, at a certain point in his life and for four long years, made his home and refuge. Where he recharged his faith, strength and energy to face professional challenges, if not the most difficult phase of his career, definitely the phase of construction and realization of his greatest dream.

My name is Adriane Yamin and I am the youngest of three sisters.

My father, Amilcar Farid Yamin, is the eldest of five siblings in a Syrian-Lebanese family. As a boy, he made a few bucks by doing small repairs – from ballpoint pen to bike tires – and by pushing shopping carts at the market near his house to go to the movies or eat his favorite bologna sandwich. Later, he started to work in the industry in his maternal uncle's factory in the city of São Paulo and was even more interested in working. His first job was in the warehouse at the Corona lighter factory, where he learned how to use thermoplastic injection molding machines. Self-taught and visionary, he designed the project for an electric shower in thermoplastic and proposed a partnership with the owner of the company he worked to develop the product. He managed, in his own words, to "make an egg stand, as Columbus did" when, at the age of 18, he saw his fiancée pouring pasta with boiling water into a plastic colander. Surprised by the fact that the material could withstand such temperature, he developed a technology to use the same material in the manufacture of showers. The idea was so successful that, when he turned 21, newly married, Amilcar opened his own company, "Duchas Corona", which soon became a large metallurgical industry. He was able to turn his life's obstacles into an opportunity of success.

My mother, Marilene Rocha Yamin, is the daughter of Portuguese immigrants and had only one older sister, aunt Marilda, my godmother in baptism. Her family sold roasted coffee at the Municipal Market of São Paulo in the thirties. The business prospered and became a company that initially was called Café Rocha and then, after merging with another group, was renamed Café Jardim. My mother, who was always praised as a beautiful, charming, lovely woman, was very dedicated to our education and family harmony.

From left to right: Christhiane, Lenise and I

My mother with me in her arms when I was 1 year old, at the door of our house, on Rua Pedro

At the time of my birth, dad's company was on the rise. We lived in a house located in the northern part of the city of São Paulo. At that time, children used to go to school from the age of five. Thus, I had plenty of time to watch the street movement until I turned five. I have the memory of spending hours glued to the gate's railing, AMAZED to see the boys walking down the street with those soap box carts and to hear their excited screams with the adventure, speed and emotion.

Me on the railing of my house on Rua Pedro

Lenise, my older sister, also remembers that time: "When were little, we lived on Rua Pedro, in Tremembé. We lived there for five years. Ayrton's family lived down the street. That was how my father and his father, Mr. Milton, met. The boys commonly rode soap box carts on the street, in front of our house."

Shortly afterwards, but still a little girl, I realized how much my father missed having a son who would accompany him on certain activities. That was when I found an opportunity to get closer to him and enjoy moments of exclusivity, when I could have him all to myself. That is how my passion for sports and other activities began, at that time considered as a male preference, such as watching the F1 races.

It is Stela Yamin, my cousin, who talks about my adventurous side: "Dri was intense, she was very special. She was a very sweet, extremely cheerful and playful little girl — and she is all that up to today! Totally fearless and with wide laughter. I have pleasant memories of her when she was little, there was no game that she did not like. She was very tomboyish, she used to touch the worm when she went fishing, she rode a motorcycle, rode her bicycle!"

I also had a lot fun playing soccer. In fact, I would rather have a ball in my hands than any other toy. I thus ended up discovering a certain ability for sports as a girl. This made my father proud, which encouraged me even more to push my limits. Christhiane, my middle sister, was also good at sporting activities and I wanted to be as good as she was, although I was two years younger. When I realized that this was possible, that is, not even age could stop me from trying harder, I started looking for other challenges. Thus, I found out early that I wanted to overcome my limits. I felt pretty good about myself when I reached my goal, although shyness camouflaged my aspirations.

Farm life also influenced my way of being. When I was just a little girl, dad acquired his first cattle farm, his greatest passion to date. The whole family had to accompany him there every weekend, without fail. This included holidays and school vacation.

Partial view of the lake at Fazenda São Judas Tadeu, in Atibaia, SP

Going to the farm in Atibaia City meant freedom and a lot of naughtiness or, in other words, games and fun were guaranteed. In addition to dealing with the cattle, which my sisters and I watched closely, we could ride a horse or a gig, fish in the lake, climb trees and eat fruits taken directly from the tree, go to the chicken coop searching for fresh eggs, plant and harvest vegetables grown in the garden, swim in the pool, ride a bike, play with balls, play tennis or, as we often did, use the tennis court to guide a small red convertible car with a white longitudinal band, powered by gasoline with two-stroke engine, which fitted up to two people weighing 50 kg. There were no restrictions on our outdoor activities, much less on our imagination and creativity. We wore shabby and comfortable clothes that we left on the farm, and to walk on the pasture, we had to wear rubber boots to avoid problems with snakes and poisonous insects. Atibaia is a mountainous city and has a cold and more humid weather, like Campos do Jordão City.

Another lesson I had the chance to learn by going to the farm was living with all kinds of people. It was natural for us to live with everyone with no distinction: From personnel who managed the herd to other breeders and political authorities, present in the "elite cattle" exhibitions (as this category is called) of which we were part. Once, at a national exhibition in the Curitiba City, I remember I received a trophy, an award granted to a cow in that dispute. When they announced the name of the Grand National Champion cow and the name of its breeder – in this case, my father –, at his request, I went to the platform to receive the award, I greeted the people and thanked for the trophy in a natural way, as I had already done on other occasions. I was probably about nine years old and I received the trophy from the hands, along with an affectionate kiss on the cheek, of the then Vice President of the Republic, Aureliano Chaves.

Later, dad acquired another farm, more suitable for handling cattle, because of the flat topography, with a milder and more sunny weather. That was the one that was most frequented on weekends until I came of age: Fazenda São Judas Tadeu do Chapadão, located in Porto Feliz City, countryside of São Paulo.

As my sister and I grew up, our routine continued to be that way for a long time. However, enjoying this paradise had its counterpart: We could not go to parties or travel with friends. We were unable to participate in any event that took place over the weekends. For sporting school activities, for example, to which I was called up, I could only participate if they were held during the week – I could not even dream about the scheduled games to which I was called up on weekends! Perhaps, as a result, instead of developing my skills in some specific activity, I ended up expanding the range of sports activities, always taking advantage of the opportunity for new ones that appeared randomly in my life, such as nautical sports, for example, that I learned when my family acquired an apartment and a boat in Guarujá, on the coast of São Paulo. It was a way to face new challenges and experience the feeling of pleasure of being good at that, thus compensating for the frustrations arising from the limitations imposed by the rules at home.

The convenient solution my parents found to solve the concern related to our social interaction with friends was to take them to spend the weekend at the farm. My parents created a kind of "microcosm" full of fun, delight and news. There, we were almost always with cousins, uncles and grandparents. That way, they combined what is useful with what is pleasant: We could play and have fun, but in a completely safe place and under their control. Deep down, they feared the wave of kidnappings that swept across the country in the mid-1980s.

My aunt Miriam Zarif, also known as aunt Muruca, remembers that time: "Adriane has always been very transparent. She is authentic. She is what she is. She was born in a kind of cradle made of gold. My brother was not famous, but he needed security because he was doing very well. He was a father who protected his daughters, especially her, who was a little girl. They had a pressing fear of kidnapping."

Oblivious to my parents' concerns at that time, my goal was to have fun.

As a teenager, I also watched closely the struggles of my older sister Lenise in trying to convince my parents to loosen their tight grip on us. There was no deal. Despite successive discussions, the rigidity of family rules, the conservative values and my parents' convenience always won, as they wanted to have their daughters around without giving up on their stay on the farm.

I came to the conclusion that it was better to adapt to the situation and calmly accept the setbacks of the conditions imposed.

After all, as mom said, "being happy is a choice;" so, I decided to enjoy all the good things surrounding me. Today I understand my parents' attitudes better – they were always with the best of intentions. Anyway, I know that although I lived a childhood somewhat isolated by this glass dome, quite alienated from the reality, still – or precisely for this reason – it was wonderful.

We were a model of the perfect family! A rigid and demanding boss, but affectionate and generous. A constantly present and very zealous mother. She has always been a volunteer in day care centers for needy children, and later she founded one in partnership with her friend Regina Zarif. Every week, she participated in the work, that consisted, among others, in the development of support activities for mothers to learn handicrafts. Thus, inside their homes, they could generate some extra income that would improve their family budget and they would also receive guidance courses with notions of hygiene and family planning. This was all one of mom's way of giving back socially and, above all, a gesture to thank God for the blessings we received: Harmony, health, prosperity.

Before the institution was founded, sometimes, as a girl, I accompanied mom – at her insistence, it is true! – in the volunteer work she performed at other daycare centers. I was a little scared to fail to meet the expectations of so many needy children, who showed such eagerness for affection and attention. It was not easy, but going back home brought me a feeling of gratitude for what my reality offered me.

Moral and religious principles served as pillars for the education my parents received and, consequently, in the instruction they gave us. My grandfather Farid, who was a dentist and came from Lebanon to Brazil at the age of twenty, always told his children that "it is not the names that makes a man, it is the man who makes the name" and "when you have a problem in your life, look for the answers by looking at how nature works". He believed that it would be possible to find the answer in the nature, in the dynamics of tidal cycles or even in how a bird builds its nest. Grandpa Farid is even mentioned in a book in Lebanon. At some point in his life, the Lebanese received French authorities and were forced to sing the French anthem, which made him urge people to sing the Lebanese anthem; it was their land, after all. He also experienced adverse situations, such as locust invasion, which resulted in food shortages. Therefore, while he lived outside Brazil he had an inhospitable life, but when he got here, he came across the natural abundance of our country and was delighted.

For all this, because of their immigrant background, their religious teachings and lived experiences, they taught us to prioritize actions that would result in the common good, more than in the individual.

Faced with some injustice, my mother would guide us metaphorically: "If someone slaps you on one cheek, offer the other cheek also." We could even hurt ourselves, but never, under any circumstances, do this with others... Another thing mom always told us: "Do not fight, girls! How can we build a world without wars if these fights happen indoors?". Beautiful, but an impossible idea if followed in isolation.

My father, on the other hand, prioritized the family core. "FAMILY FIRST," he said. And he clearly raised the three of us to be devoted wives and mothers. He said: "Nothing is more blessed than begetting a life, and this is a woman's divinity." He said again and again that he hated vulgarity. He also never encouraged us to study; on the contrary, he always discouraged us towards autonomy, freedom, and self-sufficiency. He kept us under his wings and his protection. If we had any rude attitude, he would tame us by saying: "A woman must be like a flower and be treat as such! Rudeness is a man's thing, and men are stupid beasts." Also, he would not allow ourselves to be weak in spirit. When he saw us in a conflict or in a vulnerable situation, he would repeat: "Be strong, darling! When God is for you, no one can be against you! And He will always be beside the truth." Those words really renewed my confidence. In case of slander or injustice, we heard: "Calm down! Truth always comes out. Out of debt, out of danger! Keep calm and serene that things settle by themselves. Just watch it!". He was proud to tell everyone: "Life makes everyone stumble, but I raise my daughters to fall on their feet!". Although they provided us with every possible protection from the dangers of the outside world, our parents demanded of us impeccable conduct; weakness or bad choices were not allowed.

Dad used to say again and again that the birth of each daughter had given his life a leap in professional career, as if God blessed him for it. I remember that, when I was a child, before he left to work, he would kneel by his bed and read excerpts from a little book by Saint Jude Thaddeus, to whom he was a devotee, although nowadays he also turns to Our Lady, who, according to him, for being a mother, "provides help with more promptness and kindness."

"Whoever speaks the truth do not deserve punishment," my Mom would constantly say, to encourage us to be honest in any situation. In other words, any truth, however bad, was better than a lie. And she would guide us saying that right or wrong was an individual choice, because "everyone has a little angel and a little devil telling us what to do. Thus, each one of us chooses which one to listen to." We also heard about the virtues we should cultivate, such as patience, gratitude, humbleness, generosity, honesty, justice, among many others, as an obligation of all people to build a better and more civilized world. We were encouraged not to value what is outside, but the content of the human being and its best inner potential.

Other frequently uttered phrases, depending on the situation, were: "Let not your left hand know what your right hand is doing"; "Do not do to others what you would not want them to do to you"; "No one is better or worse than anyone, we are all brothers"; "Tell me who you are with and I will tell you who you are"; "Do not cast pearls before swine." I learned, at an early age, the prayer to ward off fear: "If Jesus goes with me, I'll go anywhere! And if Jesus is with me, who can be against me?," and that would strengthen me.

With this kind of guidance, how can we not develop a sense of justice, humbleness and responsibility? Unquestionably, character-building guidance was the greatest asset I could have inherited from my parents.

Chapter II

We were a few days away from the end of 1984, in Angra dos Reis City, staying at the Porto Aquarius Hotel, where dad used to moor the boat directly on the pier, almost leaning over the pool of the property. Our boat was, for obvious reasons, named Corona. My aunt Muruca tells: "My brother's boat was more like a ship than a boat, and there were a lot of pretty girls there!".

On this trip, we were a group with four other boats of my father's friends, with families and guests, as we had already done in other years. They were: Uncle Vidal (we could not travel without him) with his Santa Maria boat; Uncle Ivo, Uncle Roberto Zarif and Uncle Zé Callil.

At that time, my sister Lenise was dating Eduardo, who had been introduced to her on a previous trip by Uncle Vidal. However, unfortunately, in the 1984 season, Dadô (as we called him) was not with us due to the recent death of his father, Mr. Omar Abdelnur.

My aunts Nádia and Miriam were there too, with their respective families. These are some of my dearest family members who have always participated in our lives.

It was late afternoon and we had returned from the tour to one of the amazing islands of Angra, as we did daily. I was at the stern of our boat, which when moored was facing the entire social area of the hotel, when I noticed some movement on the pier, very close to where we were. My sister Christhiane and my cousin Andrea came on board with an air of some fresh news.

"Dri, dad is talking to that Brazilian guy who race at F1."

"Which one? What is his name?" I asked.

"I think I heard Ayrton," said one of them.

"Hum. I do not know who he is! Show me, which one is he?" I wanted to know, stretching my neck and trying to identify him in the middle of the group. They were on their feet chatting about fifteen meters from where we were. I always had a bad memory for names, but a great photographic memory.

"Go see him. He is talking to our uncle. There!" Dea suggested, as she has always had a kind of fan mania.

"I won't! What will I do there? I am shy!" I replied and stretched my neck again.

"Go there, you silly! So what? What is the problem? Your father is there!" Dea encouraged me.

"I won't!" I replied, making light of it and disguising how shy I was. "I do not care about it! Whatever..."

When I looked at that direction again, I realized it was too late. Each one had gone one way and he, whoever he was, was gone.

Despite my discreet posture, my curiosity had awakened and my sister noticed it.

"See, you fool? Now he is gone! Serves you right!" she reprimanded me, acting as a know-it-all older sister.

I shrugged. It was pure juvenile curiosity, after all, "knowing him is not going to change my life at all," I thought pragmatically.

At that time, I was fifteen, and I only had had one crush when I was thirteen, which lasted two days because of a failed attempt of kissing. I pouted my lips out and, for three seconds that seemed endless, the boy licked my whole mouth. I was in shock. I spent that night staring at the ceiling, horrified by the experience. Needless to say, that flirting ended there.

After some time, I shared this experience with my sisters and my cousin Dea, who was a year younger than me, and they laughed a lot at me. I ended up becoming a laughingstock and got a reputation for being a fool. For me, that was no problem, I had fun with them and laughed at how ridiculous that situation was. But they explained to me what they knew about the kissing mechanism. Especially Dea, who loved kissing and yearned to live the new experiences that arose in adolescence.

It was a time when you did not often see real kisses on the TV, and when a hot kissing scene appeared, my dad would tell me to change the channel, shouting:

"Change this crap!"

After this unsuccessful kissing experience, I met the platonic love. I fell in love with guys in my older sisters' classes who obviously were not interested in the youngest Yamin. Only later did a crush invited me a few times to go for ice cream near our house. But for a moment I panicked with the idea that he would want to kiss me and came up with an excuse not to go, buy some time, and maybe, some courage. He obviously did not know about my conflict and ended up giving up on inviting me, annoyed with my neglect. Thus, my reputation only got worse. When I turned fifteen, I was the only one in my group of friends who had never had a great kissing experience. I did not find it very funny then.

That night, in Angra, the whole gang gathered at the hotel pier to go to dinner, when someone asked dad:

"Why were you talking to that guy?"

That was the question we all wanted to ask. Then someone added:

"Who knows him?"

All of us, daughters and nieces, were familiar with my father's reserved lifestyle, and for that very reason, we thought it was not likely that he knew the race driver. But to our astonishment, he replied:

"I ran into him today at Praia dos Macacos when I went out for a walk and I asked him if he was Milton's son. I explained where I knew his father from and we found out that, by coincidence, he is very close to our hotel. So, I invited him to come and eat something with us whenever he wanted. He ended up visiting the hotel with a friend and we met again here, on the pier. We talked a little longer, and when I heard they were here alone, I invited them to a ride on the boat with us tomorrow," dad replied matter-of-factly.

"Is he coming?" one of us asked.

"I don't know!" my father replied, raising his voice, a little impatient with so many questions. And completed: "I told him we are leaving tomorrow at 10 am; he comes if he wants to."

We were surprised. Dad did not use to invite young men into his domains, especially where his "little girls" were. He was more like a "pit bull". But then we came to understand that his intention was to be kind to the guy, who was going through a difficult time; he was the son a longtime acquaintance, for whom my father had admiration and respect, he considered him an honest man and a good head of family. I took the risk of asking one more question, intonating the idea of pure sports curiosity:

"Dad, they said he is in Formula 1. Who is he? I cannot remember!"

"It is that guy that was on the news a little while ago. He had a facial paralysis and does not know if he can continue on the races anymore."

That was it! My photographic memory worked. In a flash, I saw the TV scene of a young man approaching and getting into a car in a hurry, trying to avoid the cameras and photographers walking towards him. During the scene, the reporter presented the condition that put his career at risk. The technical name was Bell's Palsy. I must have remembered all this on the spot because when I saw him on the TV, I thought: "What a pity! He is so cute."

For strategic reasons, we did not risk asking any more questions in order to avoid my dad getting angry. He is not very tolerant for questionings. We were all excited about the news, but disbelieving that he would show up the next day.

After waking up, as usual, we went to the hotel restaurant to have breakfast and schedule the day. Moments later, we went all on board, each group in their yacht, starting to move for the departure. I do not know what the others were thinking, but what I thought was: "Oh, he did not come!".

Sailors went to and fro to loosen the boat's moorings and retrieve the anchor for the initial maneuvers. Suddenly, the maneuvers suspended, which made me and the others on board surprised.

I decided to go out onto the right side of the boat to understand what was going on; me, the tomboyish girl of the house, always attentive to maneuvers. I then saw a small speedboat stopped at the bow of the boat with two young men talking to the sailor. I soon realized that it should be that driver followed by a friend. The boat left, causing ripples, and the speedboat followed us on the wake, the central part of the trail in the water left by the vessel, where the sea is smoother and more suitable for sailing.

When we got at the beach in the island we chose, while the boats organized to anchor in pairs, the small speedboat waited at a safe distance until the sailors finished the maneuvers. That day, our group was made by my family, Uncle Vidal, Uncle Roberto and Uncle Ivo, with their respective families and guests. Usually, as determined by the safety rules of navigation, the largest boat – which, in this case, was Uncle Vidal's – anchored first and the other smaller boats paired up on the sides, one at a time, placing the fenders between them to protect the vessels. All the boats anchored and the speedboat could approach the stern, where we were gathered – and where we would do so whenever the maneuver was completed.

Dad had the speedboat tied to our boat so that the guests could come aboard. As it is common in these situations, we made formal presentations, with a certain amount of general embarrassment. My father was the host and, with the help of my Uncle José Carlos, a motorcycle rider in youth, he introduced Ayrton and his friend called Júnior to all of us and the other people on the other boats.

I hurriedly jumped into the sea. I was really anxious to be in that transparent water of Angra dos Reis. I used to look forward to the shutting down of the engines of all vessels for safety reasons. And I did not bother to go down the steps to the sea: I jumped straight away, wherever I was. The feeling of diving in sea water, even today, is one of my greatest pleasures.

The presence of the young men caused different reactions in the girls. I, for example, proved that Ayrton was my type, despite the facial paralysis that left his face's expression a little strange; my cousin Andréa, on the other hand, at that first moment was attracted by Júnior's beauty, as she had said at the time and now confirms: "Dri and I are almost the same age. Our parents were always together, as my mom is her father's sister. So we always traveled together and were very attached. Also, we studied at the same school and were in the same class. She was my best friend, regardless of being my cousin. On New Year's Eve in 1984, when we went to Angra, we were the youngest on the boat. We were not in the mood to flirt, but in the mood for fun. When we met Ayrton and his friend Júnior, we were very distracted. But Ayrton seemed interested in Adriane from the start. From all the girls on the boat – there were many cousins and friends –, I told Dri: I think he is flirting with you! She said: As if. It took her some time to get it. The fact is, he went straight to her and everyone was kind of in shock. Then everything worked out! They started dating there in Angra. At the time, I found Júnior, Ayrton's friend, very cute.

But we were very young and we did not imagine that two guys could come alone on a speedboat and be interested in us. We thought 'it won't be with me'. That was kind of the idea."

Aunt Muruca complements: "I do not remember many details, but I remember Adriane's posture very well. On that occasion, we were on my brother Amilcar's boat, preparing wonderful appetizers. I said: Isn't that Senna? Amilcar said yes and that he was the son of an acquaintance of his. Of course he was invited to enter the board! But Adriane was sunbathing and did not seem interested. He and his friend Júnior got on the boat, full of people, and we were talking, including the younger ones. But Adriane was on her own."

In front of all those young people together, Ayrton noticed that some wore Corona T-shirts, made for a campaign with Sócrates, the soccer player who played for Corinthians. Uncle José Roberto, who worked at the company and was a great supporter of Corinthians, was the one who convinced dad to prepare a campaign associated with the team.

Sócrates, in a campaign for Duchas Corona, with the brand's T-shirt. Later, Corona sponsored Corinthians for some time.

My other uncle, José Carlos, organized the end-of-year games, and he had brought many T-shirts to the group. Thus, Corona party was created for the traditional boat procession on the first of January.

Ayrton was a Corinthians fan and asked him a T-shirt, as if to fit in, and then put it on.

Uncle Zé Carlos' first action was to gather the group on our boat to take a photo and record the moment, which was a big event for him, as a Formula 1 fan. People positioned themselves at the stern of the boat and some sat on chairs, while Ayrton stayed on his feet. I watched at distance, as I was shy and did not want to get closer. People called me and I still resisted the idea, because the space left was right next to Ayrton. And then he called me:

"Come here. Come on!" And he complemented his words with a gesture of welcome with his hand and I, although embarrassed, placed myself next to him.

Renata, Zé Carlinhos, Júnior, I, Ayrton , Marquinhos (hidden), Best, Cris, Dea and Kaco (on his knees)

Ayrton and I on the boat, in a separate conversation

"Why didn't you want to be in the picture?"
I answered:
"Because I was embarrassed to put myself right in the middle of you two." I meant him and Júnior. "It might give the wrong impression!"

Aunt Nadia tells: "Angra was the main attraction in the region and Ayrton was famous, but far from what he would become. He was a skinny type, while Adriane was flashy, but he had that feeling and was totally in love. When a man falls in love, we know. He goes after the girl and does not give up. He pleases her. What Ayrton could do, he did. Another relevant thing, for Adriane, is that for us of Arab descent, it is important that our parents like him, and my brother liked him. My sister-in-law, although not Arabic, was strict and did not make it easy. But Ayrton was very close to our family and to his parents, so it was easy to convince everyone."

After taking the photo, I decided to swim again, and my cousin Andréa and my sister Christhiane followed me. We swam from the boat to the beach, as we did every time in this type of trip. These beaches are only accessible by boats, and

33

it was an adventure for us to be on a deserted beach, surrounded by native forest. That was the beginning of the fun.

I went back to the boat a while later to get the diving masks and fins – we wanted to explore the marine life among the rocks and shores – and I noticed that the conversation with Ayrton about the backstage of Formula 1 remained very exciting among the adults in Uncle Vidal's boat, where the men were gathered.

When we returned – my cousin, sister and I – from that dive, a light lunch was being served and the group had split up, each in their own boat. Therefore, my father and uncles were back to our yacht, along with Ayrton and Júnior. We ate in an informal and relaxed way, each one in their own timing, that is, no time to start or finish, although none of us intended to overeat and compromise on nautical games after lunch.

In a more relaxed atmosphere, everyone started to cheer up. Júnior, Ayrton's childhood friend, was studying Agronomy in São Paulo countryside, and he told very funny stories. He was one of those who made fun of his own mistakes and blunders and cheered up the whole gang. After telling one story, Ayrton, laughing, reminded him of another one to be told. Júnior was affectionately called "Antifuro" by his longtime friend.

Since everyone was satisfied and it was time for new activities, my sister Lenise came into action – she has always been the most sociable of the sisters and the only one of us who had a relationship: She dated Dadô — and suggested that we swim to the beach again. Then we all dived at the same time. I swam looking straight ahead, with my head above the water, at a gentle pace to be able to chat along the way, then I was surprised by a voice, not very familiar at the time. I noticed Ayrton was right behind me, swimming very close. My shyness and fear that he would want to talk to me, at that moment, made me dodge and speed up to create greater distance between us – if possible, I would like to hide under the sand, because the situation intimidated me.

When we reached the beach, the group got together for a quick walk through the sand. I continued to discreetly dodge Ayrton. On our way back to the boat, I decided to swim by dipping my head in the water, classic swimming style, so I would not have to talk.

Once on the boat, someone suggested we go skiing. Ayrton loved the idea because of all the sea activities, skiing was his favorite and his speedboat had exactly the function of pulling ski. I realized that it would be my moment to impress him because I was very good at skiing and had an excellent posture – that was generally the comment of those who saw me playing any sport whatsoever, due to my physical potential. However, we used to ski pulled by the yacht's lifeboat, and the speedboat had a much more powerful engine. I was afraid of embarrassing myself, but still I faced the challenge.

Andréa, Christhiane and I got on Ayrton's boat with our ski in our hands.

"Do you slalom?" he asked, impressed.

"Yes, we do," my sister and I said as we held the slalom ski.

Dea had just joined the mess. Clarifying: Slalom is a word for skiing on the water, pulled by a boat. It is the most popular type of water skiing that exists, monoblock skiing, in which the skier's two feet are attached to a single ski.

Júnior started the speedboat and pulled Ayrton, who slalom-skied wonderfully well. When he went back to the speedboat full of himself, I said quietly to my sister, but with the intention that everyone would hear:

"Chris, go ahead, I do not even know if I will have the courage to go, because I have not skied for a while and I do not want to embarrass myself."

She instantly jumped into the water. I noticed that my sister skied well, pulled by the speedboat, and I gained confidence, feeling more psychologically prepared for the adventure. As soon as my sister returned to the boat, I congratulated her:

"Wow, Chris! You did well!"

"Now it is your turn. Are you going?" She asked.

I replied softly, pretending it was just for her to listen and so that the expectations were as low as possible, so I would not disappoint anyone. Not even myself...

"Oh my God, what a shame. It is in God's hands. I hope I will not embarrass myself!"

Chris did not reply, although she knew I skied as well as she did. That way, those who did not know me, like Ayrton and Júnior, believed I did not ski at all. I jumped into the water ready to overcome myself and I was surprised at myself: I do not think I have ever skied so well in my entire life! The challenge really stimulated me. I liked to show off in sports, I confess.

When the speedboat picked me up in the water when I stopped skiing, I climbed aboard, as if nothing much had happened and felt the silence and everyone's eyes. As I removed the life jacket we always wore as a safety measure, my face showed an expression of disguised enjoyment and a mischievous smile that gave me away. I looked out from the corner of my eye at Ayrton and noticed he was also looking at me the same way, smiling. He told me, as he prepared to drive the boat:

"Yeah, you said you were afraid of embarrassing yourself, huh?" As if he said: "You made the fool out of me, but I got your trick."

I believe that was when we started to perceive our mutual attraction. I felt more confident, which eased my shyness and stopped me from dodging.

When it was time to go back to the hotel, preparations to lift the anchor began. They returned with us the same way as we went: Each one on their own boat.

Close to the hotel, while we prepared to dock, Ayrton's boat approached. He thanked us for the trip and accepted the invitation to have dinner with us. They would just go home to take a shower and soon be back. It made all the "single ladies" happy, who, discreetly, ran to get ready for the boys, including me.

When they arrived, Ayrton and Júnior climbed aboard and we stayed at the stern of the boat to watch the pier's movement while we waited for everyone to gather for dinner. Our parents and uncles had not arrived yet. That was when we, the young ones, had the opportunity to chat.

"So you won't be able to race anymore?"

"No, I will able to," Ayrton replied.

"And why did they say you might not? Wasn't it because of what happened to your face?"

"It was, but at first we did not know what caused the paralysis or if it was reversible. I had to see several doctors before I found out," he replied patiently.

"And did you?" We took turns asking questions, curious.

"We did! I had an inflammation in a kind of tube, on the right side of my head," he said, touching the spot with his hand.

"which compressed where the three main nerves, called trigeminal, pass over commanding the facial muscles, which caused the paralysis."

Someone asked if it was reversible. He replied:

"Thank God, it is! So I can race again. The team that was hiring me did not want to sign a contract until they had the report proving my conditions to drive."

"Ayrton, do you know how long until you get your movements back?" I asked.

"It is already getting better, my movements are coming back slowly. The worst has passed, now it is just a matter of time," he replied with a crooked smile as he looked directly at me.

During this conversation, I could observe his face more calmly. When he spoke, he only moved his left side, unaffected by the paralysis, pulling his mouth in that direction, while the right side was almost inert. Sometimes he closed the lid of his right eye with his fingers to lubricate it, as it was still difficult to close it without help. But when he was quiet, while his whole face relaxed, we could not notice the paralysis; and I thought: "He is so cute this way." I loved that good-guy face. He was my type! Actually, he reminded me of Fábio Júnior, who at that time was in Brazilian soap operas and was the "Romeo" of TV and, of course, I was fascinated about him.

Once everyone was ready, they called us for dinner at the hotel restaurant. We started looking for our shoes to wear. Whenever you enter a yacht, it is customary to take off your shoes. We were moored in a place where the sea barely swayed, but still, it was necessary to put them on sitting down, so as not to risk losing balance.

In this movement, I decided to wait. I went to one of the booths to borrow a lipstick from my aunt, believing that, when I returned to the stern, they would all have disembarked. But when I came back, I saw Ayrton sitting, while everyone else was getting off the boat. I walked slowly, sure that he would get up to follow the rest of the group and I would be free to put my shoes on. But he did not, he remained seated.

At that time, it was fashionable to wear long skirts down to the shin or baggy dresses with a narrower hemline and shoulder pads – we looked like "potato sacks" –, accompanied by the famous Keds sneakers. Definitely, the ugliest fashion I have ever seen in my entire life was right in my teens. What can I do?

Anyway, I got "that" pair of sneakers and Ayrton did not move in front of me, just watching me. I sat in the chair opposite him. It seemed like endless seconds, as I did not know how to put them on in an elegant or even more feminine way. After all, until recently I was just a clumsy tomboy. I had the brilliant idea of putting both sneakers on and then crossing my legs leaning forward to tie one, then crossing my other leg to tie the other. A true lady, while he appreciated and waited for me to finish getting ready for us to disembark. I do not think I was breathing under his gaze.

Another problem: Disembark with that dress with narrow hemlines. At that time, we did not have those little bridges, so we had to jump. I was afraid that the hemline would hold my leg when I jumped and that I would smash on the floor; or else I might not fall but tear the goddam dress. Even though embarrassed, the solution was to lift the dress as little as possible to make the jump easier.

For me, despite the desperation, it was a happy ending and, for him, I am sure he thought everything was normal for a very fine girl...

We all had dinner together; the young people on one side of the table and the adults on the other, and at some point the subject of each other's age came up. He was nine years older than me. I thought it was great! All cleared up.

Later, Ayrton and Júnior left. After arranging our schedule for the next day, everyone went to bed. On our way to our bedroom, Dea commented:

"Dri, I think Ayrton has a crush on you."

"No way, Dea!" I was afraid to believe in his signals, I did not find that logical. Even though I knew I looked older, what would that twenty-four-year-old guy see in a fifteen-year-old girl? Especially him, who was not lacking in attention and intentions from older and more charming girls around us.

The next day, we repeated the script.

We were all set, there was no longer that formality or initial embarrassment. Conversations flowed and Júnior acted as a sort of attraction. It was at that moment when Ayrton told us that, for intimate friends, he was called Beco, a childhood nickname, and asked us to call him that way. My uncle Zé Carlos gave Corona T-shirts to everyone who did not have one yet.

Júnior and Becão — that was how Júnior called him – had been friends since they were children and had the same socioeconomic background. However, with his parents' divorce, Júnior struggled financially. That is why Becão, a sympathetic friend, brought him close. They were more than friends, they were like brothers.

Undoubtedly, Júnior was a pleasant company: He was always smiling, participating in all programs and helping in whatever was needed, attentively and in a good mood. He was like a counterpoint to Beco, owner of a shier temper, even though he was playful. He was a true friend who was never intimidated by Ayrton's career rise; on the contrary, he was thrilled with it. You could feel the trust and complicity between them, even when flirting.

Everyone was very comfortable. Both of them fit naturally in our family's way of being and became part of the group.

We went snorkeling; I took the opportunity to, once again, show off my sports skills for Beco, who stayed on the surface, while I, with an excellent and trained breath-hold, went down to the rocks and tried to stay underwater as long as possible. I was used to do that, but I know that, at that time, I did a great job diving, imagining he would be watching. And it really was like that! While he remained close, I pretended not to notice his presence.

Beco and Júnior participated in the day's schedule and, with their lively presence, they encouraged the boys on the boats who accompanied us, as well as dad's friends' relatives, to come aboard our vessel. After all, everyone was a little afraid of the "pitbull" boss. One of the boys was flirting with Chris, and the other one was flirting with Dea, but they both maintained respectful posture and attitude.

Later on that December 31, 1984, Beco and Júnior were invited to join our group at the hotel where we were staying, for the New Year's Eve party. As they already had scheduled a party, they invited us to go with them and we asked my father, but he gave us a strict "no", based on safety issues: Going out at night in a small speedboat? No way! Dad was afraid that we would have problems navigating between the islands of Angra, where there are many rocks submerged deep enough to wreak any boat's hull, and the speedboat had no radar. Therefore, my father reinforced the invitation:

"You are both very welcome to spend the New Year with us. But I cannot allow my daughters to sail at night under these circumstances."

Ayrton then said he would stop by at the other party and then meet us at the hotel. Deep down, I thought it was a kind way of saying that he might not come.

I also remember that Dad had made a promise to stop smoking. His last cigarette would be smoked minutes before midnight. And he spent supper with the last cigarette in his hands. Later he told us that he could not even smoke that last cigarette, as he was really determined to give up the habit. He used to smoke two packs a day, but he managed to keep his promise.

At night, everyone was wearing white clothes. I was wearing a circle skirt, a blouse (no shoulder pads, whew!) and a gypsy-style sash on the waist; most women had those three-quarter skirts and loose blouses (with shoulder pads), while men wore shorts. We all had our spirits properly prepared for what a new year brings.

We sat at the table, adults on one side, kids on the other. We had a lively supper, but Ayrton did not show up... Every minute felt like an eternity and took my hope that he would come away. My heart was aching and I thought that it was nothing but an illusion. To disguise it, I pretended to be excited in accompanying the group. I did not want anyone to notice my stupid desire of having him there "with me".

Damn, feelings are so intense when you are a teenager! I could barely breathe and berated myself for having believed in such nonsense. I did my best not to show my inner conflict.

I did not want to play a pathetic role, especially in front of the pretty girls in the group.

Suddenly, the warning:

"Hey guys, it is ten minutes to the New Year!"

And they started to play those typical songs, which say goodbye to the past year and wish a happy new one. I got into the mood, decided to turn the page and put the frustration aside. After all, "What has passed, has passed"... At that point, everyone was on their feet, singing and dancing to the music. My aunties, always very lively, pulled us onto the dance floor and danced with us, as if it were a waltz.

"Five minutes to go!" Someone announced at the microphone.

I was dancing and playing arm in arm with one of the women of the family (I am not sure which one, as we were all on the floor) when I saw Ayrton arriving in a hurry. He passed through the table of our group, greeted those who stayed there, half-waving, looked toward the floor and came straight toward me. With a satisfied smile, he took me by the arms and we began to dance with our eyes fixed on each other. It was a magical and unexpected moment. As if there was nothing else around us. Of course, everyone was stunned — after all, the year before I was just a little girl —, and the fact that he walked so confidently and purposefully toward me made it explicit to me, to my family and everyone in the room that he was there because of me, and my suspicions were right.

Ayrton ran to be by my side at midnight.

It was AMAZING.

"When it was five minutes to midnight, Beco arrived, as in a romantic movie, in which at the last moment the Romeo appears as by magic. Then we danced the rest of the night" (first note I made about Ayrton in my diary), on Dec. 31, 1984*

Ayrton and I on the dance floor on New Year's Eve 1984-1985

Note: All "personal diary notes" follow this layout

For a few moments, I was in a state of grace. I was on cloud nine. Spinning around on the dance floor with Ayrton, on a magical night like the New Year's Eve, gave my life, from that moment on, a new taste. Our story was born.

He awakened in me a whirlwind of delicious sensations with his impetuous and breathtaking way, pulling me to dance in those last minutes of 1984, which made me tenderer, sweeter and womanlier.

"Ten... nine... eight... seven... six..." They announced over the microphone the final seconds for the new year.

He and I exchanged affectionate but formal greetings. We separated for a few moments to wish everyone, individually, a happy New Year. As we were a large group, it was too many greetings!

My parents did not mention Beco's explicit preference for me. He had maintained a thoughtful, respectful and irreproachable attitude. As they had nothing to complain about, they chose to observe what would happen. After all, they were always watching us.

It was amazing how Beco knew how to handle that situation. He understood my family's dynamics, he knew how to act, and that allowed everything to flow naturally. We danced together all night.

Suddenly, I realized we were all accompanied by our pairs. Chris with Zé Eduardo, Dea with Marquinhos, Vidal's nephew. But I can barely remember Júnior that night. To be honest, with so much magic happening to me, that is all I remember happening around me, with other people.

At the end of the party, I asked:

"Are you going with us to the boat procession tomorrow?"

"Unfortunately, I have already scheduled this thing with the group from the other party."

Beco and I said goodbye as friends and each of us went to our own bedroom.

The next day, we left on our boat to watch and participate in the traditional procession in the bay of Angra, which brings together many boats, some of them decorated with allegories honoring Iemanjá (mother of all orishas; queen of the ocean).

I wanted to find Beco in that crowd, because I knew he was there, when I saw someone waving from a tourist schooner. My cousins and I waved back when we saw it was Beco and Júnior, in pirate uniforms in the middle of a huge group, barely fitting on the boat. When we looked at each other, my cousins and I laughed at their precarious situation. I told them:

"Serves him right! This is because he is not here with us..."

After the procession, my parents spoke on the boat's radio with other friends and decided to go to a different island. As the boys were with the schooner group, they went to the other side and we did not meet again that day.

"We went to the procession and I did not see him the rest of the day (damn it)" - on Jan. 1, 1085

Since the beginning of that summer, I had felt that people started to approach me with curiosity. Everyone was somewhat surprised to see me, as my body had evolved a lot over that year. They said: "Wow, you look different! You've grown up! You are a woman! What did you do? You look like a woman!".

But now, the general comment was about what was going on between Ayrton and I; always discreetly, as nobody commented on this subject in front of my parents, including the adults. Curious and even more surprised, everyone wanted to know and give their opinion: "He seems so nice!", "Is anything going to happen with the two of you?" I did not reply, because I did not know yet what would happen between us.

The conversation with the girls about the events of the New Year's Eve, the night before, was focused on Dea kissing Uncle Vidal's nephew, Chris getting along with Zé, who had been flirting with her for some time... As for me, I was not even sure what to say. When I was alone with Dea, she asked me:

"Hey, Dri! Did you kiss?"

"Not yet," I replied with some disappointment, knowing she was talking about the long-awaited kiss on the mouth.

That was when Andréa brought me up to date on what had happened that night.

"Dri, you know Christhiane was crying last night..."

"But why? Wasn't she with Zé?" I asked.

"She did. And I was with Marquinhos. We kissed, he is very cute, it was really cool. But then, after we said goodbye, before going back to our room, we escaped to smoke a cigarette... That was when Chris said, crying: 'Never a new guy on the group ignored Lenise and me and went straight to Adriane!'"

In Dea's own words: "Dri and I were the youngest on the boat, which was full of women. None of us was ugly, but we were not a Miss Universe. Corona boat was known as the women's boat... a boat with ten women draws the attention! So all the new guys, friends who came with friends, usually flirted with Chris, Tata or Patrícia, who were the oldest. And we were both "little girls". But Ayrton went straight to Adriane, and everyone said: 'Wow, the guy is flirting with Dri!' Even she was surprised: 'Is he making fun of me?' It took her some time to believe it."

Andréia is one year younger than me and, of course, she felt affected by Chris' comment.

"What does she think? That we are invisible?" She finished indignantly.

"But she was crying when she said that?" I asked. "Doesn't she have a crush on Zé, after all?"

"Exactly, Dri! I didn't get it either. All I know is that she cried..."

"Come on, Dri! My turn had to come one day," I commented, surprised I did not notice Chris' interest in Beco.

I was not only sad because I knew very well how painful that frustration my sister was feeling was, I was also confused. I did not want such a special moment for me to be a disappointment to her. I knew Chris was sentimental, because she had broken up with a boy she liked a lot, Otávio, because of my father. And the fact that Dad welcomed Beco with such affection was something that caught her attention.

But for the rest of the day, everything felt normal. Chris and the girls continued with their flirtation. Relieved to see that my sister was well, I minded my own business, delighted to remember what had happened to me. Although it was not much, it was something new and unexpected for me, much more than I could had dreamed of. I was already happy to have been noticed by Beco, even though I had no idea of what would happen from then on. I might never see him again, but

I would forever keep the delicious memory of those moments.

Otávio Torres, Christhiane's ex-boyfriend, remembers what it was like to date a Yamin at that time: "I met Adriane through her sister, Chris. I met Senna at the farm, in Porto Feliz, some time after. Dating a Yamin was complicated, especially Dri, who was younger; her father was terrified of exposure. Mr. Amilcar knew that if the media knew anything, they could go after her. He has always been hard line, dating was not easy, he always had to hide it and we spent the weekends in Porto Feliz."

The next day, early in the morning, Beco and Júnior came with a speedboat a little before the usual time, to ensure that we would not miss our schedule. I obviously LOVED it! Since New Year's Eve, I felt like bursting with joy, with those new feelings bubbling up inside me, but I did not want to let it show.

Always in groups, we skied, swam, dived. In relaxed conversations, Beco and I would discover a little more about each other's lives. I learned he had an older sister and a younger brother. I also learned that he traveled a lot and was out of the country most of the time. About me, he learned I would finish middle school that year, and that almost every weekend I would go to my father's farm.

He explained that he was sharing a "microapartment" in England with a couple of friends, Maurício Gugelmin — another driver who did not race at Formula 1 yet — and his wife Stella. He also told me about Monaco's race, in which he worked a miracle with his previous team, Toleman — it was not a top team at the time —, and even under rain, he managed to climb the F1 podium, taking the second place. About the head of my family, my father, he said he was also a winner: He had gone beyond what could be expected from a boy from a simple family, a visionary who reached success alone. We concluded that we both had a conservative education, based on strict principles and that, despite the achievements and privileges, we lived and acted with simplicity.

I believe that from the beginning there was a mutual admiration between Beco and Dad, but as Beco seemed interested in Dad's daughter, both had to act very cautiously. On the one hand, my father who, despite his gradually growing admiration for Ayrton, did not find it fun to have a twenty-four-year-old guy interested in his fifteen-year-old daughter — and he's not the kind of person who needs to verbalize his displeasure to make himself understood; I know he did not believe that it would work out. On the other hand, Beco felt more and more captivated by that bossy figure. He loved to feel that, whoever he was, he would have to follow the rules to approach Mr. Amilcar and earn his trust. After all, Ayrton also had a strict father.

"We went out for a boat trip. Beco went with us, we swam and dived together. When we got back to the club, he surprise me: He gave me a red sweatshirt. I wore the sweatshirt at night. Solange* took a movie for us to watch and, with an unexpected courage, I pulled Beco close to me. I could barely pay attention to the movie, as my attention was directly linked to him (amazing)." on Jan. 2, 1985

*Uncle Vidal's daughter, daddy's friend

Lenise says: "It was a surprise, as Dri was a girl and she has always been very lively, calm and happy. She was our little girl and we were surprised when she started dating."

That night, when we gathered after dinner to watch the movie, everyone settled into the room on our boat, where there was a U-shaped sofa in front of a built-in television with a VCR. I sat in the far-left corner, where the sofa had a backrest at elbow height, with my back to a glass wall that faced the stern of the boat. When I realized, Beco was sitting next to me and our knees were touching, but the sofa ergonomics did not allow our bodies to get closer, as I was sitting in the curve. The lights were off. The movie began; Beco, leaning his elbow on the back of the sofa, slid his body towards me. Of course I just pretended to watch the movie! He leaned in until he rested his arm on mine, even though his body was bent over in an uncomfortable position. He touched his little finger on mine, I returned the touch and we ended up caressing each other's hands. After a while, although loving "it all", I was bothered by his discomfort. So I pulled him gently by the arm so that he could make himself comfortable, and he leaned back against me, being wrapped in a hug. So, with my right hand I caressed his right arm, while he rested his head on my shoulder; we stayed with our faces glued together throughout the movie. This was the first affectionate physical contact we had. As soon as the session was over and before the lights were on, we moved away.

Aunt Regina Zarif says: "Adriane was a happy girl and she met Ayrton. Her father was more delighted than she was. Amilcar came to tell us: Do you know who was on the boat? Ayrton Senna, the racing driver! He was excited because he was a fan and also his father's friend. Then Ayrton felt interested in Dri, the youngest daughter... the expectation would be Tata or Chris. But it was Dri, the little one!".

Then everyone got out of the boat, each one going to one side, and we sat at the pier in plain sight, in front of the boats, to have a one-to-one conversation.

"Dri, think carefully before we start having anything, because my life is very complicated, I travel a lot and it is not easy... I will be away for a long time."

"I have nothing to think about!" I replied sweetly.

He looked at me, surprised by the calm and assurance of my answer. I responded unafraid because of my inexperience, that is true. But I was sure I wanted that to go further. Obviously, we were physically attracted and I saw no barrier to having him close to me at that moment. The only thing I was sure about was that we had several affinities and we liked the same sports. He accompanied me and I accompanied him, because we had the same restless pace; there seemed to be no differences between us: Neither in age, nor in lifestyle, nor in education at home. I never needed to explain the reason of our dynamics for my family. Also, he never questioned the rules; he knew, however, the conduct he should have towards my parents. I felt comfortable in his presence and he did too in mine. An inexplicable connection.

"Look, I have two lives: Ayrton's and Beco's. They are completely different lives. I professionally, and myself, in my personal life. Beco has nothing to do with the world of fame that my profession brings. I drive because I love what I do."

He wanted to prepare me for what was to come. He did not want me to be intimidated by Ayrton's public person. On the other hand, I immediately understood that I was being placed in Beco's life, isolated from his professional life, the fame, the party life brought by Formula 1.

After a short pause, he continued:

"Dri, I think I should ask your parents for permission for us to date."

"For God's sake, don't do this!" I was not sure what my parents' reaction would be. I continued: "No guy has ever asked my parents for permission to date my sisters! They know there is a flirtation, but they pretend they do not notice..."

"How come?" Beco asked. I explained:

"Firstly, my parents do not usually allow my sisters to go out alone with any guy, just with someone from the family or in a group. Secondly, they do not like any kind of intimacy in their presence: Not holding hands or anything! We have to act like friends in front of them. They prefer to observe from a distance so as not to look like they are consenting to that." I continued:

"My sister Lenise, who is now setting her engagement date, is more comfortable in front of them because it is no longer a flirtation."

"And how do we do it? We say nothing to your parents? Don't I account for it? They must know I mean well!" Ayrton argued.

"We can act as friends in front of them and then we see what happens! I have never had a boyfriend. My experience is what I witnessed with my sisters... If I ever feel that Dad expects you to say something to him, I let you know. But say nothing now, they did not bring it up with me."

"You have never had a boyfriend?"

"No!" I replied, a little awkwardly, remembering the mockery I suffered because I had never even kissed on the mouth. Which, of course, I did not mention.

Once that was all cleared up, he told me in short about the last romantic relationship he had had, months before. He commented that the girl (I do not remember her name) had made him suffer, which caused the breakup, but at the moment he was alone, free for a new relationship.

When we said goodbye, I thanked him once more for the sweater he had given me. As soon as he was out of sight, Dea came with that look of curiosity.

"So, Dri, did you kiss?"

"Damn it... Not yet!"

"Oh, Dri! I cannot believe it, he obviously has a big crush on you! I saw you guys cuddling on the boat during the movie,"

Dea said. "Yeah, I do not know why... He has not tried anything yet. But of course, there are always people around," I replied, annoyed.

I told her about the conversation we had, Beco and I, and she found his concern very cute.

"It was amazing to be so close to him and know his intentions."

I completed: "But kissing... not yet."

Suddenly, people were coming closer to hear the conversation and speak up: Marquinhos, Chris, Zé Eduardo. Feeling exposed, I felt annoyed and in a bad mood. They began to say: "Maybe he is too cautious because you are so much younger than him?"; "Maybe he did not find the opportunity to get closer?"; "Maybe he is trying to be too respectful?". And finally, the one that got me worried the most: "Maybe he is afraid of not being able to kiss because of the facial paralysis?" From then on, the atmosphere of that night, which had been great, was over.

I said good night to everyone and, before leaving, I had the chance to make separate comments with Dea.

"Ah... I cannot believe it! What a bad luck, just now that I am really looking forward to kissing someone, someone who I am sooooo into and the guy is also into me, it won't happen? Holy crap! Now what?"

I forgot to comment that my "perfect family" was a foul-mouthed. And, among us young people, out of earshot of adults, under extreme circumstances, we would unload the complete repertoire.

"Wow, Dri, indeed. Holy crap!" Dea completed. I went to bed so that the next day would come fast.

Morning came and with it, Beco came too. He left his speedboat for Júnior to drive and went with us in our boat.

We had a day full of activities. But the funniest thing about that day was the socks Beco was wearing because of his sunburned foot. Note: The night before, he had worn flip-flops because he could not put his shoes on. Oh, and I almost forgot: Under the socks he had passed Hipoglos cream!

We all had fun with it, including Beco himself. Another similar aspect of him with my family: Not taking himself so seriously and being able to laugh at his own ridicule. It was amazing! Of course, at that moment, no one messed with him much yet. After some time, as everyone became closer, Beco did not find it very funny that they did this to him, although he messed with everyone himself, truth be told.

Ayrton, with his "socks" and I in the side aisle of the boat

"It was Luciana's birthday. We wanted to visit Do Frade Hotel, but Zé Eduardo's father ruined the activity. (I was wearing Mom's purple dress)" - on Jan. 3, 1985

José Carlos Duarte Filho, Kaco, recalls the detail of Beco's crooked mouth: *"Dri and I are cousins. So we have always been very close. My mother is her father's sister. At the time, I was about ten, eleven years old. I always got along very well with Dri and I remember, when we were in Angra, that my father said: Look at that Formula 1 racer boy. I did not even know who he was, meaning it was the beginning of his life as a driver. The fame, the harassment, did not exist yet. We had a personal contact with him. We knew Beco, not Ayrton Senna. I remember he had a crooked mouth. In the beginning, we made fun of his with this mouth issue. Anyway, we knew him, but we did not pay much attention. It was nothing more than a person who raced at F1, which I did not know very much. That was the beginning. We were there, in Angra, and it was something that happened by coincidence."*

For everyone's disappointment, we could not, even under Luciana's birthday as an excuse, get out of the total control of our parents — especially Beco and I, who were watched all the time. We had had the idea of celebrating Lu's birthday at the Do Frade Hotel when everyone would finally manage to find some freedom. But Uncle Calil prohibited it, worried that we would drive from one hotel to another, hitting the road at night.

Uncle Zé Calil told his son Zé:

"Are you crazy, son? Are you planning to drive at night on this road, with a guy who is a car racer? What are you thinking he is going to do? Drive slowly? No way! You are not going!"

He ended up frustrating everyone's expectation. I thought: "That is it! Another full day and night under full surveillance."

We celebrated Luciana's birthday right there, where we all stayed. It was our last night in Angra. Unlike the other nights, Beco and Júnior did not seem to intend to leave, and it was getting late. My parents, certainly tired of waiting for everyone to leave, asked Lenise, my older and unaccompanied sister, to keep an eye on us, girls, and just come to sleep with us. Of course, we all felt more comfortable once my parents were out of sight... Beco took the opportunity and called me:

"Come here, Dri!" He took me by the hand and led me to the prow through the side aisle of the boat, the only place where we could have some privacy. We left the pier and the hotel behind and all that was left was the darkness of the sea in front of us.

Standing on the prow of the boat, he gently pulled me closer and at the same time brought his face close to mine. Calmly, he touched his soft lips on mine. He braced his hands on my waist and kept me close to him. We caressed each other with our lips and, slowly, this act was transformed into a kiss: THE kiss! At first, I was afraid I would not know how to act, so I decided to respond to his movements, hoping that my inexperience did not ruin that long-awaited moment. I would just reciprocate and follow his movements. It was delightful.

Although it lasted about ten minutes, that kiss sealed our relationship. So I found out, as a relief, that his paralysis and my inexperience would not be an obstacle for both of us.

"Dri, tomorrow I will go back to São Paulo and so will you. When I get there, I will reach you."

I nodded with a smile and we said goodbye. After all, it was late and the next day would be long. Of course, when I returned to the girls, the kiss became the subject of the end of the night.

"I started dating Beco and had my first kiss (2:00 am). IT WAS SO GOOD" – on Jan. 4, 1985.

Only when I lay down to sleep did the thought occur to me: "How is he going to reach me? Did he take my phone from someone?"

The next day, everyone was in a rush early in the morning to pack their bags, to check out from the hotel, go on the boat trip from Angra dos Reis to Guarujá, where the marina was, and from there drive to São Paulo.

Beco, who was going to drive to São Paulo pulling his speedboat in a trailer, stopped by the hotel in the morning to say goodbye to everyone. He ran to find me on the boat and ask for my home phone, which he had forgotten to ask the night before. I smiled and ran for pen and paper to write down the number.

55

I soon realized that he was left-handed, as he wrote down the addresses with their respective São Paulo and London telephone numbers. As I saw he had written down all the data, I decided to do the same. Then I realized that he was writing something else on another sheet of paper, in a way that I could not read it. I let him finish. I gave him my data. Before he hurried away, he stole a kiss while handing me his data and a note. He asked me to read it later, with a mischievous little smile. As soon as Beco left, I read the note he had given me and I was stunned by his words:

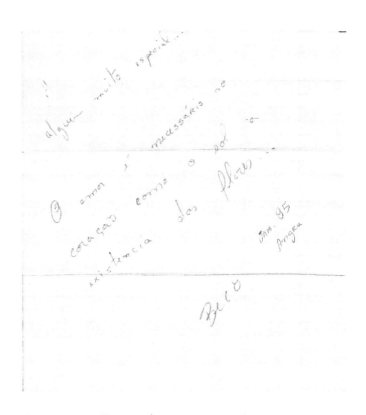

"With great affection /To a very special person... Love is necessary to our heart like the sun is to the flower's existence..."

I read the note several times, trying to believe what was happening to me. That was unthinkable, not even in dreams I thought it could happen. If I had considered something similar, it would not have been so perfect. I was numbed with the feeling that the world had stopped. To be the Prince Charming, all he needed was a white horse.

On my trip back to Guarujá, which took about six hours of navigation, I had plenty of time to understand everything that was happening to me. I felt like I was watching a movie. I showed Lê the note, in an attempt to convince myself that it was real. Too good: Beco was handsome; we had immense affinity; he entered my life through the front door, brought in by my father, who knew his origin and upbringing, whose family he admired and respected. Not to mention that Beco could understand the conservative and old-fashioned (even back then!) dynamics of my family. On top of that, he liked the same sports and games as I did! We also had the same energy and enthusiasm.

My cousin Stela classified our relationship as a a-mile-a-minute relationship: "Ayrton was extremely nice to her, a real partner. They were always coming up with something and doing sports: skiing, jet-skiing, motorcycle riding. It was a mile a minute! We went to the farm every weekend, they spent their holidays in Angra. They often took my uncle's boat in Guarujá and went to Ilhabela, and then stayed at my father's hotel. At the time, I was nineteen and F1 racing took on another dimension. I would not miss one. He was such a close idol. Dri was intense, very beautiful and special. Those were definitely memorable moments, full of emotion."

The more I thought about what was happening to me, the more the notion increased in me that everything was bigger than any fairy tales. The lives of Cinderella, Snow White or Sleeping Beauty and Rapunzel had had more obstacles than mine: I had no stepmother bothering me, no curse had been cast, I was not an orphan, nor was there a witch following me! Only strict parents...

These analogies, though comical, were frightening; so I started to put my foot on the ground. How can I be sure he is going to call me when we get to São Paulo? Not even in fairy tales had the characters been so lucky! I began to experience an anguish I had never felt before; fear that the dream would turn into a nightmare. Thinking about it today, I can say that the feeling I had was identical to that of watching a romantic movie, where everything is so perfect, harmonious, wonderful, that it seems improbable and, as the plot develops, you are sure something will happen.

I realized that the concern was not mine alone when one of my aunts said: "Be careful, Adriane! Sometimes, summer love doesn't stay." I sought a solitary corner on the boat and isolated myself. I was distressed and afraid. It had all been so amazing, but I knew I had to prepare for the possibility of getting frustrated: This was likely to go no further. I cried. I had left Angra on cloud nine, but when I got to Guarujá, I found myself prepared for any possibility. We unloaded the boat and continued our journey by car for another hour and a half to São Paulo.

Chapter III

The first thing I asked to the housekeeper, as soon as we arrived from our trip, was: "Has anyone called me?" The unusual question made her startled. She was used to the family routine and that questioning was unprecedented.

I was alertness: Whenever the phone rang, my heart raced. I did not want to let it show, but deep down, I counted every minute.

Some habits in my family may seem unthinkable nowadays. For example, only my parents' bedroom, the TV room and the pantry had a telephone, even though we lived in a spacious apartment and each of us had our own bedroom. Because "nobody should have nothing to hide"; television was in a room for us to watch the programs together. In other words, we barely had privacy in family life, but we were protected from the "trespassing" of the terrible outside world. Meaning that my parents intended to preserve the innocence of their daughters' childhood and youth. Life was what it was, without so many options and choices. My sisters and I lived by my parents' rules. If we questioned any of these rules, we would hear the following from my father: "I do not care what others do or do not do, you are my daughters," and also: "If you act like some "random" girl, you will be seen and treated as such. I do not accept that, because my daughters will know how to give themselves to respect."

"I stayed home all afternoon. At night, Beco and I, Dadô and Táta went to the Gallery, we danced, talked and drank champagne. P.S. I really like Beco." — on Jan. 5, 1985.

As soon as we went back from Angra, Eduardo, Lenise's boyfriend, came from São Carlos, where he lived, to see her because he could not be with us on New Year's Eve. They wanted to dance and invited me and Ayrton to join them. It would be an opportunity for the boys to get to know each other; it was also a way for me to go out with Beco, and Lenise knew it. My sister's suggestion was to go to the Gallery, where Dadô was a business partner and had easy access. When leaving home, Lenise, as an older sister, determined: "Let's go in Dadô's car."

I remember I was afraid of being barred from entering because of my age — which would be a blunder —, but I took the risk, as I knew I looked older; and it worked out.

We entered the Gallery and took a corner table. The atmosphere was strange, it was a new situation for me, as well as for my sister and Dadô, who had known me since I was a girl, that is, since yesterday. We told him about how we had met Ayrton in Angra.

They ordered champagne and we all drank it, including myself, because I already had that kind of freedom at home. Dad preferred that we learn to drink under their care and learn to measure the effects of alcohol inside our house.

At that time, nightclubs had more lively songs and, for some short periods, romantic songs to dance together. Thus, when slow music began, Ayrton and I went dancing. The song Careless Whispers, by George Michael, marked that moment. I felt something very special, as if nothing and no one but the two of us existed in the world; as if time had stopped and thoughts had ceased to exist; a strong feeling of connection between the two of us, nothing I could explain in words.

After the sequence of slow songs, we returned to the table, but in a more relaxed mood. We sat on an L-shaped sofa: First Dadô, then Lenise, I and Beco. After some time, during our conversation, Ayrton rested his hand on my right leg, close to the knee, with no second intentions, just an attitude signaling to the others that he was with me. It felt normal for me, but my sister, out of breath, wide-eyed and unceremoniously, immediately took it away, much to the surprise of all of us. Ayrton looked at me, not understanding the reason for that gesture, and I shrugged, meaning I did not understand either. Noticing our astonishment, Lenise properly justified herself:

"Listen. You are exposing my sister. She is only 15. How can you put your hand on her leg? What will the others think?"

He kept looking at her, not quite understanding, and I asked:

"So what? What is the problem?" And Ayrton added:

"She is my girlfriend! We are not doing anything wrong. I am not disrespecting Dri."

"How come? You are an older guy and she is a girl,"

Lenise argued, outraged and uncomfortable with the scene. And she continued: "You are targeted by your profession, you are exposing my sister!"

As a five-year-older sister, Lenise speaks of her concern for Adriane: "Ayrton was my youngest sister's famous boyfriend, and I was not sure if he was really going to be with her. That was even our family's thinking. My sister is important to me. I had nothing against him, we just were not close. We got along, but he was my sister's boyfriend. Just like that. And Dri was fifteen at the time and I was twenty. So I was at college and she was at school. There was a big age difference between us and I worried about her. But I got married at the age of twenty-one and moved to São Carlos. I began to spend less time with them."

Ayrton and I looked at each other, embarrassed by her attitude. So I looked at her, frowning, and I took Ayrton's hand with determination, and put it back on my leg, in the same place, saying:

"Yes, he will have his hand on my leg! Because yes, I am his girlfriend! Why other people seeing would be a problem? Nobody is doing nothing wrong," I concluded, turning my back on Lenise.

She fell silent. She swallowed hard because neither she nor the other members of my family were prepared for any of that. The rapport between me and Beco, despite our age difference, was much more natural than my family's adaptation to our relationship. After that, the atmosphere got weird among the four of us and we were rather embarrassed for the rest of the night. Dadô tried everything to relax the atmosphere again, but he had no success.

We kissed a lot when we got to the hall of my apartment then we kissed a lot again on the exit. We were learning about each other's ways and everything was going well. The other day, when Beco called me, we talked a little and I invited him to come over at night.

Dadô had returned to São Carlos to pack his bags. The next day, he would travel to Europe, serving his family's business. Coincidentally, my sister Lenise had also invited some friends to watch a movie. So they were there when Beco came to stay with me. Everybody ended up watching the movie together, and we had no chance of talking alone or getting closer.

"I was like crazy waiting for Beco's call. At night, he, Pedro, Bragança and Reis came to watch a movie and left." — on Jan. 6, 1985.

The next day, my sisters and I went to dinner with Dadô, then we accompanied him to the airport until his departure. I was sad, because that day Beco did not call me. This sudden silence made me no good. He probably had not expected to find other men in our house the night before, even though they were just friends and my parents were there.

"We made our farewells for Dadô, but we could not see Bambino." — on Jan. 7, 1985.

When Beco arrived, after calling me and being invited to come over, we watched TV together with my family.

"Hum. I feel like eating Arab food," my father said at one point.

Beco promptly offered:

"Leave it, Amilca, I will get it with Dri," that is how he called my father.

64

"That is right!" I said, jumping off the couch. I rushed to take everyone's order before my parents had time to think. I did not want to miss that chance to go out with Beco.

"Okay, darling, go! Grab money in my pants pocket in the..."

"No, Amilca, leave it to me," Ayrton said before my father finished the sentence.

"Hey, darling, go get it..."

Again, before my father finished the sentence, Beco took me by the hand.

"Come on, Dri! Amilca, we'll be right back."

My mom only had time to speak when we were already on our way to the front door:

"Come back soon!"

We left excited with the chance of getting a little bit of privacy. When at home, everyone was in the living room together, talking and watching TV. We were not alone for a minute.

Along the way, we talked about what happened with Lenise, the other night at the Gallery. I said the subject had finished right there at the club. We talked about other amenities and what our routine would be like.

"I will have to travel to training in England the next 15. I need to set up the car and integrate with the team and the mechanics. There will be lots and lots of training throughout the year, Dri, which will keep me away for long periods. It is not just traveling to get in the car, race and return to Brazil; that is just one part of the job."

In the face of my attentive silence, he continued:

The races are the result of a lot of hard work with mechanics to make the necessary adjustments to the car."

I tried to learn about his routine with the new team, Lotus, from then on. In the middle of this conversation, I blurted out that I had been upset with him the day before. Perhaps because   I felt more confident in our relationship, I said:

"You did not even call me yesterday; it is your minimum obligation as a boyfriend."

"Hey, wait a moment..." he said, interrupting me. "The day I feel it is an obligation to call you, I will not call you anymore. I only call you when I feel like talking to you because I like you," He paused and continued, annoyed: "And let me tell you something else: The woman who is with me, if she really loves me, will never ask me to stop racing."

We were silent for a while on our way back home. I particularly realized the childish way in which I had placed my expectations. I felt he was right, because this is the only way a relationship makes sense: No demands or obligations, just the desire to be with the other person by free will. I thought about that conversation and reconsidered my position, even though I kept a long face and was still upset that he had not called me. With sweetness and courage, I told him:

"You are right, I am sorry, there is no obligation, I think I did not express myself well. I think the proper word would be 'consideration'."

My statement eased the discomfort, but we learned a lot about each other in this dialogue.

To ease the atmosphere, I said:

"But you have to give me a hand, I am a beginner, I have never dated, I am learning!"

He gave me a wide smile, followed by his typical laugh, finding the comment amusing. And it was! As a grown man, living in a world of adults, he found it incredible. Especially for the way it was said, so calmly and acknowledged. I was not ashamed to say the truth. Honestly, I realized I would make a fool of myself to pretend I was an experienced woman and I knew our situation was comical. So I took advantage of it to make fun!

I added:

"I had not even kissed. I am learning with you!"

That was it! He opened his mouth and let out another laugh:

66

"So you mean you had not kissed anyone yet?" I made a face of indifference and said:

"I had not, so what? Do you think I flirt with everyone?" I continued in my strategy of commanding the situation. I made fun and acted as important.

He started tickling me to make me laugh too. I could not stand it and we had a nice laugh together. I tried to look offended again, but I could not hold back the laugh any longer.

When we got home, everything looked normal. We had dinner and talked to everyone. But we took a loooong time saying goodbye. It became a habit: We took advantage of the fact that we were out of the family's sight in the hall. Or in the garage at home, where I would accompany him. So, little by little, our intimacy grew.

"We went shopping for dinner. We talked." — on Jan. 8, 1985.

Our friend Reginaldo Leme, reporter and sports commentator, elucidates the beginning of the conflicts between Ayrton and Piquet that occurred in parallel with my story at that time: "It is a lie that Piquet vetoed Senna at Brabham. Piquet told to me and Galvão, in the presence of Lucia (Galvão's wife at the time, now deceased) and Carmen Sylvia, my wife, at a dinner in Northampton, England: 'It is all settled, I am going with Ayrton. This conversation occurred before Senna started working with Lotus, at the end of 1984, in a hotel in England. Even Bernie Ecclestone (then one of Brabham's owners) admits that, but then a sponsorship fight happened in Brazil. Apparently, someone on Ayrton's behalf, at his request or without him knowing, went looking for Golden Cross, Piquet's sponsor. Golden Cross' director called Piquet and told him: They came look for me, on Ayrton's behalf. On many occasions, I struggled and managed to get the two of them side by side talking. I myself brought up a subject that I knew they would like and the talk would go on freely. In one of these, we were on our way back from Bali to Australia. In Bali, Ayrton had skied a lot (I filmed this with a very old camera that Club Med lent me, and Globo TV has these VHS tapes in their archive), and Piquet also liked to practice it. These guys live from the adrenaline that feeds them. Any challenging sport, they would do it. It was during the First-class flight that I put them side by side talking about nautical ski. I even went away to make them feel comfortable and talked for over half an hour without mentioning automobilism. I was sure I had contributed to trying to 'fix' their relationship. Before F1, in 1983, Ayrton won a Formula Ford race in 2000, in Germany, Hockeinheim, and on the same day, Piquet won in Formula 1. Ayrton went and congratulated Piquet, who accepted the handshake, but was a little cold. That same night, having dinner with Ayrton, he told me: 'I went there to talk and congratulate your friend and he was cold as hell with me.' My answer: 'Ayrton, you should not expect any other behavior, he is like that!'."

On the following days, our dates were no longer daily due to Ayrton's contracts with some sponsors in Brazil and the details of Lotus' contract, pending since the confusion at the end of the previous year, due to his facial paralysis. Now, after the end-of-year parties, his professional activities should be resumed.

Excerpt from an interview given to Veja magazine on 09/25/1985

VEJA — *Como você enfrentou o pro-blema da paralisia facial que o afetou no início do ano?*

SENNA — Foi bom para sentir o quanto somos insignificantes. Por mais que você programe sua vida, a qualquer momento tudo pode mudar. Na época eu tinha acabado de assinar contrato com a Lotus, o passo mais importante da minha carreira, e de repente senti minha profissão acabada. Eu mesmo, como pessoa, me senti balançar.

VEJA - How did you face the facial paralysis problem, which affected you at the beginning of the year?

SENNA - It was good because I could feel how insignificant we are. No matter how much you plan your life, everything can change in a minute. At that time, I had just signed a contract with Lotus, the most important step in my career, and I suddenly felt my career was over. I, as a person, felt me balancing.

One day, when were alone at the TV room at home, my dad came to start a conversation, in his own way:

"So, how is it, darling? What is that? I have not said anything so far because I thought this was not going any further. Ayrton is a grown man and has a crazy life. He is always surrounded by a lot of people in this environment that is not ours, and you will not be able to follow him, because you are just a kid. I do not like this!"

"Dad, he knows all that! He is aware of the limitations and we talked in Angra." I told him all the conversation Ayrton and I had had about his life, about being a public figure, and also about him questioning me if he should ask my father permission to date me.

"Not bad, dear! But it does not solve the problem."

"Dad, I told him what it would be like and how things work at home. He is aware!"

"Indeed. I admire his family. I know his father, an honest man, and I have always heard good things about him, a man respected by his friends. As you know, we lived on the same street when you were little, in the North Zone of the city. They lived two houses up, across the street. I invited Ayrton to the boat in Angra because I learned from my friend Benigno, who also lived on the same street and is a friend of Milton, that his son was racing in F1. When I saw on television about his paralysis, I was upset with the boy's situation. But I could not imagine any of this! Now what?"

"Oh, dad! He is totally respecting me! We know what the situation is. But we get along well and I like him. We will not do anything wrong. He is accepting to be with me under these house rules, which is not easy for him. But he respects, he understood, and accepted."

"All right then! I will talk to him, to make everything very clear. And it will be on my terms. He will be your date. He will be very welcome at home, in our company. But I do not want any intimacy in front of me, nor do I want to see you going out with him alone. You are only going out with your sisters!"

"Come on, dad, only with my sisters? They already told me that they will not be the third wheel! What do I do? I was the third wheel their whole lives for them to go out with their boyfriends. Will you force them?"

"No! But you can also hang out with your closest cousins and friends! I will accept him as a date...
Is that clear?"

"Ok, dad, but he did not ask permission to date me in Angra because I did not let him! I have not seen Chris and Lenise's boyfriends ask permission to date them."

"Your sisters are older than you and their boyfriends are not that older than them. You are ten years apart! He is a grown man; you are a kid who knows nothing of life."

"Dad! He is respecting me and understands the situation. I commented it would be a "flirt" and he was amused by that. And we are nine years apart, not ten!"

"Okay! This is fickle. Soon each one will take their own path. Meanwhile, it is going to be the way I said. Understood?" He frowned and concluded: "I will have a serious talk with him when we go to the farm!"

"Ok, dad."

The first of many surprises Beco would make along our relationship: The day he went to England I received flowers with a card:

I was breathless when I saw the flowers; I have never imagined such a caring attitude. I had never got flowers from anyone other than my family and on celebrations. Not to mention that I was a little confused, wondering how he had found time to come from Santana to this flower shop near my house, in Jardins neighborhood. Because at that time, it was not easy as it is today, when we can buy flowers online and send them anywhere in the planet. So even that required planning, and he should probably be at the airport to fly to London.

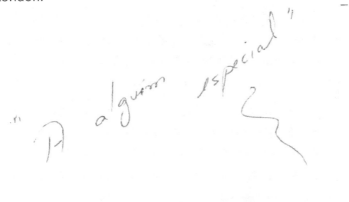

"To a special someone."

71

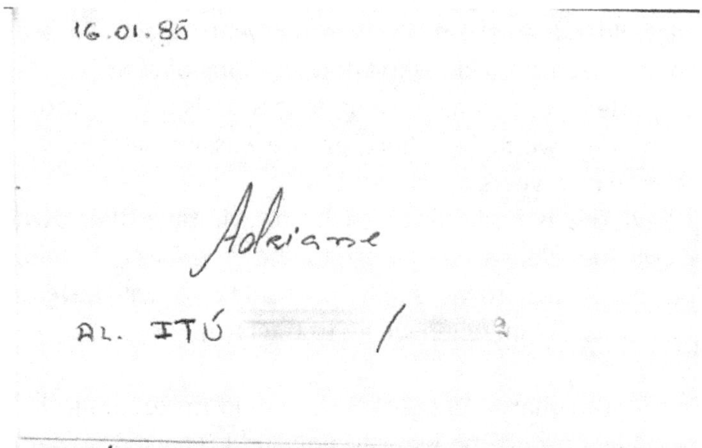

16.01.85

Adriane

AL. ITÚ   /   ₂

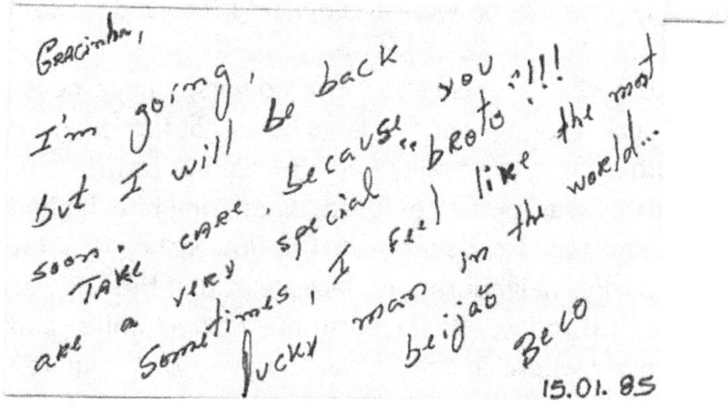

Gracinha,

I'm going, I will be back soon... but I will, because you ?!!! Take a very special photo, I feel like the most lucky man in the world... sometimes, beijão Beco

15.01.85

In fact, I was very happy with everything about Beco. His acceptance of my family's restrictions on our age difference; his constant respect, affection and kindness towards me; his high spirits and playful way of a boy. I felt cared for and safe with him.

A few days later, I received the first correspondence from Beco; actually, the first correspondence in my life — an identification card with his name printed on it.

Adriane . . . .
AL. ITÚ
São Paulo - Capital

CEP. 01421

By air mail
Par avion

BRAZIL

20.01.85

Gracinha,
Um dia desses, num almoço com meus patrocinadores em Londres... lembrei muito de você, estava na mesa. Este cartão, identificava meu lugar, decidi guardar como recordação. Ai vai um pouquinho de mim com "carinho and respect".
TAKE CARE Beijos Beco
20.01.85

"Sweet,
One of these days, having lunch with my sponsors in London, I thought a lot about you... This card was on the table identifying my seat and I decided to keep it as a memory. Here is a little piece of me with "caring and respect".
Take care, kisses, Beco. 01/02/85"

73

AYRTON

Ayrton Senna

"To a special someone"
"BECO called" — *on Jan. 31, 1985.*
Wow! My heart beat fast when someone called at home: "Dri, phone for you, it is Beco."

Not used to dating on the phone, I did not even know where to start the conversation so as not to let it show how excited I was. But I took the phone in my hand, took a deep breath...

I tried to keep a calm voice. Deep inside, I boiled with excitement and expectation, my heart beating so hard it seemed to explode.

"Hello. Beco?"

"Hi, Dridrica. How are you? How are things?"

"Everything is cool. How about you? I loved the flowers!"

He laughed and said:

"Did you, doll? Great! Everything is well here. Busy. I have been training a lot with the new car and I am still adapting to the new team. Did you get my letter?"

We spoke slowly, with no hurry, but a saddened tone gradually grew.

"I did."

"Yeah! I think it takes about seven days for the mail to arrive from England to Brazil…"

"It has arrived!" I thought about how many days ago I had received the letter and concluded: "I think you are right, it has been about three days…"

"Gosh, Dri! I have been missing you; and that day my heart sank… I thought about you a lot!"

"I love it! I have been missing you a lot too. When are you back?" I asked cautiously. I was afraid of sounding like I was hounding him, but the tone of voice was casual, so as to show only curiosity.

"I do not know the exact date yet, I can only schedule it when the team and I think that all the possible car adjustments in the short term are completed. Then I escape to Brazil… I do not know the car very well and they do not know me, we are learning how to exchange information, I have to give everything from me now, keep myself focused."

"And how is your face?"

"Getting better. I can almost close my eyes without help, but by GP it has to be a hundred percent. Here I have no problems, because during practice I stop many times to talk to the mechanics about the adjustments and I can rest my eyes for a bit."

"That is good. I am happy to know."

"Yep! Drica, I cannot fool around, but as soon as I can, I will be back. Tell everyone I sent hugs."

"Ok, I will. Take care, Beco. Kisses."

You take care of yourself too, doll! Kisses."

At Carnival, I traveled with my family to Guarujá, where we had an apartment, and I received a call from Beco, from London.

Here, I need to do an observation. The rules regarding the use of telephone and television were the same in Guarujá, with the difference that there we had two devices: One upstairs, in the social area, and the other in my parents' bedroom, downstairs, in the intimate area. The solution to have a minimum of privacy when we got a call was to take the phone to the toilet and, for that reason, the connecting wire of the device was quite long.

Another detail: At the beginning of our relationship, every other week, he would call and tell us what he had done during that period, about his Formula 1 training and his travel plans. Unfortunately, the advantages and facilities we have today with cell phones did not exist, and international calls had poor quality and were very expensive. That time it was like that. We talked as usual and caught up with the news, then I felt a change in his tone of voice and he said, in a very serious way:

"We have to have a very serious conversation." I asked:

"What happened?"

"No, nothing happened, Dri!"

"Can you anticipate the subject?"

"I cannot, Dri. When I arrive in São Paulo, we will talk."

I noticed he was not going to say anything else, so I decided not to insist and we said goodbye.

"I will be there soon," he said, adding: "I miss you."

In response, I said almost voiceless:

"I miss you too."

After we said our goodbyes, I hung up the phone and went back into the living room to put the phone back. My mother, seeing the sad expression on my face, asked worriedly:

"What is it, little girl?"

"Oh, mom. I don't get it! The conversation started off normal, but he said we need to have a serious conversation."

"But wasn't the conversation normal?"

"Yes, mom. It was. I did not understand. Did I do something wrong?"

My dad listened to our conversation, but he stayed there as if absent from what was happening.

It was a sacrifice to have no information about that serious conversation; it seemed he would never arrive in São Paulo! One day, noticing my affliction, dad commented at home:

"I heard he was once married..."

No, dad, he is too young! Is this what he wants to talk to me about? Does he have a child?" I wondered, trying to find something else through dad.

"A child? I do not think so!" he replied.

"But if he is divorced, then what is wrong? Why such a mystery?" I said, confused. "No. It must be something more serious, he told me in Angra he had suffered with an ex-girlfriend three months before, not an ex-wife; it must be something else."

My father immediately changed the subject, he did not want to extend this conversation. After all, he did not want to make further comments about our probable relationship and preferred to stay out of it until he was sure it was going ahead.

Chapter IV

Soon my classes began at Santa Maria school. I was then entering the eighth grade, the last year of middle school. Although it was a school run by Canadian nuns, it had a modern methodology at the time, called constructivism. They were addressed by Sisters and had different habits from conventional nuns: They dressed in a three-quarter-sleeve white shirt, light blue skirt with a length of a palm below the knee, black moccasins and their hairs were exposed and cut very short. They spoke fluent Portuguese, although their English accent was strong. There, we had British English and religion classes, in addition to the basic subjects, but we also had orientation classes, which, among other subjects, talked about sexuality in pubescent grades.

I entered this institution in the fourth grade of elementary school, which was practically dominated by the Yamin family. There was always a cousin or sister of mine in one of the grades. Every beginning of school year, when student and teacher presentations were necessary and I used to be number one on the attendance call, I soon heard:

"Adriane!"

"Here!" I would reply.

"Who is Adriane? Raise your hand!"

When I raised my hand, I knew it would be followed by a comment...

"One more Yamin! Wow, again! I have taught..." and there came the list of names. "Who is your sister?"

I would reply, tired of the sameness of every year. On the other hand, it was great: Nobody would mess with me; in case of any problem, I would have many Yamins to help me.

Over the years, I began to respond differently to the call.

"Adriane Yamin?"

Before they asked me, I would add:

"Here! I am Lenise and Chris' sister, Mônica, Stela and Andrea's cousin, but it is not over yet. There are more Yamin coming."

Then the teacher said:

"Um, I taught your sister or your cousin," and so on.

I also loved the school's size and distribution. It had an extensive green area, and all classrooms were on the ground floor, flanked by large corridors with access to their respective entrance doors. Alternately between these rooms, there were garden patios. Inside the rooms, an entire wall of giant windows overlooked these gardens. It was very common for me to get distracted in class seeing the birds outside.

The areas for sports practice were also wide and mostly outdoor. To access them, we had to go through a bridge over a small river that cut the land. During our entire stay there, we had the feeling of freshness of being in a country house, away from the madness of the city of São Paulo. Everything was beautiful.

I only focused on studying at the end of the year, because I knew I could make up lost ground — it was pure trickery! However, the thing is that I loved that school.

It also had a large chapel in the heart of the school, a diner, a cafeteria, science and arts and music rooms etc.

That year, 1985, I had a different feeling at the beginning of classes. Everything was familiar: School, friends, family around, but something was different... When classes ended the year before, I still felt like a child, but not anymore: I felt finally part of the world and no longer isolated from it, in a tight corner; it was as if I had gained breadth. I became more focused on my school activities, my self-esteem increased and, of course, it was all because of Beco.

I would not talk to anyone about my relationship, much less who he was. At a certain point, I was only confident enough to tell I was dating a guy I called Beco, but I avoided details. I was an expert in discretion, after all, my parents raised me from a very young age so that I would not spread that my father owned Duchas Corona Company — which, at the time, had many ads, including on the TV. Much less saying what we had or didn't have, as they said: "It is the man who makes the name and not the name that makes the man".

As a matter of fact, we lived simply, despite the comfort; we did not value the excesses, but the content and virtues that should be cultivated. While studying at Santa Maria school, my greatest joy was being known as one of the Yamins. I was really proud of my sisters and cousins.

Besides my family, the only friends and classmates who knew about my relationship were the closest ones, Raquel and Natalie, whom I made swear not to reveal my little secret, which I kept as a treasure.

The only thing I hated about that stage of Santa Maria school was the fact that I had to wake up every single day at half past five in the morning, to be there at seven, because of the distance. I had to get up before the sun came up for many years.

On a common day, we were at home and my mom came to my room to see what I was doing. When she realized she was not interrupting anything, she talked:

"What's up, dear? How are things at school?"

"All right, mom! The beginning of the year is calm."

"So you have no school work to do?"

"Not today."

"Dear, I want to talk to you about something serious. Your father already talked to you about Ayrton, but some things have not been said and that is why I am here."

"Go ahead, mom."

"You are dating a grown man, who is always traveling, and we do not know where that will lead. But you know he is a mature man and you are not a mature girl, you are very young and inexperienced."

"I know mom, so what?"

"So that he, as a man, has the needs of a man."

"Um…"

"And you are very young and you know what I think about virginity! I hope you listen to your mother and marry as a virgin to be valued by your husband. We want what is best for you!"

"Okay… and?"

"And you know he is going to go out with other women to satisfy the needs of a mature man. He will do to others what he cannot do to you. But you have to preserve yourself. We do not know where it will lead, his life is not easy and it will be full of harassment."

"Okay mom, I get it, I will not do anything wrong. Beco and I like each other, and he never crossed the line. We would not even have this chance, would we? You are always around. It is annoying! We cannot even have a conversation alone. We just back away a little bit and you are already after me like a siren. I feel embarrassed. After all, he is a man and everyone is around. We want a few moments alone. Not to do anything wrong, mom. I just want to have some time to talk, kiss… nothing else. He is going to be away a lot. And when we are together, won't we even be able to talk in peace? I am going to want at times to have his attention for me and he will want to have my attention for him. It is complicated!"

I was being honest; with so many obstacles making the relationship difficult, I would not risk ruining everything… even though it was little, that little was a lot for me! And I added:

"Mom, take it easy. I get it. You are right! I am not a grown woman and I will not act like I am. But it is too much."

"Dear, it is a new situation for everyone and we will adjust it. I trust you! But we must be together, okay? What is the problem? Do you want to hang out? Call someone and you can do it. Not alone by car! Not alone at night!"

"Okay, but can't I steal a kiss from him? Around you, I cannot even hold hands with him. It will not be a surprise when he gets fed up with all this! And what do I tell him?"

"Tell him to do to others what he cannot do to you. He will understand!"

After a long, deep breath, I said:

"Okay, mom, do not worry! But it is not going to be easy… it is a lot. I have talked to dad too and I cannot count on my sisters to accompany me. You have seen it. They have already told me not to count on them."

The conversation ended there. She had said what she wanted to, but no one knew yet how to make work what was not supposed to happen… we would have to find out together.

As soon as Beco arrived from his trip, we arranged for him to come over, even during the day, because I could no longer stand all that suspense to have "the" important conversation he had mentioned in the phone call.

After saying hi to my parents, we went into the living room to have some privacy and a private conversation. I was completely anxious and wanted to put an end to that mystery. It was the first time I wanted to have a conversation alone with him without feeling a little afraid to take that attitude towards my family. It may seem silly, but it is an important detail within the context in which I lived.

I noticed that his face was much better than the last time we were together.

I immediately asked, without any delay:

"So, what is this subject you want to discuss with me? What is going on?"

"Oh, Dri! I know you have a traditional family and your parents look after you, and they may not accept one thing in my life… And before we continue this, as this fact can become a problem between us, I need to clarify why I do not want to have a secret and I want to take you seriously. I do not want to ignore anything that might, in the future, call into question my honesty with you."

I was getting more and more nervous, while he did that introduction. What could be so bad about him? I even thought he would want to break up with me. He seemed embarrassed and was quite afraid of what he had to say. I rushed him, afflicted:

"Speak up, what is it?"

"It is just that I was once married."

My first feeling was of relief: Phew! But then it occurred to me to ask another question that worried me:

"But did you have children? Are you a father?"

"No, I am not a father. But I am afraid your parents will not accept that. I wanted to make it clear soon."

A new feeling of relief came over me. I said:

"But my father already told me that he had heard you had been married."

Then Beco asked, surprised:

"So your father already knew it?"

"He told me he had heard about it..."

"And said nothing else?"

"No! He made no further comment."

Beco remained silent for a few moments, as if he had said what he had to say and felt relieved. I got interested in the subject, obviously; some questions popped into my head:

"But what happened? You are young... You have married and already got divorced?"

"I was joining a new team, one I really wanted to join, and the contract required the driver to be married. As I had a girlfriend and I liked her at the time, I thought it was good to get married."

"So you used the girl."

"It is not like that, Dri! I did what I thought was right; I was very young, I was twenty-one. But I also suffered from it all. It sounded a good idea at the time, I was very lonely in England."

"Oh, poor thing! It must have been hard."

"I am not proud of it, I did not mean bad, and I did not calculate this. It was an impulsive marriage, I was not prepared and it turned out everything went wrong, it was not anyone's fault. My mistake was rushing into proposing."

Then I asked:

"You just signed a contract with Lotus and you are not married; why did you need to be married before and now you do not?"

"Each team adds in contract clauses that it deems necessary to require the driver to do his part. There is a lot of money involved, Dri, although it is another racing category. I was very young and at the time this was a requirement. The team would not give me such an expensive car without certain contractual guarantees. I was just getting started and I accepted the demands they made," he paused for a second and continued:

"Even today I have certain contractual demands, but others."

I asked if she knew that situation, because I then put myself in her shoes. He replied:

"Of course! She knew everything about my life then."

"But why didn't it work?"

"Oh, I don't know, Dri! Life was tough at that time, no money, I had a lot of appointments, I think she felt very lonely. But it got to the point that when she saw me resting on a day off, she started to make noise, vacuumed the house, knocked the vacuum on the door etc., just to wake me up!"

I kept silent, imagining how lonely she probably felt to take such an attitude; at the same time, I thought that was not enough reason for a divorce. I made no comment, I did not want to enter the privacy of another woman's life. But that was registered in my mind.

Beco also mentioned that his marriage lasted less than a year. I realized that his ex-wife was not the same person he had recently broken up with, as he had mentioned in Angra dos Reis. The subject naturally faded. And I was glad to see that the long-awaited conversation had nothing to do with me, and my father had not imposed any restrictions on it. Thus, relieved, I thought: "Let's move on!".

We went back to the TV room, where my family was gathered and we all stayed together. I noticed that the movements of his face were much better, as he now could blink his right eye— with some difficulty, but without the help of his hand.

After Beco left, I commented with my father:

"Hey, dad! You were right, the subject really was that: He was married some time now, but it did not last a year. He got married very young and it did not work out. He had no children and that subject is finished in his life."

Dad looked at me in silence and the subject was never mentioned again. Page turned!

At that beginning of our relationship, we talked a lot. We were both curious about some aspects of each other's life and had a constant desire to get to know each other better. In an exchange of questions about studies, Beco told me he studied at Rio Branco school and that studying was not one of the things he most liked to do. He said he had been an average student, but he had no choice. Just like me! His parents made it very clear that they would support him in his passion for racing if he had a proper performance at school. Therefore, he was very careful to have average grades, as he was sure he would be penalized in the worst possible way: Being prohibited to practice automobilism.

It was the same for me at home: We had no benefits without first doing our obligations. Responsibilities first, whether you like them or not! And then we could have the benefits, just as it works in adulthood. This requirement aimed at teaching us to have courage, responsibility, willpower and, above all, satisfaction of feeling that we could reach our dreams on our own merit. Both he and I understood this condition as something important to our education. That is why Beco and I walked arm in arm with our principles, learned within our homes: "No pain, no gain".

On the weekend after Beco's return to Brazil, we went to Guarujá. He and Antifuro (as Beco called his friend Júnior) stayed at Braguinha's house, Ayrton's friend. During the day, we went to Enseada beach by boat. We had the same ritual as in Angra, but on that trip we did not have Beco's speedboat to pull us with slalom. We ended up renting a speedboat for that.

On board, my family accompanied by their "sons-in-law", Ayrton and Dadô, with relatives of the Zarif family

Ayrton slalom-skiing on Enseada Beach, pulled by the rented speedboat

That is me slalom-skiing on the same day.

That day, my brother-in-law Dadô was with us. His favorite hobby was scuba diving to catch lobsters in their burrows. He then found a new companion for this activity:

Antifuro. Beco was never interested in diving, as he had pressure sensitivity in his ears.

When they returned, I remember Júnior showed me a huge lobster they caught, full of transparent bubbles glued to the abdomen, in a salmon color, which I learned were lobster roe.

Eduardo, showing his eccentric features, came back happy, smiling and every scratched. Júnior told us, laughing, about Dadô's prank trying to reach the lobster. He said the burrow was tight and Dadô, plus the tank, did not fit there! He ventured in anyway and caught the lobster, but he struggled so much getting out that got totally scratched.

Dadô would laugh about it too, but my father got suspicious. After all, he was the captain in charge of the vessel and did not want anyone to get hurt. He made a point of protesting to make it clear that it was not the least bit funny and that he hoped the incident would not happen again.

As soon as dad walked away, Antifuro, with the tip of his fingers, took the lobster roe and put it into his mouth! When he noticed our disgusted expression, he added, laughing:

"What?! Don't you eat caviar? This is caviar!" he said, walking towards those who did not like the idea, offering the roe.

The most remarkable thing that day, and I am happy to have his photos, is that at a certain moment, when Beco was in the inflatable dinghy (small boat) and I was standing on the mat next to those who boarded and disembarked from it, we heard from inside the boat, on the radio that had been on all day, the Careless Whispers song. I immediately remembered the strong and engaging feeling I had when we danced, Beco and I, this song at the Gallery. When I looked at Beco, entertained by that daydream, he was looking directly at me. With a soft smile, he said:

"Do you remember, Dri?"

Unbelieving that that moment had also marked him, I had to ask:

"Remember what?"

"Yeah, Drica... the song we danced that day at the Gallery," he said, as if reading my mind, understanding the reason for my question.

In a low voice, as if trying to say just so he could hear or read my lips, wide-eyed and flabbergasted, I said:

"You remember!"

He had felt it too! I looked away. I put my head down to close myself into my thoughts. Deep down, I wondered how that was possible. Why among many other songs we danced that day, he wanted to remind me of that one especially?

That had been a month ago. He had already traveled and returned to Brazil, so many things had happened to him since then, and we had never said a single word about it. It was a magical moment in my life and even today it is. That proved for me that we silently enjoyed that strong feeling together. This obviously became "our song".

Chapter V

Once, at the farm, we had all spent the day at the pool. At a certain moment, when few people were around and Beco, dad, mom and I were sitting around the table on the main balcony, Mr. Amilcar decided to dot the i's and cross the t's.

"Listen, Ayrton. We have a few things to arrange. You are a grown man, a public person, and Adriane is a girl who is finishing middle school. She has her student life, friends, school parties and she will not be able to accompany you. You will be away most of the time, and my concern is for my daughter's image and privacy. I want to preserve her life. You chose a career of exposure, but she did not. This is not part of her life and I want it to stay that way!"

"I am glad, Amilca, that you mentioned this. I also think we should have this conversation. I really like your daughter and understand and respect the situation; I hope to gain your trust and you can rest assured that I would not harm her. I have the best of intentions."

I was just watching the conversation with wide eyes, waiting to see the result of that.

"I see! "Don't get me wrong, we all like you very much, I have a great respect for your father, but please know that I never invite boys on the boat; when they come, it is because the girls invited and they are their friends. When I started a conversation with you on the beach, in Angra, was because I knew you were Milton's son. You are a well-bred boy, I know. But I could not imagine any of this! The admiration I have for your family and your professional life is one thing, my daughter's life is another."

"Amilca, I thank you for your affection and I assure you that I will preserve Adriane; I will not mix Beco's life with Ayrton's. And I am here and want to be with Adriane as part of Beco's life."

"Good to hear that. I am glad. We are done here," said dad and then continued: "What about your father? Does he raise cattle yet?"

For everyone's relief, the conversation took another direction. Afterwards, Beco and I talked about it, alone.

"Damn it! Amilca is an angry man! Didn't I tell you I should ask for their consent?"

Even though I was super proud of my father and feeling super loved, guarded and cared for by him (my hero), I also believe that things had limits!

"No, Beco! It is nonsense. I have never seen any guy asking them to date my sisters. I talked to him about us 'dating'. I think this is reasonable for now. We will not be able to go out alone, I tell you in advance. We will not even be able to hold hands in front of them. We will be as crushes for them. Is that okay?"

"Okay, doll, let's see how it goes."

"After all, I am not just any cheerleader!" I said, looking snobby, playful and defiant.

"Certainly not! Oh, if only you looked at me! But can you at least be my number 1 fan?" he said with a mischievous and playful look.

"I will think about it carefully!"

"Come here!"

He pulled me by hand to the room where he was hosted. I froze, because that was a forbidden area. With the bedroom door held open, he pulled me to sit on the edge of the bed, removed the gold necklace he wore around his neck, opened the lock and took out a small letter he used next to a rectangular plaque with a religious image. It was the initial of his name and mine.

"Dridrica, give me your chain."

I took it off and handed it to Beco. He opened the lock and with some difficulty, having to use the teeth to shape the bond to pass it through the chain lock, he put the letter A he carried with him, and said:

"This is for you to carry with you and feel that I am always close to you."

I responded to his attitude with a sweet look and smile.

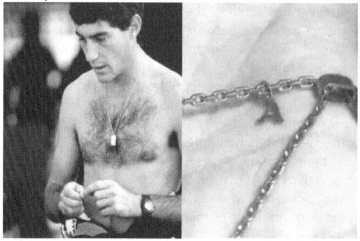

Beco with the chain he always wore and the pendant with the letter A he put on my chain

This pendant market the memory of one of my friends, Renata Belém: "I remember some gifts Ayrton gave Adriane, like a Rolex and a golden letter A that he wore and put on her chain."

"Adriane! Daughter!"

"Beco, we had better get back to the living room, they are already looking for me!"

"Gosh, Dri! It is a hard control, huh?" he said, surprised.

"Let's go, Dri!"

As we approached everyone, Beco said, laughing:

"Wow, Marilene," he laughed, "you look like a screwdriver!" he said, making swirling gestures with his hand, as if he were tightening a screw. "Controlling everything!"

My mother put her hands on her hips as if she was going to scold, gave a smirk and replied:

"That is right!"

From that day on, one of Beco's diversions was to provoke his mother-in-law, as if he was going to steal her baby girl. And hers, it was to show how much she would guard and protect me, whether he liked it or not. Mutual provocation!

Aunt Nádia Zarif, my father's sister, recalls these moments with emotion: "Beco liked to mess with Marilene; as she was hard line, he called her a screwdriver. He was crazy about messing with her, and she accepted it. She took it as a joke, of course, but she did not make it easy."

Rosangela Martinelli, a friend since high school, remembers how my family life was: "Adriane has always been a family girl; so to say, a girl who has always been preserved by her family and parents. Ayrton recognized that in her. He saw Adriane as a strong girl and as someone to marry with. He respected her a lot and was always very careful with her. He faced a challenge, because Adriane's father was angry to the extreme. Everyone was afraid of him, because although he was a very nice person, he commanded respect, and was not easy for Ayrton! He must have liked her a lot to face that close marking. Adriane was very young and her parents were afraid that she would get hurt, because he was on the rise in his career. Those were the most important years of his career, from my point of view, because he was winning races and building his career. In fact, they were together when he won his first World Championship in 1988."

That weekend, on the farm, we even played soccer, which was not common, because there were hardly enough men in the house to make two teams. But that day, besides the couples, we invited some employees that worked on the farm to make two teams. A disaster, they were all hopeless! Out of all the sports Beco had practiced with us, that was definitely the worst.

Everyone made it easier for Mr. Amilcar's attacks, "the boss". And they laughed their heads off, because you really could not get into a competitive mood — it was too many bad players together. Except that my father took advantage of the hierarchy and thought he was really rocking it, but his breath let him down!

The hopeless players: Beco and Mr. Amilcar

From left to right: Beco (kicking the ball), Kaco (in the background), farm employee (in pants), Mr. Amilcar, with his leg up, Júnior (on his back), farm employee (on goal) and Dadô.

In a blazing summer sun, around one in the afternoon, that could not last long. My aunts got into the comic game mood and packed a first-aid kit. When my father could not stand running any longer and stopped for a breath of air, my aunts sprang into action. A Styrofoam box with a red cross made of duct tape, a hope to drag someone who was injured, a plunger to revive someone who is out of breath and a bottle of water to avoid dehydration, among other gewgaws they invented. The game ended there. It became a joke. Everyone laughing. My aunts are great!

Aunt Nádia "rescuing" the boss

On our way back to São Paulo, Beco proposed:

"Let's go to the movies tomorrow?"

"Let's go!" I replied, really happy!

"Mom, Beco asked me to go to the movies tomorrow, can I?"

"You already know you cannot go out alone, right?"

"What if it is in the afternoon?"

"Talk to your sisters!"

After two incisive refusals:

"Mom, they said no way! Now what?"

"If you go on foot, you can go to a movie nearby, in Paulista   Avenue, alone with him. Not by car!

"Okay!"

Thank goodness, I did not have to explain too much for Beco to accept going to the movies on foot. It was really close to my house.

However, the third time we went to the movies together, everything happened exactly the same way, but the moment we were leaving, it started to drizzle. He obviously told us to go by car. It seemed obvious! I thought: "I will not tell him we are not going by car because I cannot ride in the car with him. This is too much! It is drizzling, we cannot walk. I find it offensive for me to say such a thing. How embarrassing!"

I swallowed hard, glanced up at the windows at the top of the building, to see if my mother would be spying from the fourteenth floor. I saw nothing, got up my courage and got into the silver Escort XR3, the latest super sports type from his sponsoring company, Ford.

On the way back home, still in the car, after making out at the movies, he commented:

"Dri, we are dating... I am a man, with a man's needs..."

Damn, I thought, I have seen it all!

"And you are young. What are we going to do?"

"I am very young and you are a grown man. Do to the others what you cannot do to me right now, but please do not let me know at all!" I replied, properly trained by my mother and free from inner conflicts. It was too many new demands for a teenager like me to handle.

Beco did not come into the apartment, and as soon as I set foot in the house, my mom asked:

"Adriane! How was it at the movies?"

"All right, mom!"

"What was the movie about?"

I told the plot of the movie. She asked:

"Did you get caught in the rain?"

I did not resist it! By the questions and the tone of voice... she knew.

"No, mom, I did not get caught in the rain because Beco drove to the movies with me."

"Oh, I saw it! I looked out the window and you have broken my order. How can I trust you? This is not what we agreed."

I stopped the speech firmly and a little scared of mom. She looked like Cinderella's stepmother and not my mother. That was enough!

"Mom! I know I failed to comply with your order, but it did not make sense for me to tell Beco we could not go to the movies in the afternoon, by car, alone. Last time I managed to disguise, but it was raining! How will it be, mom? For me to go out with my boyfriend, I have to convince my sisters, but they will not go! What if it rains? I cannot go from here to there by car with him? Either you learn to trust me or you are going to ruin my relationship! And we are not doing anything wrong. What a nonsense! You saw it was drizzling and said nothing? To make it worse, you spied on us from up here to put me to the test? To catch me in the act? That way I will not be able to date! I have no courage to tell Beco we cannot go to the movies alone by car, even on a rainy day. If you want, you can tell him. Or I will keep going by car from now on!"

I turned away and stomped off to my room, breathless and indignant. Conclusion: She never had the courage to tell Beco, and I could, from then on, go out with him in the car.

In daylight, of course!

At night, in São Paulo, we used to go out with Júnior and a friend of mine; that way, we could stay a little out of my parents' sight. We once went to a place at the end of Oscar Freire Street — I do not remember the name, but the logo was a train car — with dim lights to give the couples some privacy. It was a place specifically to go in couples, have a few drinks and kiss comfortably. Beco and I would not stay apart all night, we kissed and whispered, as if no one else was around; it was an opportunity to make up for lost time and discover sensations that I did not know until then. Ayrton caressed my mouth, neck, ears with his warm and soft tongue; he was very affectionate and skillful and took me completely out of my orbit! Nothing else existed in the world for at least an hour and a half. I went to the moon and back about twenty times. Afterwards, we returned to this place a few times.

Chapter VI

On Beco's twenty-fifth birthday, on March 21st, 1985, we went to a nightclub, to an event organized by one of his sponsors, on Rua dos Pinheiros. He set up a scheme with a van so that the entire group of my family could go together and stopped by my house to pick me up. I remember that Júnior, my sister Christhiane and my cousins Patrícia and Andrea were there. But before we go to the party, we stopped by a workshop in Pacaembu to get his helmet. He had left there to be painted by Sid Mosca*.

My cousin Patrícia Kaiser, whom we affectionately call Patu, remembers: "That day, Ayrton saw for the first time the definitive painting of his helmet for the F1 season of 1985."

That same one! Which he would wear throughout his career and would become a symbol of patriotism and struggle for an ideal.

The yellow tone of the 1985 helmet was lemon yellow.

*Cloacyr Sidney Mosca (in memory), Sid Mosca, was a driver before starting to customize racing helmets.

We joined the party promoted by John Player Special by a side door and, before we reached the main hall of the club, Beco asked us to wait in a corner near him while he would give a TV interview about the event in his honor. After the interview, we entered the room with the privacy of the dim lighting in the club and, as soon as they announced his presence, Beco told Júnior, before going up to the stage:

"Take care of my girl, I will be right back!

On stage, Ayrton greeted everyone and, after singing "Happy birthday to you", he thanked everyone and returned to the floor where Júnior and I awaited.

The first person Beco spoke to was Júnior, to whom he asked:

"Where is my girl?"

"What girl?"

Although we were in the dim light of the club and the sound was loud, I heard their dialogue very well. I was very close to them. I hesitated to speak up, confused by Júnior's doubts about who Beco was referring to. That was the first high-regarded event related to his profession that I had attended and I watched silently.

"My girl!" Beco insisted, thinking he might not have heard. Júnior looked at him without answering and apparently not knowing who it was.

"Gee, Júnior what do you mean which girl? Adriane!" he said, impatiently. At that moment, I reached out to him, relieved and satisfied. Beco opened a smile and hugged me. We stood still in the same spot on the floor, holding each other, both facing the stage as we watched a show. But I did not get Júnior's attitude.

The party also marked the memories of my cousin Andrea Duarte: "It was a party at a nightclub, Pool Music Hall. They announced his helmet. We picked it up where the guy painted his helmet. He rented a van and arranged for everyone to come along. When we got to the Pool, it was not possible to leave the van. It was crazy the number of reporters and photographers. I said I could not get out of the car and Dri agreed. We drove and entered through the side of the club. It was like that; we had to live with him as if he were a normal guy. But it was very crazy for me. Everyone around him, a lot of photography. Then he found a way and left us in a reserved box and left us in a box and complied with all the formalities. They sang Happy Birthday, introduced the new helmet and he gave interviews. About two hours later we left by the side of the club. Nobody saw us leaving."

After the show and because of the appointments for the next day, the group left together. At that time, I did not wear much makeup and wore discreet clothes. But that particular night, I wore a straight skirt and a thick V-neck blouse, which I wore without a bra so not to show the strap. When I got out of the car, in front of my house, Beco reached out to help me, I leaned over and it was at that moment that I felt a breeze go through my blouse, which were exposing more than I meant to. Instinctively, I used my hand to hide the exposed cleavage. We looked at each other for a few seconds but said nothing.

Then we went to the farm, and I gave Beco a kite as a birthday present (picture below at the farm), as well as a pair of Zoomp jeans. This brand was the hit of the moment in Brazil!

That weekend at Chapadão farm, I decided to say something to Beco that was bothering me. He used to call my father Amilca. It may seem silly, but if there is one thing that I learned in my life is respecting the hierarchy. Otherwise, it becomes a mess! I know Ayrton treated people the same age as my father with whom he worked as equals and even had authority over them, but that did not sit well with me. I asked:

"Beco, it is Mr. Amilcar, and not Amilca. He is my father and not a colleague of yours and should be treated as such. Do you mind?" I asked, a little nervous, but in the sweetest possible tone.

"Of course not, Drica, it is just that I did not know! I call my parents Záza and Miltão.

"Wow! The day I meet your parents I will not be able to treat them like that! I was raised that way and this is why I decided to tell you. But I appreciate your attitude in understanding my point."

I gave him a warm hug, pleased by his calm reaction. Nothing became a problem or unnecessary nitpicking for us. On the contrary, everything was easily solved. After all, the difficulties in getting together were many and demanded mutual effort, affection, respect, care and tolerance! But those were difficulties apart from the relationship. Between us, there was no complication in any aspect of the relationship, although I was younger than him and we dated almost at distance. Beco knew the difficulty I faced to be with him and I was moved by the difficulty he faced to be with me. Certainly, it was love based on overcoming existing difficulties. I had never felt so loved by anyone.

When we, the younger ones, were talking in the fireplace, virginity theme came up. When we were alone, Beco commented:

"I do not care about this female virginity thing. I have never had a relationship with a virgin woman."

My mother said that virginity was the greatest gift you could give anyone you chose as a husband. So, believing that, I told him:

"But I do care. I was raised that way!" and I closed the subject.

At another moment of the same weekend, there was a comment about Princess Stéphanie of Monaco. At that time, she was young and was always in celebrity magazines for being considered the most rebellious of the family and providing good images for the paparazzi. When he heard about her, Beco said:

"I met her and her family in Monaco when I got the second place on the podium in Monaco last year (1984). They have a tradition of holding a gala dinner on race night, to receive the top three drivers and their teams."

"Wow, that is nice! And what is she like?" someone asked.

"Oh, I don't know, I did not pay much attention," he said, smiling.

"There were a lot of people I wanted to meet, important people to my career, team owners, representatives of the main sponsors, FIA people, just important F1 people. As a newcomer, I had this opportunity thanks to that rainy day," he said laughing and proud of his achievement with Toleman.

Quiet, listening to that and imagining the trouble I had gotten myself into, I visualized the scene of my Beco surrounded by women much more interesting than me! How long would that boy want to stay with me? Who was I? What kind of woman would he have a chance to be with? Damn it! Princess of Monaco?

Those thoughts, especially in the first year of our relationship, put me in touch with myself. Which was great, because it kept my feet on the ground and I had no illusions about holding him to me. The only guarantee I had of his affection would be that he would come back to me if he wanted to. And I had better not expect that. Or it could be bad for me. So whenever he left, it was a real farewell to me. I did not know if he would come back. During his painful absence, I tried to live my life as normal as possible. I was terrified of people knowing about our relationship, afraid that he would show up with another woman. I did not want to go through that constraint! Because of that, I thought my father had been a genius in requiring to keep me anonymous. I was grateful to him that, in addition to protecting me, gave me the opportunity to take a risk with such an unlikely relationship.

My aunt Miriam was always very skeptical about our relationship: "It is not that I did not like their relationship. But I did not like the future I saw. I watched over Adriane. It is not that she was better than him. But I thought she was young and deserved a more present guy. I used to say: With him, she will always be a poor rich woman. For professional reasons, I believed he would never have the opportunity to give her the attention she deserved. What was the point of being in a castle but alone?"

A wise and fun advice I received from my mother helped me a lot in the beginning of my relationship with Beco: "When you have nothing smart to say, it is best to be quiet. Quiet people can go smart. But once you open your mouth, there is no going back! Better to let others be in doubt."

Because of our age difference, I was terrified of being a fool or a child in front of him, and I was very careful when saying anything. Absurd self-control for a fifteen-year-old.

I was always playful and very tomboyish; people at home noticed that I acted cautiously in front of Beco. They were amused by the girl who suddenly intended to behave like a lady. In my fantasy, he was a prince charming who deserved a princess.

As usual for relatives, they would denounce me by making fun of me. For example, on Saturday nights, on the farm, it was customary to serve mozzarella pizza on pita bread, which were made right there. We used to eat a lot of vegetables, fresh from the vegetable garden, and we ate pizza with cheese and crunchy dough, covered in seasoned lettuce. I decided to eat it with knife and fork in the presence of Beco...

"Wow, Dri! So fancy! I do not recognize you! Are you eating pizza with cutlery?" my sister said in a sarcastic tone, intending to expose me.

Everyone at the table turned their attention to me to see how I would get out of this, including Beco, although he did not understand it at first.

"I am!" I replied, playing dumb, giving a simple answer to an unimportant question, but controlling myself not to laugh and hoping to end the matter there.

I discreetly looked around and found that some were already eating the pizza with their hands and to my bad luck, they liked the dirty trick with me. Then someone else teased:

"But you love eating it with your hands! Why are you using a fork?"

What an unpleasant situation they put me in. Totally gave me away! I tried to act polite, but I knew they would not let me get away with this. Beco understood the situation and decided to participate:

"Explain it right, Dri!" and laughed his slow laugh.

Already full of that, I did not let it go. I said calmy, resting the cutlery on the table:

"You know what, Beco? I was the one who had the idea of filling the pizza folded in half with a lot of salad inside," I said, showing how to do it, "like that! See? It is easier if you eat with your hands."

I said, brazen-faced, as if I was being didactic. Beco did not take his eyes off me. With a funny face and surprised with the twist, I still bragged:

"It is so tasty that everyone adopted it! I was trying to be polite in front of you, but as they have already given me away, I will eat with my hands anyway. You should try it, it is delicious."

I took a good bite to finish my demonstration. My parents smiled, proud of the flexibility with which I got out of that situation. But the bastards would not miss an opportunity to turn me in. Just as I had done hundreds of times with my sisters, just like a good youngest child who must drive the older children mad, as well as the brothers-in-law and cousins. In fact, they were getting their own back on me.

And this vegetable pizza became famous among visitors of the farm, as aunt Nádia says: "Adriane was very funny. She taught Beco how to make a sandwich that later became a routine in his life. We always made it on the farm. We used to put mozzarella on the pita bread, as you do in a pizza. Moreover, there was always a big salad on the table. Dri used to make a huge sandwich, with a lot of vegetables inside, and we would talk to her in private: Adriane, it will look bad for you. But then he did just the same. It became a huge sandwich pizza. He imitated what she did, in an identical way! This marked us. He ate healthy food. He would never eat too much of anything and loved this sandwich Dri made. He was a measured person. He ate normal. And loved eating vegetable pizza. It is delicious! They have to patent: Adriane Yamin's pizza: pita bread with a ton of vegetables inside. It was very funny, because when eating the vegetables, the seasoning leaked out. We would laugh our heads off with their sandwich. It was a fun and very enjoyable time."

Chapter VII

It is worth recalling a moment remembered by my uncle José Carlos: "Ayrton was doing a tire test in Rio de Janeiro, and I was there. A discussion occurred in the Lotus team: He was going to take the first laps and was already in the car when the boss said: You are not going now.

He left the car with the steering wheel in his hand and went to check how many kilometers per hour Elio de Angelis was driving. Afterwards, he went back to the pit and was furious. Ayrton was supposed to leave at that moment, but they made him go afterwards. When we got back to the hotel, he went upstairs to shower and we went downstairs to have dinner. Then we sat on a bench and as I noticed he was down, I asked:

Are you tired, Ayrton?

When you drive from São Paulo to here, you get tired, don't you?

Yes! I replied.

You come at a hundred kilometers per hour and I drive at three hundred; it is really more tiring.

The other day, we came back from training and I had dinner alone, but I found him at the hall, walking back and forth.

What is it?, I asked.

He replied:

I have to have dinner with the President of the National Bank, Magalhães Pinto, and he will piss me off, not to mention that whole bunch of children he has who will ask me for an autograph, and I want to rest!

He was like that: Although exhausted, he did not hesitate to comply with his commitments with his sponsors, especially those who supported him from the beginning."

At the Brazilian Grand Prix, Jacarepaguá racetrack in Rio de Janeiro, on April 7, 1985, Ayrton started in fourth place, but had to abandon the race on the lap 48 due to electrical problems.

But what bothered me most on that occasion was to see published in the press photos of the model Monique Evans sitting on his lap. I commented to my mother:

"What the hell! We got off to a good start with this fame thing, didn't we? Public figure? Or publicly available person?"

"Dear, get used to it, this is his life! It is no use complaining."

"The love story is not important, what matters is being able to love"

Quote from the "Little Prince" that Adriane wrote in the 1985 booklet, customized for each driver, and which Beco gave her so that she followed the schedule and information about the GPs at each circuit.

When Beco came back from the GP in Rio, we went to the movies in the afternoon. Already settled in our seats, I noticed huge blisters on his hands. Alarmed by that, I asked:

"Beco, what are you going to do? Will all races end like this?"

"Do not worry, Dridrica, this is no problem. I will figure it out!" he said with a smile.

Imagining the pain he must be feeling, I instinctively kissed the blisters carefully, one by one, as if that could soothe his pain.

Before Beco left for Europe, we all went to the farm. At the beginning of our relationship, we met there, because I went with my parents. But after a while, we would go together in his car, he and I in the back seat, kissing from São Paulo to Porto Feliz, with Júnior driving, who also stayed alert to see if Mr. Amilcar's car was not in the surroundings. Loud music and interior rearview mirror out of sight for us to have some privacy. This is how we managed to have a little fun, with no pressure from my family controlling us. We could do almost nothing without some company! And when we went out, we had to deal with harassment from the fans. Later, when our relationship was steady and Beco had gained some confidence from my parents, we would go alone on the road, kissing the entire way all the same, but he would go driving slowly and I would lean over him, with my back to the wheel. One of the requirements for him to choose the car model of the brand that sponsored him here in Brazil, in addition to the luggage space for his model airplanes, accessories and tool box, was space and comfort, so that I could lean over him in a way that the gear would not hurt me. After all, it was as much privacy as we could get together and we could not waste it. Thus, he started to use automatic cars, even though he preferred the manual gear, which provides greater control of the car and allowed incredible maneuvers from time to time. Bye-bye, sports cars, and long live the automatic gear!

The problem of being with Beco on the road was when other drivers recognized him. Every time we ran into people with powerful cars, they would start provoking him to go drag racing. A real hell for those who wanted peace to make out. Thus, he preferred to travel with a big car — we would be out of the ordinary line of sight and be comfortable on the dirt road.

When we arrived at the farm, I said:

"Thank God, Beco! Will it be like this? I do not mind taking pictures together, but did you need to have Monique Evans sit on your lap?" I said, annoyed.

He replied, laughing:

"Dridrica, it was full of photographers around and she jumped into my lap! What else could I do?" gesturing with his hands. "The photographers were encouraging her, then she also sat on my lap, pulling my hands around her to pose... I froze!"

"Look, I would love to be there with you. But you know I cannot. But that is not working!"

"Dri! I am there for work, not for that sort of thing. It happened! I was caught by surprise. Such a thing has never happened to me before. It is the first race of the year and people are curious about me, and it was in Brazil. I did not expect so much attention on me." He finished the sentence holding back a laugh, finding my jealousy amusing but afraid I would be scared.

"Look, Beco, you will have to be more careful and prevent this kind of thing from happening again. I know you are there for work and focused on what you do, but the harassment is strong and you have to figure out how to handle these girls who want to create news. That won't work! And how do I look at my family? Take it easy!" I said, annoyed.

"Dridrica, you are right. I will be more careful from now on, but I am sure this initial fuss will calm down because of the professional attitude I have in the pits."

"Please, it is hard enough for me not to 'exist' and not be able to follow you, do you think I do not really want to be there with you? And now this? Help me, okay?" I said in a pleading tone.

"Deal! And no more talking about it," he decreed.

I did not hear about episodes like this anymore, because Ayrton avoided photos with models in the pits. It was also a matter of not being used and not hampering his concentration on race days. Gradually, Beco was learning how to deal with fame and how to not push his luck or get into trouble, as he used to say.

About this GP in Rio, Beco told us that the mechanics played a trick on him during training.

"Those Englishmen wanted to get me! When I left the pit to the track, I had the car's traction tires off the ground and it took me a few seconds to realize why the car was not moving," he said, laughing. "I looked around and the naughty ones were holding back their laughter, pretending not to know what was going on. When they saw that I realized the prank, they lowered the car and I went to the track.

From then on, he could barely keep talking because he was laughing so hard, and all of us laughing at his laugh...

"When I got back to the pits, everyone was attentive to see my reaction, but I pretended that nothing happened. They did not know who they were messing with!" He laughed his slow laugh and continued: "As soon as I left the racetrack I got blue aniline, a syringe, and candy, which they would not refuse! At the hotel, I prepared the sweets. On Sunday morning, when I arrived at the pits, I dressed up and kindly offered candies to all the Englishmen. Too bad not everyone accepted! They all got blue mouths and then they told they were peeing blue for two days."

Then we all laughed hard.

I received more flowers with a card on the day Beco boarded to Europe. He traveled to the Portuguese GP and I, from then on, found out how hard it was dating long-distance. Mainly because I was completely in love with that handsome guy, with a good character, cheerful, kind, loving, admirable and very present in my life when he was in Brazil.

Chapter VIII

1985 Portuguese GP was special. In Friday's unofficial practice, Ayrton set the best time and, on Sunday, won his first victory in F1. It was a very exciting race in the rain. He started from pole position and won from the beginning to the end.

"Beco, in addition to beating the track record (Estoril), won the Grand Prix in Portugal" – on April 21, 1985.

After climbing the podium, Beco gave an interview, very moved, to Reginaldo Leme, thanking everyone who supported him and gave him the structure to get there: Parents, siblings, agent and "my girl".

I was out of breath. I was watching the interview in the TV room of the farm, with the whole family together. They were all surprised and stunned, until a funny one said:

"Who is this girl?"

That was it! The magic feeling in the air ended and we dispersed. A few moments later, Beco called:

"Hey Dridrica, what's up?"

"Beco, congratulations! The race was awesome! You did it! Whoooo!" I said, vibrantly and happily.

He asked:

"Did you see the interview I gave after the race?" I cautiously replied:

"I did, I watched the interview and the entire race!"

"Well then! Didn't you see who I dedicated the race to?"

Honestly, I did not know what to say about that loving gesture of his. I started to cry softly with emotion and gratitude.   That was all for me?

"Hello!!! Is anyone there?"

And before I had time to answer, he added:

"Dridrica, I am calling so that you have no doubts, even though you do not give me a chance," he laughed his slow laugh, "that it was for you that I dedicated my first victory, along with my family. My very special girl, who is already very important in my life."

I cried my eyes out, unable to say anything for a few seconds, and he was laughing across the ocean, probably imagining my crying face. But he knew I was crying with emotion! He knew this was a gesture that would give one's girlfriend a heart attack, because I was so proud of the boyfriend I had. When I managed to put my things together again, I spoke, still slurring:

"Wow, Beco! I did not expect that. It is a good thing you called to confirm," I said, half laughing, half crying. "Because it was hard to believe you did that. So it really was for me?"

"Of course, Dridrica!" he replied, laughing, "It is for you to see how important and special you are to me. I called you to know and be sure it was for you."

A brief silence. In fact, our silences always contained one million words. As Saint-Exupéry put it, "What is essential is invisible to the eye". And I humbly add: "and inaudible to the ear".

"Beco, I do not even know what to say... Just... come back soon for us to celebrate. I miss you so much!"

"Okay, Dridrica!" Things are crazy here. I am calling you from a motorhome and I cannot talk anymore. Take care, we will talk later. A huge kiss on 'my girl'."

"I wish I were there with you! Congratulations on that beautiful victory. Kisses."

At the time, in the farmhouse, we had three wired phone points: One in the TV room, where we watched the race; another in the living room; and another in the kitchen. Incredible though it seems, I picked it up on the kitchen, imagining I would have "some" privacy. As if! During the entire phone call, my relatives surreptitiously circulated around me, trying to catch something from my conversation with Beco. But I was already used to it and it was useless to complain, as it was impossible to change my family behavior. On the other hand, I also understood that everyone was delighted with Beco and thrilled with his gesture. So I decided to share with the fans:

"I cannot believe it! Beco called just to say that I am the girl to whom he dedicated the victory."

"That is nice, dear!" my father said, visibly pleased.

It was hard not to love Beco, he was extremely seductive. He liked to make surprises that took anyone's breath away. And everyone who lived with me ended up, in a way, also being taken by him.

After this public declaration of love, Beco had to deal with the curiosity of the press, as journalist Reginaldo Leme recounts:

"It was a very long interview. He had won for the first time in F1. And he was talking about a lot of things about the race, mainly, but also about his life. Then they asked him who he was dedicating the race to. He said again: To my girl! But who is "my girl"? — everyone asked him. But Ayrton was precise: I cannot say, but you will know one day. This interview was conducted at the racetrack, but then we had dinner together. In fact, that was the day when Tancredo Neves died (Tancredo Neves had just been elected president of Brazil at that time). Galvão and Armando returned to Brazil that night. We had dinner at *Guincho*, a very well-known restaurant, with several Portuguese friends. In the restaurant, we spoke again and again about *my girl*. But Senna said he would say nothing else".

That year, I had taken him to a recording of *Roda Viva* TV show — not in the show in which he participated, but in a recording in which I took him precisely to show him how it was then go out to have dinner with friends and partners. The questioners, along with me, were Bob Coutinho, Carlos Rios, Ricardo Montoro, Fernando Braga, my friends and partners in a bar. I only took Ayrton because I knew how he would be received by the audience. He had no idea, but I thought I had to show this guy to the media, I had to make Brazil know this man. He had just won his first race in F1, with black Lotus in Portugal, 1985.

That night, when his name was announced, people stood up and applauded. Before the show, people would meet in a large hall, with many guests. It was always a special evening, and when they announced his presence, the applause was lively and continued for a few minutes. I got close to him and said: *See why I brought you here?* He did not say thank you, he did not say anything. I knew he was like that, but I was satisfied. When we left, he just told me: *Do not bring me to these places, I want to stay in my house,* to which I replied: *Why did I bring you? But did you see?"*.

Shortly afterwards, when Beco and I went to attend the opening of Reginaldo Leme's bar, in São Paulo, the following photo was published by a newspaper in the capital.

Luizinho Coruja/Ed. Azul

A namorada do campeão

A "minha garota", a quem Ayrton Senna dedicou a vitória na F-1 domingo foi descoberta ontem: é a estudante paulistana Adriane Yamin, 19 anos, na foto antes da corrida. Página 15

Photo published in Estadão taken by Luizinho Coruja.

The champion's girlfriend We found out yesterday who was "my girl", to whom Ayrton Senna dedicated his victory in F1 on Sunday: The student Adriane Yamin, São Paulo, 19 years old, in the photo before the race.

And it is Reginaldo Leme himself who tells the details of that night, when he met me: "I did not know her yet, but I knew her family. Some people called her his 'sweetheart'; at fifteen, it is normal to be called 'sweetheart', but you were his only girlfriend, and he took you very seriously, that is just how he was. We met for the first time at the opening of the bar *Talento Jazz*, on Avenida Faria Lima, which was mine and my partners — and friends to this day, Ricardo Montoro, Carlos Rios, Bob Coutinho and Fernando Braga. I had made the invitation to Ayrton a few days before, but he was very aloof to that sort of thing. I insisted: *Look, I know you do not like it, but it would be important for me having you there.*

Armando, his agent, helped and said: *You have to go, Becão.*

Then, they went! We stayed at a table with Gugelmin. I even have this photo. He wanted to leave early and I went with them. There was a very large L-shaped staircase; it was the most beautiful part of our bar. We started to go down the stairs; I was coming last and the reporter Ana Maria, who had a TV show with her name, Ana Maria, from 9 to noon on Jovem Pan Radio, arrived. She spoke about everything there, except about sports. Whatever the reason, she decided to have an interview with Ayrton. I had never seen her in my life, but I knew who she was because the show was famous. We had barely started down the stairs — he, Adriane and I — when she walked right up to him: *Ayrton, I am Ana Maria, from Jovem Pan. Can I have a word?*

He said: *No, I am not talking to anyone,* and continued down the stairs.

I went down behind him and looked at her, who was on the way. I went down about three steps and I heard her say: *Wow, is this the impression I am going to take from my idol Ayrton Senna?*

I kept going down and when we got outside, I told him: *Ayrton, this Ana Maria is not a sports or automobilism reporter, I do not know if she is going to ask you about sports, her show is about varieties, food, family, and I just heard her talking about how disappointed she was. If I were you, I would have a word with her!*

Then he took a few steps back and talked to her. It was a matter of five minutes, while I talked to Adriane, from a distance. This has already happened outside the bar, on the street. A photographer came and took that famous photo. I had a friend photographing the event, but inside (he was the one who took the photo of the table with Senna and Gugelmin). But this one that showed up outside? I have no idea who that boy was. I took Ayrton and Adriane to the car and when I got back, the photographer was still there. I asked him what he was doing and he replied that he was always at the door of famous people parties. I do not remember if he told me his name. But I never saw him again.

What I do know is that this photo was published in Estadão Journal. Precisely because we were at a time when Ayrton was a little off the media."

Right after the Portuguese GP, I sent the following telegram to Ayrton:

119

It took a long time for Beco to return to Brazil. It took a lot of practice for him to set up the car. But in the meantime, I received a letter from him:

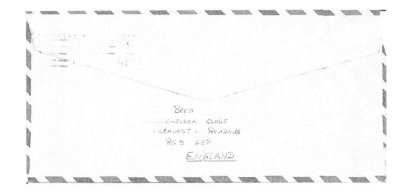

Friday 19th April

PRACTICE DAY 1

Off track	On track
7	7
8	8
9	9
10	10 Practice (untimed) 10.00 – 11.30
11	11
12	12
13	13 Qualifying (timed) 13.00 – 14.00
14	14
15	15
16	16
17	17
18	18
19	19
20	20
21	21

Saturday 20th April

PRACTICE DAY 2

Off track	On track
7	7
8	8
9	9
10	10 Practice (untimed) 10.00 – 11.30
11	11
12	12
13	13 Qualifying (timed) 13.00 – 14.00
14	14
15	15
16	16
17	17
18	18
19	19
20	20
21	21

Sunday 21st April

RACE DAY

Off track	On track
7	7
8	8
9	9
10	10 Practice (untimed) 10.30 – 11.30
11	11
12	12
13	13
14	14 Race Start 14.30
15	15
16	16
17	17
18	18
19	19
20	20
21	21

ABC Design Norwich

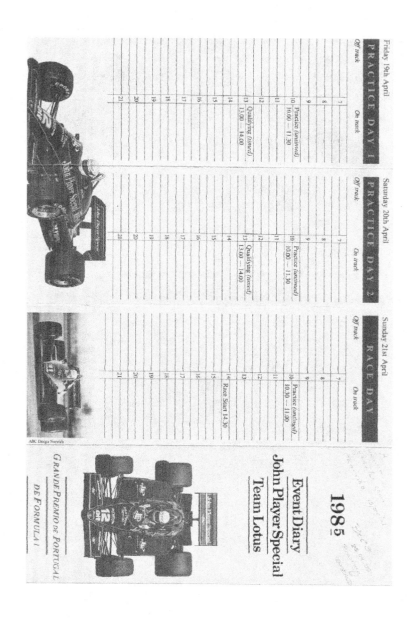

1985

Event Diary
John Player Special
Team Lotus

GRANDE PREMIO DE PORTUGAL
DE FORMULA 1

EVENT

Grande Premio de Portugal
19 a 21 abril 1985
Autódromo do Estoril
Alcabideche

CIRCUIT

LOCATION

Maps reproduced with the assistance of Pascal Stephens Limited.

Arrow Series

DETAILS

4.359 km 2.703 miles
Lap Record: Niki Lauda McLaren MP4 1984 1 min 22.996.
Pole Position 1984 Nelson Piquet Brabham 1 min 21.703.

TIMETABLE

Friday 19th April
Practice (untimed) 10.00 — 11.30
Qualifying (timed) 13.00 — 14.00

Saturday 20th April
Practice (untimed) 10.00 — 11.30
Qualifying (timed) 13.00 — 14.00

Sunday 21st April
Practice (untimed) 10.30 — 11.00
Race start 14.30
Number of Laps 70
Race distance 308.85 kms./191.913 miles

WORLD CHAMPIONSHIPS

Positions after 1st round

Pos	Constructors	Points	Pos	Drivers	Points
1	McLaren	9	1	Prost	9
2	Ferrari	6	2	Alboreto	6
3	JPS	4	3	Elio	4
4	Renault	3	4	Arnoux	3
5	Ligier	1	5	Tambay	2
			6	Laffite	1

INFORMATION

Portuguese Grand Prix

Team Lotus. Chairman and Team management: Hotel Palacio, Estoril, tel. 268 0400, tlx. 12257
Other Team personnel: Sintra Hotel Estoril, Km.6 Estrada Nacional 9, Autodromo, Estoril, tel. 269 0720/9, tlx. 16891
CSS Tony Jardine, Hotel Palacio, Estoril, tel. 268 0400 tlx: 12257

For further information contact: Noel Stanbury, Hotel Palacio

UK TV and radio coverage:

Sat. 20th April
Radio: BBC Radio 2 Medium wave (693 kHz/433 m, 909 kHz/330 m) Sport on 2 (1053-1600) Practice reports.

Sun. 21st April
TV BBC2 "Sunday Grandstand" (1230-1930) Live coverage from Estoril is scheduled. BBC2 "Grand Prix" (1930-2200) Recorded coverage and highlights.
Radio BBC Radio 2 Medium wave "Sports desk" reports on the hour starting at 1500.

HOSPITALITY

Portuguese Grand Prix

The Team's Mobile Home will be situated in the Formula 1 paddock. A telephone will be installed.

MOBILE HOME TEL NO
(?) 284 4053.

FUNCTIONS

Portuguese Grand Prix

A Team dinner has been organised for Saturday evening in the Four Seasons Restaurant, Hotel Palacio. Time 7.30 for 8.00pm. Invitations will be issued at the circuit.

Minha Dri,

Passei uma semana e tanto, não é pra menos, depois de vencer em Portugal foi tudo bastante relaxante !!!

Voltei na terça-feira de Portugal, mas minha vontade mesmo era de pegar um avião p/ o Brasil na noite do domingo da corrida, afinal, não esqueci da champagne que o Armikka disse tia colocado na geladeira após o Rio de Janeiro!

Esta quase feito o negócio da nova casa, mas após a compra, será loucura total p/ mobiliar em tempo suficiente p/ que mudemos até final de junho, em especial pois embora seja uma casa nova tem algumas coisas p/ serem modificadas e que necessitam de cuidado e tempo.

Tenho uma série de treinos programados entre as corridas e nem sei como vai ser p/ encaixar uma escapada ao Brasil, but don't worried, I will find the way to make it possible to be with you ... isso mesmo, é bom ir treinando seu inglês, escuta moça!

Lembro de você com saudades, embora esteja com o tempo curto p/ pensar muito sinto sua falta.

Sabe, embora nosso relacionamento seja curto e de certa forma difícil (pelo fato de viajar muito), gosto bastante de nós dois juntos, te respeito sobre maneira e tenho um

124

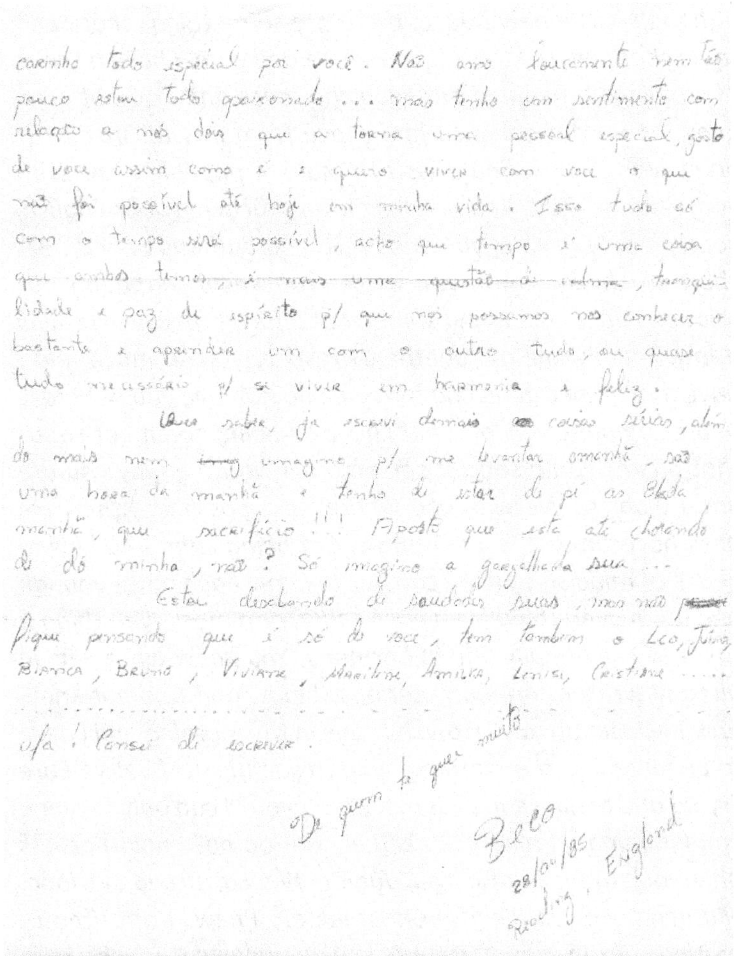
carinho todo especial por você. Nós [illegible] nem tão pouco estou todo apaixonado ... mas tenho um sentimento com relação a nós dois que a torna uma pessoa especial, gosto de você assim como é e quero viver com você o que não foi possível até hoje em minha vida. Isso tudo só com o tempo será possível, acho que tempo é uma coisa que ambos temos, ~~é mais uma questão de calma~~, tranquilidade e paz de espírito p/ que nós possamos nos conhecer o bastante e aprender um com o outro tudo, ou quase tudo necessário p/ se viver em harmonia e feliz.

Quer saber, já escrevi demais coisas sérias, além do mais nem imagino p/ me levantar amanhã, são uma hora da manhã e tenho de estar de pé às 8h da manhã, que sacrifício!!! Aposto que está até chorando de dó minha, não? Só imagino a gargalhada sua...

Estou [illegible] de saudades suas, mas não fique pensando que é só de você, tem também o Léo, [illegible], Bianca, Bruno, Viviane, Marilene, Amilca, Lenise, Cristiane ....

Ufa! Cansei de escrever.

De quem te quer muito

Belo
28/04/85
Reading, England

"My Dri, I had a long week. Of course, after winning in Portugal, everything was very relaxing!!! I returned from Portugal on Tuesday, but what I really wanted was to take a flight to Brazil on Sunday night, after all, I did not forget the champagne Amilca told me he had put on the fridge after Rio de Janeiro! The business with the new house is almost done, but after buying it, it will be a mess to put furniture in enough time for us to move by the end of June, especially because* *although it is a new house, there are some things that need to be changed and this requires time and care. I have a series of trainings scheduled between the races and I do not even know how I am going to find space for going to Brazil, but don't worry, I will find a way to make it possible to be with you... that is right, you had better go practicing your English, young lady! I think of you and I miss you. Although my time is short to think, I miss you a lot. You know, although our relationship is recent and somewhat difficult (because I travel a lot), I really like us together, I respect you so much and I have a very special feeling for you. I do not love you like crazy or am completely in love, but I have a feeling about both of us that makes you a special person, I like you the way you are and I want to live with you whatever is possible; I think we both have time, it is just a matter of being calm and having peace of mind so that we can get to know each other enough and learn everything from each other, or almost everything it takes to live happily and in harmony. You know what, I have already written too many serious things, and I do not know how I will get up tomorrow, it is one in the morning and I have to be up at 8 in the morning, what a sacrifice!!! I bet you are crying and feeling sorry for me, aren't you? I can only imagine you laughing... I miss you like hell, but do not think that it is only you, there is also Leo, Júnior, Bianca, Bruno, Viviane, Marilene, Amilca, Lenise, Christhiane... Phew, I am tired of writing. From someone who likes you so much Beco 04/28/85"*

The race of May 5th was the San Marino GP in Italy, and Ayrton again started in pole position. But he had to leave the track for lack of fuel. Refueling during the race had been banned since the 1984 Championship, and the fuel tank capacity had been limited to 220 liters — an attempt to indirectly control power through consumption.

The day after the Grand Prix, he called me:

"Hey doll, what's up?"

"Everything cool! How about you?"

"I am fine, it is just hard to get back to Brazil. They are scheduling a lot of training sessions, but I am already getting familiar with the mechanics and the car to make the necessary adjustments. Dridrica, I know this is difficult. I miss you..."

"Too bad you had to leave the race!"

"I was upset, but after I won in Portugal, I am even more focused!"

"That is great! Another pole, congratulations!"

"Thanks, but what about you? What have you been doing?"

"The usual, living my life, school..."

"Have you been going out?"

"Only on the birthday of some friend, when I can go. I wake up really early, you know."

"You have a nice, soft voice..."

"Oh, I am a little tired, but your cheerleader misses you. When will you have some time for me? We have not seen each other since Portugal! I would like to thank the winner in person..." I made the remark by playing charm, in a provocative tone.

"I think I will soon be able to go to Brazil soon. I will try to stay there longer. Hang in there, Dridrica."

"Come quickly!" I asked.

"I have to go now, Dri, it is late, it is four hours later here than in Brazil and I am calling from the hotel lobby, you know how expensive international calls are. Calling from the lobby is more affordable. Tomorrow, I go back to England to practice and then Monaco. I will have a good chance to come back, doll. I will be there real soon!"

"Take care, okay? Kisses."

"Kisses, Dridrica."

A few days later I received a postcard from him:

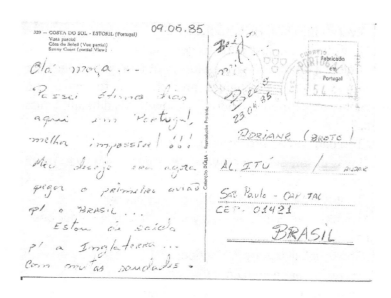

"Hi lady... I had great days here in Portugal, It couldn't have been better! I wish I could take the first flight back to Brazil... I am on my way to England. Miss you a lot."

About a week after receiving Beco's postcard, Monaco GP took place, in Monte Carlo. New pole position and he left the race again, but now due to engine problems.

Senna fans will have to apologize me, but I was thankful. I was apprehensive about the dinner at the Palace, hosted by the Grimaldi Family, for the top three in the race. And, at least this time, he would not participate. Phew!

Otávio Torres managed to express my situation well: "Dri was jealous and it was impossible not to. Ayrton was immensely exposed! We saw on television that he was harassed all the time and she was kind of upset, but they had a pact that no one could know about their relationship. It was a very complicated situation for Adriane; she saw everyone after him, but she could not publicly appear beside him because of her family's imposition. I think it was more because of her family than because of herself."

Chapter IX

The month of June was a very fun time for my family, because many friends would spend the weekend with us on the farm. But in that year of 1985, I had one more reason: Beco! There, we all had a lot of fun together. During the day, we played tennis, went to the pool and rode a motorcycle. In the evening, we played cards— many different games, depending on the number of players.

My cousin Renata Yamin remembers these moments of leisure: "I am five years younger than Adriane, and when they started dating, in Angra, I was still a child. Beco talked more to the adults and teased the boys, my cousins. To make it worse, I was shy. But I remember that we used to play cards on the farm after eating pizza. He liked sports, was very disciplined, went jogging every day and was very playful with Dri and the boys. It was a time of a lot of fun, when funny news was frequent."

On the first weekend, my brother-in-law Dadô took to the farm a small motorized plane that flew in circles, held by a flexible rod, in a diameter of five meters from the conductor. It became the biggest fuzz of the season, and Beco quit using the kite I had given him as a birthday present, because he was delighted by that small plane.

Heloísa Abdelnur recalls the friendship that put Ayrton and Dadô together, her late brother: "I still have my brother's planes, including the plane that Beco gave him, they are my souvenirs. They had great affinity; everything that one liked, the other liked too. Aeromodelling was one of the activities that brought them together the most. But they also had a taste for the sound of the engine. Ayrton once gave my brother an outboard engine and then he built a speedboat. So Beco came here to ride this speedboat on the dam lake*. He would stay at our place and we used to do a lot of fun things around here. It was very nice."

*"Broa Dam", in Brotas, countryside of São Paulo

We had a lot of fun during our stay at the farm, but my heart was still tight and missing him, and I was thirsty for more moments alone with Beco. I felt we were together, but apart. As he was always very kind and wanted to please everyone, he did not notice that I was sometimes isolated in a corner of the social area of the house, hoping that he would come and find me. It is also true that whenever we were close, we managed to caress each other, old hands or rub our feet under the table during meals, run each other's fingers through the other's hair when were on the motorcycle—that is why we rode a motorcycle so often... not to mention the kisses we exchanged whenever we had a chance. But on that particular weekend, he was in the group mood and in the mood for fun.

Cousin Patu does not forget those moments on the farm: "We would make the biggest mess. Sometimes, Chris, Adriane and I would go into Ayrton's bedroom in his absence and take his and Júnior's bed frame off; sometimes, we would put corn under their sheet. We even got to sew the hem of their pajamas once. This was all to have fun and mess with them. When they went to sleep, they noticed but pretended that nothing had happened. Always after a day or two we had a fightback. They would put toothpaste on our shoes and stuff like that. Then, in the morning, we would bang pots on their bedroom door to wake them up and cycle of fun continued. It was a mess."

That time, I had been so anxious about meeting Beco again that I even had a fever—this occurred later on some other occasions as well. I suffered in silence, but my mom realized that it was related to his arrival. My body gave me away.

It was cold that Saturday at the farm, and due to my feverish state, I had to content myself with watching the games without actively participating. The girls messed with the boys and vice versa. Lenise never participated in these games so as not to suffer with fightback; she stayed out of it and growled at the slightest sign that she might be the next target! My other sister Christhiane, on the other hand, was really excited to mess with Beco and Júnior. They committed in misdeeds, and I, isolated and recovering. At certain times, when the sheriff was not around — that is, my mother — Beco would escape the games and come to steal a kiss from me.

Everyone at the lunch table, Jacoto (Antifuro), Beco and I.

At the same time, in the background, my uncle José Carlos, aunt Nádia, Lenise and Dadô behind Jacoto

He and I

From left to right: Stela, Márcio, Beco, I and my sister Christhiane

On Sunday I woke up without a fever and could participate in some activities. I even planned a prank with Beco against my mother, who had the habit of using hair curlers with the help of aunt Nádia. I warned my aunt beforehand and went into action. Mom. She had a scare, and her face when Beco took the photo made that a hilarious moment.

Aunt Nádia and my mother Marilene

Aunt Nádia remembers the episode, laughing: "That day, Adriane arranged for Ayrton to take a photo of her mother wearing hair curlers. I obviously accepted the prank! And they made a funny record for posterity. It was a fun prank. The kind Ayrton liked to play."

On that trip to Brazil, Beco had given me a bag full of Sergio Tracchini brand products, who sponsored him: Sports outfits, sweatshirts and jerseys, beautiful sneakers like the ones he wore. My mother could not control herself and said:

"Dear, be careful! A man who gives so many presents is usually doing something wrong!"

"What can I do, mom? Do I have a choice? Weren't you the one who advised me to tell him to live his life as a man? So why are you saying that now? I do not get it!"

"No, of course, I just told you to be careful."

"Okay then! Be careful about what? Do you think it is easy for me? Don't be such a party pooper right now."

"You are right, darling! I am sorry. I know it is hard and I do not want to see you suffering, but you were the one who chose to date a man in that situation. I do want you to fool yourself, I am just trying to spare you."

Beco had come to Brazil with many appointments in a two-week interval and already needed to leave to dispute the Canadian GP. It was our most sad farewell until then. For the first time, I had the feeling that that relationship had no room to flourish. Not in my life, not in his.

"Beco, I do not know how we are going to work! You were away for two months, spent very few days here. I understand you did your best, but I cannot see how we are going to make it work!" I said in a tearful voice and completed: "I miss you so much and I keep counting the days for you to come, but what for? To be close to you but unable to have a conversation? It is like torture! I do not know what to do."

"Dri, I have been coming to Brazil a lot more often than I used to, I live in England! In every gap in the team schedule, I have been coming here to be with you. Unfortunately, this time I had other work commitments in São Paulo."

Apparently upset by my sadness, he gave me a little kiss and left with his head down. The next day, I received flowers with the following card:

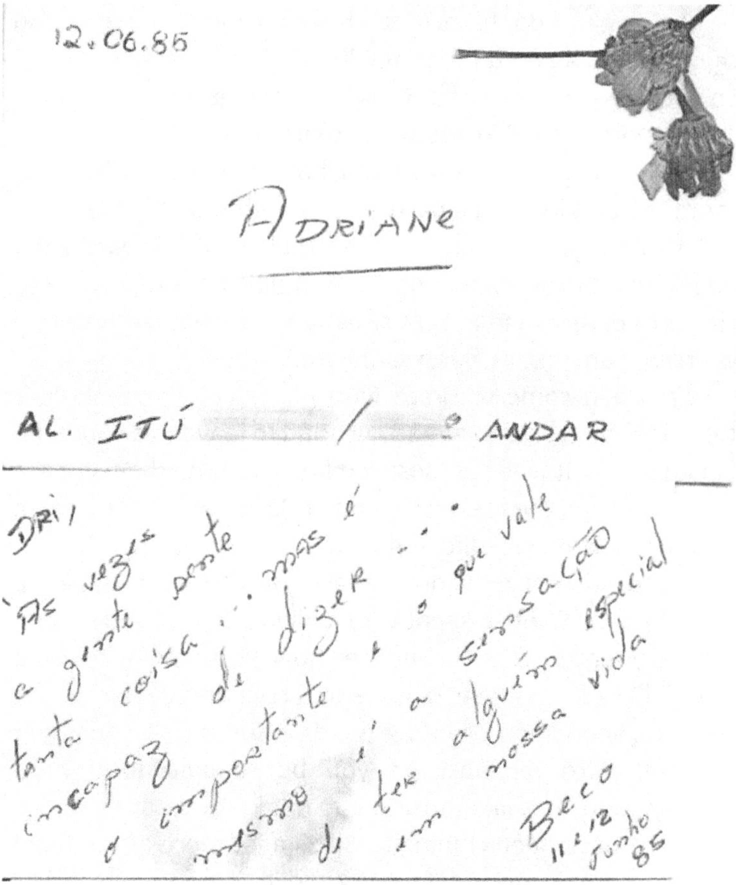

12.06.85

ADRIANE

AL. ITÚ [illegible] / [illegible]º ANDAR

DRI,
Às vezes a gente sente tanta coisa... mas é incapaz de dizer... o que vale é importante, é a sensação mesmo de ter alguém especial em nossa vida

Beco
11 e 12 Junho 85

"Dri, sometimes we feel so much but we cannot even tell... but what really matters is having someone special in our life."

I also received, on that occasion, a promotional photo that Ayrton had taken the year before, which I immediately put in my datebook, with the following dedication on the back:

*"A souvenir from your top 1 crush. To a special someone,
with a lot of love"*

If things were not very exciting for me, they were for my sister Lenise: She had been officially proposed by Eduardo. Dadô's family lived in São Carlos, countryside of São Paulo, and my sister should prepare to live there after the wedding. He had three siblings: Marzo, Alexandre and Heloísa. Their house was quite busy, thanks to the presence of the girlfriends of brothers, cousins, and family friends. A very nice, fun and welcoming group. At that time, we started to travel there some weekends so that Tata could join Dadô's family and get acquainted with São Carlos. We were welcomed with great affection by Aunt Irani, Eduardo's mother, who would pamper us with delicious food. Mrs. Irani is a very elegant and dear lady who provided us to experience memorable moments with Ayrton in her house during that period.

I watched the Canadian GP on June 16th and imagined the frustration Ayrton must have felt when he started second in the race to finish in 16th position. It was stressful to participate in a dispute with a car that was unable to fight for the top positions, especially for him who was very competitive and demanding with himself. It was time to take it easy and try to finish the race, no matter what.

Right after the GP I received the following letter from Beco:

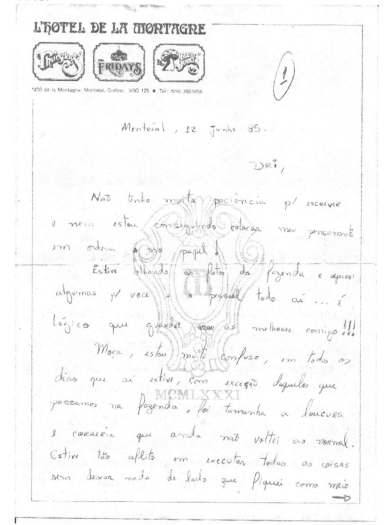

alucinado e ainda hoje (cousa 24 hs depois de ter saído do Brasil) estou como a (flutuando com uma sensação de que esqueci de alguma coisa. Uma coisa é certa, foi tão pouco tempo que nós nem tivemos sequer uns minutinhos a sós e isso com certeza é uma das razões que estou me sentindo insatisfeito com minha ida ao BRASIL.

Saí de sua casa aquela noite com um aperto no peito, me senti naquele instante a pessoa mais impotente do mundo, por mais que pensasse em algo não conseguia e não consegui encontrar uma saída p/ aquela situação. Tudo o que queria era ficar com você um pouco num ambiente onde pudéssemos conversar sem interrupções ou preocupações de que a qualquer instante alguém apareceria na porta da sala. Você percebe que ninguém de nós dois cometeu nenhum crime, talvez crime seja uma palavra

L'HOTEL DE LA MONTAGNE

(2)

1430 de la Montagne, Montréal, Québec. H3G 1Z5 ● Tél.: (514) 288-5656

muito pesada a ser usada, mas quanto mais penso a respeito nosso mais tenho a sensação e de que é ~~necessária~~ somos altamente controlados, caso contrário vamos cometer erros gravíssimos. Meu Deus do céu, já temos tão pouco tempo em que podemos estar em contato direto, na verdade esse é um problema causado de certa forma por mim mesmo, pois sou eu quem viaja e leva essa vida maluca, portanto não é sua culpa ou responsabilidade absolutamente se temos esse tipo de problema, tão pouco de teus pais já que quando analizo mais friamente, deve ser uma barra p/ eles gostando da maneira que gostem de vocês três, saberem que a ~~~~ uma de suas filhas está se envolvendo com um cara que já foi casado

que vive inter viagins o tempo todo e que
leva um tipo de vida digamos não dos mais
desejáveis p/ uma família tão unida como a
de vocês.

No fundo a situação é como é e
desde que se tenha calma, e bom senso,
respeito mútuo e logicamente amor entre nós,
não existirá nada impossível que não se
possa resolver, o tempo é na verdade no
momento o melhor remédio p/ ~~~~~~~~ o nosso
caso.

Sabe, não quero que fique muito
preocupada com tudo isso que escrevi, fiquei
muito angustiado esses dias todos aí no Brasil,
senti uma necessidade enorme de te participar
e desabafar o que ~~~~~~ estou sentindo e
acredito muito em sua capacidade de agora
mais do que nunca, não deixar que isso modi-
fique a sua atitude ~~~~ a nosso respeito.
Encare como um desabafo necessário, e coloque
isso de lado e vamos em frente que a gente tem
uma longa caminhada, ok!!

A verdade é uma só, mas sou pessoa de normalmente cruzar os braços, especialmente quando existem coisas a serem feitas, gosto de ir a luta e contribuir de alguma forma p/ que elas aconteçam e quase sempre rapidamente, entretanto por essas linhas você pode ver que tinho muito ainda que aprender sobre mim mesmo e PROCURAR melhorar muito essa defeito que tenho que é a tal da "paciência" essa é a palavra chave de minha personalidade e muitas vezes deixei de obter sucesso profissional e pessoal por não conseguir dominar essa vontade, essa ansiedade tremenda que faz parte de mim.

Nossa, estou cansadíssimo, acho que aqui está um pouco de mim do fundo do coração.

Como te disse, me despido de ver aquela noite com muitas saudades, como se não estivesse ao seu lado por longo tempo

Cuide-se bem

você é muito importante

Beijos.

"Montreal, June 12, 1985.

Dri, I have no patient to writing and I cannot put my thoughts in order on paper! I have been looking at the pictures from the farm and I chose some for you and your people... of course I kept the best ones for me!!! Lady, I am very confused. Every day I was there, except for that one we spent on the farm, everything was so crazy and busy that I am not back to normal yet. I had been so distressed in trying to do everything without ignoring anything that I got kind of crazy, and even today (after 24 hours I left Brazil) I still feel like floating with the feeling that I forgot something. One thing is for sure: time was so short that we did not have time for ourselves, alone, and this is certainly one of the reasons why I am unsatisfied with my trip to Brazil. I left your house that night with my heart aching, I felt the most powerless person on Earth. No matter how hard I try to think I cannot find a way out of this situation. All I wanted was to be with you somewhere we could talk uninterrupted or without worries that at any moment someone would show up at the door. Do you realize that none of us have committed no crime - maybe crime is a very strong word to use, but the more I think about us the more I feel that we are highly controlled; otherwise, I would make very serious mistakes. My God, we have so little time when we can be together; actually, this is a problem I caused myself, because I am the one who travels and lives this crazy life, therefore, it is not your fault or responsibility if we have this kind of problem, neither is your parents' fault, it must be tough for them once they like you and your sisters the way they do, knowing that one of your daughters is having a relationship with a guy who have already been married, who is always traveling and who takes a lifestyle that is not the best one for a family that is united like yours. Deep down, things are what they are and as long as we stay calm and have judgement, mutual respect and of course love, nothing is impossible to solve. Time is actually the best medicine for us. You know, I do not want you to be worried about what I said, I was very

144

distressed these days in Brazil, I felt an huge need to let you know and speak heart-to-heart to you what I am feeling. Now more than ever I believe in your ability not to let this change your attitude towards us. Face this as a necessary confession, put it aside and let's move on because we have a long journey ahead, okay?! The truth is that I do not usually just stand idly by, especially when there are things to be done; I like to fight and contribute somehow for things to happen and usually quickly; however, based on these lines, you can see I still have a lot to learn about myself and try to fix this problem I have, the "patience", this is the key word of my personality, and I often failed in having professional and personal success because I could not control my urge, this huge anxiety that is part of me. Wow, I am really tired, I think this is a little about me, from the bottom of my heart. As I said, I said goodbye that night already missing you, as if I had not been with you for a long time. Take care. You are very important. Kisses Beco"

Beco called me from England and he was furious with the result of the photo development of his last visit to Brazil.

"Adriane, you have no idea what your cousins got up to! I was completely embarrassed when I received the photos from the development man. I am mad at those kids!"

He broke off the scolding when he noticed I was laughing on the other end of the line...

"Did you know? And you didn't tell me? I made a fool of myself!"

"Ah, Beco... it was a joke! They had so much fun wasting your roll of film with nonsense that I did not have the heart to get involved. C'mon, don't be angry!"

"What? You say that because you were not in my shoes. I always leave my photos to develop in the same place, and the man who does the job sees all the photos."

I burst out laughing. I could not help imagining his face.

"Beco, didn't you take a photo of my mom with curlers on her head? Well, then! You guys play tricks on the younger ones all the time! Sorry, but it was funny," I said, amused.

"Have you seen all the photos they took?"

"No! But I saw some that were totally okay! That is why I did not get involved!"

Which ones did you see? Because some of them I prefer not to tell you what they were…"

"Um… I saw them taking closes from the big toe, silly details of the house and they would laugh hard imagining your face when you saw them. I thought it was a good joke."

"Well, there were photos of embarrassing objects," he said more calmly. "You have no idea of my face when I got the photos…"

Then, still laughing at my cousins' prank, I said:

"Look! You keep setting a bad example for the kids, and they ended up joining in the fun. Unfortunately, they got carried away, but they are kids. They did not think the developer would see the photos too, they just thought how surprised you would be when you saw those photos. Sorry I did not warn you! The photos I saw them taking were no big deal and they had a lot of fun doing it. Too bad they passed the point, huh? But what kind of photos did they take that were sooooo embarrassing?"

"Look, for you to have an idea, one of them showed the "natural calls" of someone who seemed to have eaten an ox!"

He said that unable of holding back his laugh and we burst out laughing together.

"Beco, I am so sorry for such an embarrassment, and you are right; it must have been troubling for you. What do you want me to do?"

Look, this is what we are going to do. When I go to the farm, I do not want to sleep in the same room with those kids anymore. On top of everything else, they make a huge mess in the bedroom, leave everything on the floor and do not even flush when they use the bathroom. As you can see, it is not at all pleasant."

"I can imagine! I know my little cousins well..."

"Hey, Dridrica, you will not tell them anything, okay? It is like nothing happened! I won't let your cousins have this satisfaction. And from now on I will keep an eye on my camera."

"Okay, will do. In the end, I was the one who had the most fun in this story, then!" I said, laughing. "But I will not say anything about that, I promise. Miss you."

"Me too, Dridrica, but I will be there real soon! Next time, we will find a way to have more time together and alone."

Marcelo Yamin Abdo, also known as Chélo, confirms what would happen in the bedroom the boys shared with Beco on the farm at that time: "I was thirteen at that time, I was a 'teen-ager' and we had a lot of bad jokes. Important: Ayrton did not sleep in a separate bedroom when he went to my uncle Amilcar's farm; he would sleep with us, the brats! He had no privileges at all. I will talk about one event of which I am not proud, but that is real. It is even a little disgusting... One day, we were at the farm and it was auction time. My brother and a cousin left to set up a sign indicating the access to the site on the dirt road, and he passed by the boys driving a Sulam Blazer wagon. He passed and suddenly stopped. My cousin found that weird. He put the car in reverse, drove up to the boys and greeted them. When he set up the gear to go, he threw some rain of sand on us. Beco was like that, very funny and playful! But on that day, he had a payback. He had a digital camera, but with film... if I am not mistaken, it was a Canon. An amazing camera! Because he really liked taking photos. He left this camera in our room, because he was sleeping there, and then we did some kid thing. One of my cousins was taking a shower and another was using the toilet. We started taking photos of our private parts and that was it! Very focused photos of the parts of each one; we took too many photos and then we put the camera back to where it was. It must have caused a great mess, as Ayrton Senna probably ordered this film development somewhere and those photos certainly came to his attention. I remember he was riding a pedal boat on the lake and we were playing in the bedroom and we said: Let's take a photo to fuck him up? We took the camera and took the photos. It was a hell of a joke! It was a very dirty idea we had that day. We even took pictures of the shit, and I told them not to flush the toilet. He must have been really pissed."

My cousin Márcio, known as Chim, was also together at many of these moments and he says, laughing: "I remember that earth bath; he was on Rural Prata road, had a big car, then he sped up and threw dirty on us. He loved to tease us and we teased him too, but he did not like it and was cranky. There was the bedroom thing; I was thirteen and Kaco was about nine or ten. I said: *Kaco, let's get some Sergio Tacchini stuff?* I still have one sock kept here, from our idol, who I loved. And Kacão replied: *Let's go! He is sponsored and pays nothing.* So Kaco got it, I do not remember what, I got two pairs of socks and a yellow Sergio Tacchini polo shirt with the black emblem on the chest. Kaco said: *Chim, it is free! He pays nothing, he does not buy any of that.* I answered: *Oh, great, he will earn more later.* And then we took it! I also remember the tricks Beco played. Once, our female cousins were in the pool and he said: *Chim, go grab the toothpaste.* I grabbed it and we enter the girls' room; he was very attentive: He very cautiously placed the toothpaste on the end of the sneakers so that they only noticed when they stepped on the floor, he did not leave a single drop visible and repeated this in many sneakers. Once he put a stink bomb in their bedroom; he loved these pranks. In sports, we played street cricket on the grass, and he hated losing, he would not accept that; he would go crazy and we would make fun of him, just as he would make fun of us. This camera thing with Kaco: I think we unloaded all his film, took pictures of our legs, ass, dick and whatever else, so that when he developed those photos, we discovered that we destroyed the whole film in the camera. We slept together a couple of times at most. Sometimes, when he would get mad at us, I would fart there and everyone would run away. The idea was to make some fun, but he was pissed! And we kept talking at night while he wanted to rest. But we were kids."

My grandmother Catarina, now 99 years old, remembers Ayrton at that time and shares with us:

"He was kind of quiet, did not talk much; I even told Drica that one day, here at home, he was talking on the phone and I had a maid who stayed here for 30 years, Margarida, and she talked to him, because he was nice. If you talked to him, he would answer, but sometimes he seemed a little cold; so, that day, Margarida came running to him, who was still on the phone, and said: *I am your fan*. And he said: *Thank you*. She said: *I would like an autograph.* He signed the autograph, completing: *With pleasure*. She ran away, happy, and then left to dinner. I remember he did not speak much, he listened more than he talked, and was a very good person.

My son loved him and they got along really well. He came here for dinner twice, but we met more at the farm and we talked normally; he was very kind and everyone was open-mouthed for him."

Chapter X

In the USA GP, in Detroit, on June 23rd, Ayrton started again in pole position and had the best lap in the race. But on lap 51, the brake system has failed and the wheel has locked and he lost control of the car, having to abandon the race. He was on rain tires, but not a single drop of water fell during the entire race and the rules of the 1985 championship did not allow tire changes during the race.

The day after the Detroit Grand Prix, I wrote him the letter below:

S.Paulo, 06/24/85. Beco,

I am pretty sure you did not like what you saw when you developed the photos from the farm. I tried to warn you, but it was a very well-thought-out joke and I would not dare to spoil it, no matter how sorry I felt for you.

Honestly, I did not understand why you did not say anything to me on the farm about everything you told me in the letter written on 06/12/85. Instead of, as you say, making small talk, or when we were alone in front of the fireplace.

Why didn't you take the opportunity to say everything? I noticed your indifference towards me the day you arrived at the farm (the day you spent playing with Dadô's little plane), which in a way occurred, because I did not sincerely feel the longing I mentioned several times. And the worst thing is that I did not do something I wanted to (I do not know if you remember) to watch you play airplane! But I did not say anything, hoping there would be an explanation for that situation (but there was not). And I do not want you to think that this is a demand on my part, it is just that I was not in the mood to be around you and not receive any kind of attention. I felt like I was the only one missing you. Honestly, I hope it was not your intention to show such an importance, but some things will change in my attitude towards you, and they have already changed as a result of this event.

I also want you to take it as a heart-to-heart talk, because I already feel better by telling you a few things that go through my mind (I hope I was not rude);

Apart from the first day, you were the sweetest guy and I really enjoyed the other days, too bad I was apathetic because of the fever. As for the last day at home, at night, when you were saying goodbye (what a horrible word), I felt safe for the first time in thinking that I am important for you (at least a little), and I felt much more relaxed because of this. You have no idea how good this is to me.

After having thought about all this, I came to the conclusion that we lack dialogue and we have to say things out at the moment they cross our minds, so that we can resolve them right there. That way, we will not have unclear thoughts about each other's attitudes.

Becão, do not blame yourself for not being able to see me constantly, as this was a choice I made and I believe we will both be strong enough to accept this situation. The best we can do is enjoy each other's lives while we are far from each other. As you said, we have a lot of time ahead and I hope that both you and I make the most of it whatever way is best.

We have already talked about this and you know I am not at all opposed to you enjoying your life as you please and I will do the same (of course).

Ah! And please do not forget to ask me what I think of what you wrote about the problem with my parents (since I am not used to writing letters, not even books).

I want you to promise me to forget everything I wrote in this letter and that unfortunate day, because when I finish this letter, I will forget. Agreed?

Let us just think about what we can do from now on together, with very good vibes. From one of your fans,

Dri, Doll, Beauty, Etc.

Of course, I meant to seem tough and easygoing, and a little sarcastic. By saying I did not oppose him to "enjoy your life as you please and I will do the same (of course)", I was just camouflaging, because it was not easy for me to know he could be with someone else. But somehow, I was trying to get on with my life naturally and, on July school vacation that year, I planned to travel to Europe for the first time with my sisters. It would be a marathon: We would visit twelve countries in twenty-four days. My mother even argued with my father for him to consent with the trip, but everything was finally settled. I was really excited!

Before my trip to the Old World, I would still see Beco, who was returning to Brazil after competing in the US GP. He got here on Wednesday, the 26th, and I was at the farm with my family and some friends, spending the first vacation days. We then agreed that he would go there on Friday. But then he decided to go on Saturday, as he wanted to spend a little more time with his parents and nephews.

Figuring he would arrive at the farm before lunch as usual, I woke up early. I took a shower and dressed one of Sergio Tacchini coats he had given me as a gift. I chose the prettiest one and it was similar to the one he used to wear. By 10 am, I was ready and waiting for him, believing he would be as excited as I was for our reunion.

Hours passed and I was on the lookout for any sign of his arrival, such as car noise going down the cobblestone street or the roar of an engine or a horn. Anyway, a smoke signal or whatever! I had all senses on alert for the long-awaited arrival of my boyfriend, for whom I drooled over and even burned in fever, but who spent most of the time away...

Despite the cold of the season, it was a beautiful day with blue sky. Expecting him to arrive at any moment, I stood around the pool, pacing back and forth. I started to sweat in that dark colored coat, but as I did not want to spoil the outfit, I decided I would not take it off until Beco saw me.

I started to feel annoyed because the perfume and freshness of the bath was already gone. Ding-dong... Ding-dong... Ding-dong... I heard my mom ringing the bell, announcing that lunch was on the table, as usual. It was already two-thirty in the afternoon. I gave up on welcoming him as I had imagined.

The joy of waiting was over. Expectation is the mother of disappointment. We had lunch and around 4 pm Beco arrived with Antifuro.

I welcomed them politely and kindly, but with no enthusiasm. Everyone said hi and I showed them the room where they would now be staying, answering Beco's request that he no longer wanted to stay with my cousins, because of the photos they had taken with his camera.

This is us in the fireplace room on the farm, wearing coats branded by his sponsor

Sometime after Beco arrived, we gathered in the fireplace room for dinner. It was very cold that night and we all sat there talking. He commented to my father:

"Wow, Mr. Amilcar, people are recognizing me more and more out there. It is impressive how far my profession can reach. I did not imagine that everything would happen this fast!"

"Yeah, Ayrton! I hope you realize the responsibility it brings. Our people suffer a lot, they have a very low self-esteem. Misery and unemployment are big problems in our country. And your name reaches countries abroad. Out there, they see us an inexpressive country, they think only indigenous people live here. Of course, they only see bad things on the news about us, and you as a Brazilian, are representing us abroad."

"Did you know that, the other day, a guy jumped in the track at the end of a race to give me a Brazilian flag? And it made me want to stop and pick up the flag."

"Well, you should do this! Why didn't you pick up the flag?" my dad asked.

"Oh, I had no reaction at the time! I was not sure what that would cause," Beco replied.

"So, next time it happens and you feel the urge, stop and pick up our flag. With that attitude, you will carry the entire country with you. We have an unfortunate image. Suffered! And you must realize the privilege of getting where you are now and your responsibility as our representative to the world. We have to be grateful to God for the privileged life we have, we cannot forget the ones who were not so luck," dad said.

Everyone gathered in the fireplace room for a snack, from right to left: Uncle José Carlos, my cousin Kaco, Dea, my father Amilcar, my mother Marilene, I and my sister Cris

On the other end of the sofa, at the same moment, our friend Ana Lucia, Jacoto and my cousins Mônica and Patrícia

He and I

Beco was silent for a few moments. He was certainly thinking about the responsibility as a public man his career imposed.

I know my father was one of the men he most respected and admired during his life and I believe this conversation forged a bond between them. As for dad, I know this conversation represented an opportunity to help raising that brilliant young man. I love it when an enlightened person meets another enlightened being and together, they produce even more light.

About other aspects of F1, Ayrton told us that night that he was not happy with being the second driver of the team. He complained that Elio de Angelis, the first driver of Lotus, was always the priority and had the best car. He also complained about the obligation to let Elio de Angelis overtake him and give way in case of dispute for the podium. Beco also told us about the electronic fuel injection adjustments to be made by the team in the pits through computers connected to the car. That way, it was possible to help regulate fuel consumption during the race. However, the power / fuel consumption relationship could determine in the pits the performance of the car and the race result. Therefore, he was still afraid that it would be possible to manipulate the final result of the races. Not to mention the problems that Beco already had with the car itself: Sometimes it was with the suspensions, sometimes the brakes, sometimes the gear. This was all under the strict control of FIA, which set a limit on the final weight of the car. Most rules were made to encourage the technological development of the drivers, balance the difference between the competing teams and ensure the safety of the drivers. Thus, it was important to delimit the final speed of the engines and not just encourage the new technologies to be developed. Electronic fuel injection, for example, was used and tested in F1 before it was produced at scale in common cars; before, we used the choke to start the engine and manually regulate the fuel injection in the engine.

I also remember Beco criticizing the problem of oil leakage from the cars and the dirt on the track that would impregnate the visor of his helmet, which, in the race, impaired his eyesight. This was solved with removable visors fitted to the front of the helmet. And, above all, he complained about suffering from dehydration during the race. He left the car completely weakened, losing over two kilos per race and suffering from terrible cramps. To try to circumvent this problem, they included a straw inside the helmet with access to the driver's mouth and a slot inside the cockpit of a container with liquids, so that they could get hydrated, but it was not enough considering how tired they would get during the races.

For all these reasons, it was extremely important the monitoring of his physical trainer and nutritionist. When we were on the farm, we trained together, Beco and I. At first, he made a journey of about three kilometers on a dirt road, and I went as far as I could. But he asked Nuno Cobra, his physical trainer, to prepare me a training session and then, even when Beco was absent, I would run regularly in order to improve my physical condition and be able to keep up with him when he was in Brazil. I did not want to disappoint him, I wanted to reciprocate his care and affection for me, as he always encouraged my development in a loving way.

While my sisters and I were embarking for Europe, on July 7th, Ayrton started in second place at the French GP, at the Paul Ricard circuit, in Le Castellet. I remember Beco was worried about the car's fuel consumption because the engine was powerful, but with a bad fuel economy, he was afraid not to finish the race. Which actually happened! But for another reason: The engine broke down on lap 26.

Two weeks later, coincidentally on the same day as the Great Britain GP, July 21st, my sisters and I disembarked in London, but unfortunately, we did not arrive in time to go to the racetrack to watch the race. In Silverstone, Ayrton started in fourth place, took the lead on the second lap, but his car broke down on lap 60 with problems with the electronic fuel injection — dry failure — and abandoned the race.

On Sunday, day of the race, and on Monday, Beco left messages at my hotel until we were able to talk on the phone and agreed that he would come the next day to pick me up so we could spend some time together. I was very excited about this reunion and counted the hours until I could see him. He still lived in an apartment in Chelsea Close at the time.

BONNINGTON HOTEL	BONNINGTON HOTEL	BONNINGTON HOTEL
LONDON, WC1B 4BH	LONDON, WC1B 4BH	LONDON, WC1B 4BH
TELEPHONE MESSAGE	TELEPHONE MESSAGE	TELEPHONE MESSAGE
DATE 21-7-85 TIME 9:12 Pm.	DATE 22-7-85 TIME 5:30pm	DATE 22-7-85 TIME 523
TO Room 523	TO	TO
MESSAGE Ayrton called and said he will call later tonight	MESSAGE Room 523 Mr Ayrton called His phone No ... call mr Beco mr Beccrie	MESSAGE Phones I will try again later this afternoon mr Ayrton
TAKEN BY 36128	TAKEN BY 36154	TAKEN BY 31460

When Ayrton arrived at the hotel, we were already in the lobby deciding where my sisters would go while I was with him. Suddenly, Christhiane shouted:

"Hey! This is my purse!"

She had left her purse in another room in the lobby to talk to the concierge. It all happened within seconds. The thief was already leaving the hotel when Ayrton, without blinking, ran after him, shouting:

"Drop it!"

And disappeared from our sight. A few minutes later, he returned with the purse in his hands.

"Look, you have to be careful! Where there are tourists, there are people watching!"

"So, how was it?" we asked. "Did you catch the thief? Did he have a gun?"

We were excited and curious to know the outcome. Beco said:

"I did not reach him, but when he realized I was close he dropped the bag on the floor. Here in England, armed robbery is a very serious crime; so they are pickpockets at best. Anyone caught stealing a purse has the same penalty as if they robbed a bank if they have a gun. Here the law is not easy!"

"Phew! That scared me!"

However, the funny thing was what my sisters heard later when they went to a restaurant at the top of another hotel; right at the entrance, there was space to leave their coats, which is quite common in very cold countries. Someone said in English:

—"Be careful, keep an eye out because they are Brazilians!"

That day, I was prepared to go to Beco's house and have some time alone with him, without no one looking after us. Unfortunately, he did not even suggest that. I hid my disappointment but was frustrated, even though I knew he wanted to avoid breaking the rules previously set for our relationship.

I got into a navy-blue BMW on the left side, while he drove on the right (the opposite side we drive in Brazil).

"Wow Beco, that is weird!" I said, laughing. "Why is that?"

"Yeah, it is weird at first, but I am used to it now! As far as I know, this is because in the Middle Ages they used the sword with their right hand, and it was the best side for a counter-attack; it was where the man would sit to most effectively protect his family or some load in his carts, then in their carriages and finally in their cars."

"Cool! But I think it is dangerous. Just today I was almost run over when crossing the street. It was a narrow two-lane street and I looked first to the side I am used to; that is, the opposite side where a Ferrari was coming from. That was close! When I saw the red shape, I backed away quickly out of reflex. Not even the rearview mirror touched me because I actually lifted my arms and bent back to give me more space. I got to stand on tiptoe."

He laughed by picturing the scene and said sarcastically:

"Wow, Dridrica, that must have been a beautiful ballet move! But be very careful, this is dangerous for any tourist here. Try to stay alert!" he completed and laughed even more. "Too good you are a great ballet dancer and got away with it."

I laughed too and did not pay attention to his teasing. I believe one of the reasons we had such an harmony in our relationship was that I knew how to laugh at myself and made fun of the situations I experienced. He loved to laugh at me!

"Wait a minute! Any tourist, my ass! I would be run over by a Ferrari. This is not for any tourist. It would be a very chic run over. Think of the success it would be in Brazil! Or do you know anyone who has been hit by a red Ferrari?"

He laughed but did not answer my question, as if he did not want to encourage that nonsense, and I insisted:

"Do you know anyone or not?"

"No, Dridrica, I do not." And knowing what I would say next, he admitted: "See? This is not for any tourist!"

While we were chatting away, we wandered the streets of London until we passed by a building with the sign House of the Guinness Book. He got interested right away, ambitious that he was, he had already broken some speed records on some tracks. We parked the car and went inside. But Beco gradually became discouraged when he realized the place meant to unusual records and exotic situations. He left the place disappointed.

So we decided to go to the movies. At least we could kiss and make up for the lost time. Then he took me back to the hotel. I did not say anything, but I was furious! When there was not a lot of people around us in Brazil, there was him, trying to be responsible and correct. What the hell!

I am not sure why I did not tell him what I intended at that date, whether it was out of pride or inexperience. But I had dreamed of living that rare moment of freedom with a lot of romance and passion. It was clear to me, at that moment, that for him we were no more than crushes. And although I was in love with Beco, I decided to slow down my desires and take more care of my life. I believed that his self-control was a lack of desire to be with me. Where was the romance? It was all black and white for me, and desire, frustration, joy, sadness were very intense. After all, I was a teenager living the story of my first love. And I could not see how hard it was for him, who had made a commitment to my father and felt compelled to keep his word.

My sisters and I continued our trip through Europe until the end of July and Beco went back to his training routine.

At the German GP, Nurburgring race track, on August 4th, Ayrton started in fifth position, but left the race due to a break in the axle half-shaft suspension on lap 27.

If, on the one hand, Beco had been facing problems in recent races, on the other hand, his financial situation was getting better, and this allowed him to move, at that time, from his tiny apartment in Chelsea Close to a comfortable house on the outskirts of London.

I now draw the fans' attention to the race on August 18th, the Austrian GP at Osterreichring. One of the most thrilling races in Ayrton's career, in my opinion. He started in 14th position, went to the tenth on the first lap and moved to the sixth on the tenth lap.

But the emotion in this GP was intense since practicing. The car had several problems in the adjustment that affected its performance, and they had very little time to adjust it before the race start. Ayrton did not start well, so the recovery during the race was impressive. The feeling I had was that, at any moment, on that fast track in Austria, the car would have some problem. But it held up until the end of the race, even with the strong pace Ayrton had imposed, and after many about-turns with the other cars that were in the lead, he took second place on the podium.

On the 25th he was in the Netherlands GP — Zandvoort. Ayrton started in the fourth position and took third place on the podium.

As the few people around me found out about my relationship with "Senna", school friends I lived with at the time changed their attitude toward me. It was as if I was being scrutinized in a curious way; other friends looked at me with admiration; however, they all seemed to want to understand what was special about me to win over "THE MAN". Now I could no longer be that silly, tomboyish girl, because people had expectations about my behavior, and I insisted on doing whatever I had to do to deserve being Ayrton's girlfriend. Not to mention that I wanted him to be proud of his choice, just as I was proud to have him by my side! Unfortunately, I also had that feeling that some were waiting for a chance to criticize: "How can a man like Ayrton choose a girl like that?" That was it! My freedom was over. I had to be more rational because of that situation and I gained more responsibility for my attitude with our relationship.

Truth be told: I had no idea why that amazing man always came back to me and treated me like a treasure. I knew I was interesting, despite my age, but I thought I was no match for the models that surrounded him. I did not know yet how to dress properly, make up, etc. I had to learn so I could accompany him, but I was not intimidated by that. He met me with a clean face and natural hair and liked me that way! I was cheerful, sweet, polite, challenging in sports and from a very nice family. I felt there was a natural and inexplicable affinity between Beco and me. When we were together, I felt calm and safe, I trusted him entirely, I was not afraid of what was to come, whether I could handle it or not. These questions popped into my mind sometimes when he was not in Brazil. When he was here, everything was right, as Beco did his best to be with me most of the time.

Today, as I look back over our history, I realize that the biggest problem in our relationship was the excessive control we had to deal with. Although understandable, it was complicated for a romantic relationship. And when were away from each other, longing was just too distressing. Phone calls and letters were the options we had at that time to communicate.

"Hi girl, I am in a hurry with the new house... In addition to the races, the trips to everywhere, changing hotels, baggage and airports, I cannot stand it anymore! I am finally managing to finish some races but the car is not good enough to win. As usual, if the letters or phone calls do not come from England, nobody listens to each other... I miss you - it is useless to say. Just yesterday the moon was gorgeous and I thought about you a lot; it sounds too romantic, but that is who I am, it does not matter. I want so much to see you and be with you, one way or another we are getting by, and I expect to go to Brazil *soon, I can't barely wait for it. Miss you a thousand, Kisses from your crush Beco"*

At the Italian GP, in Monza, on September 8th, Ayrton started in pole position and finished the race in third place. Lucky streak had come! He started running strategically and won some championship points. He also now had a more balanced car, but the problem with fuel still surrounded him and he had to manage it in order to finish the races.

Chapter XI

My birthday was getting closer and Beco could not be with me, because of the Belgium GP at the Spa-Francorchamps on September 15th. But it was worth it! He won the race. He started in second place and won his second victory in F1, in a race played in the rain that confirmed the title he received as "The King of the Rain." With that second victory, he settled in Lotus, and the idea of being the second driver began to change as the team's attention turned to him.

And on the 17th, I received a card (below) with a birthday gift: A beautiful gold chain with a fixed octagonal pendant and a diamond with five points in the center. I really liked it; I admit I did not expect such a nice gift!

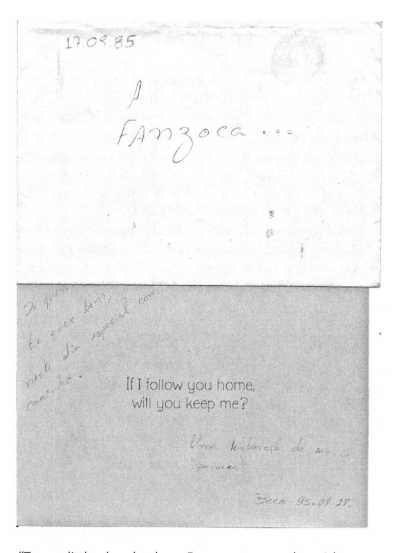

"To my little cheerleader... From someone who wishes you well on this special day, with a lot of love. If I follow you home, will you keep me? A souvenir from your "crush". Beco 09.17.85"

I practiced at school, before Physical Education class the training that Nuno Cobra, Beco's physical trainer, prepared for me contained ten minutes of brisk walking, ten minutes running, and another ten minutes walking. We had three classes a week with varied activities, sometimes volleyball, handball or basketball, sometimes athletics. That worked for a while, but when my classmates started wanting to run with me, the teacher forbade me to keep practicing there. I tried to argue that we were not getting late or disrupting class and that that activity was related to Physical Education. But there was no deal, I had to follow her order. So I began running only on weekends and, of course, I would run with Beco when he was at the farm. But he was physically developing much better and I could not keep up with him all the way, only part of it. This was frustrating for me at the time, as I was not only proud of how easy it was for me to practice sports, but I did not accept physical limitations in any activity I tried to do. The thing is that it was impossible for me to follow the so-dedicated Beco as an equal in running practice. However, we practiced everything else together. I am sure one of our affinities was the energy and aptitude to accompany each other in whatever it was. Beco was restless, just like me!

On October 6th, Ayrton competed in the European GP in Great Britain, at the Brands Hatch circuit. He started in pole position and finished second, behind Nigel Mansel. Soon after, I received a mail from him:

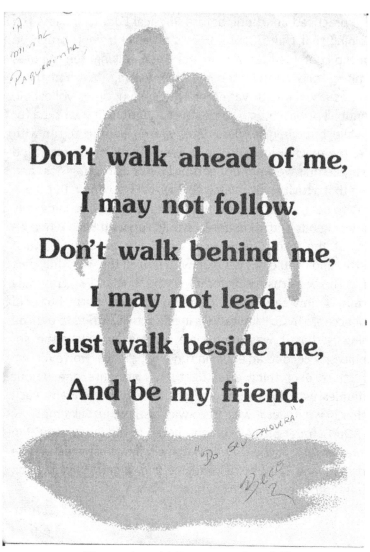

Don't walk ahead of me, I may not follow. Don't walk behind me, I may not lead. Just walk beside me, And be my friend.

"To my 'crush' From your 'crush'"
Card received from Beco

This time Beco surprised me and came to Brazil right after the GP, to stay for just seven days. In addition to the F1 agenda, he was moving to his new house in Esher. Even with such a short time, he came to see me. Those trips were tiring because of the jet lag. He explained to me that the body takes at least two days to adapt sleep to the local time zone. Thus, four days in Brazil would not be enough to rest and then go back to Europe and adapt again to the time zone there.

In São Paulo, Beco kept his word and we stayed together every day. The daytime schedule was going out to lunch or a movie. In the evening, we would go out for pizza or ice cream or stay home watching TV with my family.

The evening we went to Monte Verde Pizzeria, Chris and Dea went with us. It was not busy when we arrived, but they asked us to wait a bit at the bar. We sat on high stools, fixed to a concrete step. When they called us to the table, I, at the time very young, wanted to play the "confident woman", like in Hollywood movies. After all, I was with that handsome boyfriend, a grown man, who made me full of pride and who did not go unnoticed anywhere.

I swiveled along with the stool feeling glamorous to the opposite side of the counter. I wore flat shoes with a very smooth leather sole. Awesome, so far! I forgot about the bar step. When I was going to put my foot on the floor, I stepped on the corner of the step and fell to the floor on my knees, in high speed. I could not lean anywhere to break my fall and all I had left to do was to use my arm strength to avoid me from literally kissing the ground. But even so, I touched my mouth to the floor. I got up as fast as I could and found Beco standing in front of me. He had had no reaction to the scene. I jumped on his neck to hide how embarrassed I was, and also because I did not know how my mouth looked.

"Dri, are you alright?"
"I am, Beco, just give me a minute."
I continued hugging him, while mentally looking for a way out of the shame I had just starred in the pizzeria. Bravely, I let go of him and, with my back to the room, I asked, upset:
"How does my mouth look like?"

"Did you hit it? It looks fine, I cannot see anything."

"Great! So, let's go to our table, I think I am okay, the worst has passed."

My companions tried their best to hold back their laughs, but after a while, my lower lip started to swell and that was it, they burst out laughing. Beco laughed a little too, but he was more concerned about my mouth because it was now obvious I was hurt.

"Damn it! Can you stop laughing?" I asked them.

"Your mouth is swollen, Dri!" one of them said, laughing even harder.

I used my hands to check how bad my mouth was, and Beco kindly asked the server for some ice.

"I am fine, Beco, thanks. I just want to forget what happened, can you stop laughing at me? It is enough!"

More laughs. I decided to wait for them to finish having fun. But when they talked to me, they looked at me with my mouth more and more swollen and that was it! They burst into laughter again. I do not usually care much about my blunders, never did, but I was there as a big girl now! My boyfriend, with the beginning of his fame, attracted the eyes of some people in the place. My situation was not the best.

The day before he left, after we had dinner at home, I was really sad to know that he was leaving soon and we would not see each other for weeks. I had the idea of going out for ice cream. I asked Beco privately and he agreed right away! I asked my parents if we could go to the ice cream parlor Swensens, as we did before, and that we would be back soon. With their agreement, Beco soon offered to bring ice cream for everyone.

"Don't, Ayrton! Do not worry about this. Go get ice cream, but do not take long as it is getting late!" my father said.

"Okay, Mr. Amilcar, we will be right back!" Beco said.

Wow! Such an advance. An escapade alone at night? That was awesome! Although those were our last moments together, we were excited by the achievement of this new situation. With my father's permission for us to go out alone, Beco also received a key to access my building's garage, where he could park his car safely while he was at home. I went out with my boyfriend feeling like an adult, finally!

We had ice cream and, on our way back, we parked the car in the garage. The parking space was in a corner at the back, in a very discreet place. There, we kissed passionately as if we missed each other even more during those few days together. Suddenly, I felt a light, unexpected touch of his hands caressing my breasts. Startled, I backed away, hold his hand gently. Embarrassed, I said:

"Beco, I am not ready yet!"

"It is okay, Dri!"

A few seconds passed. Noticing how embarrassed I was, he gently cupped my chin to lift my face so we could look at each other and kissed me gently.

"Sorry, Beco, you took me by surprise!"

"It is okay, Dridrica, do not worry, we have all the time in the world. It is just that since that day your blouse opened when you got out of the car... do you remember? I saw your breasts for a few seconds and that image stuck in my head," he said sincerely, rubbing my chin.

At the same moment, I remembered the day of his birthday party at the Pool Music Hall Dance Club, when we looked at each other as I noticed the opening of my shirt. Surprised by the disclosure that it had been imprinted on his memory, I said:

"So you saw it all that day?"

"I did, Dri!" he confirmed with a mischievous smile.
Confused and aware of my inexperience, I could barely look into his eyes. Although I reacted spontaneously, I was completely embarrassed by the situation. I was with an experienced man and I reacted with my usual inexperience. However, knowing that he saw me as a woman and was attracted to my body was amazing to me. It awakened my

femininity and sensuality even more, like a flower that little by little blossoms into the sun.

"Dri, we had better go upstairs."

Carlo Andrea Bauducco, my friend, knew we used to make out in the garage: "I was her neighbor, lived with my parents and was about twelve. I knew her, knew and watched everything because I was an unconditional fan of Senna. After we found out he was coming to the building, that he dated Adriane, I was on the lookout. He had a nice car. He came with a Mercedes van, at the time Brazil did not accept imported cars, so this was everyone's sweetheart. We stayed there, always waiting for him to arrive to use the elevator together. I remember he wore the brand Sergio Tacchini a lot, and I asked my parents to buy a sweater of that same brand so that I would look like him. Like every boy at that time, I was crazy about Senna. So it was more like wanting to see the idol. I did not have much contact with Adriane. Actually, it was like that, the spying thing when they came at night, being around, waiting for the elevator and pushing the button to see if it would stop there. He was super nice to the kids. What I remember is that Adriane was very discreet and really young! F1 stopped and he came quite a lot, and they would have some fun together in the garage. In fact, the janitor's son was always the one who told us when they arrived and we would rush to go see them. It was a kid thing to spy on, nothing serious."

Beco traveled the next day to resume the F1 competition. At the South African GP, in Kyalami, on October 19th, he started in fourth place but had to leave on lap eight, due to an engine breakdown!

Finally, the 1985 Championship final with the Australian GP, in Adelaide, on November 3rd. Ayrton started in pole position, but the car engine broke again, but at the end of the race, on lap 62.

That weekend, I was with my sisters in São Carlos, staying at Dadô's family house. It was a big house, in the country, very close to the city of São Carlos. But we spent the day at Broa dam, where the Abdelnur family owned a summer house in front of the dam to enjoy the various leisure options the place offered. My brother-in-law had a speedboat to ride around the dam (the one he set up to use the engine he got from Ayrton), and mainly, to pull skis. Although Miguel Abdelnur, Eduardo's cousin, preferred to "sole" — a sport modality in which the skier slides with the soles of his feet —, while the rest of the group skied with skis. On this dam, there was a club with a floating ramp for the most fearless skiers. In addition to water skiing, we also had access to a hovercraft and cross buggy.

In the evening, back at the house, we were all gathered to watch the race in Australia that would start at two or three in the morning that Sunday, due to the time zone. As I was exhausted from the sports-filled day, I managed to stay awake until part of the race, but I could not help but falling into a deep sleep in front of the TV. Of course, people made fun of me because of that, I was always under the spotlight on that matter.

A few days after the Australian GP, I received a letter from Beco:

"DRI,

Estou em Melbourne
e tinho uma pequena
viagem de apenas 24 hs.
a frente até LONDON.

Devo testar o carro
na França ainda este mês
entre 18 e 22 de novembro
e, não vejo o momento
de voltar ao BRASIL,

Quer dizer que a moça
andou conversando bastante

Com a Dona Marilene? Isto
está me parecendo uma gelada!
Mas estou muito curioso, se
é o que você quer fazer!!
Pra variar o motor
quebrou na corrida, mas
enquanto durou deu p/ se
divertir!!!

Morrendo, desabando
de saudades
Beijão Beco
06.11.85

"Dri, I am in Melbourne and I have a small 24-hour trip to London. I will probably test the car in France this month, around Nov. 18-22, and I can barely wait to be back to Brazil. So, I have heard you, young lady, have been talking a lot with Mrs. Marilene? This sounds like trouble! But I am really curious, if that is what you want to do!! The engine broke during the race as usual, but I could have some fun while it lasted! I miss you as hell Kisses Beco 11.06.85"

Senna won fourth place in the Championship with a car that was inferior to the other drivers who were behind him, like: Elio de Angelis, fifth placed; Nigel Mansel, sixth placed; Piquet, eighth placed, to name a few. A surprising result for a twenty-five-year-old beginner. With this achievement, the eyes of the world turned to him.

Beco finally returned to Brazil. He always asked my opinion after each race and I gladly gave my feedback. On the other hand, I felt he also enjoyed sharing with me his achievements. Unfortunately, this time, when he entered the subject, we were talking in front of my family and I responded as if I had watched the entire race. Not to be mean, just not to disappoint him, because I really knew how the race in Adelaide had been and had legitimate interest in Beco's affairs, my boyfriend.

"How come, Dri? You fell asleep!" someone said, overhearing our conversation.

"Dri... did you sleep during the race?" Ayrton asked me.

"Oh Beco, I tried to watch it all! But I was so tired that I fell asleep in the living room. I could not help it," I replied sadly.

I looked around and saw that some were amused by the situation. I cannot remember which one of my relatives gave me away, but I was in an awkward situation. I looked like a liar and for no reason. Although good people, my family is extremely critical and did not let anything go unnoticed. My effort to deal with family dynamics and make that relationship flourish was not appreciated by many. That did not look well for Beco or for me. After that, although we still talked about it, he stopped asking my opinion about every race. And in subsequent years, he also did not give me more material with information about the championship, like what he had given me that year. In that episode, I was disappointed with my family because of one's attitude and everyone's acceptance. I had to comply with the rules imposed while being watched by everyone, all the time, but did I need to be refuted that way? That was totally unnecessary.

In the first days of Beco's vacation, I was still finishing school and had to study for final exams. But I knew we would have plenty of time to be together until the early months of 1986, with only short breaks for his professional appointments, so I was very happy.

Although very tired, Beco arrived in Brazil with a feeling of accomplishment. It had been an amazing year. Despite a few moments of frustration, he gained more confidence in his ability to get where he wanted to in F1. He stopped being the second driver in the team and bothered top veterans throughout the championship, meaning that he managed to prove himself despite the problems in the car. But now it was time to rest, relax and let go of all that madness.

That year myself, I had an exemplary performance at school, unlike previous years. I believe that with Beco's presence in my life, I started to take myself more seriously, because I wanted my boyfriend to be proud of me. I also longed for my parents to see me as a grown-up, sensible girl, so I would gain more of their trust and more freedom with my babe.

The whole family, including uncles and cousins... I was excited to spend the vacation on the farm. And this time New Year's Eve would be there!

My sister Christhiane had got back together with Otávio, who hadn't had much contact with Beco yet, and this time at the farm would give the opportunity for that. Which actually happened and they became great friends.

Beco was super excited to take his newest toy to the farm: A small remote-control airplane! We had already played with my slotcar (yeah, I had one), with my father's remote-control cart and a remote-control speedboat that had the JPS team's colors and logo — which was actually really cute! Later, he also came up with a cross-type cart customized like his F1 car. But now, the fuzz of the moment was the small plane.

It was light, made of white Styrofoam, with a battery-powered engine. Dadô, my brother-in-law, was maddened by the news. In fact, all the boys who shared the news were acting like children. The first and also the most exciting flight came after they carefully studied how to assemble and operate that fragile toy. The best place to takeoff and landing was chosen around the house, and everyone was ready for the inaugural flight. It was an atmosphere of celebration and new adventure. Now, besides breaking the limits in nautical sports, we would also explore the sky, with aeromodelling. Wow! Beco was focused on his first flight, after having tested the commands of the little plane to memorize the timing of the remote control he had in his hands, imagining the movements he would cause in the air.

The remote control was similar to that of the cart and the small speedboat we had played with before: Square, it had two levers, one moved back and forth to be operated with the thumb of one hand, and the other moved sideways with the thumb of the other hand. In the cart control, the lever that moved back and forth was to accelerate; the other, for making curves. It provided a good sense of motor coordination.

So, thrilled with the new toy, Beco began carefully accelerating the engine to pick up enough speed for takeoff. As the track was made of grass, even though it seemed flat for the activity, it held the wheels a little, making it difficult to gain speed. He slowed down, stopping the first takeoff. That plane was too light for that grass track.

So Beco, Dadô and Júnior decided to throw the small plane like a paper plane, but a volunteer would have to run and throw it to increase the chances of success. Without enough speed, it would fall. Antifuro was assigned to the task. Júnior began to run with the small plane in launch position, Beco gave full speed through the control and the plane was released; it kept flying somewhat staggering up and down, back and forth. Beco instinctively made with his body the movements he wanted the little plane to perform, trying to stabilize it through the control in his hands. It was a big journey! Everyone was afflicted with the imminence of a fall or collision. Beco chose to bring the plane back to try to land, which was really difficult, because when the plane came towards us, the control command was reversed! He commanded to the right and the plane went to the left. Crazy!

Beco landed badly, but with no major damage. As soon as he managed to land, he burst out laughing! And he jumped out, like a boy, to see the damage on his toy. He and Dadô, who also could not look without touching it, checked the situation and used a tape to fix the small damage. They talked about a remote-control adjustment, called trim, to improve the command of the aileron in the small plane.

They did again the whole procedure and this time the flight was not so bad, so to speak. But when landing, the plane went down faster than the first time and somersaulted on the ground! This time, with greater damage, they decided to repair it more calmly and use the glue from the airplane kit. They sat around the table in the pantry and exchanged information about the flight adventure, excited. That was repeated during those summer days until the small plane could no longer fly, such was the damage made.

Uncle José Carlos Duarte remembers this very well: "Beco had the ability to please people, but he was very selective. I remember one event in the farm with the model airplane: His plane fell and broke down; at night, we sat at the pantry table to fix it. Then he gave me a part for me to assemble, I did it and gave it to him. He saw it was perfect and gave me another part. I was very good at assembling things and I did it right. As Dadô did not do it right, he was rushed, Beco would not give it to him. He was selective when he needed someone. He always chose who would do better."

The following weekend, Beco took a new plane to the farm. Now made of very thin plastic! The fun was such that

Dadô had the brilliant idea of demarcating the track with pieces of Styrofoam; he took a huge one we had on the farm, cut it in pieces that were fixed by sticks, passing through and sticking it in the grass in order to delimit the "runway". So much fun!

Otávio Torres confirms Beco's availability to us: "We became very good friends because we spent much time together. Every break he had in the season, he came to Brazil. We ended up spending almost every weekend at the farm when he could be here. And we had a hobby in common. He, Dadô and I used to fly model airplanes. We would spend the whole night assembling the model airplanes and the next day, in the morning, instead of going to sleep, we would fly!"

Beco, Dadô and Júnior with the second plane. Behind them, on the ground, the landing track marking with the pieces of Styrofoam

A peculiar story of this second plane: A long, loose wire would serve as an antenna to receive the command signals from the remote control. Beco did not know how to affix it, and it would not be wise to fly with the loose wire. The manual provided no explanations and the adhesive tape would impair the stability in flight, due to its weight. I followed everything closely, and realizing his difficulty, I said:

"Beco, make a hole in the rear fuselage of the plane and put the wire in it, affixing it with a drop of glue."
He looked at me not understanding my suggestion. I pointed out the place where he could pierce because of the length of the wire, without interfering with the wing and "aileron" commands.

"Just make a hole and pass the wire!" Beco, still confused, asks:

"Dri, and how am I going to pierce this?"

"With a hot needle! Heat melts plastic, doesn't it?"

"How am I going to do this?" he asked, still confused.

"Wait, I will get a needle!" I said, moving away.

I came back with a regular sewing needle in hand and asked for a pair of pliers from his toolbox.

"Done! Now you hold the needle with the pliers so you will not burn your hands and put it in the stove's burner to heat it until it turns red, then just pierce the plastic."
He put the plan into action and sometimes stopped and looked at me quizzically. I smiled at him showing confidence and so it was, until the fuselage hole operation came to an end! Not satisfied, he asked:

"Where did this idea come from? How did you know?"
Beco was surprised that I knew the needle trick, and I was surprised at his surprise at such an obvious thing! I felt like a genius with such a simple thing!

"I don't know, Beco! Didn't you know that heat melts plastic? With a needle, you would not run the risk of damaging the entire region to be pierced. And you still have control over the optimal hole size. You have never been a child? You have never played with burning and watching the reaction in different materials?" I concluded.

Soon, the planes got bigger and more powerful, with engines powered by kerosene. Beco, on his first trip, came back with new paraphernalia, improving his hobby with model airplanes. He started to specialize. By this time, Dadô already had his own small planes, and this hobby was really becoming a passion among the boys in the house.

My cousin Mônica defines our relationship as follows: "Speaking of the couple, my cousin Adriane and Beco, as Dri called him, they were happy, they matched, had a really soulful communication; it was very beautiful for us to see the couple from outside. They were always fine, there was harmony between them. I felt that it was real love and that was what impressed me the most. Happy moments they spent with everyone together. I think, in a way, we were privileged to have lived with him, this wonderful, charismatic and kind person he really was. Our family was conservative. So, boyfriends had to have this relationship of respect with all family members. The importance my uncles gave to family life, this union that extended to the uncles, cousins and grandparents, formed a very strong family bond; it is one protecting the other. I think Beco felt what Adriane has, how she was raised, this love nest that our family is."

Beco always brought his camera and, at his request, Júnior did a photo shoot of us, of course with Beco tickling me. One of my favorites is this:

But there were more...

On Christmas Eve, Beco met me at my maternal grandparents' house, Lídia and José Gomes da Rocha Paes, who lived in the same region where the Senna da Silva family lived. That was the opportunity when he also met my mother relatives. And the next day, Christmas lunch was at my paternal grandparents' house, where he already knew almost everyone in the family. He always came to me, wherever I was. On Christmas and other holidays, it was no different.

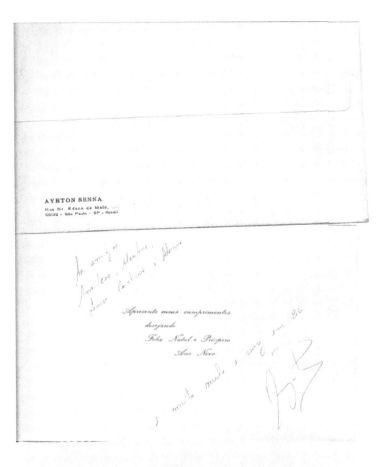

1985 Christmas card, sent by Beco to my family

"To friends Amilcar, Marilene, Lenise, Cristiane and Adriane I present my congratulations wishing you a Merry Christmas and a Happy New Year. Health and peace for 1986."

A letter I wrote to Beco on 1985 Christmas:

I know you were and are important to me because you make me feel special (sometimes) and feel like I have things inside of me that I did not think I had. This year, you helped me to mature (a little bit) and face the future a little more seriously, like "What will I do with my life?".

Most importantly, you warm my heart so much that, sometimes, I have to throw a big bucket of water to keep it from catching fire.

A small part of what I feel, For you

I...?...YOU

Merry Christmas Adriane

Stickers pasted on Beco's gift packages. He could not skip a little joke

"From: Beco/ To: Dridrica Merry Christmas and a Happy New Year! From: Beco/To: Drica I hope these little fats do not get in the way"

Chapter XII

We all went to Chapadão farm to celebrate the turn of 1985 to 1986. In the photo below, from left to right: Júnior, Amilcar, Grandma Catarina. In the background, Leonardo, Beco and I excited about the new beginnings and dreams of the new year.

In the photo above, from left to right: Dri, Dea, Aunt Marlene and Chris in choreography

It was ten days together at the farm. My father told Ayrton he looked "green", as if he was not healthy… Certainly, as a result of the hard year. Beco had a metabolic nature that did not store energy easily, that is, he was thin even though he ate everything. So, Mr. Amilcar nagged him to eat foods with plenty of vitamins, minerals and proteins, and forced him to drink bee's honey with royal jelly — a powerful natural energizer to recover energy.

Despite the usual activities on the farm, Beco was calmer. Not so worried about his usual races, as it had happened all year. It was vacation time. I did not even hear about F1. Total peace! The press, however, would not forget. Of course! It had been an extraordinary year for Senna.

In fact, those days were really nice. We had lots of activities, lots of chatting and small planes — while they could still fly, among drops and patches. Júnior was present and he told us some funny events about Beco and him. One of them involved a joke played with a friend they had in common. They put a cube of chicken broth into a shower. This was one of the funniest pranks I have ever heard! Can you imagine someone taking a shower in chicken broth? Júnior also revealed that, since they were young, they used phrases from romantic songs to act like a poet in notes and letters they sent to girls. But sometimes they forgot what they had written and to whom, repeating phrases and making gaffes that made it easier to see the fraud and thus breaking hearts. Júnior's participation in conversations was always relaxed and light, which made the environment very pleasant. Leonardo, Ayrton's brother, was also with us. Although shy and quiet, he also had fun with us and was always a welcome presence. Both Júnior and Leo spent just a few days with us at the New Year's celebration.

"1 year together, which I believe will not be the only one" on Jan. 4, 1986.

After some time at the farm, Beco and Júnior spent a few days with us in Guarujá, but again they stayed at the house of their friend Braguinha. During the day, we would meet for the usual boat trips.

Once, we stopped the boat at Iporanga beach, with crystal clear waters, but darker due to the color of the sand at the bottom, with a very calm sea, perfect for skiing. On another occasion, we stopped at the end of Enseada beach, where the waves are milder because of the protection of the peninsula, and Beco and I went diving near the rocks to watch the local marine life. We were with snorkel and diver fins. Occasionally, I would dive a little deeper to take a closer look at something that caught my attention from the surface. Beco kept an eye out for my movements. At one point I surfaced, still not knowing exactly where he was, and continued swimming, when I felt a voluminous touch on my body behind. Although I swam like a fish, I was always terrified of sharks, after all, this was their natural habitat! I was taken aback by that unexpected touch and had the

194

instinctive reaction to pull away, terrified. Only when I felt safe did I stop and look back to find out what it was: Beco had his head above water and looked back at me, with his diving mask on, astonished and very embarrassed at my reaction. I realized then he had advanced on my body for fractions of a second. I stood there, looking at him with my heart almost escaping through my mouth; but after the initial fright, I burst out laughing. He smiled, still embarrassed by the situation he had not foreseen, as his intention was quite different.

"Gee, Beco! You almost scared me to death! I am terrified of sharks and I did not expect this one," I said, gulping down water with laughter.

About the Formula 1 Grand Prix, in addition to the new car that they were preparing for Ayrton to compete in the season, the Championship had new rules for 1986, such as the maximum fuel tank capacity of 195 liters, and the maximum displacement of 1500 cm3 with or without a compressor.

Obviously, Beco took advantage of these trips to Europe to go after the novelties in model airplanes in stores there and came back excitedly with new equipment and accessories to assemble them on the farm.

At the farm, Beco helping to prepare Dadô's model airplane for the flight with the help of Mr. Amilcar, whose curiosity and participation did not last long! In the back, the Sulam silver station wagon with the small plane under it

The planes were getting bigger and more powerful every day, now with kerosene-powered engines. My brother-in-law Dadô and Otávio were maddened by the news Beco had brought from this trip, such as a little electric rotor to start the engine that used to start only if you forced it with the tip of your finger.

In England, this hobby was much more widespread and developed than here. And, at that time, nothing could be imported to Brazil. Also, customs control was very strict. Only a famous boy like Mr. Ayrton Senna da Silva would have some perks and comradeship from customs agents and manage to enter the country with a trunk full of parts of a new plane, as well as accessories and other knickknacks model airplanes, like glue (the optimal glue to guarantee repairs was essential to continue the game).

Dadô already had several deep cuts on his hands from when starting the plane's engine, turning the propeller with his fingers. Actually, Beco was amused that Dadô, with that way of his, had an unquestionable intelligence for engines, but as reckless as he was, he was always getting hurt! That is why Beco immediately tried to give him the electric roto brought on this trip, as well as the trunk itself, when he noticed that Dadô's eyes sparkled when he saw it (I believe the Abdelnur family treasures this trunk to this day with affection).

At that point, Dadô had found a supplier in Brazil and had also bought a new airplane when Beco arrived from England. He did not want to be left behind and would search everywhere about here; he even ordered a custom-made wooden box to carry all the necessary tools and accessories — he had built in a small panel that indicated the electric discharge and the battery charge level of the rotor; hence, he was amazed by Beco's news. And so they got more and more excited, united and friends. Later on, Otávio also joined the fun and this hobby became a real passion among the boys in the house; they could not wait to be together on the farm to enjoy the fun.

Marcelo Abdo, my cousin, never forgot his adventures with model airplanes, and he had a good reason for this: "One thing I like to remember about Beco are the planes. I started tinkering with model airplanes because of him. Dadô, my cousin, married to Lenise, Adriane's sister, introduced model airplanes to Beco.   He had a peculiar driver-characteristic:

He drove both ways, right-handed or left-handed. Ambidextrous! The plane's rudder is in the left hand, and he used it in the right; the elevator was in the right hand, but he used it in the left. He reversed the controls depending on the gift he got. For example, with Japanese model airplanes, the control sticks are reversed. That was fascinating about him! He would crash planes like hell, he would fly over and was very crazy. He challenged himself. One day, he flew over a short track with eucalyptus trees at the end. Dadô, who was his "coach", said: *Dude, Beco, watch out for the eucalyptus*!

Then he started to play tricks until the plane crashed at the tip of the eucalyptus; then there we went, the kids, helped to rescue the plane. All that was left was the engine and a few pieces of the fuselage. He was pissed, not about losing the plane, but about the lack of control. He would challenge himself and was disappointed when he failed."

At that time, a new pizzeria had opened in the small town of Porto Feliz, and one night we went to see it. There were me, Beco, Jacoto, Chris, Otávio and Andrea, who remembers what happened there: "The boys decided to bet who could eat the most pieces of pizza; and whoever won would not pay the bill. They started by eating pizzas of various flavors, but at one point, they only ordered mozzarella with little cheese so that they could eat more pieces. Otávio won when he ate his 23rd piece and the competitors gave up. They ate so much pizza that they were feeling sick on our way back home. We were in Beco's pick-up truck and they suffered with each bump... all in the name of the competition! Even though they were in pain, they would burst out laughing at the situation."

fev 86

Late afternoon at the Chapadão farm, Beco and I in love

The year of 1986 was, for my family, focused on the preparations for my sister Lenise's wedding with Eduardo. We traveled a lot to São Carlos, where my sister would live after the wedding. And when Beco was in Brazil, he traveled there with us.

It was also the year I started attending high school, at "Colégio Mackenzie". New school, new friendships. My best friends from that time are Renata Belém, Rosângela

Martinelli, Ana Lúcia Correa, Eliane Zavataro (Lita) and Patrícia Winard — some friends I still keep today.

In February, we only had a week of classes before the Carnival holiday. But it was enough time for us to exchange personal information and detect affinities. Of course! As teenagers, the first subject we wanted to talk about after "What is your name?", "Where do you live?", and "Where did you go to school before?" was: "Do you have a boyfriend?" As usual, I replied that yes, I had a boyfriend, a guy who was older than me, named Beco.

In our conversations, I soon realized that Patrícia, the oldest among us, already acted as a grown woman; from a liberal family, she had no problems talking about any subject related to men. She spoke in a calm and mature way about that, which made me, admired, feel free to talk to her about my personal matters. It was at this stage that I started to broaden my horizons. I started to unravel other life options that helped me make my own choices, without feeling guilty or vulgar.

Although we are three sisters at home, unfortunately, it would not be acceptable among us to consider attitudes or secrets that would go against my parents' rules. They probably lied about certain topics so that their secrets would be safe. These rules were an extension of a certain naive hypocrisy introduced by my parents, who until recently had guided me as if they were almost a religion. But it was no longer good for me!

On the first opportunity I had alone with my friend Patrícia, in Mackenzie's courtyard, I commented in a discreet voice:

"Pati, sometimes I feel like an idiot! Beco is nine years older and I was raised conservatively. There are times when I do not know what to do. The other day we were kissing and he touched my boobs. I was terrified! I did not know what to do and I pushed him away. Afterwards, I was ashamed, because that was a reaction of a little girl. I know he hangs out with other women, because we have already talked about that and I really do not feel prepared..."

"Calm down, Dri!" she interrupted me with a smile. "It is super natural! What is wrong with him touching you? Caresses are part of a relationship! And you must go as far as you feel prepared. No one has nothing to do with it. It is your body! And you must know what is best for you."

"Sometimes I am afraid of letting my parents down. But I am also afraid of losing Beco to a woman who can give him what he wants. I feel like an idiot when I am around him!" I said, coming clean about my feelings.

"Dri, do what is best for you... it is super normal that he touches your breasts!" she said, laughing. "You are not a vulgar girl because you and your boyfriend touch each other. You guys have been together for a year now. Do not be silly!"

I took a deep breath, kind of relieved to take off some of the shackles and the shame for my situation in front of my friends.

"Thank you, Pati. Do not talk about our conversation to anyone, okay?" I asked.

"Do not worry, Dri!" she assured me.

On February 11th, I went with my mother's family to my grandparents' house, in Itanhaém. We used to spend Carnival at the Yacht Club there. My cousins Ney and Fernando were older, so we could go to the ball with them. The ball was destined for sixteen-year-old people onwards, but as I looked older, my parents allowed me to go with them since I was fourteen. We only returned home after sunrise. Before 1984, I used to stay home, upset, watching the samba schools on TV with my grandmother Lídia.

That year, my cousins Ney, Fernando, Patu, my parents, sisters, aunt Marilda and uncle Ferdinando, grandparents José and Lídia and Otávio, Chris' boyfriend were with me. Lenise's fiancé was not there, as it would be his last Carnival being single and my sister thought it was great! Beco did not go either, because he was abroad.

Fernando Kaiser, my cousin, remembers the events in that time: "I have been living with Adriane since I was little. Especially during school holidays; we would go to the farm, to Itanhaém or Guarujá. And she did not change a thing during her relationship with Ayrton. The interaction was the same. We would mess a lot during Carnival. It was a time when water was poured from a tube on cars passing by on the street. There was also a train that transported people from downtown to the beach, and it was open. During Carnival days, when the train came, people would pour water, eggs etc. on it. And so did we: Adriane, her sisters, my brothers and I would throw water on the train. At night, we would enjoy Carnival at the Yacht Club. It was very nice, with a very familiar atmosphere."

Since childhood, it was in Itanhaém where we learned all kinds of prank. Buckets of water or a clog would fall over heads when opening doors, pepper were put in the food, nylon string was tied to the lampposts in front of our house. We were just waiting for an unsuspecting person to come. We made blowguns with aluminum TV antennas, which we used to secretly shoot beans at pedestrians. It was a mess that sometimes caused some trouble. But it was generally pretty fun. All day my cousins' friends came in and out at my grandparents' house, amazing! We played cards, War and Battleship. My grandmother patiently taught us knitting and crochet.

But that year, with all of us growing up, the mood for pranks calmed down and we agreed to go only one night to the ball. Among the four days of Carnival, we chose the third night as the best option. Not as crowded as the first night, not as empty as the last night used to be. With the help of my mother and my aunt at sewing, we made Greek-style costumes to create a Carnival block of our group. Made of white satin, the coats were open at the sides and the length was a hand above the knee. We decorated the costumes with blue sequins on the belt, on the shoulders and on the hem of the coat in the shape of typical Greek checkered waves. The girls would wear bikini tops, under their coats, and everybody would wear shorts and sneakers. On the day of the ball, we were playing cards in pairs at the dinner table, and around five in the afternoon, when the summer sun was starting to set, Ayrton walked into the door, all of a sudden. He had traveled to England to practice with the new car for that year's championship, and I had no idea when he would return to Brazil. He had called me on Saturday, in Itanhaém, but at no time he considered spending Carnival with us.

I was sitting facing the front door. Confused, I stood there in shock, holding the cards in my hands while everyone stood up to welcome him. In my mind, several questions were asked about how he had gotten there! Soon after, when he had already greeted everyone, I stood up to greet him, trying not to stumble on my own feet and to show the calm I did not have at the moment, while everyone looked at me looking accomplices in that endeavor.

At one point, he calls me to follow him to the front porch of the house:

"Come here, Dridrica!"

When we were alone, we hugged each other tightly and kissed passionately. Beco said:

"Yeah, Dridrica... I got you! You did not expect this one, did you?"

"Wow! I really didn't! How did you end up here? Weren't you traveling?" I asked.

"I was, but I returned to Brazil yesterday morning. I called you on Saturday just before I got on the plane."

"But how did you know where my grandmother's house was?" I asked.

"Ah, now you want to know too much. This is a professional's secret! And a professional does not reveal their sources."

"Geez! You will give me a heart attack!"

Beco looked at me with a smile of satisfaction, like someone who has accomplished a great feat. And for me, that is how I saw it: A great and delicious feat! How can I not love a man like that, capable of so many surprises and who spared no effort with love gestures?

"But Dri, I have to go back today, I just came here for a kiss and to give you what I brought you from the trip."

As soon as he finished his sentence, he pulled me by the arm so we could sit on the front step of the house and handed me a small black rectangular box.

When I opened it, I saw it contained a watch made of metal with a dark blue background, with the famous YSL logo intertwined. I thought the watch was beautiful and very elegant.

"Wow, Beco! That is beautiful! But why?" I said, trying to put the gift on my wrist as he enveloped me in a hug.

"Because I know you like watches and it reminded me of you the moment I caught sight of this one, in the duty-free shop. I could not wait to give it to you and see your silly face with all the surprise..."

"Geez! How cocky you are. I am the one who deserves it all!" I said, laughing, but with an air of snobbery. "It is not easy at all! Stand you? I must be a heroine! Not to mention that bunch of women hitting on my boyfriend! Puff..."

He laughed his slow laugh and said:

"But I only care about my silly girl, my number one fan, whom I miss so much!"

"Oh, but you are leaving today? Please, stay..." I asked fussy, and leaned my face against his chest. "You do all this and just leave? That is not fair!"

"I did not say I am leaving now, I just said I have to go today." he replied.

"Beco, I will not be able to use the watch right now, it is a little too loose and I will have to have it adjusted. But it is amazing! I love it!" I said, happy for the gift, thanking him with a tight kiss.

Some time later, I put on my costume to go to the Carnival ball. While disappointed with the situation because I wished he could stay, I was convinced that he would be even more disappointed than I was, knowing I would have a long and fun night without him.

Dressed up, with makeup, a nice hairstyle and wearing that costume that opened on the sides, I showed up happily in the living room so that he could see what he would be leaving alone in the middle of the Carnival party. I did not mean to do something wrong, but the man's imagination would be in my side.

Wide-eyed, he said laughing and trying to disguise the annoyance:

"Wow! Are you that beautiful just for Carnival?"

I replied with no mercy, smiling, and without disguising my provocation:

"Oh, yeah! I would rather go to Carnival with my boyfriend, but as it will not be possible, I will have to be content with having fun alone!"

We had a small snack before heading to the Yacht Club. Although I was already sad for spending so little time with my Beco, I tried not to show it. All ready to go, Ayrton said goodbye and when we split up in the cars, he suggested:

"Dri, come with me, I will drop you off at the club and leave."

"Okay, so they will all fit in one car!" I replied with some indifference because I was annoyed.

Júnior, Beco and I entered the Escort, which was now white and convertible! When we got to the club, Beco asked Júnior to give us five minutes alone to say goodbye, who excitedly said:

"Okay, Becão! I will take a look at the ball entrance and be right back!" Beco calmly looked for a place to park the car.

"Well, Drica, we have gained a few more minutes to make up for the lost time."

Patrícia, my cousin, remembers this too: "We all went to the Carnival ball together, except for Dri, who stayed outside the club with Ayrton."

After many passionate kisses, he said:

"Wait, I will be right back!"

He jumped out of the car towards the club's lobby. He disappeared from my sight for a few minutes and then returned running, saying excitedly:

"Dri, I am going to park the car in a more discreet place for us to have some privacy."

"What about Júnior?"

"He is in the hall and will stay there until later. That way we will have some more time for ourselves."

He drove somewhere not far from there, but very discreet. We started to make out again, now even more freely in our hiding place. I stopped, watched his eyes blaze, and brought his hand toward my breasts. He gently continued the suggested gesture. That light, gentle touch left me completely off the planet. Of course! A new and delicious sensation for me! Noticing my reaction, he continued touching me for some time, delighted with what it had caused me. Suddenly he stopped and said:

"Dridrica! What got into you? Why is that now?"

"I have been talking to a friend and she laughed at me, saying that this is super normal and no big deal! I have had this in my mind since that day, remember? I wanted you to touch me!" I replied in a soft voice, rapturous by the incredible sensation my body had been subjected to.

We spent hours enjoying the new touch. I, turned on with every movement of his hands, and he, turned on with my sensitivity to his touch, with passionate kisses on the mouth, neck and ears. It sounds excessive, but that really made me ecstatic!

"Wow, doll! You are so sensitive. That way you leave me so into!" (An expression he used with me many times, which meant "into you", "hooked".)

At one point, we got tired of the position in the car and went out into the canal. I sat on a parapet with my back to the wide canal and we could not get away from each other. We were enjoying each other until dawn, when we decided to wait for the group near my grandparents' house so that my parents would not notice my absence from the group. We stayed in the car parked on the corner of the street, waiting for everyone to arrive from the ball, already tired and leaning against each other.

"Dri, why don't you ever touch me?" Beco asked.

I thought about the answer for a moment. In fact, I had not thought about that possibility yet. But ashamed to say this, I said:

"I do not know, I do not think it is fair to tease you, knowing I cannot go through with it."

"Do not worry, I will never force anything and we do not have go through with it. That is not how it works! You can touch me without worrying about it."

Half a word is enough for a wise person, said the wise people, and I got the message. What made me feel more secure, above all, was the unconditional love he devoted to me. For he did not retreat before any obstacle, whatever it might be. He loved me for who I was, with all my concerns of age and limitations of my family context.

It was almost daylight when he came over to kiss me again and this time he led my hand and I tried to touch him through his clothes. I was not sure how to do it. Geez, it was so hard to excite a grown man, with my glaring inexperience! But the car with the gang on their way back from the ball approached and we quickly pulled ourselves together. I thought: "Thank God I will not have another embarrassment and will have some time to deal with this matter." Our night, in addition to being amazing, was the first step towards getting greater intimacy.

Different from my fears, I did not feel vulgar, nor did I have the impression that I had been frowned upon by my boyfriend for it. I loved being touched! I then realized that I could do whatever I felt prepared to do and he would enjoy. We got out of the car and said goodbye:

"Dridrica, see you in São Paulo," Beco said, with a mischievous smile.

I entered my grandparents' house along with my family, and Beco returned to São Paulo with his friend Júnior. No one asked me or made any comments about my absence from the ball, which made me feel respected by them.

One weekend after Carnival, we were all at the farm when a motorcycle arrived, it was Beco's, a motor scooter by Piaggio.

"Dridrica, come see what I brought to leave here on the farm for our motorcycle rides..." He took me by the hand, excited to show me his prize.

"That is beautiful, Beco! How did you get it?"

It was silver and at that time you could not find a scooter in Brazil.

"Piaggio gave me last year; they would give one of these at each race to the driver who took pole position throughout the championship. As I did seven poles, Dridrica," he laughed with happiness, "I won seven of these, but I only brought two of them to Brazil: This one and a white one, to stay at home for the guys."

"Cool! I have seen a lot of this type of motorcycle in Italy, it is so cute!"

"Shall we test it?

"Of course!"

Beco got on the bike, and I waited for him to start the Scooter. I had already realized that it was very different from my Yamaha 180, which my father had given me a while ago, as well as he did for each of my sisters, so that we could ride around the farm together. He also looked at the details, exploring the possibilities. He turned the key on, made sure it was in neutral to start it by using the bike's pedal (for those who do not know, at that time engines started by "popping the clutch", using a pedal/lever). Noticing that there was no gasoline in the engine injection, he immediately looked for the "choke" (it was the feature that controlled the fuel injection flow; when we opened it, more fluid entered the spark plug, which made it easier to start), tested again and soon the engine ran (usually, you had to wait a little with the engine running, to "warm up" a little and only then regulate the choke to normal flow, thus preventing the bike from "flooding" — too much flow in the injection would make the bike turn off by itself and then it would take more time and effort to "unflood" and turn the engine on again; we detected what had to be done by the sound of the engine. These are things from a time when the modern wonder of such an electronic injection that automatically regulates all of this did not exist.)

"Come, Dridrica!"

I got on the motorcycle and we rode around the farm. During the ride, he shared with me the operational details of the bike:

"Look, Drica! This bike is different. The gear is on the right hand, can you see these little dots? They are the indicators of each gear and the neutral. Clutch is also in the right hand. On other bikes, it is all on your foot. Watch out, you need to get used to it!"

I stayed behind, keeping an eye on Beco's explanations and delighted with the news.

"The brake too! Unlike the others, you brake here, look," he said, pointing to an access pedal with his right foot. "You need to feel how the brake responds, be careful!"

And so that was our first Scooter ride. When we got back to the farmhouse, he turned off the bike for us to get off and showed me the detail of the support pedal. In order to the Scooter be stand upright when stopped, there was a double pedal under the motorcycle that suspended the front tire in the air, as if it were a lever making a tripod with the rear tire.

"Got it, Dridrica? Now it is your turn."

I was amused since the beginning by Beco's concern to guide me on how the Scooter worked. I knew about motorcycles because I always had one to ride on the farm and I also had a natural curiosity for everything, including engines and all of its novelties. But mostly, I was amused by his excitement about that toy, which he had won as a prize for his great achievement. I wanted to honor him, and happy, I immediately accepted the challenge:

"Yay!"

I sat down and took the bike off the tripod, while Beco guided me beside me:

"Dri, turn the key on. See this light on the panel? It is because it is in neutral, you can start it."

Even though I was clumsy with that pedal, I immediately started the engine and, as it was already warm, I had no problems with the choke. "Now just ride it!

Remember the clutch is here now! Go, engage the first gear and try to go slowly to feel the clutch. Go alone," Beco said.

I loved the challenge and wanted to do well, even though I was sure that, with my experience with the motorcycle I had, success was certain. I got out carefully enough so that the bike would not die right at the start, which would have been a plateful for my instructor's mockery. From then on, it was me and the bike, I was calmly testing the gears, trying out the news and adapting to use. I soon realized that the balance in the curves was different, probably due to the proportions of the axle and the size of the tires. Beco watched me proudly.

"Well done, Dridrica! You are pretty smart, aren't you?"

I gave him a smug smile, but I was focused on getting back to where I started, because I did not want to abuse the perk. I stopped, turned the engine off at the key and then put the bike on the pedal by myself. I could not hold back the temptation to do it all by myself. Do you remember that sometimes and in some ways I like to show off? Well, then! I would not miss the opportunity to take a ride on the Scooter. Usually, when we went out on my bike together, I would hitchhike because it was a great time to cuddle with him. Not to mention that this was his Scooter and, therefore, I was very careful when riding it. That was my logical deduction.

They called us to lunch, I thanked him for his kindness, satisfied with a tight hug, happy for his achievement, for his enthusiasm and for sharing this moment with me.

Of course, after lunch it was time for model airplanes. But this time, Beco took the boys first to take a look at the Scooter, as they were also curious about the news that had been the topic of the lunch. Right after that, they decided to play with the planes and, before I walked away from the bike, Beco stopped and said:

"Why don't you practice riding your new bike a little more?"

"What do you mean, my bike?"

"Dridrica, I brought this bike to you, you silly fool. Hellooo!" he laughed.

"Oh, Beco! Come on! I cannot believe it!"

"Why not, Dridrica? I know you will take good care of it for me..."

Speechless and unresponsive, I stared at him not knowing what to say.

"Go there, Dri! The key is in the ignition, go practice while I go see Dadô and Otávio losing their pilot's license.

He walked away and I tested a little more my new, precious toy. Later, I parked the bike and told my father.

"Dad! Beco gave me his Scooter, the one he won on pole!"

"That is nice, dear! But we already knew he brought it to give it to you."

"Huh? How did you know?"

"This motorcycle arrived in Brazil and we had to license and put a plaque in it. Ayrton called me to arrange the documentation, but we put it in my name because you are a minor," dad said, pleased with Beco's attitude.

That is me, on the brand-new bike I got from Beco, my boyfriend. 1985 Pole Award.

I was moved by my family's connivance in the face of such a special surprise. I thanked my father with a hug and went to meet Beco, at the head of the runway for the model airplanes. I waited for one of them to finish their flight, because it was always a tense moment. When the flight was completed, I ran towards him. I wanted to properly thank him for the gift. I wrapped him in a nice hug, before Dadô and Otávio got closer, and told him:

"Thank you for the amazing surprise. I really did not expect it!"

"We played you just right!" and laughed his slow laugh.

We kissed with affection and before I ran back to my gift, I provoked:

"Let's figure out a way to celebrate properly later, just the two of us."

And we celebrated in the best possible way for us.

Still on this vacation, on another visit from Beco to Itanhaém, he went with Júnior to spend the day with us, and they took the speedboat in a trailer to pull the water ski. We skied on the river in front of the Yacht Club, but then we decided to go to a more distant beach called Cibratel. We drove there, along a two-lane road that was a straight line. We stayed for a short time and, on the way back, I remember my sister Lenise was with us in Beco's white Escort XR3. That day, he drove like a madman. There was heavy traffic in our direction and he overtook vehicles in a way that seemed impossible for us, mortals. In small spaces between the cars that were coming against us, he would go out to overtake them and return to our lane, fitting the car into a tight space for it. Crazy! Even I, who loved adventures, was apprehensive, even though I noticed his total control over the car. Lenise was furious with his attitude, which made her feel in danger, but he refused to be stopped in that traffic and continued to overtake the cars even under her protests. That was the only time he did such a thing in my presence, because my sister complained a lot, very annoyed, as soon as we got to Itanhaém. When he sought my help with his eyes, I reprimanded him:

"Yeah, Beco... you were too much this time. It is one thing for you to take a risk by yourself, but taking a risk with other people in the car?!"

Lenise remembers this event: "Once we went to Itanhaém and I was in the car with them. My God! I do not remember what happened, but I was scared to death. He became famous at home because he was stupid on the roads and bad off the tracks. I found it dangerous to be in the car with him."

Another day, we were leaving the house in a group with this white car; it was a rainy day and Beco decided to play it fun. Around the corner of my street, there was a steep descent, and he, pulling on the handbrake, went practically all the way down the street with the car on the wet asphalt. He kept control of the car in the handbrake in one hand, with the other on the steering wheel. Although I found the things he was up to exciting, as he showed total mastery, I did not compliment or encourage him to do this kind of thing, I knew it was risky. It was just few times that he took liberties of messing with me in the car.

About twenty days before the Brazilian GP, we were all at the Chapadão farm and my cousins, Beco and I left for a motorcycle ride through the area. Marcelo Abdo, my cousin, recalls what happened that day: "One day, we left for a motorcycle ride around the farm. I was with Chris' Yamaha 180, my cousin with a DT, Dri with her 180, and Beco with the Scooter that you needed to change the gears with your hand. The Scooter was a small motorcycle, terrible for riding on a dirt road. We left the headquarters and headed towards Pilão, which had a steep road and, at the end of descent, just before the curve, there was sand. We sped up and Beco came on the way down with that Scooter, hit the sand and tumbled. The Scooter's side was scraped and he almost had a dislocated arm. Can you imagine? Ayrton Senna falling off a motorcycle that, by contractual clause, he could not even be riding on, and he gets hurt? At that time, it was a hell of a concern and a great mobilization for not letting the press know about what happened."

My cousins, instigated by the adventure of riding with Beco, ran off in front of me. I kept at a safe distance, watching what they were going to do, when I saw Beco sliding the rear of the bike to the left and tumbling to the right in a fall, it was all too fast. The others were further ahead and it took them a while to realize what had happened, but I went right by his side to help him. I stopped and quickly got off the bike:

"Beco, are you alright?"

He was already getting up, with a distinct expression of who was in pain. I looked for a sign of injury throughout his body.

"I am fine, but I hit my arm and I think I got hurt." Meanwhile, the boys approached to help.

They lifted the bike off the ground, but seeing that he was safe, the mocking began:

"What's up, Becão? Did you kiss the ground?"

"What the hell! I decided to brake right here, in this soft land, and the rear wheel slipped, I could not get my balance back, and that was it! I went to the ground."

The boys laughed and said:

"We need to teach you how to drive..."

He, all covered in dirt, noticed few scratches on his leg and some bleeding on his right arm, but I was worried because he seemed to be in pain in his arm. The bike had its paint and handlebars scratched by the fall. We soon decided to return home, but Beco, with wounded pride, insisted on riding back.

When we got home, he rinsed his body, changed his clothes, and we treated his scratches, but the pain in his arm did not ease. We put ice on the spot, put on proper muscle sore ointment in an attempt to find some relief, and finally we bandaged his arm and got him a sling to immobilize his movements; we also gave him a pain reliever. Having done everything in our power, we sat down with the whole family that was waiting for us for lunch. After we reported it to everyone, my father worriedly suggested:

"Ayrton! You should go to São Paulo to take an X-ray of the arm."

No, Mr. Amilca! I am sure it is nothing serious, I am just worried if I will be well enough for the race in Rio. If I cannot race, I will have to pay a monstruous fine because I got injured riding a motorcycle; I am contractually forbidden to ride a motorcycle and, worse, prevented from driving injured."

"Damn, bad luck! Let's hope everything works out," my father said trying to comfort him.

To break that tense atmosphere, I spoke, taking long pauses between words to raise expectations about what I wanted to say, seriously and gesturing and looking from side to side with each pause:

"Look... I am super worried... I do not know how we are going to solve this situation... That is not possible, guys...

What a bad luck... This is very serious... My brand-new motorcycle is now scratched!"

Everyone started to laugh, and every time he looked annoyed, afraid of what was to come, I used the same strategy and ended by telling him to calm down that everything would be all right.

Thank God, as soon as Beco arrived in São Paulo, he went to an orthopedist who confirmed it was just a dislocation. He had his arm immobilized for a few days, but removed the band a few days before the GP to regain his normal movements. That was close!

I have a record of a note of mine, written on March 12th, 1986; something I would never send to him. We were in São Paulo during the week, and my notes make clear my anxiety to be with him, my annoyance when he was so close and did not look for me, even if it was just for a day. If I were to sum up feeling in a single word, it would be frustration.

It is curious to note that, one day after putting down on paper what was troubling me, even though I had not said a word about it, Beco sent me flowers, but this time he was not leaving the country. That surprised me a lot! The most he could tell was that I was distant and reserved, because that was my attitude when I was upset with him. We did not argue with each other, but shared a silent connection I did not understand, as if we could see into each other, an inexplicable mutual understanding.

"Dri, Miss you a thousand!
Beco, March 13, 1986"
Red roses with the card

Chapter XIII

The 21st was Beco's birthday and the first day of training at the Brazilian GP. We could not celebrate together, once I could not go to the race in Rio de Janeiro.

That year, he became the first driver at Lotus. His teammate the year before, Elio de Angelis, moved to another team and was replaced by Johnny Dumfries.

The Brazilian GP was on March 23rd, in Jacarepaguá. Ayrton started in pole position and won second place in the race, in a doubleheader with Piquet. That year, Brazilian top models could not reach him in the pit. To my relief, things were falling into place. Soon after, he returned to São Paulo and we could spend some more time together.

Renata Belém, my friend from school, remembers how she found out who Beco was, my boyfriend, and how was her interaction with him back then:

"I started Mackenzie's first-year high school in 1986, and Adriane was in my class. We met and became close friends and ended up making a nice group: We would go out to dinner and go to the movies in São Paulo, spent weekends at her farm or at my house in Guarujá. It was a group of six or seven girls. We knew she had a boyfriend, but he lived abroad. When he was in Brazil, she would not go out with us.

After a while, we learned that Adriane's boyfriend's nickname was Beco. But she had some photos of Senna signed on the back by that Beco guy in her diary. She claimed to be a fan of the driver and that her boyfriend had gotten a picture of him. I started to suspect.

One day, we were at Mackenzie's door together, she was waiting for Beco and I, for my father. Then she became embarrassed and said: Oh, do not bother to what you will see, he is a little older, and we kept looking at the cars that were the same as my father's and the same as her boyfriend's,

which she said was a red Escort XR3. But my father arrived first and I left.
I asked my dad if Ayrton Senna had a red Escort XR3, and he said he did. My dad knew this because he read magazine articles and saw a picture of Senna in the car, and I put the stories together.

The next day at school, I stated to Adriane: I know who your boyfriend is.

She confirmed it and asked me to keep it a secret. I agreed and said nothing to no one, but the fact is that, on that day when Beco picked Dri up, Mackenzie's people saw Senna at the school's door and everyone wanted to know who his girlfriend was. In fact, I think Adriane was afraid to tell people because her father was very worried about linking her name to his, thinking this would be bad for her. So, as far as Adriane managed to, she kept it a secret. The comments increased and people in Mackenzie found out that Dri was Senna's girlfriend. But she did not know that at the time. She only knew that now when we met again, as adults, then she said, surprised:

"Hold on. Nobody spoke to me at the time. Damn it! I had no idea everyone in Mackenzie knew it!"

"Everyone knew and found out who you were..."

"Is that why no one approached me? No one flirted with me? They just kept looking from afar..." she laughed.

"Do you remember how it was at Pizzeria Monte Verde? A hilarious scene! There were you, him, Ana Lúcia with her brothers and me. Paulinho, one of Ana's brothers, was sitting next to me, looked at Senna and said he thought they had gone to college together, and I told him to look again and imagine him wearing race overalls and a helmet. Paulinho immediately realized who was with us, a line of people formed to come ask for an autograph. Then you guys got up to leave because you could not eat and asked me to pay the bill. But he was super nice and talked to everyone."

We went out other times with Senna. I remember we went to the Gallery once when everyone was at Dri's house; in another event, it was just her and me; we also went once when Júnior was together. We used to go to Adriane's house and everyone would go out together. When we went to the same place, we went in the same car.

When I dated Júnior, we used to meet at Dri's house. We would go to the lobby together, but each couple would go their own way and, on the way back, we met again and went up together to her apartment to drop her off at home.

Imagine my situation: I had nothing to do with this story, had a normal life, meeting a simple, very funny guy, good and bouncy person, but who was famous! Once, Lita, Adriane and I were waiting for him to pick us up at home to go to the farm. The phone rang and dad answered, on the other end of the line, Beco asked if Renata was at home. Daddy asked: 'Who asks?'. Then he capped the nozzle of the device and said quietly, smiling: I am talking to Ayrton Senna.

Anyway, I remember Adriane's difficulties in dating someone who was abroad longer than here, in publicly assuming the relationship because he was ten years older than her and having to deal with harassment from fans and the press. I sometimes went with them to the farm when he was there; he was really a very nice person, happy and playful, like a kid. He was always messing with everyone, if you get distracted in a conversation, he would tie your tennis lace for you to trip. He used to play a lot with Adriane's brother-in-law at the time. So, inside a "protected" environment, it seemed like everything was really cool. Her family was very fond of him.

I also remember the Scooter he imported to Brazil and gave her as a gift, and it stayed on the farm.

For all that, it was nice for us to go to her farm, there they were free to live their relationship without a journalist or photographer around."

As a perk of being sponsored by the brand, he had available some versions of XR3 Ford, and at that point, Beco changed the car again, but now for a red one. He did not stay long with the white convertible, which I thought was the prettiest of the three, and I have no idea why. I found it impolite to ask questions or give my opinion.

My friend Renata, when she was dating Júnior, celebrated her birthday at her house on the very day that Beco had arrived from a trip. Besides some friends, Beco, Júnior, Leo and I were present, who joined us to use the opportunity to meet new girls. At certain point, sitting in the same chair in the dining room — I was sitting with my back to him and between his legs —, Beco rested his face on my shoulder, which I adjusted for support, and he fell asleep, so tired he was. I felt sorry for him, but at the same time I was happy to have a boyfriend who was such a partner, who agreed on everything and was always ready and willing to have fun.

He and I: Prank prepared by me, that night with my friends

Photos taken that day, at my friend Renata's house

My friend Rosângela also remembers how she found out who was my mysterious boyfriend and talks about it:

"Dri just said she was dating an older guy and that he lived abroad, but I did not know who it was. One day at Mackenzie, I even saw a guy in a blue cap and sunglasses leaning against a tree that was in the courtyard in front of the building and near the exit. Then I heard someone commenting: Guys! Senna is there! Where?, I asked. He was there in a cap, under the tree! Then I missed Adriane, and I asked myself: 'Where is she?' I was told she had left with her boyfriend. When I looked in the direction of Rua Maria Antônia exit, I see her leaving hand in hand with a guy in a cap. And that was when I put things together and found out she was dating Ayrton Senna. She, very discreet, said she dated Beco, but that was how I found out who Beco was. I saw him other times when he passed by the school in the red XR3 to pick Dri up."

Undoubtedly, Chapadão farm was our weekend getaway when Beco was in Brazil. Because we really felt free and safe there, and we also had many leisure options.

Exactly because of that, it was where we lived memorable moments with our closest friends and family. In fact, Saturday after lunch was the time for "kamikaze" flights of the model airplanes. Of course, after the nap of his father-in-law "Mr. Amilca", whose bedroom was right at the head of the "runway" and the planes' engines, more powerful every day, were very noisy. For this activity, Beco had the company of his brothers-in-law and partners, Dadô and Otávio — Júnior was not always there.

My cousin Kaco comments about their interaction: *"I remember Beco always had this playful spirit with his other brothers-in-law, Otávio and Dadô, who were very playful too, so everyone joined in and we played, it was always a party."*

One night on the farm, after dinner, we were watching a TV report about the Amazon Rainforest. While they showed the aquatic life in its rivers, Dadô boasted that he knew all those fish because he had taken fishing trips with friends in the area. He said he once caught "so many kilos of this and that" fish. Making fun of him, Beco and Otávio said that was "fishermen's talk", that is, a typical exaggeration of those who fish, when the pink dolphins appeared in the report... a kind of dolphin from great Brazilian rivers, with pink skin, almost white, like Dadô! That was it! Ayrton shouted:

"Look, Dadô is there! Dadô, they caught you in the act!"

That was it. Everyone laughed. Including Dadô, who was a very nice and playful guy; he laughed a lot. He liked being the focus and pretended not to mind being messed with. The one who did not like this at all was my sister Tata, his fiancée, who would soon come to his defense. Otávio still laughs today when he remembers it: "Dadô's nickname was given by Beco, because he had a pinkish skin tone. Then, Beco nicknamed him as Pink Dolphin. He was really pissed when Beco called him that. We laughed a lot with this pink dolphin thing, because Dadô was very uptight and Senna was a big joker. So we did not miss a chance to make fun of him."

Dadô himself liked to tell jokes about country bumpkins, because he lived in São Carlos, countryside of São Paulo. When he wanted to be funny, he twisted his tongue and made his accent heavy, and both Beco and the rest of the group was amused by that. He came with little jokes, like: Do you know how a robbery happens in São Carlos? Hands in 'e air, 'is is a 'obbery, gimme everythin' in a-thousand-dollar bills.

And added:

There, the chicken goes cock-a-doodle-doo, the chick goes bah-gawk, the cat goes meowr and when a stone falls into the water it goes plonks.

Everyone would laugh, including himself! That was when we found it even more funny, by his way of being. Whenever there was a new audience among us, he would repeat the same little jokes and burst out laughing.

After a while, Dadô took revenge on Beco and gave him a nickname. Because of his big ears, Ayrton was nicknamed as Topo Gigio, a character from an Italian children's TV show. So Beco would call Dadô Pink Dolphin and would hear Topo Gigio in return. Obviously, Beco did not like the nickname at all, but he was aware that "those who do it, take it back", and these "niceties" were limited to them in moments of mutual provocation.

My father, on the other hand, never let his guard down. He did not like to accept jokes so as not to lose the respect of his sons-in-law. He really liked Dadô and called him that way; sometimes, when he heard someone calling him Pink Dolphin, he would give a disguised little laugh. As for Beco, my father always called him Ayrton, there was a lot of affection and respect between them!

A few days later, Beco resumed his routine in the F1 Championship in Europe and I returned to my regular activities.

The Spanish GP took place on April 13th, in Jerez de La Frontera. Ayrton started in pole position and won his third victory in F1. He won since the beginning! He was more strategic; with the authorized change of tires that year, he surpassed Williams' cars, which had far superior engines to the other competitors.

That same day, Beco called me:

"Hi, Dridrica!"

"Beco! When they called me saying you were on the phone, I almost could not believe it! What an amazing race! I did not think you would be able to finish the race, let alone hold the lead. That was a hard game!"

"Yeah, Dridrica, that was close. But you did not count on my cunning!" (Making fun of the phrase by Mexican comedian - The Red Grasshopper)

"That's it! That's it! That's it! That's it!" (I replied as the same comedian, but in the role of Chavo del Ocho.) "Well done! It was awesome! I did not believe the car would last until the end, it was breathtaking!"

He laughed and said:

"Dridrica, I almost could not take it! I am sore all over! I almost could not get out of the car." He laughed again. "Lifting the trophy and the champagne on the podium was a martyrdom!"

"I can imagine. I am so proud of you! Wow, what a race! But are you in a lot of pain?"

I dehydrated, did the almost the entire last lap with cramps all over my body, and now I am crooked!"

"Wow, now what?"

"Yeah, Dridrica, and you are not here to take care of me! I have to put everything back in place, I will need a massage, find a professional to put me back together and get some rest; I need to be brand new in time for what is to come."

"Oh, damn! I wish I could be there to take good care of my boyfriend..."

"Yeah, doll, I miss you so much, that is why I had to call you today."

"Beco... be back soon, okay? I miss you a lot too."

"Dridrica, take care, be good! Watch out for falling rocks!"

"Um, um, you be good too! Once again, congratulations on today's win. I will watch out for falling rocks. I am sending you those delicious kisses, from your proud biggest fan!"

"Take care. Delicious kisses on your mouth which I miss so much!

"Kisses."

It was at times like those when I realized the pivotal role I was playing in his life; a growing responsibility that made me, at sixteen, gradually let go of the tantrums that, although not apparent, I confess happened inside me. Despite my young age, in adolescence, with my hormones and body adapting to adulthood, that still caused me a serenity in relation to the man I loved, who also loved me and counted on me. I felt that this was bigger than myself, that something else, up there, was in charge.

In the words of Uncle José Carlos: *"It was a very good time for Adriane, where she matured a lot, maybe faster than normal for her age; she grew much faster than she would have in a natural way. It was too fast, she was a tomboy, stayed with us playing and having fun, but suddenly she had to take the leap to date a world idol; that is what marked Adriane. Long before Adriane met Ayrton, she already knew how to dive, how to play pool, street cricket, she rode motorcycles on the farm and rode horses. She always participated in the games, but she was no longer Adriane we met before she met Ayrton. She was sad when he was not here, but that is part of every relationship, especially when the person is far away; you travel and are away for three days and you get upset, imagine staying away for three months."*

The day after the GP, I wrote and sent Beco the letter below:

April 14th, 1986

Hey pervy,

You have no idea how important I felt to you when I got your call on the race day. I would like you to know how I wished I were close to you, massaging your aching arms and cuddling you so that you sleep in my arms like a baby, after such a physical effort. In short, I wish I could take care of you, as if you depended on it.

I think I am the proudest crush in the world, do not ever lose that determination you have and that I admire so much.

Come back soon, I cannot wait to hug you strongly.

I miss you so much that I am collapsing.

Insatiable yours,

P.S.: Do not get used to it because I do not usually write this stuff for my fans.

Days later, I got this letter:

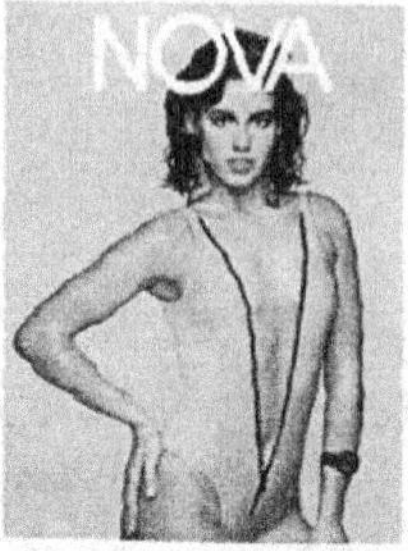

AUSTRIA,   23/04/86

①

Oi Dri°,

Pensei tanto em você que
provavelmente escrevi uma dúzia de
cartas "mentalmente é lógico"! Você
deve ter jogado uma peça daquelas
mismo!!!

Daqui onde estou não tem telefone que ligue ao BRASIL, mas amanhã
já estarei na Itália e tudo bem.

Após a corrida da Espanha fui p/
a Inglaterra mas assim que cheguei lá
imediatamente no dia seguinte peguei um
vôo aqui p/ a AUSTRIA, pois ~~entre~~
meu ombro direito, coluna e pescoço não

228

tinha muita coisa funcionando, fiquei
aqui apenas dois dias pois em seguida
tinha uns treinos a fazer na Itália
p/ o G.P. de Imola. Treinei ali os
2 dias e retornei novamente aqui p/ a
Austria e agora volte p/ a Itália p/
o G.P.

Aqui onde passei todo esses dias
é um Hotel de um preparador físico
AUSTRÍACO que ~~cuidou~~ cuidou no passado
da equipe AUSTRÍACA de SKI e recentemente
até o ano passado do NIKI LAUDA. É um
CARA EXCEPCIONAL, entende uma barbaridade

do corpo humano, é especialista em coluna, preparação FÍSICA e NUTRIÇÃO, ele realmente sabe muito sobre o nosso corpo e foi a única pessoa que podia dar um jeito em mim.

Com tudo isso, a única conclusão que dá pra tirar é a de que, do dia que saí do BRASIL estive em casa na Inglaterra uma noite apenas e sabe como é não foi possível dar assistência a "todas minhas fãs" IN ENGLAND !!!

Nem vou dizer de saudades pois sei que você não liga mesmo, não é?

A propósito, não se importe com a foto no papel é apenas "uma das fãs"!!

Aliás, preciso falar urgente com o anti-furo p/. ficar sabendo se tem tomado conta direitinho de ... !!

Quer dizer que não acreditou quando te disseram que eu estava no telefone no ~~domingo~~ domingo após a corrida da Espanha, sua "bobeca" se soubesse a vontade que estava de te ver e dar uns beliscões ... se bem que eu falo, falo e nunca tenho coragem de te dar uns apertões, quero dizer,

apenas alguns carinhosos, também
já imaginou se nem os apertões carinhosos
eu tivesse a coragem de dar, acho
que me tornaria monótono, já
pensou tudo certinho sem nenhuma arte,
acho que não sou o único que
precisa de emoções fortes, não é?

   É incrível quando penso que
estou longe de você a apenas 15 DIAS,
parece uma eternidade! Talvez seja
porque ainda tem várias semanas pela
frente até que possa voar p/ aí e
isso não ajuda a cuca da gente.

Tenho estado meio pirado, quero dizer, um pouco mais do que já sou, tenho que ir mexendo as coisas com outras equipes pois meu contrato com a Lotus acaba no final deste ano, graças a Deus tenho algumas opções abertas, mas a responsabilidade é tanta no sentido de não errar na escolha que fica difícil decidir, existe inclusive a possibilidade de continuar na própria Lotus, o negócio é ficar de cuca fria mas é justamente o que não consigo fazer,

⑦

tem tanta coisa passando pela minha
cabeça ao mesmo tempo que fica
até difícil separar as coisas.

Hoje estive numa Igreja aqui ao
lado do hotel, e resolvi entregar nas
mãos de Deus e tenho certeza que o
que for melhor de uma forma geral vai
dar certo.

Como é, o Otavio já deteuu
o avião dele ou ainda não terminou de
montar? Qualquer coisa diga a ele pedie
ao ~~Aado~~ boto cor de rosa uma ajuda,
tenho certeza do resultado !!! Catastrofe !!!

⑨

Quanto mais escrevo mais agonia
me dá, puxa você esta me fazendo uma
falta daquelas, toda a culpa é do teu pai,
diga a ele que estou reclamando!!
~~quero~~ Quero dizer, deixa pra la, sabe como é,
da de ele dizer que então vai dar
um jeito, prefero que ele não tenha
nenhuma idéia brilhante, pois ali esta o exemplo
pratico de como tamanho não é documento.

   Mocinha, saudades mil,
Eu te .... do teu paquera!
                      Beto

"Hi Dri,

I thought so much about you that I probably wrote a dozen of letters, in my mind, of course! You must have cursed me!!! From where I am, there's no phone calls to Brazil, but tomorrow I will be in Italy and it will be okay. After the race in Spain, I went to England, but as soon as I got there, I immediately took a flight to Austria, because among my right shoulder, spine and neck, not many things were working; I was here for only two days because I had to practice in Italy for the Imola GP. I practiced there for two days and came back to Austria and now I will go back to Italy for the GP. I spent all these days here in a hotel by an Austrian physical trainer who in the past handled the ski Austrian team and by last year was taking care of Niki Lauda. He is an exceptional guy, who knows a lot about the human body, is an expert in spine, physical preparation and nutrition, he really knows a lot about our body and was the only person who could help me. With all that, the conclusion I can take is that, since when I left Brazil, I stayed home in England for one single night and you know, I could not talk to "all my fans" in England!!! I will not even mention how much I miss you because I know you do not even care, do you? By the way, do not mind the picture on the paper, it is just of "one of the fans"!! In fact, I need to urgently talk to Antifuro to see if he has been taking proper care of...!! So you mean you did not believe when they told you I was on the phone on Sunday after the race in Spain, you silly fool? If you knew how badly I wanted to pinch you!! I mean, just affectionately. Can you imagine if I could not even pinch you affectionately? I think I would probably become monotonous; can you imagine? Uptight, no art, I think I am not the only one who needs strong emotion, am I?

It is incredible when I think that I am only far away from you for 15 days, it seems like an eternity! Maybe it is because there are now several weeks ahead until I can fly back there and this does not help my mind. I have been a little crazy, I mean, a little more. I have been needing to deal with things *from other teams, because my contract with Lotus ends the end of this year, thank God I have some other options, but the responsibility is such, in the sense of not making mistakes when choosing, which makes it harder to decide. I even have the possibility of staying in Lotus. What I need is to rest my mind, but this is exactly what I cannot do, there is so much going on in my mind at the same time that it gets hard to separate things.*

Today I went to a church near the hotel, I decided to let God decide it and I am sure that it will happen what is best. So how is it? Has Otávio destroyed his plane yet or he haven't finished assembling it? Tell him to ask Pink Dolphin for help, I am sure of the result!! Catastrophe!!

The more I write the more agonized I get, you are sorely missed, and this is all your dad's fault, tell him I am complaining!! I mean, let it go, you know, I do not want him trying to find a solution, I prefer he does not have any brilliant idea, because he is the living example that size does not matter.

Lady, I miss you a thousand, I ... you,
Your crush, Beco."

Honestly, Beco did not exaggerate when he said in the phone call that he had problems with his shoulder, spine and neck. After all, those are the most demanded anatomical parts of a Formula 1 driver.

San Marino GP took place on April 27th, another pole position — the tenth in his career. Although he started well, he left the race on lap 11 with a broken wheel bearing.

Beco returned to Brazil!

Uncle José Carlos fondly recalls our moments at the farm: *"Once, at night, we started a game of hiding things; I remember hiding Ayrton's jacket in the freezer, and no one found it, until someone went to get ice there and found it. But it was an innocent thing, brother to brother, cousin to cousin, a very healthy moment. Everyone had fun, went into the pool, played soccer; I also acted like a kid, even though I was older. And Dri would do so too. At playtime, Beco pull your shirt, trip people up, hold them, he was a kid!"*

Otávio, happy with his new model airplane

Otávio tells us an interesting story, which Beco quoted in the letter he wrote to me on April 23rd: *"My first model airplane was brought by Ayrton. I am an engineer and I have always liked to assemble and disassemble things. So, we ended up interacting more together on the farm and I said: This is really cool! When he was starting to fly and brought the kits, we spent the whole night assembling or repairing model airplanes, then one day he asked: Wow, Otávio! You like it so much; do you want me to bring one for you?*

But it must be a pain to pass it through customs, buying it abroad... let it go, man!

It is fine, it is very easy for me!

I also remember that, when we were in São Paulo, we would go to Interlagos, because he had a good relationship with the board there and they would open the racetrack for

us to fly, and it was just us, at the racetrack, flying the model
airplanes."

When we were in São Paulo, the days I had classes until the afternoon, Beco would pick me up from school for lunch together, near Mackenzie school. We used to go to a snack bar called Sujinho ("Dirty" in an ironic way), in the neighborhood of Higienópolis, or anywhere else far away enough that we would not find students from my school. We wanted to have some privacy and keep our relationship out of my surroundings, out of my school routine. Anywhere was good enough, it could even be in a bakery, to have a quick snack and have a few moments to date and chat. We were careful even with this: He would park his car at a distance from the school entrance and we would stay there together until the last possible minute so that I would not miss the class. It was all timed. Sometimes, we would meet again the same day at my house, in the evening.

On May 11th, at Monaco GP in Monte Carlo, Ayrton started in third, led the race for seven laps and finished in second. For me, that was a very painful night, thinking of my boyfriend all loose, at the Monaco royal ball, knowing that among the sisters of the Grimaldi family, one of them was known for keeping an eye on "single" drivers. While here I would go to bed early for class the next morning. I was left to my own luck and having faith that, if we had been together for some time and he came back missing me more and more, it was because it was worth it being together.

In the interval between races, training sessions were scheduled for the teams for adjustments and tests in the car. In one of those training sessions, at the Paul Ricard racetrack in France, his former Lotus teammate, Elio de Angelis, had a fatal accident. That was really unexpected and everyone was taken aback. The fragility to which the drivers were exposed in those powerful cars and the danger to which they were subject at all times became clear.

After this tragic accident, knowing how lonely Beco's life was, I decided to write him a note. I was feeling more and more confident and safe to open my heart to him. Besides, he also knew how nice was the surprise of receiving a letter:

My pervy,

I cannot wait for you to return to Brazil, I am dying to kiss you, to feel your arms squeezing me tight, to look at you, to talk, to talk nonsense, etc., etc., etc.
I miss you more and more. And that makes things harder than they already are, so make sure you come back soon, okay?
I need you.
1000 kisses
By: The Needy One

On May 25th, at the Belgian GP at Spa Francochamps, Ayrton started in fourth and finished the race in second place. With these results, he was deservedly leading the championship.

After the race, Beco got a break in the F1 calendar to come to Brazil and, as soon as he got here, we spent the Corpus Christi holiday in Guarujá and had news on this trip. My father had purchased two Kawasaki jet skis: A red one, which was ridden on your feet, and a white one, with a bench in the middle. That was supernew in Brazil!

We left by boat with the jet skis on board and when we stopped at Enseada beach, we all jumped into the water watching those toys. Ayrton and Dadô tested the equipment to find out if they worked and how they worked. When it was my turn, I chose to ride the red one, which seemed easier to climb, and while I was putting on the life jacket as a precaution, I was told:

"Dri, be careful, the more you accelerate, the more stable it becomes and the easier it is to turn. If you slow down, it will not turn!"

Beco in the water, next to me, said:

"Look, here you start and the accelerator is here. If you fall off it, it turns around on its own, it is no use swimming after it, you wait for it to come back to you."

"Okay, can I go?" I replied to speed up that class.

"Yes. Be careful, Dridrica."

I started the engine, accelerated and climbed on my knees on the jet board. I felt how the equipment worked for a while, tested the balance and it seemed very easy, so I risked standing up. Perfect, by then! I was riding beside the boat, and at this point, I noticed that the boat was close to the rocks at the water's edge. I accelerated to turn and found it difficult, so I accelerated even more, intending to dodge the rocks, but I could not turn enough to get away from them, which were now quickly passing by my side. Then I realized that I could not even fall there! Because I saw submerged rocks passing under the jet that were far enough from the hull, but if I fell, my body would sink deeper and I could be seriously injured. I hardened and forced the jet out of that risky situation. As soon as I saw no more rocks under me, I slowed down and, holding the jet, I threw my body back like an anchor. Out of danger, I caught my breath, climbed back onto my knees in the jet and rode slowly until I got closer to the boat. I jumped from the jet into the boat with my heart racing! Everyone had watched my adventure from a distance and were frightened:

"Adriane, you are crazy! Riding that fast near the rocks?" my father yelled from the top of the boat.

"Do you think I meant to do that? When I saw I was approaching the rocks, I felt it was difficult to make the curve, so I slowed down! Because I was told I had to accelerate to help stability in the curve, but it did not happen! And I accelerated more trying to turn," I spoke with my heart racing, shaking a lot.

"Drica, but at that speed you could not turn!" Beco said, next to me.

"Okay, now I know that. It scared the hell out of me!"

Everyone noticed how nervous I was and I closed the matter, but decided to take more care in the guidelines. After all, no one had mastered those machines yet. My dad decided:

"As you do not know how to do it properly, you will ride towards the open sea. No riding it near rocks and boats!"

When I calmed down, Beco invited me to ride the white jet with him.

"Shall we go together, Dridrica?"

"Can we do it in pairs?" I asked.

"I think so!"

We jumped into the water and, before climbing the jet ski, Beco said:

"Drica, you stay in the front, grab that handle, climb up from behind, I balance the jet in the water, you start it, accelerate a little, I get up and take control."

"Ok!"

I went up at once and grabbed the handle that was close to the handle bars; I sat down, turned the jet on, which was quite narrow, thus unstable when stopped, accelerated to steady my balance, Beco put his arm around me and grabbed the same support handle and climbed up. When he was already sitting, he held the handlebar where my hands were and said:

"Now leave it to me!"

We were gaining confidence. I held on the handle to let Beco ride as he pleased, and that became a real fun for both of us. Later, when we had mastered those ingenious toys, he played the devil when he was with me. The more he ventured in the curves, the more I burst out laughing, knowing he was risking taking us down. From then on, he only rode a jet ski by himself when I was on the other jet. Otherwise, he would rather have his misdeeds with me! It was a lot of fun, especially when we hit the water. Another fun thing we always shared.

As the jets belonged to my father, Beco had to be careful not to take over them, as the others wanted to make use of them too! But there were so many activities that this was no problem. While some did one thing, others did another, and we took turns. Truth be told, he was very careful with the jets: He used fresh water at the end of the day, zeroed the gasoline in the carburetor, applied oil to keep the engine protected from rust; anyway, he did whatever was necessary to ensure its full functioning! When there was any problem, he and Dadô bent over the engine, disassembled and assembled it again, until it worked well again; they performed all the necessary maintenance. They looked like two children playing, a real fun.

Francisco, Dadô's friend from São Carlos, also remembers this time in Guarujá: *"When Eduardo and Lenise started dating, he had a speedboat that was in Guarujá, in the same marina as Amilcar's boat. I also had a speedboat there, and we ended up meeting when we went diving or booked an activity. Adriane and Ayrton were also there, and that is how I met them.*

Once, it was very funny. We were in Guarujá and were invited to a friend's birthday party in Peruíbe. Dadô had the most coveted car at the time, a Passat Pointer, the first national car with an Ap 2000 turbo engine turbine, whose platform was a little better than the others. It was a stable car and good to drive. Ayrton was with the Santana Quantum van, Adriane's parents', which also had an Ap 2000 engine but was not a turbo, a much heavier car that shook a lot. At that time, roads were not like they are today, that is, divided highways. It was a damned little road, like Padre Manuel da Nóbrega Road, that went along the sea. In addition to the traffic of dump trucks carrying rocks, it was full of potholes and you could find everything passing along the way: from dogs to bicycles. We left together — me in Dadô's car, who also drove well, and Ayrton with Jacoto. We left and Dadô made the great mistake of passing by him and honking. He started accelerating the Santana Quantum and, in a route of about 80 km, he arrived an hour before us. That is when the driver's story starts. When you think you will not be able to overtake someone, due to the perception of distance, speed and space, in addition to how close the other vehicle is, when in doubt, you brake. Ayrton did not do so, he accelerated. He knew he could overtake us because he mastered it. That is why he won races in the rain: Because he knew he could go, what limit he could reach."

On the following weekend, we went to Chapadão farm. On Saturday evening, we decided to have dinner together at a famous restaurant in Itu, a town next to the farm, which had parmigiana steak. We split into some cars. Beco asked Dadô to drive his new rural van — one of the first closed-cabin SUVs in the Brazilian market —, which he used to go to the farm.

Dadô and Tata took the front seats; Beco and I, the spacious backseat. My brother-in-law enjoyed driving the car, the brand's launch, and talked to Beco about his impressions when driving. I was sitting behind the passenger and Beco laid on his back the full length of the backseat, resting his head in my lap. I started to caress his hair as I usually did, believing he wanted to take a nap. But Beco lifted his arms like he was going to put them under his head and reached the back of my leg... I was wearing a short skirt that evening. Their conversation, between Eduardo and Ayrton, was flowing normally and I felt Beco's hand slowly moving up my leg to my thigh. An inner heat began to rise through my body and I was attentive to his movements. I noticed he was reaching with his hands for space between my leg and the car seat. Instinctively, oblivious to any thoughts of refusal, I crossed that leg over the other to surreptitiously make room for that curious hand. All in a kind and loving way. I did not think about stopping him, although Tata and Dadô were in the car. I was only attentive to change position if one of them looked back and I started to make quick comments with my sister, especially. It was the best tactic I could find to stop her curiosity from spying on what was going on in the backseat.

When Beco saw I crossed my legs, he realized he could move forward. Quietly, counting on the night's darkness, he touched me. Obviously, I had never been touched before and we were in a position that did not allow much movement, it was all too tight, but I remember my whole body starting to shake and I could not see anything anymore. Suddenly, someone asked me something... and I, completely out of orbit, had to made an enormous effort to respond in a voice that would not give me away. In fact, it was really difficult to speak at all! If they found my answer strange, they could turn their back thinking I had not heard well. I finally managed to articulate a short sentence in a slightly shaky voice. All while my body reacted to the pleasure I was experiencing for the first time at that touch. Even my breathing had to be painfully controlled.

At one point, when we were already entering the city and the street lamps appeared in front of me, I gently pushed his hand away. He got the message. I had another five minutes until our destination to pull myself together and catch my breath. Not a word was said between Beco and I during dinner, not a look, not a malicious gesture on his part about what had happened, but we were one hundred percent connected that night. He knew this had been the first time for me and must have noticed the effect it had on me. I, in turn, remained quiet, as I was a little stunned by what I felt from his touch. Kind, he waited for me to say something. It was a whirlwind of the new sensations that I had experienced and needed time to assimilate. I felt as if my body dissolved in the middle of that wave of pleasure caused by Beco's hand. It felt like I was no longer there, but levitating and floating with pleasure. This is how we got closer and closer at each stage of our intimacy.

After dinner, on our way back, someone else wanted to come in car with us, but Beco asked Dadô to drive. That was when he pulled me close to him, wrapped his arm around my shoulder in a warm hug, and I leaned my head back against his chest. When we arrived at the farm, after everyone got out of the car and before we did, I pressed my face to his and whispered:

"Beco, I do not know exactly what you did to me, but it was amazing! Please do it again, but with no one around. It is too risky. We have to make time for ourselves."

I pulled away and we looked at each other deeply for a moment. We got out of the car before Mrs. Marilene or someone complained about our absence.

"He was becoming very famous and was already loved; he had won several great prizes, he could be with anyone, any woman would be interested in him. He really was a very interesting person, but for me it seemed like he did not have eyes for anyone else: He liked Adriane a lot and preserved her. He never meant to offend or hurt her; they had normal discussions about their relationship, but managed to be okay. At the time, he had many appointments that prevented him from being permanently with her, but he wanted her close. We even went to the Gallery together, he was kind of quiet, shy, but always very polite and kind; especially with Dri. One day, we were at her house and left to buy some sfihas on Pamplona Street. So we went with Beco's car. When we got there, neither I nor Beco got out of the car, only Adriane; I think she was just going to pick up the sfihas they had ordered. But in the meantime, pedestrians passing by began to recognize him. We were in a blue Mercedes that barely existed at the time and attracted a lot of attention. They started wanting to talk to him, asking for an autograph; I was

even scared by that, it was all too fast. Thankfully, Dri arrived when the buzz was starting; she got in the car quickly, Beco said goodbye to everyone and we went back to her house. They also went to a party at my place.

One day, we went to the pizzeria Monte Verde together, which was on Juscelino Kubitschek Avenue. We got in before him, he came in right after, but there was a moment when the restaurant owner had to close the doors of the establishment so that we could have dinner quietly. We were at a large table and had to eat quickly to leave."

These were the impressions my friend Rosângela had about Ayrton while spending some time with us.

A few days before Beco left to resume F1 competitions, we went to the movies to watch Nine 1/2 Weeks, with Kim Basinger and Mickey Rourke, at Iguatemi mall. The movie touched us, for the hot and sensual scenes. When we got to the parking lot, he opened the passenger door for me to get into the car and could not help himself. No sooner had I sat down than he came to kiss me and laid down on top of me. I returned his passionate kiss, but at one point we both stopped. It was as if we asked ourselves "What are we doing?". In daylight, in a public place! I did not expect such an intense reaction from him, but I was also under the influence of the sensuality and energy of the movie.

So we decided to go to home. We were silent for most of the way until I said, as if my feeling spilled out of my mouth:

"Beco, I love you."

It basically slipped out of my mouth, something we had never said each other before; I only thought about the consequences of it after I had said it. I had done my best to keep my feelings under control so I would not get hurt, afraid he would know I was one hundred percent into him. Although he was present whenever possible, he had his mistresses and was most of the time away. Silence remained, but both our minds were blowing. He also did not want to give himself in completely for reasons contrary to mine: He was always traveling and I could not go with him, besides, he could not even count on me as a woman! That would be a disaster for both of us. And what would it be like for the two of us to indulge in this feeling while he, as a man, "needed to go out with other women", would he feel guilty? I know he had good feelings for me and risking breaking my heart was not in his plans, but the thing is, we were already pretty connected, emotionally. A very delicate situation for both of us. I loved that man so much and I could not hide it anymore. We said goodbye a little stunned that day. Funny thing is, we were stuck together when we could be together, trying to touch each other even if in hiding, in front of other people: Hands, feet, a stolen kiss... always connected. Beco knew he had someone waiting for him, happy to follow all his deeds, but there was a certain lack of commitment in our general situation — or you could say, a limited commitment. And this thing of assuming our love for each other dangerously crossed that fine line that kept us safe.

Of course, afterwards, every time I listened to the theme song of that movie playing on the radio, Slave to Love, I remembered our moment and felt my face blushing and getting warm and a secret desire to give myself to him.

The next day, before traveling to Canada, Beco came to say goodbye, saying he did not want to miss the opportunity to see me, even if it was just to spend a little time together and kiss me goodbye.

Shortly after his departure, I got flowers with a loving card. For the first time, he wrote the word "love". Until that June 11th, letters, notes and cards were more cautious with vague adjectives. He wrote "your crush" or used three dots to insinuate some stronger feeling. But never before had he declared his love.

ADRIANE
AL. ITÚ

11.06.86

A minha Paquera !
Com amor de
Beco " Já estou com saudades "
11.06.86

"To my crush, With love, Beco. I already miss you
06.11.86"

The next morning it was Valentine's Day and I got more flowers:

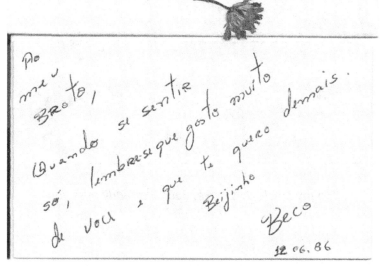

"To my doll, When you feel alone, remember I like you a lot
and I want you so much. Kisses, Beco 06.12.86"
*Of course those two cards were written on the same day and
one complemented what was written on the other.*

At the Canadian GP, in Montreal, on June 15th, Ayrton was in pole position, but Nigel Mansell forced his way through the start, firing ahead, and he got the second position, trying to hold the other cars behind him. It was a tough race for Lotus due to the superiority of Williams and McLaren engines. He finished the race in fifth place.

The US GP occurred on the 22nd, in Detroit, and Ayrton had an emotional win. He started in pole position, but in the first tire change he lost positions, came back in eighth place, had an amazing recovery on the street circuit and won the race. For the first time, he stopped on his way back from the celebration to pick up the Brazilian flag from a fan. Brazil exploded with joy, while I had the privilege of knowing where his motivation for taking such an attitude came from.

We were at the farm watching the race and I said, surprised:

"Dad! Look! He took the flag!"

Some of those who watched the race with us that day were also present during the conversation between him and Ayrton about picking up the fan's flag when celebrating the victory. And the "boss", Mr. Amilcar, began to cry silently, moved by the joy that Beco's gesture brought to thousands of Brazilians who were watching the rebirth of the pride of being Brazilian. For a matter of seconds, all misery, fight, violence and crisis we faced in our country were forgotten. Seeing a Brazilian guy shining out abroad and proud to be Brazilian was a thread of hope for all of us. It was a magnificent moment that gave even more impetus to the love of fans who now turned him into an idol: Ayrton Senna from Brazil.

For Beco, it was surprising to receive so much love from his fans and the repercussion it had from then on. No doubt, it was also an increasing responsibility. But by that time, he was confident enough in his ability and believed he would not let the crowd down. A historic day in his career for sure! It is a privilege for me and my family to be part of this moment and history.

On July 6th, the French GP took place at the Paul Ricard circuit, in Le Castellet; Ayrton started in pole position, but when breaking in a corner, his tires were locked and he left the track, abandoning the race.

Right after the race, Beco made a day trip to Brazil.

We were in Itanhaém and he went to spend a day with us there. My cousin Patu remembers how it was: *"We were in Itanhaém, where my grandmother had a house, where we spent part of our childhood and adolescence. One day, he went to see Dri and my grandmother made him lunch, but people started showing up around the house — it was a house in the street — so he soon left. Poor grandma, the intention was not bad, but she played a joke and ended up being unhappy, because Ayrton's car had span in the curve in a race, and during lunch, grandma said: "But are you blind?"*

I also remember this comment: *"Listen! Didn't you see the curve in front of you? Are you blind?"* I laugh remembering this scene. Grandma Lídia, as a typical Portuguese, was unaware of the art of subtlety, but it was not that bad. It was good, once in a while, for someone to do something like that with him, getting him off the pedestal, and there was no meanness on her part! He was embarrassed, but laughed with us at that awkward situation the dear little lady, looking like Mama Claus, had put him on.

Fernando, Patrícia's brother, also remembers this day: *"Once, Adriane took Ayrton to Itanháem and told us the day before, at the end of the day. My mom and grandma rushed to prepare lunch and they wanted to cook a good dish, so they bought shrimp and made shrimp risotto or stroganoff, something like that. It was pretty cool, he spent the day with us, and my mom and grandma were tense, because they wanted everything to go right — after all, a famous visitor like Ayrton... —, but it all worked out. After lunch, they went out for a walk on the beach that was nearby, but they gave up because before reaching the beach, some pedestrians recognized him and began to approach and gather, they had to turn around and return home. Then they went to the club. I have a picture of him with the president of the club, who was called Horácio Tanze and wanted to take a picture with Ayrton; Dri did not want to be in the picture. But he left for São Paulo before nightfall because the news spread around and people started to gather around the house, trying to see him."*

Ayrton with the then president of the Itanhaém Yacht Club. (Photo courtesy of Fernando da Rocha Kaiser)

Chapter XIV

It was July vacation and I was on the farm with my whole family when Beco came for a quick visit, coincidentally on the same day when my dad was having the visit of a team from DBO magazine, specialized in cattle. The news coverage was because dad was an award-winning breeder, known throughout the country for his excellent work. They had the interview initially in my father's office, then, after lunch, the team of reporters went to the headquarters to take photos on the lawn in front of the house, for publication.

When the team noticed Ayrton's presence, they were surprised and took some time to understand the unexpected context of that situation. Of course, we did not explain anything, but the journalists realized that he was the interviewee's son-in-law and was completely familiar and comfortable at the farm. Noticing the photographers' excitement, Ayrton offered to take some pictures with him and the animals selected for this coverage. Beco rushed to change clothes and look more like a farmer, to please his father-in-law. When he saw that my father was wearing a hat, he did not think twice: He asked me to borrow one of dad's hats. Ayrton's appearance as a cowboy for the photos was a very fun moment for everyone, including himself. These next photos were not published in DBO magazine, but were provided by Ayrton himself, who secretly included us in publications about his personal life, and thus, honored and publicized the strength and passion of "Mr. Amilca".

As it seemed that Senna himself was the cattle breeder, they ended up being widely publicized later in other news. But it does not take much to notice in the photos his lack of skill in holding the cattle's "halter".

Beco, dad and his favorite calf squad

Beco with Amilcar's calves

"Travels from Brazil to Brands Hatch" — on 07/10/1986

On October 13th, Ayrton competed in the Great Britain GP at the Brands Hatch circuit. He started in third position, but the car's gearbox broke on lap 27 and he had to leave the race.

Right after that, on the 27th, he had the German GP at the Hockenheim circuit. Ayrton started in third and finished the race in second place. And, secretly, he began negotiations with the Japanese who owned Honda engines.

He escaped to Brazil as soon as the race was over! Beco did everything he could to have a schedule that made it possible for him to have, if not two, at least one full weekend with me, wherever I was. This time, we went to São Carlos.

At this stage, with my sister's wedding day getting closer, we often accompanied Lenise there. Beco had already consolidated his friendship with his brother-in-law, whom he said was about to "get himself into hot water", referring to Dadô's wedding.

Ayrton's presence in that area was new and when the closest friends of the Abdelnur family found out about his stay at Broa's house, they showed up there. This obviously included Dadô's siblings and cousins.

That weekend had been full of news and adventures. My uncle José Carlos tells us how it was: "We were at Broa dam when one of Dadô's cousins, Mig, came with a cross cage car, laughing a lot. Ayrton drove the car, but first he tried the gear, the steering, the pedals, and took the first lap. Only then he did a burn out. He was a guy who knew what he did: He first analyzed the car's behavior and the land; if it was me, I would just floor it. When he came back, he instructed Mig: In the curve, you do it like this and you change the gear before, like that. In other words, just a little ride and he already knew the car. Something I learned from him was to close one eye when I am about to enter a tunnel. As soon as I enter, I switch eyes and after a hundred meters I open both eyes. On my way to my house in Mairiporã, there is a tunnel, and whenever I go there, I do that, and wow, it is perfect." Ayrton used the trick of closing one of his eyes when entering the tunnel to, in the shortest period of time, adapt his vision to the low incidence of light during the races.

In addition to the cage car, we also had a parachute or paraglider, the kind of parachute that flies pulled by a cable connected to a speedboat. I of course wanted to try it and I thought it was awesome! Even though it was only once, the guys who had already ridden it gently gave way to those who hadn't had this experience yet.

On the way back from Dadô's house in São Carlos, where the boys decided to resolve some matters with him there, on the way to Broa, uncle Zé Carlos recalls a fact: *"We were on our way back from Dadô's house, in São Carlos, and Beco was driving his car in front of me. Suddenly he stopped at the side of the road and went down the bank. I stopped right away and saw there was a vehicle down there and he had gone to help the guy. Ayrton was like that!"*.

It really was a wonderful time in my life and probably in Beco's life, because wherever we went, there were always exciting, different and cheerful activities, and we loved it!

We entered the month of August and Senna went to Hungary to compete in the Grand Prix for the opening of the track in Hungaroring, on the 10th. He started in pole position and finished the race in second place.

The Austrian GP took place soon after, on the 17th, at the Österreichring circuit, and Ayrton started in eighth position, but left the race on lap 13 when the car engine broke down.

Twenty days later occurred the Italian GP in Monza. Ayrton started in fifth place and abandoned the race at the beginning, because the car's transmission broke down.

After five consecutive Grand Prix in such a short period, Beco managed to find a break to celebrate my birthday. But as soon he got in Brazil, I found out I had a contagious disease.

My mom was sure that all three daughters had contracted measles at the same time when we were little, and she never thought that I could be unprotected against it. However, the truth is that I had to stay in bed from the first day Beco arrived until the day he left. It was distressing! After a very long absence, I was missing him as hell and crazy to see him again.

Only on September 17th Beco visited me because I was turning seventeen. He entered the intimate area of my house for the first time to see me lying on my parents' bed. I was in their bedroom because it was the only room with TV, and it helped me pass the time while I recovered. He came carrying flowers for me, but he did not approach, afraid of catching the virus. He sat down on a chair beside the bed.

"Hi Dridrica, so it means the little baby got measles, huh?" he laughed his slow laugh.

With a sad smile, despite the little joke, I replied:

"I have not seen you in such a long time and just now I got this crap! And you arrived a few days ago and only came to see me today? Were you too busy? How worried you were, huh?"

"Oh Dridrica, I am disappointed at this too! I came to Brazil to see you because of your birthday and we were already too long away. But I have professional commitments! I know it is not your fault you got sick, but I did my best to be with you. I just cannot risk contagion; I have professional commitments!" he repeated.

That harsh reality in the life of the man I loved made my heart shrink even more. His professional commitments took precedence and limited our horizon of possibilities. He sensed my disappointment but was silent as he had nothing else to add. I wished he would go away so I could cry alone, I was holding back my tears the best I could. The wait to see him again had been long and I really felt heartbroken.

"Drica, I am leaving. I will let you rest... get well soon, okay, young lady? Take care of yourself, I want to see you brand new when I come back. Then we will be able to make up for lost time. I will be back as soon as possible, I promise.

He gave my forehead a quick kiss and walked away. I broke down crying and only stopped when my tears dried. It was only then that I fondly observed the gift Beco gave me with the flowers: A pearl necklace interspersed with fine gold rings covering the little knot among the pearls. Beautiful! Very delicate.

The next day, Ayrton traveled to Europe and I received flowers again with the following card. He went to the Portuguese GP, in Estoril, which took place on the 21st. He started in pole position and finished the race in fourth place.

"To my sick doll, With love, your Beco.
… I will be back soon, so take good care of yourself so can be well soon enough. Kisses 09.18.86"

After his longer visit to Brazil and with my health problem, it seemed that our relationship was paused since July. I do not know how we handled that situation! But Beco kept his promise and quickly returned to Brazil, now with enough time for me to forget the previous episode and regain joy in our reunion. We were having more and more sneaky escapes alone, which was not ideal but it was the best we had! Meetings at night on the farm after everyone had gone to their rooms, motorcycle rides stopping at strategic locations and making out in the car on the way out or on the way to the garage at home... Always paying extra attention so as not to let it show. That was how our intimacy increased, as well as the urge to find new opportunities to be alone. We never had much time, neither much comfort... That is probably why we managed to postpone what was inevitable, but the desire grew more and more. I became aware of my body with him and I learned about his, like that, little by little.

Who followed this routine of our relationship was my cousin Andrea Duarte: *"He was very affectionate with Adriane, and acted like a prince. He was the perfect boyfriend for her! They really were very in love. Whenever possible, he came to Brazil to be with her. If he had only three days off, he would come here. It must have been very tiring, but he did it. He insisted on being together with everyone because he understood it was a family relationship. They went out at night to nightclubs, but they brought her cousins together. He really liked her and was subject to the conditions imposed by my uncles. But when you are a teenager, your emotions are on fire, and I know this was a dilemma in her mind. At that time, at our age, when the relationship had more than a year, it did not stop in kissing! Intimacy grew and there came a time when we could no longer control the desire, and I say that from my own experience."*

At that time, I was sure Beco missed me and wanted to be with me, because we used to arrive in Brazil having already planned what we would have to do to get those precious moments alone — due to the restriction we still faced of going out alone for more than going to the ice cream shop.

Ayrton was already in contact with people from Honda to bring the engine to Lotus next year. He had revealed in a private conversation at the farm that he had received an offer from McLaren for 1987. But he preferred to bet on Honda's engine and I remember I said:

"But Beco, why don't you go to McLaren, that already has a top car and team?"

He explained that Lotus lacked an engine that could withstand the race and he really believed in Honda's, because Lotus car was good and would be even better the next year with the new technologies. Furthermore, he said that if he went to McLaren, he would be the second driver again, so he would prefer to stay with Lotus as the first driver. Also, if he managed to bring Honda's engine, all he had to do was running after the championship. But obviously McLaren must not have made an offer in amounts that Lotus could not cover that year.

On October 9th, before he left to Mexico and resumed F1 racing, Ayrton sent me the telegram below:

"Now instead of roses, I send you one more little piece of my heart. Beco."

I watched the Mexican GP on TV, on the 12th, with a high heart. It was the second last stage of the 1986 Championship and, at the Hermanos Rodriguez racetrack, Ayrton started in pole position. He climbed to the podium in third place despite driving a car that fell short of his abilities, and that bothered me. However, what mattered most to me at that moment was that he would soon be back to my arms.

During Beco's absence, I went to São Carlos for the weekend with my sisters and, on Saturday night, we decided to go to a nice nightclub in a neighboring city, Ribeirão Preto. I remember I was wearing a root braid that day.

There, a tall, handsome, and very interesting boy approached me to start a conversation when I was with Heloísa by my side. We introduced ourselves and while talking, he commented he was a reporter for a newspaper in the region, in charge of a column, and added that "probably of a subject that we were not interested in reading."

Obviously, we asked what was it about and he replied:

"I cover Formula 1."

Finding the situation funny, Helô and I looked at each other and laughed, but we said nothing. He noticed something was going on and asked:

"Why? What about it?"

"Nothing!" I tried to change the subject.

"No, I want to know what is so funny about me covering F1?" he said, suspicious and with his hands on his hip.

Feeling trapped, Helô asked me:

"Can I tell him?"

I authorized with a nod. Heloísa turned to the reporter and said:

"It is because she is Ayrton Senna's girlfriend."

The boy then imagining that this could only be a childish and bad joke, turned his back and left.

Helô and I, surprised by his reaction, were sorry because she was single and the boy was really very interesting. She ended the event by saying:

"Poor man, little does he know he lost the news scoop today!"

We laughed about it and went dancing and enjoyed the night.

Ayrton competed in the last race of the championship, the Australian GP, on the 26th, in Adelaide. He started in third place, but had to leave the race due to an engine breakdown on lap 43.

What I did not know was that he had written me a wonderful letter, missing me as much as I missed him, which I only received on the race day:

Flight Deck

Oi, moça,

A Lua cheia nestas últimas noites andou me seguindo, e com ela uma recordação de você que é difícil de controlar. Tenho pensado muito em você e as saudades estão enormes.

Talvez esta carta nem chegue antes de mim, mas estou mesmo sentindo por demais sua falta.

Quero curtir ao máximo este verão a seu lado com todos os novos brinquedo LANCHA / SKI JET / mergulho / para-quedas e como não podia faltar os novos aviõezinhos... tudo isso com muitos beijinhos.

265

Estou meio quadrado de tanto viajar, saí do Caribe e fui a Los Angeles, dormi por lá, saí de Los Angeles passei no TAHITI no meio da noite por mais de uma hora e continuei até aqui em Sidney e agora estou no Aeroporto esperando conexão p/ Adelaide.

Mesmo sabendo que você não liga, resolvi escrever, está vendo como sou um bom menino.

Nossa, estou teebado de sono !!!

Beijinhos com amor do ....

Beco

21. 10. 86
10:30 A.M.
Aeroporto de SIDNEY AUSTRALIA

Saudades, saudades saudades, saudades saudades, saudades do meu amor papeca.....

Hi lady,

266

The full moon these last nights have been following me, and with it the memory of you that I cannot control. I have been thinking about you a lot and I miss you so much. Maybe this letter won't arrive before I do, but I really miss you a lot. I want to enjoy the summer by your side as much as possible, with all the new toys: speedboat/jet ski/diving/parachute and of course, let's not forget about the small planes... all that with a lot of kisses.

I am a little crooked with so much traveling, I left the Caribbean and went to Los Angeles, slept there, stopped by Tahiti in the middle of the night for over an hour and continued until Sydney and now I am at the airport waiting for a connection to Adelaide. Although I know "you do not care", I decided to write, see? I am such a good boy. Wow, I am completely sleepy!

With love, Beco. Sydney airport, Australia 10.21.86 - 10:30 AM
I miss you, I miss you, I miss you, I miss my naughty love..."

My uncle José Carlos recalls an event on Beco's return right after the Australian GP: *"When we played cricket on the farm, we improvised wooden handles to hit the ball, but Ayrton went to the Australian GP and came back after a week with giant cricket bats. Before, we used to play with a broomstick or something, just to have some fun. On that same trip, he also brought me a squash racket and a box of little balls as a gift. Adriane was a real partner and took up everything, she took a diving course, she knew how to play billiards, rode a motorcycle on the farm, rode a jet ski. In fact, all the nephew and my children learned to drive on the farm, both motorcycle and car. Ayrton fit in perfectly in this context because he was like Dri: A partner, participative and took up all the games. I never saw them fight, but there was nothing to fight about. He was away for two months and, when he came back, it was just fun."*

The bat Beco brought sent the ball far away when you hit the target! Therefore, the game became more competitive as well. Whoever managed to hit the ball with those large and heavy bats, practically won the game. Beco would burst out laughing, celebrating whenever he managed to hit the ball out of sight, as did Otávio and Dadô — they loved screwing up each other.

My sister's wedding occurred on November 12th, with a beautiful party at Clube Monte Líbano. I was their maid of honor at the church and after the ceremony, while I watched the civil wedding, the guests were already walking towards the party hall. I knew nearly half of the five hundred guests. It took me a while to finish my part as a hostess — although we did not attend social events very often at that time, we were well educated and knew how to welcome people on those occasions. I played my role with joy on that so important day to my family, but tried to be brief in greetings, so that I could enjoy the party with Beco, who was waiting for me. However, the bride and groom's photo session began with the guests — we did not have cell phones with cameras at the time. During the party, he had the opportunity to meet other relatives of our families.

Layde Tuono, a niece of uncle José Carlos, remembers one situation of that day: *"My son Bruno, who was about five, loved Senna. He called him Eston Senna. On that occasion, my husband told him we were going to meet Ayrton. We were not sure about that, but we knew you guys had been dating for a while. That is why we decided that if he were at Lenise's wedding, we would show Bruno's drawing: A black racing car (which was the color of that year), the helmet and Ayrton with the Brazilian flag. We took the drawing to the wedding and, when we met him, we asked for an autograph. He wrote: For Bruno, with affection from Ayrton Senna. When we got home and showed it to Bruno, he was amazed, crazy with joy."*

I took the pictures of my parents, uncles, cousins and called Beco, so that he could be in this photographic memory.

When I got to his table, I was told he had just said goodbye, saying he was leaving. I then ran to the place destined to pick up the cars. I walked across the hall, past where the newlyweds were with the photographers, and ran down the stairs hoping to catch up with him. All while I wore a long dress and very high heels. As soon as I saw him, even far away, I yelled:

"Beco! Wait!"

He stopped and came to meet me. I asked:

"Where are you going?"

"I am going home! I have to wake up early tomorrow."

"Were you leaving without saying goodbye?"

"I did not want to bother you with the guests, Dri."

"Look, we will talk about this later. Come with me! They are waiting for us to take a picture with Lê and Dadô. Hurry!"

I took him by the hands and hurried him across the hall. He, somewhat reluctantly, followed me. We got there in time for the official photo with the couples. Then he greeted the newlyweds, disguised and came to me:

"Well, bye then, Dri."

"What do you mean, bye? The party has barely started! We still have to dance together."

"No, Drica, the gang is downstairs waiting for me, and you are very busy today."

"But my family will miss you."

I gave him a quick kiss and, upset, turned my back and returned to the party. On the way back to the hall, I made two decisions: I would enjoy the party even without him, and I would not excuse his absence to anyone. He could excuse himself later with my whole family!

My friend Renata tells us about the ride in Beco's car with Júnior on the way home: *"At Adriane's sister's wedding, we went home in Ayrton's car. He gave everyone a ride and it was a thrill to be in the car with Ayrton Senna driving. It was a very short route, but I remember it was really cool. He did not run the car, but played with us. He threatened to overtake cars, saying he would run so we could see how a driver does. But he did not, it was the end of the party."*

I did not get Beco's attitude, he did not even direct a compliment to me that night. I had never had a makeup made with a professional until that day. Painted nails, sculpted hair, meaning I was completely dressed up, I prepared for that day for months... It was frustrating to learn he got upset at a moment when I was in the spotlight.

Yamin family was adept at having fun with other people's gaffes, and, during the party, I learned Beco and Leo, who was also wearing a white suit, black pants and tie, were mistaken for waiters — the difference in the clothes was the type of tie: The waiters were wearing bow ties. I heard a lot of jokes at the party about it, but I did not mention. I also learned that my cousin Chim, who, like the other younger ones, suffered from the teasing of the older ones, took the opportunity to leave when Beco was standing next to my family's table.

Premeditatedly and in concert with the other cousins, who were waiting on the lookout, he acted distractedly and said:

"Sir! Can you bring me some soda? Wow, Becão! I am sorry, I mistook you for the waiter!"

And the cousins laughed before Beco could come up with an answer. Realizing the prank, he made a poker face to the kids and shrugged. But the prankers knew there would be a rematch, when they least expected it. I confess that, due to Beco' indifference towards me at the party, I felt a certain pleasure with the prank and teasing of my cousins — my family on my father's side would not miss an opportunity!

Me (trying to disguise the annoyance of the moment) and Ayrton, with the couple in the center, in an official photo

Then, the next day, Beco insisted on going with us to take the newlyweds, my sister Lenise (Tata) and my brother-in-law Eduardo (Dadô) to the airport for their honeymoon trip.

Dadô (on his back), Beco, Tata, Kaco

To the left, Júnior, me and Roberta (on her back), Leo, Dadô, uncle José Carlos and Beco, at the airport, at the couple's farewell

On November 16th, Beco traveled because he still had an appointment in Japan and in England. That is, it demanded a few more days of waiting, in addition to the completion of the F1 calendar that year, to have him by my side for longer — I was feeling annoyed by that, it demanded me a Jedi patience and strength to wait for his return. But I want to emphasize that Ayrton was the main responsible for bringing Honda's engine to Lotus. He believed in the team and made this partnership possible. The team, that year, had been promising and Beco was committed to it because he wanted to make it possible to dispute the championship in 1987.

Ten days later, Beco returned to Brazil in time to participate in the elite cattle auction dad was holding at Chapadão farm that weekend.

It was a great event and the whole family participated, and Beco even brought his parents; that was the day when I was introduced to Mrs. Neyde and Mr. Milton. They arrived at the end of the auction, which had started early in the morning. They accepted my father's invitation for the opportunity to get to know us better.

"Mom, dad, this is Dridrica!" Beco said, as he tickled me. "Dridrica, Záza and Miltão!"

I greeted Mr. Milton and Mrs. Neyde in a hug, followed by a kiss on the cheek.

"Oh, you are Adriane! I am glad we finally met," Beco's mother said, her eyes gleaming with pleasure.

"I am happy to meet you, it is my pleasure. I hope you feel comfortable and later, after the auction, I want you to follow to the headquarters so that we can talk better. Here, with this noise, it is impossible!"

"Of course! It will be a pleasure, but we cannot leave very late," Mr. Milton explained.

"Great! Beco, you know everyone in the family, make the necessary introductions and place them where they feel comfortable. I will catch up with you in a minute," I said.

I do not remember exactly what I went to do, but that auction day we had a lot of things to do because we helped with whatever was necessary. Of course, soon after I joined them during the auction, but we barely spoke at that time. We were only able to have some contact when we went to the farm's headquarters. They accompanied us there, where we met several of my uncles and aunts, and everyone sat at the porch to talk.

I was very happy to meet them and I felt honored that they had traveled from São Paulo to the farm to be with us for just a few hours, and I saw that everyone was comfortable. Beco seemed very proud to finally bring together two important parts of his life. His parents seemed happy and glad to meet that family they had heard so much about, the girl who had reeled in his son, in that place where he never missed a chance to be. Likewise, my parents were also happy with their presence that day. They exchanged stories that had occurred since we moved from Rua Pedro, when our lives were separated and we lost contact, with the intention of getting updated about what had happened since then. I also remember that Mrs. Neyde nicely brought us a cake she herself had baked at home, which was named Bolo Beliscão (Tweak Cake), and I loved it. It was a cake made with a pile of balls stuffed with raisins, covered with cinnamon and sugar, very fluffy and moist with a rum syrup, which you would eat with your hands by detaching the balls one by one. It was a success!

My uncle José Carlos also remembers this cake: *"I met Beco's parents, Mr. Milton and Mrs. Neyde, at the Chapadão farm and it was very nice. On that occasion, his mother brought a delicious cake she used to bake, a cake with balls."*

We did not talk much, because there were a lot of people around and a lot of good conversation among the older ones, so Beco and I just listened and enjoyed that moment. Unfortunately, they had to leave before the sunset to avoid the road at night. That day, the bonds of affection between the families were formed and, those who witnessed, were also delighted by how sweet and elegant Mrs. Neyde was and how excited Mr. Milton was. They were people like us.

Uncle Clóvis was also there and recalls: "I Met Milton and Mrs. Neyde, Ayrton's parents, at a cattle auction on the Chapadão farm."

Just like my grandmother, my father's mother, who recalls that day and other details: *"His parents also came to the farm, where I met them, very good people. They liked Adriane! When he went to the farm, he skied there in a lake, or used to fly a small plane, with a childlike way, I remember it well. I once told her: Adriane, go and stay with him, he just skis all the time.*

And she said: Let him ski!

He was very distinguished, polite. Today, boyfriend and girlfriend kiss and hug in front of their fathers and mothers; they kissed, but never in front of others. I cheered for him, who did not cheer for the idol Ayrton Senna? He was nice, I had nothing bad to talk about him."

Tweak Cake Recipe
2 tablets Fleischman yeast (30g),
2 tablespoons sugar (50g).
1/2 cup warm milk
750g wheat flour
200g margarine
4 eggs
150G pitted raisings
Sugar and cinnamon powder to taste.
Syrup: 2 cups sugar and 1 cup water
How to prepare: Mix the yeast, sugar and milk and let it rest for 10 minutes. Separately, mix 100g margarine with the eggs and 3 cups of flour taken from the 750g. Add the yeast. Mix it and add flour until it no longer sticks to your hands. Leave it to rest, testing the balls in the water glass. Take pieces of dough, fill with raisins, make balls and pass them in the remaining 100g melted margarine; then, in a mixture of sugar and cinnamon. Place the balls in a greased baking tray with a hole in the middle until it is finished.

Make the syrup adding the sugar and water and cook for about 10 minutes (the secret of the syrup is not to stir). Pour half of the syrup in the tray on the balls and cook it. Regular oven for about 25 minutes. Remove from the tray and pour the rest of the syrup over the cake. Filling is on you: Chocolate, guava...

After my birthday, Beco tried to reconcile his appointments with our relationship. At that time, I noticed he used a pad of paper that he kept in his pocket. In the notepad, he wrote down his scheduled appointments, and during the day he ticked off those already completed or, if there was something new or any changes, he wrote them down. At night, he used a new sheet to update the next day's appointments and tasks, with the help of his secretary when needed. It was like this, looking at this little notepad, that he said he would like me to accompany him to a dinner that had been scheduled with an executive or perhaps a reporter from "TV Cultura". I said yes because I was also willing to combine our time together with his professional activities and invited my sister Christhiane and Otávio to come with us.

A Mercedez-Benz van that Beco bought some time ago had arrived in Brazil, and it was also brought as a "prize" to being able to pass through the strict customs control. It was brand new, metallic navy blue, beautiful, there were no cars like that in Brazil; the rare luxury-branded cars that rode in Brazil only entered as a personal asset of ambassadors residing in our country, and therefore, they were worth a fortune around here. Can you picture seeing a car like that in the middle of the traffic and with Ayrton Senna driving? It could not go unnoticed, and it had its counterparts.

So, on Monday night, December 8th, Beco stopped by to pick us up in his blue Mercedez — Chris, Otávio, and I — and we went to a restaurant on Haddock Lobo Street. There, we met with a couple and a TV Globo reporter. After introductions — I do not remember their names anymore —

, at dinner, I recognized the girlfriend of one of them. She was a girl I had seen several times at Daslu, a famous luxury women's clothing store in Brazil at that time, and I believe she was responsible for the decoration of the store or something. Her companion was precisely the executive from TV Cultura and there, at dinner, he invited Beco for being interviewed by a group of journalists in Roda Viva TV Show, which was then led by Rodolfo Gamberini. Thus, trivial conversations ceased and the focus became the interview with the F1 driver.

"So, Ayrton. Shall we schedule the interview in Roda Viva?"

"Let's give it a try! It depends on the agenda!" Ayrton replied, shrugging after his typical laugh.

"Look, you choose the reporters to ask the questions and if you want to invite a beautiful woman for the interview, it is totally okay!"

Beco laughed and asked:

"Really, huh?" And looked at me as if he was amused by the situation.

"Of course! Do you want to invite Luma de Oliveira? Who else?" said the guy, adding fuel to the idea to get the interview.

Beco laughed and said:

"Luma is nice! Luiza Brunet... Monique Evans..." Ayrton said, enjoying the situation and trying to remember the name of those "celebrities" highlighted in the media.

"Yes, you can! Whoever you want to invite, we will do it!" the guy said, making fun of me, with the help of the other reporter.

Beco laughed again before accepting the invitation:

"All right then! I will send you my agenda so we can schedule the recording day and the list of reporters I like and the list of beauties..." he could barely contain his laugh as he said the last word.

The list of "celebrities" seemed to go on forever, but I can only remember these names. Ayrton pushed the envelope, thinking that at some point I would laugh too. And it would have been a lot of fun if we were among friends, but I found it embarrassing that Beco, my boyfriend, put me in such a situation among strangers. And worse, in front of my family! The TV guys liked the inelegant joke, to say the least, even though they had just met me. Of course, I managed a grim smile as I was not amused, but without looking unfriendly, but since I am transparent as Ayrton himself was, my face must have shown the displeasure. But I did not say a thing!

Even the guy's girlfriend was embarrassed by what they were doing in front of me. She actually went wide-eyed, ducked her head and looked at me furtively to see how I was reacting to that, expecting some reprisal from me. I just looked at my sister and Otávio, as if saying "That is so ridiculous! Look at the situation we got ourselves into!".

After dinner, we said our goodbyes and I got into the car with my mouth shut. Ayrton felt my silence and, playing dumb, asked:

"Dri, what did you think of dinner?"

"I found it super fun!" I replied sarcastically. "It sure was for you, wasn't it?"

"Oh, Drica! Stop that. It was a joke!" he said, insisting that I be amused and laughing like I was foolish and jealous.

"Geez! Your joke was super cool. When we are with my friends, who you do not even know, I will talk in front of you about the hot famous men out there that I would like to meet! And we will all laugh at you. I bet you will find it super fun, won't you?"

"Oh, Dridrica, do not overreact! It was no big deal."

"No problem! When it is your turn, I want to see you having fun when I treat you like a fool, okay? It will be super cool!" I finished with a tone of someone who was going to get revenge and wanted to see if he would dare to complain.

Ayrton was silent by imagining himself in such a situation. He was quiet and apparently realized he had gone too far. When we said our goodbyes, he said in a soft voice:

"Sorry, Drica, I had no bad intentions, it was just a joke!"
I replied in a sad voice:

"Bye Beco, we will talk later. But please do not ask me out to make me go through a vexatious situation like this. Never again! You will play this kind of disrespectful joke away from me. If that is what you call a joke! That guy, who I do not know who is and I do not care about, was very rude, because if he does not know anything about your private life, as an adult, he should be careful with the bullshit he talks about in respect to whoever was there with you. Now, you, acting like that? Going with the flow as if I were nothing for you? Honestly! Good night."

That night, Beco understood that he had a girlfriend who knew how she was supposed to be treated and that the fact that he was famous and everyone laughed at any nonsense he might say did not mean I would too. This episode was important to define how would be our relationship with the world outside the boundaries of family Rocha-Yamin from then on, as a couple.

We spent a few days before Christmas at the farm and, on this trip, my cousin and I went with Beco in his new car, along Castello Branco Road. At a certain point, a little after Km 50, towards São Paulo-countryside, in a long curve that divides a high hill, Beco said:

"This curve must have some defect!"

Dea and I looked at each other, confused by that comment, because everything looked normal on that road, so I asked:

"What do you mean, defect?"

"Every time we come here, I see vestiges of blown tires on the sides of the track," he explained.

"Wow! That is true!" Dea said, who was sitting in the backseat.

"You cannot see, it causes no damage to passenger cars, but for loaded trucks is different, due to the weight! They burst it here due to some defect in this curve," he completed.

"Wow, I had no idea! And we have been coming this way every weekend for years," I said.

Dea and I looked at each other again, surprised with what we had learned and admired with the kind of attention Beco had, a different look at scenes that sounded so ordinary to us.

The most interesting thing is that even today, thirty years later, we still notice tire residues in that same place.

Christmas celebration that year was at my aunt Nadia's house, my father's sister. Among the guests was Layde Tuono, who Beco met at Lenise's wedding party, a month and a half earlier. During supper, something unexpected happened, as Layde herself tells: *"My son Bruno, who was five at the time, went to talk to Ayrton. He was very attentive and Bruno was delighted. Ayrton was part of the family, of course everyone liked him, but we could not separate the idol from the person. I remember that on the coffee table there was a silver candy dish (called "bombonière"), it was my grandma Ada's, about thirty centimeters in diameter, whose lid was a little bigger and, at one point that night, he took the lid and made a steering wheel out of it. He seemed completely out of touch with his surroundings and mentally drove a car. My grandma noticed it and said something like: Are you driving anything? She was very spontaneous! But no one would have noticed if she had not spoken and, although he was a little embarrassed, it was clear that even there, at a Christmas party, he had his mind on the races."*

After supper, some of us left Aunt Nádia's house and went to a nightclub that was also famous at the time, named "Societá". Chris, Otávio, cousin Andrea, Beco and I spent the night dancing a little after Christmas Eve celebration.

Right after Christmas, we went to Angra dos Reis City for New Year's Eve.

On that occasion, Beco told me about some habits of the Japanese that he observed on his trips to Japan, among which, the traditional gesture of Japanese culture of bowing when saying goodbye, as a sign of respect.

He asked:

"Did you know that the Japanese speak the person's name followed by the word 'San'?"

"What does it mean?"

"It is a loving way to address another person. For example, they call me Ayrton Senna San, it is more like saying dear Ayrton Senna."

"So cute! Let's do that?" I proposed, excitedly.

"Oh Drica, stop it. Not this one," he complained. But I insisted:

"Why not? If it a loving thing, you are 'Beco San', Beco my dear, and I am 'Drica San'."

He ended up agreeing, maybe to please me, I do not know. The thing is that he immediately started repeating "Drica San", "Drica San", and found the sound of the word funny, which made the nickname even more loving. I was already Drica and Dridrica, and also became "Drica San". And he, who was Beco, became my "Beco San", because it was a form of treatment unique to us, not shared with anyone else.

Chapter XV

The last week of 1986, we went to Angra dos Reis for New Year's Eve and stayed at Porto Aquarius Hotel. We were very excited and for the first two days we went through the usual ritual.

Hagop and his wife Regina accompanied us that season and they remember some stories.

Hagop is the one who tells: *"When we arrived in Angra, I heard that Amilcar, Adriane's father, was there and I asked for authorization at the hotel to dock beside his boat. They authorized because they knew we were friends. I docked close and, immediately afterwards I was invited to board and say hi. That was when I had the opportunity to meet Senna and sat down next to the couple. We scheduled to hang out the next day and so it was in those days. I remember that on a wonderful afternoon we went to Dos Meros Beach, and all of a sudden, we saw signs of a storm, and it is dangerous there! I said: Amilcar, let's go!*

But Ayrton was playing with the jet ski and it took us a while to signalize him to return to the boat. Then the storm started and the barbecue ended up in the sea. We ended up losing several items from our boat that day. When we managed to leave, halfway there, the jet ski fell off the boat and, over the radio, I said: Amilcar, I have two children here!

The storm was too strong and I could not stop the boat, so we made circles. Amilcar asked: What do I do? What about the jet ski?

It was his jet ski. I said: Leave it and let's go!

Sure enough, Ayrton, when he heard it, jumped into the sea in the storm and caught the jet ski while we rode in circles. Then he hitched the boat again, went up and we left."

Regina completes this memory: *"It was a strong storm, but now when we remember, we laugh, right? Because the* wind and the waves crashed too hard! But Ayrton had no doubt, he jumped into the water, it was unexpected. Then Amilcar said: Hagop, let's make a circle!

Because if we stayed still, the boats would sink. Then we started to ride in circles where we thought Ayrton would be trying to get the jet ski, but that was not easy for him. So Amilcar picked up the megaphone, which was the resource he had on the boat, and started shouting: Ayrton, if you do not come now, I will leave you there!"

Hagop continues: "Amilcar was super worried! But Ayrton managed to get on the jet ski, started it and tied it to the boat. Our vessel had no radar, only Amilcar's. I wanted to leave, but I could not see a thing. It was pitch black."

Regina also recalls: "I do not know how Ayrton did it, I was scared to death! I was in the boat with my two small children, praying because it was crazy. At that time, the stern of our boat, which was a Carbrasmar 39, was covered with canvas and the wind ripped it off completely and there was nothing left."

In Hagop's memory, rescuing the jet ski was an adventure for Ayrton: "He played it cool and today is nice to remember it. The next day, he played with the model airplane in the middle of the sailboats and I took his side. He said: Do you want to see?

And played with the small plane among the sailboats, without hitting the masts. He was very skilled! After this adventure in the storm, we went out the other day and went to Sítio Forte cove; then I could talk to him more. It was the day I took pictures of him with little Hagop on his arms."

Regina completes: "He used to run on the beach. He dated, rode a jet and piloted his plane, but he always found time to run. Adriane was very sweet, a real lady; she looked like a doll. In addition to being very polite and charming, she was very close to her family! She had an understated charm that was amazing. During the year of 1987, we went to Amilcar's farm a few times, and Ayrton would not leave the *pool with her! He had good spirits, was not very talkative, except when he told some stories; but he had a lovely smile, was charismatic and very kind to people. He had exactly that same personality that everyone knew. And they were a beautiful couple."*

After a few days at the beach, Beco hurt his back and could not move. Out of the blue! He did not fall, nor did he make any move to justify such a serious back problem.

Mr. Milton, Ayrton's father, sent his twin-engine plane to pick him up in Angra and take him to São Paulo, to be examined by Prof. Adelino, a friend of my father, who was a massage therapist and holistic therapist. He had a technique for getting the spine into place, similar to chiropractic care — he understood about musculature and bone structure of the human body. He had vast knowledge and back then he already spoke of the importance of the pineal gland to modulate the sleep cycles, and the adrenal gland to balance the organic metabolism; he also used the energy of the hands to energetically rebalance the organism. He was very spiritual and had an integrated view of how the body works.

Prof. Adelino managed to unlock Beco's back and relaxed the points of tension accumulated in his muscles. And he flew back to Angra that same day, feeling better but still quite sore. He felt pain when he moved so he rested, staying reclusive, and I took the responsibility of helping him; we even took a next photo as a joke in which I am feeding him in his mouth. But actually, that day, he felt pain even with the weight of his own arms when he tried to lift them, and needed my help. It took him about three days to feel better and partially return to the activities we were used to when we were together on vacation.

Beco trying to eat by himself during rest

Me, feeding Beco in his mouth while he was at rest

But the rest was essential for Beco's recovery, as he had already scheduled training with the new car for the beginning of 1987, in Europe — he would use Honda's engine and needed to do tests for the new F1 season. The good thing was that we talked a lot during that period of Beco's convalescence. He told me of how distressed he felt during the 1986 Championship when he could not adjust Lotus car because the engine was not good enough; in fact, that is why he contacted the Japanese. It was his initiative to partner with Honda, just as he was the one who convinced Lotus to receive the engine from the Japanese company, in order to transform the car into a state-of-the-art product and on equal terms to compete with the other teams.

In those days, my heart was full of celebration, as Beco and I were celebrating our two-year anniversary on January 4th; he was having a good recovery from his back problem and we had spent the last few days very close to each other. I avoided thinking that the time to say goodbye was getting closer, so as not to spoil the moment. But life is what it is! And a few days later, Otávio, Christhiane and I drove him to the airport in Rio, so he could return to Europe and start testing the car with the new engine.

About this trip to the airport, Otávio remembers some details: *"Ayrton certainly had the gift of driving a car like no one else. In early January 1987, we drove him from Angra to the airport in Rio. He was driving with Dri at his side, Chris and I were in the backseat. It was night and it rained, the highway was on the slope of Serra do Mar, but he was driving fast. The curve was coming and he had one hand on Adriane's leg and drove with just one hand on the steering wheel, and I thought: 'This guy will not be able to make this curve at this speed', I held Chris and placed my foot on the seat, but he made the curve with the car sliding smoothly, with only one hand on the wheel. He did it on the first, second and third curves. Then I said: Relax, Chris, because it is going to be this way from here to Rio de Janeiro. No sooner said than done! He drove all the way to airport having fun, actually playing to make the curves, with the car moving smoothly along the track while he flirted. For Beco, that was a joke, literally, and he was having fun with the situation."*

After Ayrton left to Europe, we returned to Guarujá by boat, where we stayed a little longer in that month of January.

But Beco soon returned and went to the beach to meet us. Unfortunately, he would have to interrupt his vacation again for another appointment in England at the beginning of the following week. Whenever possible, he would do this: Interspersed leisure time with professional appointments and vice versa.

That weekend, my dad's white Kawasaki jet ski went down. Dadô and Beco tried to fix it, but they were not successful. As Beco would travel soon, he suggested to the men on Corona's vessel:

"I take the jet ski with me to São Paulo to be repaired and, on the way back from my trip, I will meet you in São Carlos with the equipment fixed."

My brother-in-law, wide-eyed, challenged:

"I doubt you can fix it so fast!" and laughed.

"Oh, really, Dadô? I will take it to São Paulo today, and when I get back in three days, I will bring it fixed to Broa."

"I doubt it!" Dadô challenged.

And they bet, worth a round of pizza in São Carlos.

And so it happened. Beco left the jet ski at his friend Tchê's workshop, in São Paulo City, before traveling, and when returning to Brazil, with the equipment fixed, he met us in São Carlos, with Júnior. And pizza was paid by Dadô that season, at his house, at Broa dam.

In early February, Beco again interrupted his vacation for another trip back to England. As soon as he returned, he resumed our summer schedule, meeting us in São Carlos. From there, we went to Chapadão farm, in Porto Feliz City.

Ayrton knew that 1987 would not be an easy year and would require a lot of effort on his part, because despite all the Japanese technology, Honda had no tradition in Formula 1 and would need to adapt to Lotus and the operational and functional specifications for building an engine/body. In other words, in addition to power, size and weight, the material's resistance to the temperature of the engine, which works at its maximum capacity for about two hours, was essential. Thus, even with a powerful engine, he would have to test the car extensively during his vacation so as to prepare it for the championship that year. Of course, he was a driver with extraordinary skills: He was thorough, knew how to "listen" to the engine and, obviously, wanted to remain the first driver of the team. But he had one characteristic, as a human being, that kept him at Lotus: Loyalty!

Ayrton was a loyal guy with his team, as well as with any other partnership with people or companies that believed and gave him opportunities. Had he not been a person of principles, I believe he would have gone to McLaren in 1987, in order to reach his goal of winning a World Championship faster.

Therefore, that year that was just beginning would require great dedication and great commitment, which contributed to his maturity as a driver. He knew every part and every component of the car he drove, he was tireless in his pursuit of perfection, and had great confidence in the skills of the team's engineer, Gérard Ducarouge. He was nicknamed "Velvet Butt", because he "felt" the car's performance and located the necessary adjustments like no one else.

Source www.grandepremio.com.br: Ayrton and the Lotus engineer
Gérard Ducarouge (23.10.1941 —19.02.2015) photo from 1985

In addition to everything Ayrton had to deal with, Prost stated to the press that his car would have great news and would surprise everyone that year. The teams kept the changes completely secret until the very last moment, when all the other teams had their cars ready for the championship — it was like a State secret. Right after learning about this statement from the French driver, he told me when we were alone:

"I wonder what are the news in Prost's car... What are they hiding?"

We were talking on the swing seats on the farm porch one late afternoon while he laid with his head on my lap. When I heard him say that, I thought to myself: "This Prost is cold-blooded, he does not miss a trick. He probably wants to make his competitors worried with all this mystery," and I said:

"Beco, can't you see Prost is creating a mystery? Saying his car is a mysterious wonder to make everyone worried?

Don't fall for it! He is an excellent driver, but he loves a psychological game. And if it were something innovative and really superior to what already exists, he would be very quiet, keeping it under lock and key!"

He widened his eyes, remained silent, thoughtful for a moment, and said:

"Dri, do a math for me: Six plus three, plus five, minus four, plus..."

And I added. I do not remember the numbers, but I believe he was doing the math of how much he would earn or projecting what he intended to earn in the following years with sponsorships and contracts. Suddenly, he looked into my eyes and said:

"Dri, there are three dreams I want to come true in my life. One is to be world champion. Another is to be the highest paid driver in Formula 1. The third is to marry... you."

It was the first time he uttered the word "marriage" and, I confess, I did not expect to hear that at that moment. Silently, I stroked his hair to show how glad I was to know that he thought about it and verbalized that this was his intention.

Beco and I, each on a jet, "chasing" each other on the lake at the
Chapadão farm on our vacation of July 1987

293

294

He having fun with the jet

I was trying out this "banana" type of ski that Beco brought, pulled by Júnior on the jet.

In the background, caught in the act: far behind Júnior, Beco with the red jet turned after falling

Among the changes that would occur in the year of 1987 was also the Formula 1 calendar, whose season would only start in April. Right here! This allowed Beco to come here more often. He could not stay longer because of the adjustments to Honda's engine, in England, where Lotus is based, but we could enjoy many moments together before the Brazilian GP. At that time, whenever Beco was in São Paulo, he stayed in his parents' house and we met every day; sometimes, we went out for dinner with my cousins and their boyfriends; other times, we stayed home watching TV until a time that did not interfere with my school routine; now and then, we went to the movies; but whenever possible, we went to the ice cream parlor Swensen's close to home to be alone, talk in privacy and make out in the car.

My classes started on February 9th and it was very calm, because I was already used to Mackenzie school and I met my friends again. At that time, high school was divided into three areas: Exact, Human and Biological Sciences. I chose Exact Sciences.

"Mens sana in corpore sano", I believed I had always been a fan of sports and, lately, I had been attending the gym Runner in Jardins — this unit no longer exists today. At the time, gyms were something new — before, clubs were the places people used to go for this practice — and they offered aerobics and weight training classes. I had to face terrible traffic to do gymnastics — that was the term we used — at the gym. Usually, I would go with my cousin Dea and Chris. The gym clothes followed the style of the dancer in the film *Flashdance*: Lycra pants with leggings and tights hang-glide style, very tight. However, as we were young and shy, we would wear a big T-shirt over the pants and tights.

We usually went to the gym two or three times a week in the late afternoon. We would return home at night, after leaving Dea in Paraíso neighborhood. We accessed the gym through a turnstile at the entrance, where we had to show an ID card. Just to the left was a large room where aerobics classes, which I attended, were held. One day, Chris, Dea and I were taking class when I saw Beco standing at the door, in shorts and a T-shirt, which he usually wore to run and exercise and sometimes when he went to my house without the intention of going out. He saw and giggled from afar, I giggled back and pretended it was not with me. Then he went to the guy at the reception and asked to see the place and they both went on a tour at the gym, while a group of students gathered around them. I was euphoric to finish class soon and be able to meet him.

As soon as I could, I went to meet him, but I surreptitiously stayed behind him, who seemed very interested in the structure of the gym and in everything the receptionist explained to him. Finally, he looked at me. I smiled at him and nodded to say "let's go". The boy noticed that we exchanged glances, Beco thanked him and walked away towards the exit. I moved closer to Beco and we passed the turnstile together; we only greeted when we were out of sight of the onlookers and I jumped into his arms:

"Beco San! What are you doing here?"

"Dridrica, I came to surprise you. See if you were exercising well at the gym..."

"You crazy, you did not tell me when you would come!"

"Drica San! You know I live to surprise my girl!" he laughed his slow laugh and continued: "See if you are behaving yourself!"

"I loved the surprise, Silly San! And you must have loved seeing me in this unsexy shirt, all red and disheveled!" I laughed. "I just hope nobody noticed anything, otherwise this place will be hell for me from now on."

"Let it go, Dridrica, what matters is that I came to see you, doll!"

We walked with our arms entwined and our eyes fixed on each other. We walked towards his brand-new, not discreet Mercedes-Benz. As soon as we got in the car, I jumped on him to shower him with kisses. I paused when I realized.

"Beco San, I know I am sweaty! But you were the one who chose to surprise me at the gym! Your bad luck!"

He laughed and said:

"I am used to it, you silly! We do this all the time when we are on the farm. You can grab me at will. Use and abuse me." He laughed again.

We went to my house making up for lost time and sharing the news from the last few weeks away. Beco was full of surprises.

Chapter XVI

During Carnival, we all went to Ilhabela, where my uncle Clóvis, my father's brother, has a chalet and the Montemar Inn. My parents' surveillance was not so active anymore. I had turned seventeen, we had earned their trust, and we respected the family dynamics. The group was nice and we always hung out with my sisters, cousins and Júnior. As we were a large group, we stayed at the Itapemar hotel, on the beachfront, near downtown. Our boat could anchor in an area demarcated by buoys, in front of the hotel, and we used to go and return by boat to the vessel.

Beco also took the speedboat to Ilhabela and we agreed that after he left, on Monday, Júnior would stay with us until the end of the holiday and take the speedboat back to São Paulo. As for dad's white jet, he already had autonomy by virtue of always keeping it clean and working.

He and I

Beco and I in his speedboat in Ilhabela, Carnaval/1987 - Images
courtesy of Marco Yamin

The itinerary on those days was to take the boat and the
speedboat to go to the beach and, at night, go back to sleep
comfortably at the hotel, just as we used to do in Angra dos
Reis. Whenever we went to Ilhabela, we liked to walk around
the city center and stop for ice cream. By then, however,
Ayrton had already gained some notoriety and the fans
bothered me. Because I always liked privacy — I had a nice
life, with trips, trips to the farm, and boat trips, but the best
thing was to be able to live it all freely, without worrying
about what others might say or, worse, afraid of being
photographed at any time, because I hated being in pictures,
I never looked nice! Also because I tried to smile, but my
boyfriend never missed the opportunity to tickle me or do
some funny things to make me lose the perfect pose. The fact
is that Beco no longer had that freedom, and when I was with
him, I did not have it either.

We all witnessed this turn in Beco's life, his growing
notoriety and we instinctively did not insist in going to public
places with him; the harassment interfered with the routine

301

we were used to, but we did not let him be embarrassed by it, we were all supportive. I remember that when we went to a restaurant, Beco would try to sneak in, we would choose a table in the corner and he would sit with his back to people. For all that, on this trip, we preferred to gather with friends and family in the evening in my uncles' cottage. My Uncle Clóvis recalls some moments in Ilhabela: "I had some patrician guests who loved to stay there at the cottage, and Ayrton was there — he had already won a few races. All I know is that the guys were sitting at the entrance gate of the inn and Senna passed by to look at the tennis court across the street, and one of the guys said:

Hey, isn't that Ayrton Senna?

And Beco replied:

No, no, it is his brother.

The guy said:

Come on! I know you, man!

And they ended up laughing at the joke.

Another time, Ayrton's jet ski stopped at Fome beach, if I am not mistaken, Amilcar was with the yacht, Adriane on the other jet — at that time, it did not have electronic injection, and the device stopped. And he had to carry the jet to the beach. There were some vacation homes owned by people from São Paulo, and he went to one of those and asked to the people in it: Do you have alcohol there? They recognized Ayrton and granted his request. He, as mischievous as he were, opened the jet's engine, cleaned and dried the sail, and with a buck went back to play again. And he tried to pirouette 360 degrees all the time, Dri and him playing; I remember the two of them roughhousing!"

Beco playing on a jet in Ilhabela – Photo courtesy Marco Yamin

As usual, Beco and I together on the same jet

On Saturday, we left by boat to a beach on the island about twenty-five minutes by navigation from our starting point, because the forecast was of rain in the evening. Therefore, we chose a place nearby that was safer and also allowed us to enjoy the day with the sports. The day had dawned with a sultry heat and in the afternoon the weather clouded over. There was that strong wind, typical of the region in the summer, which causes a surf in the channel between Ilhabela and the continent, right on our way back to the calm and protected waters of the yacht club.

We were with my dad's jet skis, the white and the red ones. Usually, when we were in transit, they were stuck in the boat skirts — that place near the sea, where the steps are used to climb aboard, like a small intermediate deck between the water and the boat.

In those weather conditions, they thought it best to get out of there quickly, and getting the jets back on board again would take time. Beco promptly offered to ride the white jet to our destination and I, without blinking, offered to ride the red one by his side. With the sea rough, we decided to put on the float vests for safety in that adventure. Beco and I went ahead to save time, as the boat had a much faster cruising speed than jets, especially in rough seas.

The two of us, each on a jet, before the change of weather in Ilhabela

Right from the start I realized that, for reasons of balance, in that rough sea, each jet worked in its own way, and I could not keep up with Beco. While he was more balanced on his feet, bouncing over the waves, I could not even stand on the red jet ski, which was narrower and the feet were close together in the center. Another detail: In the model I was on, the steering bar was not fixed, it had enough spring to follow the height to be ridden, kneeling or standing, and the rider's weight was all in the rear of the equipment, so as the drag was greater and less stable. The model of the jet that Beco was had fixed steering, which gave support, the rider's weight could be centralized and he could have his feet apart on the edges with the seat between his legs, providing greater balance for navigation. We had not thought about the technical problem when we left. We always used both jet skis to play and maneuver in different ways, each one with their characteristics, but never to move from one place to another with considerable distance, especially with the sea in those conditions.

I got exhausted by trying to keep up with Beco. I needed a lot more strength to balance myself, even on my knees. The navigation performance was much lower, which made it difficult to gain speed. To keep up with him, as we were close to the beaches and knowing that the boat would pass us further, due to the necessary depth, I could safely navigate and stop to rest until I reached my destination, at a possible pace for me. Beco, excited, thinking I was following him, took a while to notice we were getting farther away from each other. As soon as he saw it, he came to meet me, we paired up.

"Dri! What happened?"

"Beco, it is impossible to keep up with you in this jet! Go ahead, I am fine and safe. If anything happens, the boat can rescue me."

We were talking screaming because of the noise of the wind and the engine of the jets that were kept in continuous motion so that we would not fall; stationary would not offer stability. Believing in that, he continued on, but slowed down a bit and tried to stay close to me. Despite my athletic build and the enviable breath of someone who has always practiced sports, that endeavor at the end of the day ended up exhausting my strength and I had to stop a few times, ride for some time with my body being carried by the jet or follow at a speed that required less strength, but I did not give up on reaching our destination. I was not used to giving in to physical limitations when I accepted doing something. The boat passed by me some distance away and I pretended I was riding the jet easily. I did not accept the exhaustion to which I subjected myself. At times I thought I would not make it, I confess, but I did not give up. There was a moment when I almost burst into tears, realizing I was on my own, instead of asking for help when I could, because I imagined a shorter route. Then I stopped to rest a little and thought: "Calm down, Dri, you will make it! Breathe, calm down." I was cold, the humidity added to the wind and the rain that started to fall seemed to freeze my body, but I went anyway to the final destination. I saw Beco from a distance and looked back wanting to be sure I was really on my way, albeit far away, until the rain fell hard and we could not see anything anymore, only the figure of the earth that accompanied me a few meters around me.

It was quite a fight I had with the sea and with myself that day — like The Old Man and the Sea, by Hemingway! I arrived having cramps and down. I stopped near where I could leave the jet and end that journey to try to catch my breath and calm down, because I did not want anyone to notice the situation I had gotten myself into. Otherwise, Beco might feel guilty and that was not the case, once he ignored how difficult it was for me and the level of effort I was subjected to. Not to mention that I did not even know about the difficulties he had overcome to get there, after all, the phenomenal Ayrton Senna on the tracks was, first and foremost, a human like me.

Beco saw me and came to me, he was very worried and wide-eyed; he asked:

"Are you okay, Dri?"

"Cool!" I replied breathlessly, but as naturally as I could.

Laughing, he said to interrupt the discomfort of the fright we went through:

"Drica San, you were left in the dust!"

I forced a smile, as I was not amused either by the joke or by the situation we had been through. He was down at my reaction; I turned away and we did not talk about it anymore. I left the jet where someone could put it away and left the water along the Club beach, gathering the meager strength I had left; I could barely feel my legs and arms, numb with exertion. I took off my soaked vest as I walked while I also looked for a place to sit. I saw a relative at one of the tables on the restaurant's porch, walked towards him and collapsed into the chair.

"Hey Dri, what's up?"

"Fine, I need a Coke."

It was not my favorite drink, but I knew it would give me energy quickly — as Beco's physical trainer had already explained to me — so I could go to the hotel room to change into a warm, dry outfit.

Days later, when we had already returned from Ilhabela, Beco brought the subject and I told him what had happened that day.

"Gee, Dridrica, why didn't you tell me? I would have accompanied you," he said, using the moment to redeem himself.

"Do not worry, next time we will change jets," I said, hinting at what he might have suggested in the middle of the storm, "because with the red one I will never do that again!"

I knew it was my decision not to ask anyone for help, out of pure pride, and I looked at him as saying "it is better that each of us takes their own learning from that experience."

"Carnival in Ilhabela. I did not party in Carnival. I stayed with Beco. (It was nice.)" – on Feb. 28, 1987:

On Sunday night, people went out on a Carnival block. Everyone put on a colorful T-shirt for the block, but Beco and I did not feel like participating. The day's activities had been intense, we rode a jet ski, dived, did snorkel, swam... At night, Beco and I preferred to rest at the cottage.

To the left, Christhiane, cousins Stela and Mônica, me, Beco, my cousin Márcio and Tatá in the garden of Montemar cottage

My uncles were not there either and we had some time for ourselves, of course very carefully because someone could arrive at any moment, as the door was left open. But we enjoyed this rare moment alone.

We kissed, teased, smelling and feeling each other's skin textures, exploring each other's body with the hands; it was all very pleasant. He was careful with me and super sensitive to notice me. When I was cautious or tense about something, he would back off and on slowly, mapping out my boundaries. Although he was already an experienced man, we both enjoyed it. Maybe because, somehow, my purity in acting with him, the one you have when you are loyal to what you feel and what you are ready to do at the moment, was

308

legitimate. And he was surprised by the feeling of pleasure that his moves caused me. It was all very beautiful! I had the feeling I was living a dream and would often ask myself "Why me?", when he could have any other woman in his arms.

I confess that during that year of 1987 it was particularly difficult to imagine him with someone else. The dichotomy of relief that he was traveling for a while before I gave in completely and the painful sadness of his absence was constant. It got to the point that, given the extreme intimacy we had achieved over that year and the pleasure we felt — even though we did not come to blows —, I wanted to be his and wanted him to be mine alone. It hurt to think that someone else would smell him, touch his skin, and do more to him than we did together! I often silently wished that he wanted to take that last step. But he knew what virginity meant to me and he was cold-blooded enough to stay in control of the situation to wait for the right moment. I believe that because he was older and I was so inexperienced in every way of a male-female relationship, since we started dating, the responsibility to decided had weighed on his shoulders. After all, it was with him that I had my first kiss and discovered myself as a woman.

However, that Sunday night of Carnival, we were really tired; we dated and took the opportunity to sleep together. We were on the middle floor of the cottage, which was like a loft, where there were many mattresses scattered on the floor.

"Let's get some rest," I said.

We woke up when, later, people arrived and we went back to the first floor.

"I slept with Beco in the cottage.' – on March 1, 1987

Beco left Ilhabela on Monday, as scheduled, because he had training in Europe, and his father ordered someone to pick him up at the small airport, next to the Ilhabela Yacht Club, where we went to say goodbye. There was some buzz there, people wondering how he would go to the landing track, what time he would have to take off and, in the meantime, people were approaching Ayrton to ask for autographs or take pictures with him, we had no peace anymore. Ayrton patiently talked to all the fans and I even took the opportunity to register one of those moments. I took the next photo, where a fan and his son are in the foreground and my father, in the background, next to Beco, wearing a cap with golden laurels, awarded to the driver who conquers a victory — as he had more than one cap, he gave one as a gift to Mr. Amilcar.

To the left, my cousin Mônica and my mother, Marilene, right above, together with my father, Amilcar, Ayrton and the fan with his son on his arms

Right after that, just before Beco left, he took me by the hands and we walked towards the club's lobby looking for a private place on the way to say goodbye, when two boys of about seven to eight years old passed through our way abruptly to stop us and ask for an autograph.*

"Look, I am sorry, but I can't right now!" Ayrton replied rapidly.

310

But one of them crossed our path again and said imperatively:

"No! You will give me an autograph!"

We looked at each other, shocked by that! Beco, realizing my perplexity with the situation, and also anxious to be able to say goodbye to me, got angry at the boy's imprudence. He frowned and replied emphatically:

"No! I will not give you an autograph! Excuse me, please!"

The boy then backed off, indignant at not having gotten what he wanted. That was one of the few times I saw Beco refusing an autograph that way, but things had limits.

During the writing of this book, to my surprise, I discovered that the "boy" in question was none other than the F1 driver Felipe Massa, who tells in several interviews, having been traumatized by Senna's refusal. When he was a kid. As he tells himself in an interview for the Yotube podcast "Cara a Tapa"*:

- "I suffered a lot for that autograph he didn't give me! He was still at Lotus, when he was winning races at Lotus. Suddenly I'm at the Ilhabela Yacht Club, in Brazil, and a boat arrived. We were having dinner with my parents and a couple, me and two other children. Suddenly, the waiter says: Senna is coming! He was parking on a boat. I must have been 7-8 years old maybe. And I was still starting to race in a kart . It was a dream! I couldn't believe it! Then I and the other two children took a piece of paper and a pen and went there to wait for him at the exit of the boat, there on the pier. Then he went down with a woman... I think I was unlucky to be honest, that day, you know? Maybe the guy didn't want to show up... and there was no one, it was empty! And then he got off the boat with the woman, passed by and didn't sign an autograph, said he wouldn't give. To save it for the next time..."

We were relieved to get out of that situation and said our goodbyes quickly. We did not have time for a tight hug and a long kiss like we would have liked. He just smacked me at the Club's lobby, in front of everyone. We did not have much privacy or time to exchange words, because the audience, as ***Felipe Massa tells this story himself:**
(https://www.youtube.com/watch?v=BleaAWwaiPs)

well as the "professional appointments," awaited him on the other side of the world. But he said in my ear with affection:

"Be good! I asked Antifuro to keep an eye on you and give me the complete report! I am going, but I will be back soon, Dridrica."

I replied sadly:

"Take care, Beco San, I will be waiting for you."

And he headed to the landing track. We made our way back to the pier discreetly and, about twenty minutes later, we heard the sound of the plane's engine. I went outdoors, in front of the Club's restaurant, and noticing that the aircraft was already a good distance away, heading north, where Rio de Janeiro is, I thought: "Is he going to leave from Galeão airport? São Paulo is in the opposite direction!". Suddenly, I saw the plane make a turn to go back to where we were and I was stunned, not understanding that movement. But as the plane approached, it flew lower! Instinctively, I ran to climb the wooden bench that delimited the sea on the pier, so that Beco could easily see me, and I waved happily as it performed a low pass towards São Paulo.

Our last and exciting farewell. Beco always found a way to make up for my sadness for his constant departures. Just as I tried to make up for his physical and mental tiredness in moments of rest, following him in his favorite activities and keeping the atmosphere always light and cheerful. We already had enough emotional wear and tear because of his absence to create unnecessary problems between us.

Then I realized I was letting it show and everyone in the club watched the unintentional show we played there. I climbed off the bench, embarrassed, and put my eyes down, pretending nothing had happened and wishing I was invisible. But my heart was leaping with joy and exultant that he was mine and I was his!

"Carnival Monday. Beco left and performed a low pass the club." – on March 2, 1987

The day after Beco left, we went by boat to Guaicá beach to meet my friend Renata there. That day, Ricardo Gobetti's presence, my cousin Mônica's boyfriend, who looked a lot like Beco, bothered me. At certain angles, his face looked too much like Ayrton's. I confess it was difficult to understand that he was a double and not Beco himself. I actually could barely look at him.

After Carnival, preparations for the F1 championship began and Ayrton invited his friend Jacoto to spend some time with him in Europe. Two coincidences contributed to this invitation: His friend had just finished Agronomy college and was kind of uncertain of what to do from then on, and Beco was living in a spacious house in England. That was how Júnior took on some functions in his everyday routine, as a personal secretary for Ayrton, who did not have time to provide everything from taking care of the helmet and overalls he wore in the races, to eating. Also, it meant he could have someone close to him around the world, easing his loneliness. I remember people talking to him at home, when we learned about his decision, and his response was recorded in my memory, precisely because of how proud I was for that human being I admired so much.

"Wow! I wish I had a friend like you, Beco! Will the guy travel the world with you?"

"Well! If we do not help friends, who are we going to help? The enemies?"

At that stage, Beco was very concerned about the nutrition of his diet, and the motorhome food was weak. At the beginning of his contract with Lotus, he laughed about this situation, but the physical wear he had been facing in the races made him change his posture. Everyone in F1 envied the food served by Ferrari, whose Italian menu was considered a real feast, while in Ayrton's — English — team, it was the opposite.

Then, Júnior was in charge of arranging and bringing him a more balanced and refined food, similar to what Ayrton had in his house, cooked by a Brazilian cook, and as instructed by a nutritionist, on training days.

Chapter XVII

On Ash Wednesday, we went by boat from Ilhabela to Guarujá and then drove to São Carlos. We stayed for two days in my sister Lenise's new apartment, splicing the Carnival holidays with the weekend to help clean up the new house. On Saturday morning, we went to the Abdelnur family's house, at Broa dam, there in the area. Once there, Beco called me. "How did he get this phone number?" I thought.

"Hi, Dridrica, how are you doing?"

"Everything cool, Beco San! How about you?"

"Fine, Dridrica! What a good life, huh, young lady? All you do is traveling around? Don't you ever have classes?"

"Well! We spliced the week. Cool, huh? How about you? Where are you?"

"Yeah... I am in a hurry!" he said in a cheerful voice.

"How come?"

"I am on my way to meet my doll! Do you know who it is?" I laughed loud and replied:

"I think it is me! But how come? Are you already returning to Brazil? When are you coming?"

Now he was the one who laughed his slow laugh and said:

"I am already in Brazil, Dridrica. On my way to see you and kiss you a lot!"

"What? Are you already here? I cannot believe it! What time do you arrive?"

"I will be there in a couple of hours! Is there room for me?"

"Yes, the house is empty. It is just us here." "Awesome! You will be here for lunch. I will let people know to wait for you. Geez! Come quickly."

"I am coming, Dridrica! I will be there soon."

"Kisses, Beco San, take care."

"Kisses, Drica San."

I ran like a child about to meet Santa Claus, such was my happiness, to tell everyone the news.

Beco arrived from São Paulo by car, with a driver who soon left. The two-hour trip seemed like twenty to me, such was my joy in seeing him again. I was so happy when he arrived; we had lunch and spent the day together with the few friends and family who were there. Dadô's sister, Heloísa, gets emotional when she remembers this time with Beco: *"It was too good. A wonderful time that, unfortunately, will never come back. Ayrton was very sensitive; he looked at you and did some kind of X-ray. What I most admired about him, in relation to everything he was and represents for us, is the human being he was. A sensitive guy and concerned about the other. He was also very playful! Once, we were at Adriane's farm, in Porto Feliz, and he and Dadô were sunbathing by the pool. I showed up with Dri, I was dressed and had just taken a shower. He saw me all dressed up and pulled me under the shower. He did that, he played with you and did pranks. But he knew we would fight back. This same time, after getting soaked, Dri and I went to the bedroom, opened his suitcase, knotted all his clothes and made a huge string out of them, and I threw them in the pool. He made fun of everyone; it was a characteristic of him to play like that."*

That night, in São Carlos, Beco would sleep in a room by himself, and before going to bed, he said goodbye to everyone. He and I maintained our proper posture in front of everyone, as usual, but our hearts were racing. He got closer to me to say goodbye and whispered in my ear:

"Give it a while, Dri, until everyone is in their bedrooms, and I will wait for you in my room."

"Okay, Beco San, go to sleep because you must be exhausted! Have a good rest," I replied in a way that the curious ones would listen, disguising our intentions.

I kissed him sweetly and our eyes met, red hot. The butterflies in my stomach and that shiver that goes up the spine were inevitable! I stayed there a little longer, but then I went to my bedroom so that those who were worried about leaving us alone in the house could also sleep quietly.

I prepared myself to sleep. After taking a shower, wearing discreet pajamas and brushing my teeth, I went to bed waiting for the appropriate moment. When I heard the silence in the house, I slipped out so that my roommates would not notice my movements. And I tiptoed towards my love, the one who had crossed the Atlantic Ocean just to spend a few hours with me.

I went into his bedroom, worried about waking him up, after all, he must have been really exhausted. I sat on the edge of the bed and stroked his hair to see how deep was his sleep. Then he moved, turning to my side and, looking at me, he asked:

"Did you lock the door?"

I shook my head and, smiling, got up and went to the door. I moved the key carefully so as not to make any noise. We made out like never before. Lying down! Jesus! Even though it was a single bed, it was a real comfort for both of us. We did not go all the way, but we gave each other plenty of pleasure, happy for that moment of intimacy. I never felt vulgar with him because that was a loving exchange, as if we needed that to be happy! But I was almost in my limit, crazy to give myself totally to him, but I would never admit it. I went back to my room so he could rest and to avoid the risk of being caught.

"Beco arrived from England." – on March 7, 1987

The next day, we acted so that I could return to São Paulo with him in the twin-engine plane his father sent to pick him up in São Carlos. We wanted to stay a little longer together. My parents could not say no, moved by that man's commitment to be with their daughter.

We landed at Campo de Marte Airport, which was close to Beco's parents' house, in Santana. We just had time to arrive, take a shower, have something to eat with Miltão and Záza, and left for the airport.

Júnior was in charge of taking me home after his departure. We got to the airport and, while he was checking in, I had the opportunity to meet Mr. Armando Botelho, his manager, who was already waiting for him. We had a brief conversation:

"Nice to meet you, sir! I hear a lot about you, but only now I have this pleasure."

"Not at all! The pleasure is all mine! How are your parents doing?"

"They are great! I came back before so that I could stay a little longer with Beco and they will meet me in São Paulo (it was said in the way the Portuguese people speak: *eles virão ter cá comigo*). That coming of him was crazy!"

He observed:

"Wow! Are you Portuguese?"

"I am not. But I am the granddaughter of Portuguese too, why?"

"Because you used that expression. It is an expression of the Portuguese people!"

"Really? I did not know! I have heard it since I was little," I replied in surprise.

Beco came to meet us and talked to Armando as we walked briskly to a VIP room, dodging the small crowd that had formed around him. We went in, just Beco and I, and were surprised by the silence. I looked around and saw only three or four people inside. He sat, placed his briefcase with documents beside him and pulled me onto his lap. We took a deep breath. I was still stunned by the rush, and to assess my situation, I asked:

"Won't Júnior and Armando come in?"

"Nope, Dridrica. Now we will have a few minutes to say goodbye calmy, without anyone disturbing us."

We looked at each other and he gently pulled me by the back of my neck, under my loose hair, and we kissed, happy with the feeling that all that rush was worth it. The few strangers who were in the room, when witnessing the love scene, did not even dare to approach or interrupt us.

These surprise trips took place throughout the year; whenever he could, Beco would come to Brazil. Furthermore, thanks to Tata's marriage to Dadô, we now officially had a man in the family, a new son and a new brother. With that, certain family habits changed and we, single women, could travel alone to São Carlos or to any other place where my sister and brother-in-law were to "stand watch". Not to mention that, in Guarujá, Beco no longer stayed at his friend Braga's house, but he could stay with us in the privacy of our apartment, in the guest room, sharing one of the bathrooms with Dadô, while the other was used by the women. Thus, indirectly, my brother-in-law would be keeping an eye on the dynamics of the house, after all, my parents' suite was a little more private and they would not be able to control us. Beco realized the benefits that a good partnership with his brother-in-law would bring, which further consolidated their friendship. As for me and Beco, even under the supervision of the couple, we had much more opportunities to socialize as lovers, hugging, caressing and kissing each other without repression or having to hide. It all made a big difference. It was not total freedom, but we could enjoy each other much more.

The maximum interval that Beco could stay here was ten days, but he came even if it was just for the weekend, as I said before. I know it was tiring for him and I was delighted with his effort to be with me, especially because of the switch to Honda's engine he was leading in the team. It was a year of a lot of work. He felt responsible for the project and was focused on making Lotus as strong as the other top teams.

"We returned from São Carlos in Mr. Milton's plane. Beco returned to England", Sunday, March 8, 1987:

On Monday, my classes started and I saw my friends again. I resumed my routine, including training at Runner gym.

About ten days later, Beco returned to São Paulo. He would have his birthday that Saturday, the 21st, and we started celebrating with a dinner on Friday, which ended at Societá nightclub. At the end of that dinner, something very funny happened. My cousin Mônica was with her boyfriend, Ricardo Gobbetti, who I already said was very physically similar to Ayrton. When we were leaving the restaurant, I walked over a table with Beco, and a lady told her husband:

"Wow, but doesn't he look like Ayrton?! I think he is Ayrton."

Just then my cousin, who was right behind us, came with Ricardo. The lady's husband looked at Ricardo and said, "It is not him, but he is very similar." Mônica heard it and laughed, because Ayrton had already passed by and was outside waiting for the group to gather at the restaurant's door so we could celebrate his birthday at a nightclub.

"We had dinner at Massimo's and then headed to Societá. The group was Mônica, Chris, Serginho, Ricardo Gobetti, Beco and I. Beco was fine, it was nice to dance with him." – on March 20, 1987

The next day, I went with my family to the farm and Beco went a little later, after having lunch with his parents in São Paulo — it was his birthday. At this point, he did not miss an opportunity to be with Dadô and play with the model airplanes. We traveled with the truck, just to transport his planes and accessories to the farm.

At that time, we were looking for more opportunities for moments together, just the two of us, and fewer moments with everybody together, so we became more and more attached to each other. Our intimacy increased, not just physically, but the intimacy created by living together and trusting each other, which gave us the feeling of being an extension of the other — that is how I felt. It was a very good time in our relationship.

At the end of the day, we took a motorbike ride around the farm and surroundings on our own. We did not take long, but when we got back my sister Christhiane said:

"Adriane, where were you? Mom has asked me ten times: where is Adriane? I did not know what to say anymore!

"Gosh! We took a motorbike ride; we went close to the city and back! What is the problem?" And I left angry at the relentless watch.

"Beco's birthday. He will leave and I will miss him." – on March 21, 1987

We returned to São Paulo on Sunday afternoon and, at night, we went to Chaplin pizzeria with Christhiane and my cousins Andrea and Mônica. That was when we said goodbye, because the next day Beco would leave for Europe. As the championship had not started yet, he was coming and going. But he was eager to debut the new car, the yellow Lotus 99T — color of the sponsor Camel — with Honda's engine and active suspension. This type of suspension aims especially at cushioning the car in the oscillations of the track and leaving it at an equal height, during braking, in a straight line or even in curves, compensating for its centrifugal force, which would be used for the first time in Lotus by Ayrton and Satoru Nakajima, his teammate that year.

When Beco was out, I sometimes imagined activities we could do when he returned. I once imagined being with him lying on a beautiful lawn, in a very romantic scene. This idea never left my mind and I looked around the farm for an area that was similar to the bucolic place I had in mind. I chose a corner near the river, where there was an abandoned house, and I kept it a secret; I wanted to surprise him at the right moment.

As soon as he got back from Europe, we went to the farm for the weekend and I was prepared to put my fantasy of dating on the lawn into practice. I remember it was a beautiful sunny day and I, a little embarrassed, led him to that spot and suggested that we stopped the bike there. He, finding all that novelty strange, let himself be led. We stretch out a towel and started dating. Everything was great and the outside world seemed to no longer exist. But suddenly he turned his foot to the side and looked disgusted. He stepped on the manure and was very annoyed. The mood was over. I was embarrassed and disappointed: After so much planning, that unexpected outcome.

We walked back to the farmhouse with our heads down, and I went to my bedroom to cry hidden because I could not explain to anyone why I was sad. I was sad with Beco, who did not know how to deal with the situation. After all, the cattle moved freely through the areas of the farm, even though I chose a location in a hard-to-reach stretch. This unpleasant event made me step back from the frenetic pace we had been in, and for some time I avoided our escapades, to protect myself. I desired him every day more and more, and I thought Beco did not understand how important it was for me to fulfill that fantasy.

During his stay in Brazil, when we were in São Paulo, we also went out with my group of friends to go to the Gallery and Beco picked me up a few times at the exit of Mackenzie, now with his Mercedes-Benz wagon. He called my house in advance to notify the driver, without letting me know, and in the days I had class all day, he would come to have lunch with me at a cafeteria near the school. He was full of surprises and I loved it! I realized that he was happy with my celebration with each unexpected appearance of his.

One day, at that time, Beco invited me to spend a day in Goiânia with his parents, Leo and his niece Bianca, in order to visit Ayrton's godfather and his family. His name was Mr. Benedito. We went on a twin-engine Cessna or Senica plane that Mr. Milton had. We ate jerked beef made by Mr. Benedito, who welcomed us very affectionately. If I am not mistaken, they had some business together, I think they made ice for sale. A longtime friend of the family, he talked animatedly, which was very familiar to me as I already knew the typical dynamics of people from the countryside. I would call Mr. Benedito a "good man". Rustic, warm and welcoming, simple and happy with life.

There was also a girl there, about fourteen years old, with fair skin and hair, who was not part of that family. I was later informed that she was a big fan of Beco and asked to join the lunch. The girl did not take her eyes off me — as if I would not notice, or how you look at someone on the TV, without the slightest discretion. But I was there, in person. While I tried to participate and interact with Beco's parents and the hosts, she was there, by my side, attentive to every detail of me. Her gaze was not hostile, but I found it a little creepy and was alert. She was crazy about Ayrton, then why didn't she tag alone after him? A sinister situation to which no one was paying attention! So I figured that maybe everyone knew she did not pose any danger.

After lunch, we decided to return before dark to ensure a safe flight. We went straight to Beco's house and that was when I met his sister Viviane, Paulinha (youngest niece) and Lalli (brother-in-law). They were the only ones I did not know yet, even though we had been together for a long time.

Porch of the Senna da Silva family house, in Santana, with Mrs. Neyde and Viviane behind. On Beco's back, his niece Bianca. Sitting from left to right, nephews Paulinha and Bruno, he, I and his brother Leonardo — image courtesy of Neyde Senna da Silva

I was invited to dinner and it was the first time I was alone together with the entire Senna da Silva family, who lived in a spacious one-story colonial-style house in Santana neighborhood. Mrs. Neyde had shown me a room where I could take a shower before dinner. I remember we sat on the floor for a while, using the bed as a support for our elbows as we talked.

"Hey Drica, did you like the tour?"

"I loved it, Mrs. Neyde!"

"Call me Záza, everyone here calls me Záza!"

"Záza," I said with a smile, grateful for the intimacy, "It was a very nice day! I loved that conversation with people who has a simple and happy life. And I loved the jerked beef! I had never tried it."

"Yeah, they do it with a lot of love, and it takes a long time to dry the meat in a mild oven. They are really dear friends!"

I mustered up the courage and told her about the girl.

"Wow! That is weird!"

"I thought so too, Mrs. Neyde – Záza," I correct with a smile and added: "I have had other bad situations because of Beco and this thing of nobody knowing I exist. Women act very freely with him and push the limit, as if he were not in a relationship."

"Really? How come?" she asked in surprise.

"Once, we were all at the Gallery restaurant, celebrating my parents' wedding anniversary. We met a youth friend of dad and my aunts, and he was invited to join us as he was alone. During dinner, two "ladies" who knew our guest approached alone and, after greeting him, went straight to talk to Beco, acting like groupies. One literally leaned over me, turning her back on me and pushing me out of my position. They did not even greet those at the table. They looked like fine ladies, but they were extremely rude. We were in a family group and they were totally disrespectful."

Mrs. Neyde heard it with a surprised expression, and I followed:

"The rudeness was so striking that Carlão, our guest, apologized, embarrassed by his friends' attitude. Beco was also embarrassed and I took the opportunity to confess my irritation. I said: 'Carlão, please tell your friends they were rude, invasive and disrespectful. They are old enough to know how to behave. One of them even pushed me to make room so she could talk to Beco. Ridiculous! Please send them my message.'"

"What about your parents?" Mrs. Neyde asked.

"They watched in silence, and Beco was embarrassed by the situation caused by his fame. Carlão seemed like wanting to run away because of the shame. And as I unburdened myself, asking him to talk to the girls, they accepted Carlão's apology and talked about something else. Carlão, politely, soon left to join these friends."

"Wow, so bad!

It is not easy to be with Beco in public places. Often, unpleasant episodes happen.

What else happened?" she asked.

"Once, an acquaintance who studied in a cousin's class saw us on the beach in Ilhabela and, when she noticed Beco, she slowly approached and looked around to see if anyone would mind... He was sitting on a wall, and she sat next to him to start a conversation. The fool did not say anything! If he does not, I will not be the one to get in the way, right? I turned my back and walked away."

"What about him?"

"He left and ran after me, sure he had gotten himself into hot water!"

"Yeah, these women are terrible!"

"Don't even tell me! They are shameless. And he does not want to let his fans down! Then I am put in terrible situations. He will have to learn to set limits when he is with me, Záza!"

I then told her the most recent and regrettable experience:

"The other day we went to a pizzeria with Chris and Otávio, her boyfriend. After some conversation, the waiter arrives discreetly and gives Beco a small note. He puts the note in his pocket. I started to observe who it could be and soon I noticed the girl there in the pizzeria. He got up to go to the toilet and she promptly followed him. I got up quickly to see what would happen. From a distance I saw the girl approach him and he turned to answer her; she was trying to start a conversation. But she barely had time to exchange half a dozen words with Ayrton because he, upon noticing I was close, promptly changed the conversation and quickly entered the bathroom. The girl, frustrated and curious, looked back, and seeing me, entered the ladies' bathroom. I followed her to the bathroom and found her killing time in front of the mirror. With a cynical smile, I did the same in order to tease her, ignoring her; I checked my hair with an air of satisfaction and returned to the table. The moment Beco returned, I asked. 'Where is the note?' And he said: 'What note?' I said pointing my finger explicitly at her: 'The one that girl over there asked to give you and you put in your pocket.'

Beco said it was nothing, for me to let it go. To our surprised companions, unaware of what was going on, I explained what happened. Otávio also wanted to minimize the situation and asked me what I expected Beco to do. I said I expected him to show the girl that he has nothing to hide from me. She does not know I am his girlfriend, but he does! Then Beco said I was giving a big importance to that nonsense. So I told him to give me the note so I could read it or maybe rip it in her face! Otávio said that if I were to stay like this every time a woman harassed Ayrton, I would make our relationship impossible. I ended the discussion by telling them, Záza, that I do not care about what the girls do. I care about what Beco does in these situations, because if he does not set limits and does not respect my presence, then it is going to be impossible."

Mrs. Neyde, who was listening attentively to my report, asked:

"But what did Beco say to you after that, Adri?"

"At home, when we were alone in the elevator hall, he said I had overreacted and I asked him what he would do if the situation was reversed. I told him to keep the note he had kept so carefully. He got angry and gave me the note, saying 'Are you happy now? Is that what you wanted?' I took the note and tore it in front of him, before the elevator door closed. But then I could not resist, patched it up and read the note."

Mrs. Neyde asked:

"And what was written on the note?"

"The girl had been Miss Brazil I do not know when and said she had met him on another occasion, when she was accompanying the other Brazilian driver, but that she was his fan and then praised him a lot, throwing her bait."

Front and back of the note Beco received from a fan

"Ayrton, my name is [hidden], I met you in Germany in 1986 (I was with Nelson). We talked at Holiday Inn, you might not remember it. After that, we did not have the opportunity to talk again, but now I have the chance to congratulate you for the wonderful work you have been doing. You really had the chance to show what you can do. I am sure this year the championship is yours. Congratulations, good luck."

"Honestly, the girls are terrible! He has already fallen into the claws of one!"

I took the opportunity and asked:

"What happened to the relationship he had before me? Why did they break up?"

"Wow! That one was terrible. She did with him whatever she wanted. Thank God, he managed to get out."

She then looked at her watch and hurriedly got up, saying:

"Gosh! I did not even see the time go by. I have dinner to arrange and you need to shower. I will get shampoo and conditioner, be right back."

I loved using Beco products, whose familiar smell made me forget those stories that upset me so much. Showered, I went to the living room to meet everyone who was waiting for dinner. On that occasion, I also met the dog that Beco loved so much, which was called "Tomba-Latas" (stray dog, in English). One among many other dogs Beco found on the streets and took home. He did that since he was little because he felt very sorry for abandoned dogs that wandered aimlessly through the streets and adopted them.

I already knew Bianca, always very loving, and Bruno, a little untamable, but very polite. And that day, I met Beco's youngest niece, Paoca (as Paula was affectionately called). She should have been around four years old and was very cute! She approached me to start a conversation and said:

"Pup…"

"Sorry?" I asked, moving closer to her to try to hear better.

"Pup…"

"Paoca, the aunt did not understand what you said. What is it?" She pointed to the dog and repeated:

"Pup…"

At that time, I did not have much contact with children of that age and it took me a while to understand what Paulinha was saying. I found it the cutest thing on earth! And, like a fool, I told everyone about our "dialogue", because I immediately fell in love with her. She wanted to continue the conversation, but her mother Viviane said:

"Dear, leave the girl alone."

"No!" I said. "Leave her here with me. She is not bothering me at all."

I was loving deciphering the dialect of the little one, but her mother insisted:

"Daughter!" Come here!"

I also met Lalli, Beco's brother-in-law and father of the children. A handsome man, with dark hair, wide smile, very kind and polite.

After dinner, Beco, restive, said:

"Well, the conversation is great, but it is getting late! Shall we go, Dridrica? Otherwise, Mr. Amilcar and the "Screwdriver" will kill me!"

Everyone laughed. I excused myself and said goodbye to everyone, grateful for the delicious day and dinner. On our way to my house, we exchanged reports of what we went through that day, Beco was curious about my impressions of Senna da Silva family. Beco had calculated a little time for us to make out in the car in my building's garage. Temperature was rising between us... I needed such discernment and willpower! And to complete that special day, among kisses and hugs, he whispered in my ear:

"When I belong to you, and you to me, it is going to be crazy!"

On April 12th, the F1 season began with the Brazilian GP at Jacarepaguá Racetrack, in Rio de Janeiro, in accordance with the first phase of the new rules announced by FISA (Fédération Internationale du Sport Automobile) in October of the previous year, aiming at greater security. The two main changes for the '87 Championship were: Elimination of super-soft rating tires and mandatory use of a valve on turbo engines, which was already used in Formula Indy, to reduce engine power. Ayrton started in third place, but had to abandon the race on lap 50 due to engine overheating.

My cousin Fernando Kaiser has been there and tells us his impression: "When of the Brazilian Grand Prix, Beco invited us to go to Rio. I went with a friend and we arrived in Rio on Friday night. I tried to talk to him at the racetrack and I could not, the environment was very stressful. I only talked to him about this race a long time later, when we sat down to chat! I said: Fuck, I tried to talk to you! And he told me: Man, forget it! It is impossible in these days that precede the race. There is no way, no chance, it is such a stress at the race track. I had the impression at that time that the farm was his refuge, where he disconnected from reality. In Formula 1 environment, he was a totally different person."

After the Brazilian GP, Ayrton took a few days off from F1 training and stayed here. I had no class because that month there was a general teachers' strike that lasted two weeks. The country was in a huge crisis, inflation was out of control and wages were outdated.

Easter that year would be followed by the Tiradentes holiday on April 21st. So, we decided to go to Ilhabela by car, on the 15th. Andrea, Chris and I took a ride in Serginho Gobbetti's pickup truck. Beck would go the next day. We stayed at my uncles Clóvis and Nadir's cottage.

We spent Thursday at Praia da Feiticeira, which was close to the cottage. At night, Beco arrived with Júnior towing the speedboat and stayed at Hotel Itapamar. We all went out for pizza.

On Friday morning, we woke up late. Beco and Júnior had breakfast with us in the cottage. He and I ran to the mooring of the ferries that bring and take the cars through the channel that separated the mainland from Ilhabela. Afterwards, we both stopped by a candy shop to buy sweets for aunt Nadir, who was an excellent hostess. As I have said before, Beco was a super partner and companion, always cheerful and willing to do whatever was necessary. In fact, he never let me pay anything! A true gentleman, I barely carried a bag, because if he saw me with one, as in this case, he would say:

"Hey, Dridrica! Can you tell me where are you going with that bag?"

"Buy sweets for aunt Nadir!"

"I still did not get what the bag is for. You will carry it for nothing," he said, laughing.

"Okay, hold on."

I left the bag at home that day and we went to the candy shop, he kept a satisfied face. But, on the other hand, whenever possible I did not wait for him to pay, but I accepted his kindness for the pleasure he had, perhaps, always taking the opportunity to repay the hospitable and generous attitude of all my family, wherever he accompanied us. He was kind and polite and so was I!

He and Dadô sometimes disputed who would pay the bill when we all went out together. With dad around, they sneaked off of paying the bill before my dad knew it. This turned into an adventure between them, who was quicker and more discreet, or one would tattle the other. Dad was not very happy about it, but they were amused by everyone's surprised face when they managed to do it without being noticed.

After my parents arrived on Friday afternoon, we stayed with them at Hotel Itapemar and had dinner at Totó (a restaurant near the Ilhabela Yacht Club). After dinner, Beco and I hid on the hotel's tennis court to be alone.

On Saturday, we went to Praia da Fome and rode a jet ski with Beco's speedboat all day. I was very tired, because the sea got turbulent suddenly and it was pretty scary. But it all worked out in the end. We had dinner at Viana and stayed at the hotel bar talking.

On Easter Sunday, we went by boat to a beach that was empty. On the way back, we had a barbecue at my uncles' cottage and walked back to the hotel.

On Monday, we returned by boat to the beach from the day before and then we went to Guaicá. We had dinner again at Viana. After dinner, Beco and I went for a walk along the shore and sat on a bench on the deserted beach, just the two of us, with that breeze and the sound of the sea. We were in a rare moment of peace, in no hurry for anything, and we had a pleasant chat, interspersed with kisses and caresses. He told me about the rush of training and about various stories of the Japanese.

On Tiradentes holiday, we woke up early to go to São Carlos, while Beco went to Rio de Janeiro to, from there, embark to Italy. From the airport, he called to say he was already missing me. The longer we stayed together, the harder it was to separate.

After the Brazilian GP, the next ones would take place in Europe, with two-week intervals between them. Therefore, Beco would not come back to Brazil anytime soon. I accepted the fact and traveled with my mother and sister Christhiane to Miami. We stayed at Hotel Intercontinental. It is interesting to note that, at a time when communications were restricted to landline telephones, letters or telegrams, Beco found no obstacle to communicate with me. We had barely gotten to Florida when he called. Wherever I was, he found me! If he could not reach me, he would leave a message.

He once complained about my lack of reciprocity:

"Gee, Dridrica, don't you ever try to talk to me? You never call me?"

"Oh Beco, I can never know where you are! In which country, which hotel? I only find out when you call. Or do you intend to keep me up to date to your schedule before you leave?"

"Yeah, Dri, it is difficult, you are right, because when I go away on a trip, I do not even know where I will be staying, nor the travel dates," he concluded, looking sad as he realized that.

Chapter XVIII

At the San Marino GP, at the Imola circuit, on May 3rd, Ayrton started in pole position and finished in second place. A few days later, I received the first letter from him during that period. It was like this: He made up for his absence by sending me letters. The news was that, as I was improving my English, he used a printed letter as a multiple-choice exercise, dated 05/12/1987:

DO BECO   PARA O BESTO !!!

Dear ___F A N Z O C A___,

I miss you more than ☐ ~~Mum~~. ☒ you can imagine. ☐ ~~my Mickey Mouse clock~~. I've been counting the seconds we're apart and so far, ~~it's been~~ ☐ ~~6½ minutes~~. ☐ ~~three days~~. ☒ 27 years.

I think of us as star-crossed lovers like ☐ ~~Romeo and Juliet~~. ☐ ~~Anthony and Cleopatra~~. ☒ Abbott and Costello. Sometimes when I think about you, I want to ☐ ~~cry~~. ☒ sneeze. ☐ ~~throw up~~. I even see you in my ☒ dreams. ☐ ~~bathtub~~. ☐ ~~bedroom window~~. And whenever I hear ☐ ~~"The Werewolf of London"~~, ☐ ~~"Rule Brittania"~~, ☒ "The Mickey Mouse Club Song", I think of it as our song.

Please send me ☐ ~~a lock of your hair~~ ☐ ~~an 8 × 10 glossy~~ ☒ a used toothbrush as a reminder of you. I'll send you my ☒ underwear. ☐ ~~empties~~. ☐ ~~germs~~. I know it's not much, but it's ☐ ~~free~~. ☐ ~~all I can afford~~. ☒ better than nothing.

When I see you, I'm going to rip off your ☒ clothes. ☐ ~~eyebrows~~. ☐ ~~wallet~~. And if I don't see you soon, I'll ☒ jump off a bridge. ☐ ~~hijack a plane~~. ☐ ~~take a cold shower~~.

Wishing you ☐ ~~a good day~~, ☐ ~~a warm bed~~, ☒ were here,

Beco   12 05. 87

Ayrton had a cold and was weak when he competed in the Belgian GP, at the Spa-Francorchamps circuit, on the 17th. He had a fever during training, but took some medicine and participated in the race anyway. He started in third place, slipped around the curve and crashed into Nigel Mansell on the first lap. Out of the race and with nothing else he could do there at the racetrack, he went home to get some rest.

On May 20th, he sent a second letter in the same style as the previous one, but with a brooch attached:

Hello !!!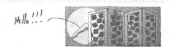

Dear sex ~~friend,~~ ~~offender,~~ ~~"e"~~ **CARENTE /**

I've decided to open up and write you everything that comes into my ~~mind.~~ ☒ heart. ~~blue-jeans.~~ I want this letter to turn you on more than ~~a bust of Dolly Parton.~~ ☒ Sylvester Stallone in boxer shorts. ~~a totally nude episode of Coronation Street.~~

DE BIDUINI !

Ever since I first saw you ~~close-up,~~ ~~from the front,~~ ~~in the shower,~~ I've wanted to ☒ discuss politics. ~~wrestle you to the ground.~~ ~~challenge you to a game of strip ping-pong.~~ But for some reason I always ~~chicken.~~ ☒ pass. ~~lose out.~~

On many occasions I've thought about inviting you over for a ~~drink.~~ ☒ pillow fight. ~~bowl of whipped cream.~~ I've even considered telling you about my ~~see-through bathrobe.~~ ~~craving for peanut butter.~~ ☒ infatuation with hair dryers.

Finally, in this very touching letter, I'm revealing the ☒ warm ~~bumpy~~ ☒ permanent spot I have for you on my ☒ body. ~~sofa.~~ ~~calendar.~~ I'm thoroughly convinced that the two of us can make beautiful ~~music~~ ~~sundaes~~ ☒ finger paintings together.

I can only hope that you will take this letter ~~seriously.~~ ☒ romantically. ~~with a large grain of salt.~~

TARADINHO ...

P.S. Don't you think I have a sexy way with ☒ words? ~~punctuation?~~ ~~ticks?~~

Handwritten words: needy girl / on a bikini! / Your pervy...

The brooch had the words "I love you." My heart exulted with happiness:

I attached the brooch on the cover of my diary

May 31st, another historic day in Senna's career, at the Monaco GP. For the first time, a Brazilian won in Monte Carlo, which is a street circuit. It was an exciting race, in which Ayrton took the lead in the middle of the race, when Mansell had problems with the car's engine and left the race. He celebrated the victory before crossing the finish line, and was called "Ayrton Senna from Brazil" by Galvão Bueno during the race broadcast. He thus achieved the fifth victory of his career and climbed the podium along with Piquet, who took second place in that race.

This time, Beco would be with the Grimaldi family as the winner of Monaco Grand Prix. Of course I was happy for his victory, but in pain again, as he would meet again the royalty at the dinner given to the Formula One drivers. Pain probably caused by my teenage imagination.

Beco returned to Brazil on the week of June 8th to spend Valentine's Day with me (on June 12th in Brazil) and we finally were authorized by my parents to have dinner together, just the two of us. Afterwards, we went to Porto Feliz to spend the weekend at the farm with the whole family. On Tuesday, he boarded for Detroit.

"Ayrton took the lead in the Championship by winning on the streets of Detroit." – on June 21, 2019

There was an unfortunate event that year, and I tell you to show how our world works, which sometimes happens to a person who has a public life and is subject of news. A journalist published that Corona's connection with Ayrton Senna was just for advertising. He came to this conclusion after having trouble installing a Corona shower he had purchased. But look at what happened: He sent a note to the company reporting the problem with the shower. So the company contacted him, sent a technician to change the shower and took it back to the company for an investigation. Obviously, Corona analyzed the shower the journalist claimed had caught fire and short-circuited in his house. Because every manufacturer needs to know if there is a problem on the production line in order to solve it, it is part of the world of industry! But, when opening the shower, it was found that the failure was due to poor installation; a technical report was made as a precaution and sent to the complainant. This shows how, sometimes, certain people mix things up and attack in a regrettable way, without first analyzing the situation carefully. As he was a reporter and was annoyed by a personal problem, he felt he had the right to attack the company and Senna in the press.

Rosângela tells us an interesting thing from that June 6th, which was our mutual friend Renata's birthday:

"It was on Renata's birthday, I think in 1987, and I was dating medalist swimmer Ricardo Prado. He was already a world record holder and had just won a medal in the Olympic Games." And Ricardo himself confirms: "I remember I was dating Rosângela at the time, Adriane's friend from high school, and I went to another friend's birthday. I had a Monza, and the party was in Jardins neighborhood. When we got there, the party was already full. During introductions, when I was shaking Ayrton's hands, he said: *I am your fan!*, and I said: *I am your fan too!* And everyone there laughed at the situation. I do not remember any later conversations between us, we were in a fun group. Then we only met again when we took the same flight from Galeão to São Paulo."

My friend Renata Belém, and Beco and I when we met the Olympic medalist Ricardo Prado

That year, Christhiane and I decided to organize a June fest — a very typical celebration in Brazil — at the headquarters of Chapadão farm on the last Saturday of June. We handmade the invitations with the help of our cousins and invited friends from all the places we used to go, as well as my parents' friends. Everyone came typically dressed, it was amazing!

My uncles organized a hilarious wedding! The bride was almost two meters tall, with natural mustaches and a fake belly: Uncle José Roberto. The groom, dwarf with painted mustaches: my cousin Kaco. The priest was Uncle José Carlos and the altar boy, Dadô.

Beco, recently arrived from a trip and, surprised by the news, took his brother to the farm with him. We regretted not having a chance to provide a typical costume. Then I remembered I had a plaid shirt at the farm and we improvised his outfit.

Guests came from São Paulo especially for the party scheduled to start at five in the afternoon. When the party was already very lively, we gathered the most excited people to dance an improvised square dance, following the lyrics of the song: "Olha a chuva! [It is raining!] É mentira! [It is a lie!] Olha a cobra! [A snake is coming!] É mentira! [It is a lie!] A ponte caiu! [The bridge is down!] É mentira! [It is a lie!]", and it was a lot of fun, for both the participants and the audience.

Crouching, from left to right: Francisco Pereira Lopes (Dadô's friend), Alexandre Abdelnur (Dadô's brother), and my cousin Miguel

Francisco with his viola

When night fell, Dadô with his friends from São Carlos and some family members played a supercool game, previously organized. They brought a trailer to the place and they all got out of it with straw hats, white suits and white pants decorated with patches of plaid fabric and musical instruments, dubbing viola songs. The trailer had funny phrases, as if it was going to be used by the "bride and groom" when leaving the party after the wedding.

After the show that lasted only two songs and lots of laughter, the wedding ceremony began. All properly prepared with the "groom" (my cousin Kaco, who was thirteen at the time) at the altar, the "bride" (my mustached uncle Bite) arrived with wreath and veil, in a fully decorated gig. The scene was hilarious in itself, but the actors made it even better. The priest's speech (my uncle José Carlos) also followed the comedy script with the altar boy (Dadô) next to him, and when he asked the expected question, "Should anyone present know of any reason that this couple should not be joined in holy matrimony, speak now or forever hold your peace", my cousin Chim, the most shameless person in the family, yelling, says they cannot get married, because he is the father of his child! Then he kidnaps the bride and they flee together in the gig. It was all very funny. After the fun, we spent some time interacting with the guests and barbecue was served, with drinks and typical sweets.

My cousin Leonardo, who was little at the time, remembers: *"From the June fest, I remember he was there and people were kind of surrounding him. Feeling suffocated, he walked away with us and set off fireworks that fell right in the middle of the cars and damaged the glass of one of them. I was closest to him during the day; he did not have much patience with me, but he liked to tease me a little. At the farm, I also remember him riding the jet ski and once he or Dadô took me to ride it and they wanted to do maneuvers, because I really shit my pants out."*

Above, the arrival of the "bride and groom" with Leonardo Senna on the right

343

Above, Kaco as the groom, uncle José Roberto as the pregnant bride, and in the right corner, Dadô as the altar boy

On the right, uncle José Carlos as the priest, friend Andó, me, Alfredo (a friend from school) and my paternal grandfather Farid (in a beret)

On the left, in a hat, Miguel Abdeldur (Dadô's cousin), the girls from the "cheeky post" (following explanation) with a heart glued to their clothes signaling this activity at the party and, behind them, my sister Lenise

My younger cousin and a friend were responsible for the "cheeky post" (*"correio elegante"*, a typical activity of this festival in which people flirt by small notes sent during the party; usually, girls were responsible for delivering the notes) among the guests. I could finally sit down next to Beco and he started receiving notes. Embarrassed with that happening with me next to him, he chuckles, reads them and says:

"You see, Dridrica! You are the only one who does not give me a chance. But these other fans won't leave me alone," he laughed.

He barely finishes his sentence and my cousin approaches us again and hands me two notes at once. Not expecting for it, Beco gets disconcerted. I open the notes not believing my luck.

"Well then, Beco San! Looks like you are not the only one who have fans!" I said, unable to help but laugh.

I excused myself and went to talk to the guests I had not welcomed yet, and only after finishing my role as a hostess I looked for him again. With some difficulty, I found him sitting on the floor, on a corner, on the side of the house, alone and isolated. I sat down next to him and saw some sadness in his eyes.

"What's up, Beco San?" I asked worriedly.

"Nothing, Dridrica! I was here thinking about life."

"But did something happen that I do not know?"

"It is nothing, I just wanted to stay on my own."

"Oh, Beco San! The party is so good, let's go and have some fun."

"You go, Drica, I will be there in a minute."

I wrapped my arms around him in a tight grip and said:

"No, Beco San, I am going to stay here with you for a while. I miss you and they do not need me at the party anymore."

We stayed there for a silent moment, contemplating darkness in the garden; we caressed each other and I noticed he reacted well to that contact. I started a conversation hoping to cheer him up, told him about the organization of the party, who had done what, then he finally seemed better. Then I said:

"Beco San, let's go to the party, but now I am not leaving you anymore! Oh, if a fan of yours decides to play it fun with you!"

He laughed, his so peculiar slow laugh, before saying:

"Wow, so angry, Dridrica! But I will love it, so your fans stay away too."

We exchanged a smile of complicity, kissed and walked back to the party just as a hired "country bumpkin" comedian showed up for a stand up for the guests. I, of course, split up between friends and boyfriend, was relieved when the party came to an end. We got together after all the guests had left to comment on the June fest, and Beco, now relaxed, had a beer. I found that funny because until then I did not know he liked beers.

346

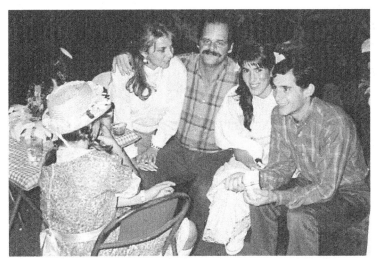

End of the party: On the left, on her back, my cousin Roberta, aunt Miriam, uncle José Roberto (now without the wedding clothes), me and Beco, talking about the party

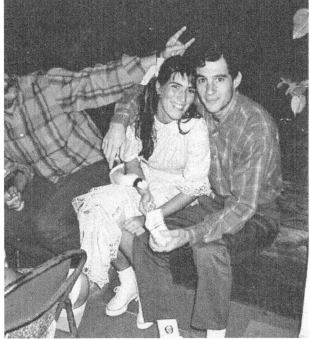

"What goes around comes around", and my boyfriend was the king of pranks, so we could not forget about the horn in the photo.

Us: Beco drinking a beer and I drinking a typical mulled wine from the party

My cousin Fernando, who graduated in Agronomy, was working at Chapadão farm that year and remembered some cool moments:

"He would greet everyone on the farm, from the cook, the cleaning lady to Adriane's father — he treated everyone as equals, he made no difference — and was very playful. He used to mess with me a lot, I always had to be a little attentive, because he would tie my pajama sleeves and other things, I had to be careful! When we were showering, he would turn off the room's power switch so we would take a cold shower. Once he put a frog in my boots (laughs). He was always up to something. Who slept together was Ayrton and Kaco, who is another cousin of Adriane's and I; it was the

three of us. Once I knotted his sock, wet it and soaked it; one was always messing around with the other. The one who suffered the most was Kaco, who was younger; we messed around together against Kaco, poor thing! (Laughs) One day, it was just me, him and Kaco in the room, then I asked: Kaco, was it you who farted? No, it was not me!, he replied. Then I said: Hey Ayrton, was it you? And he said: "Look! If it was not you or Kaco, it must have been me! And we burst out laughing.

Early in the morning at breakfast, Adriane always wanted to know what had happened and who had gotten the worst of it. On Sundays, we played soccer; at night, we got together to play something, and Ayrton was always very competitive at all times, even in card games. He wanted to win at soccer too, but we were careful, we did not want to hurt him at the game; he was in the middle of the Formula 1 championship. An injury or a fracture would be a huge loss, everyone who played against Ayrton would go slowly and tried to avoid tackling, but he did not care: He slammed, kicked, because what he wanted was to win — such a very competitive guy.

Whenever he returned to Brazil, after every race, he would go to the farm and bring a tape — it was a VCR at the time — to watch the races as a spectator and find out what happened. I sometimes watched with him; he wanted to see what he had done wrong, what could be improved, by looking from the outside.

Once, he went jet skiing on the farm lake and the engine was failing; we pulled the jet out of the water and he took a toolbox from his car. We disassembled the carburetor, cleaned and reassembled it; in fact, he was the one who did everything, I was just the assistant, looking and helping. After about two hours the jet was already running in the water.

Whenever he arrived at the farm, he always brought Adriane a gift or a souvenir, so we realized she was important and he remembered her when he was away, and he wanted to show that to her. He always showed that he liked her a lot and felt good with her, she was the company he loved to be with.

I once went with them and Adriane's sisters to the Bar do Alemão, in Itu. As it was not very crowded, there were not many fans around, but people came to take pictures and ask for an autograph anyway."

I remember a conversation I had with my sister Chris, whose relationship with Otávio was somewhat complicated, and Beco, as he had built a strong friendship with him, questioned what was going on. She, who had a more reserved temperament, just said that despite having broken up, they sometimes hung out together. And he, without thinking twice, said excitedly:

"Hmm, I love a flashback!"

I found that strange, as it had nothing to do with us, so I decided to let this matter go, but that stayed in my mind.

On that trip to Brazil, the following weekend, we went to São Carlos. In the evening, as we always did, we went into town for pizza. We were a group of about ten people. We settled at the table, as follows: Jacoto sitting at one end, with Mig and Dadô's other relatives on one side; Beco, I, Chris with her boyfriend and Lenise on the other side; Dadô at the other end of the table.

There were two girls at the pizzeria that I had met on another occasion, at Dadô's house, at a table in front of Jacoto, a little behind me and Beco. When we got there, they just made a quick gesture to their fellow citizen and did not greet the rest of the group. Shortly after we were settled at our table, I noticed some movement between Jacoto and Beco, in a parallel conversation. So I discreetly analyzed the area and noticed the girls flirting with the boys. They were blondes, with voluminous, feathering, long curly hair, typical of '80s rockers (I say again: In my opinion, the ugliest and most inartistic fashion of all time). I stayed on my own, pretending to be distracted by the conversation at our table, and just listening to their dialogue:

"Go there, Júnior! They are hitting on you."

"Stop it, Becão!"

"Go there, damn! They do not take their eyes off of you."

Jacoto looked at them, as if he were "analyzing" the material available there, thoughtfully, and Beco was completely eventful.

"Go there, damn!"

"Oh, I do not know, Becão! I am cool."

"Go there, man! Stop being silly. Look! One of them went to the bathroom, looking over here. This is your chance. Go after her!"

"Damn, Becão! I go whenever I want. Leave me alone!" he said, annoyed.

"Geez! If it were me, I would not think twice!" Beco said, in a smart, show-off and predatory way.

That was when I lost my patience. I immediately turned to him who, noticing my reaction, was startled, and I said softly so that only he could hear:

"Why don't you go? There is nothing holding you back here! Make yourself comfortable," I said as if asking him to order a soda for the server.

As I turned my face to the table, I noticed Mig's expression of discomfort, sitting across from me, because of the embarrassing situation I was exposed to. There was a heavy silence. But although I was furious, I acted normally with the other people and did not look at Beco's and Júnior's faces that dinner. I left it to my boyfriend to solve the problem he had caused, with that disrespectful prank in front of me.

Beco, who did not know how to act with me to get away with it, whispered and exchanged cautious gestures with Júnior. After all, now they knew I could hear everything they said. Their flirting ended there, such was the embarrassment to which they were exposed by me. Not to mention that they were excluded from the conversation at the table, because I wanted to make them feel very comfortable in their conversation, shrugging them off once more.

At the end of dinner, the men paid the bill and we went back to Broa house just like we had gone: Beco and I in the back seat, in Dadô's car with my sister Lenise. I sat in the opposite corner from him, very close to the door, my eyes and attention to the window, watching the city, then the darkness of the road and the starry sky. For a while, Beco did not risk talking to me, probably because there was nothing to be explained, and he did not know what my reaction would be, once I had all the reasons to be pissed off. We did not expose our "little problem" to the others, we both acted with discretion so they would not notice. Embarrassing for me, but also for him.

At one point on our journey, he asked some trivial questions and I gave him short answers so that he would not speak to himself in front of my family. I did not want to dialogue because, yes, I was very sad about what I had seen and heard that night. His last attempt to approach, so that I could not deny it without drawing attention: He lay down on the seat and rested his head on my lap.

"Drica, I have a headache," he said. Can you caress my head? Maybe it helps with the pain."

I did it begrudgingly, as I could not get away with that situation in the car. When we got to the house, I said goodbye to everyone and went to my room, along with my sadness and disappointment. I left him that way, with the embarrassment and discomfort he had caused. We both had a lot to think about what had happened.

The next day, he spoiled me a lot. He did not let me avoid him until I started laughing at that ridiculous situation. He had been an asshole, maybe even dumb! But actually, he had not done anything wrong, just talked too much. And it was like that all day: I was trying to avoid him and he was making fun of it. That was his explicit way to apologize to me. I played as tough as long as I could, but he knew me too well and knew I could not stay away for long. Thank God, I think those girls were afraid of me and never set foot in Broa house when I was there.

The fact is that Beco and Jacoto Júnior were definitely having the same behavior they used to have during their trips together around the world. He had chosen, from an early age, to focus on his greatest passion: Racing in a car! He had not had the opportunity to party like young men of his age. But at this point, with the proper financial return, his F1 career stabilized and in the company of childhood best friend, the harassment took his feet off the ground. However, he knew he needed emotional structure to overcome the challenges of the job.

I believe that, emotionally, despite my young age, I had my feet on the ground. I was sure about what I wanted, which provided me with me inner tranquility in not being distracted by what had no real meaning; it brought me stability and structure. Also, I knew who I was with and I knew the risks I took with harassment. The only thing that could keep me in that complicated relationship with an older, world-famous man was his conduct towards me. Even though he made some mistakes throughout our relationship, which, yes, hurt me, I can say that our biggest problem has never been within the relationship, but from fame and greed.

In the Bible, in the Old Testament, there is a very interesting excerpt: King Solomon, after overcoming all the challenges to build a nation alongside the woman he loved, at the time of peace and prosperity, he decided to have other women, as the time allowed. He was delighted and dazzled by various pleasures and obviously began to neglect his wife, whom he really loved and admired, his mainstay and mother of his rightful heirs.

Solomon's mother, seeing what was happening, with a wisdom brought by life, called her son for a conversation: Be careful, my son, you may lose the love of your wife, the one you love too, your partner, the one who supported you, with love and intelligence, in your worst moments. Are you prepared to lose this woman's love?

Of course not, Mom! I could not imagine my life without her love.

So beware, my son. "Quantity distracts love!".

Chapter XIX

July was a special month for our relationship, because I traveled to Europe to get to know Ayrton Senna's world up close, and we stayed at his house. We left Brazil on July 2nd, Thursday — my mother, Chris and I. Upon arriving in London, we were welcomed by Beco's parents. We had lunch with Mrs. Neyde, Mr. Milton, Maurício Gugelmin and his wife Stella, who already were in the house. After lunch, we took his new plane — by then he was earning enough money to buy it — a Learjet, heading for Paul Ricard, France, but we stayed at Petit Le Castelet. This charming, medieval town sits on top of a hill. At the end of the day, there is a flock of swallows over the valley that welcomes the sunset. It was summer in Europe and the landscape had an amazing color.

Above, me, Mrs. Neyde (Záza) and my sister Chris, at Le Castelet

At dinner on the first night at Petit Le Castelet, me, Chris, my mother and Záza

I had to control my romantic urges; that was my first trip to accompany him in his professional life, but Ayrton had a race on Sunday, so he had training on Friday. We barely saw each other at night, we just had something to eat quickly together, caressed each other during dinner and then each went to their own bedroom to sleep.

"On Saturday, Beco went before us to the racetrack. I went later with Mrs. Neyde and Mr. Milton. We went to the racetrack at noon. It is nice to hear the roar of the engines and see the drivers trying to get the best time." – on July 4, 1987

It was my first time at a Grand Prix and I was fascinated. I had access to all the locations of the paddock, where the atmosphere of expectation prevailed, and everyone there, from the drivers to the guests, the employees and the press, had only one thing in mind: To win.

On the track, it was every man for himself in the effort for the best time for Sunday's race; that was how I understood the reality and the tension to which Beco was subjected during the time periods in practice.

Ayrton Senna in Lotus' cockpit, on my first day in the world of F1

In the paddocks on the right, Chris, me, Záza and Júnior

Ayrton and I in Lotus motorhome. Photos taken when I was not paying attention. Prank set by him and his friend Jacoto Júnior:

We, in another prank

We returned to the hotel to rest, which was close to the racetrack, and it was also easy to drive to the small town. The place was small, with few floors and very cozy. I remember we all woke up from a siesta before Beco, and Mr. Milton had to throw stones at his bedroom window, which faced the hotel pool, to wake him up because we tried to call the room but he did not wake up. Then, suddenly, the "Sleeping Beauty" opened the window looking like someone who had just woken up from a deep sleep:

Mr, Chris and Mr. Milton, Ayrton's father, throwing pebbles at his son's bedroom window

"Stop it, dad! I will be there in a minute!"

"Hurry up! Everyone is waiting for you and you are there, sleeping," his father said, amused by the situation and gesturing with his hands.

I liked Mr. Milton's playful way, who despite his reputation for being angry and authoritarian, was very easygoing, always smiling or playing with me.

That evening, we all had dinner together at Petit Le Castelet, but we did not have a single minute alone. Ayrton simply could not think of anything else other than the GP, which would happen early the next morning. I understood he was focused on the race and had to sleep early. It is okay! But I was waiting for my turn...

On the 5th, I wrote down in my diary: *"French GP —Paul Ricard Circuit. We were on the track at 8 o'clock. The race started at one in the afternoon. Beco started in third, finished in fourth. We returned that same day to England."*

Me and my sister Chris in the "tent" of Lotus motorhome

Jacoto and Mrs. Neyde, Beco, me and Chris

In the picture above, Beco's house in Esher, England: My mom talks to someone who is in our bedroom window

Me, in the garden of Beco's house, taking a break from reading to watch the squirrels climbing the tree

We were all staying at Beco's house, in Esher, near London. A very nice, light, cozy townhouse. We were shown to one of the bedrooms on the upper floor, right in front of the stairs, where there was a double bed and a single bed already prepared for the three of us: Mom, my sister and me. I could not access Beco's bedroom, nor his parents'. The next day, he went to the bedroom to check if we were well settled. My mother and Chris were having breakfast with Mrs. Neyde, while I was in the bedroom dressing up to join them.

"Hi, good morning, Drica San sleepyhead," he looked back to confirm that no one was around and went into the room. "So my doll is here in my house, huh? I missed you so much!" he said smiling, already scooping me up in his arms and throwing me onto the bed.

I let myself fall, sensing his intent, and he bent over me.

"Drica, let's take advantage that the "Screwdriver" is far away," he said, alluding to my mother.

I had been waiting for that moment since I arrived and we kissed ardently until we heard someone coming up the stairs. We put ourselves together in a startle, as if nothing was happening, and he spoke in an audible tone:

"I am glad you are well settled and you have everything you need. Shall we go down for breakfast?" he said, leaving the room, regardless of who might be coming up, worried about preserving me in front of his parents as well.

Beco did not just make fun of Mrs. Marilene. He was also a joker with his own father, due to his rustic, playful and simple style.

"Dad, stop being a rube!" he said to his father, laughing. That same day, during breakfast, I learned that Mr. Milton and Beco were going on a business trip that afternoon and they would not return until the end of the next day.

I was happy to be there, but I had a fever that day. So much anxiety and anticipation since my arrival in Europe, in relation to our reunion, ended up breaking down my resistance and I spent the entire afternoon in Beco's house.

"Still in England. We went shopping in another small town near Esher, called Kingstone." – on July 7, 1987

Mrs. Neyde, my mother, Christhiane and I walked around Kingstone during the day. My mother and Mrs. Neyde got along very well these days together, and I myself had nothing to complain about. She has always been and is a sweet, warm and hospitable person — a wonderful hostess during our stay at her son's home. Now I know it is common for mothers-in-law and daughters-in-law to fight all the time because of jealousy. But

Mrs. Neyde is an exception to that rule: There was nothing in her heart that resembled jealousy or a feeling of possession towards her son; she always had a welcoming attitude. She was a person made of honey, filled with love and affection.

The interaction with Maurício Gugelmin and Stella, on the other hand, happened only on that trip and was very quick because of the couple's appointments. I had dinner with them at a Chinese restaurant in London. Menu: Shredded duck, house specialty. Divine! It was served wrapped in a kind of pancake. It was a very pleasant evening and I regretted not having had more contact with Stella, who, in addition to being busy all the time, left in the morning and only returned home at night, she seemed to be a very private person. Maurício, on the other hand, was very friendly, participative and more communicative, with that southern Brazilian accent.

"Beco arrived from his trip and we all went to dinner at the Italian restaurant (but we spent the day at home, waiting for the men to arrive: Mr. Milton, Beco and Júnior); and on the 9th: The women went to Kingstone. Beco, Maurício, Mr. Milton and I stayed home" on July 8, 1987

Me, Beco, Miltão, Maurício and Stella Gugelmin, Záza and my mom Marilene

Me, Chris and Stella Gugelmin, relaxed, helping Záza in the kitchen

However, had a fever again and this condition was repeated on a few other days during the trip. But that morning, despite this, I wanted to help Mrs. Neyde in the kitchen. Among other things, I prepared a half-frozen baguette that we put in the oven, which gave off a good smell and whet everyone's appetite, and then I washed the breakfast dishes. There was a window over the kitchen sink, and at that moment, Beco was coming by bicycle with Júnior, in the backyard of the house, and he looked at me. It was a beautiful day with sun rays streaming through the window glass that reflected off the sink in front of me and enveloped me in its light. He could not resist, stopped the bike and called Júnior:

"Come, come see it."

Beco's eyes sparkled with admiration and he opened a beautiful smile. He just stood there for a few moments. I felt in heaven at that moment, for that manifestation of ecstasy on his part and hoped to make time in his busy schedule.

That day, Maurício booked a tennis court and invited Ayrton and Júnior to a game. There was a place nearby with covered courts, and Beco, cheerful, invited me:

"Drica, do you want to join us and play tennis?"

"Let's go! But I did not bring any sneakers to wear..."

"No problem, we can buy one there!"

"Ok! I will get dressed."

"Don't be long, Dridrica!"

Beco drove us to the location with the courts. Although I tried not to show it, in my heart I berated him for wasting that time with a tennis game while we could be alone and make out. But I did not hesitate, although annoyed, and accepted the option I had at the moment.

When we got to the place, I saw several clay courts, all covered, one next to the other, and a small store with sporting goods for tennis players. I chose a white-leather Reebok with the brand lettering in pale blue. He, kind as usual, wanted to give me the sneakers as a gift:

"Dridrica, let me pay! I want to give it to you!" giving the hint that he wanted to make up for something.

"No, thank you! I brought money," I replied emphatically, to be done with the matter.

In the game, I confess, I had the devil in my body. Indignant at his lack of attention to me for not having scheduled something for the two of us to do on this day off. I served hard, hit back assertively when I was at the back of the court, I did not let a ball pass when advancing into the net, and I easily hit any ball. It felt like I was everywhere in the court at the same time, so fast I was running. I did not look at the others who must have been perplexed, especially Beco and Jacoto who often watched me play at the farm.

Nobody dared to comment, not even Beco, who, by temperament, would never accept playing silently with a ball hog. But I would not miss a ball, so he could not even complain, and I definitely played better than all of them together that day. I let go of the frustration I felt at the game and returned home with an air of satisfaction. Hadn't he prioritized tennis, after all? So I showed him how to play with heart!

Of course, when we were at the farm, we played sports, walked around, went out to eat, but we also dated and enjoyed each other, just like any couple. But not in England! We only had a few moments on our own, stolen from his intense daily schedule. Then it got boring and I felt almost like an intruder in his life there.

One day on this trip, I told him in the paddock:

"You know, Beco San, if you were not in F1 I would root for Berger."

"Why Berger, Drica?"

"I am not sure why, but he looks like he is a good person, he is talented and I also think he is cute," I made a point of saying it, showing him I knew I should not say that, but I said it anyway, as a subtle warning.

"Oh, really, Dridrica?! So you think Berger is cute?"

"I do! I am not blind, after all. He is a good-looking guy! Aren't you always surrounded by beautiful and wonderful women here? Why can't I find Berger cute?"

"It is different! But let's change the subject, this one will not do us any good, Dridrica," he said, smiling to show me he had gotten the message.

Years later, I reflected on this conversation when I learned that he and Gerhard Berger had become great friends and good teammates at McLaren.

I concluded that life is like this: An intricate game of fittings whose pieces our unconscious suggests as it identifies similarities in facts and situations that made us happy, even for a brief moment, which we usually call coincidences.

Záza, Chris, me and Paulo Casseb, who accompanied us in Kingstone

"We went out with Paulo Casseb to visit London and go shopping. Beco took fourth place in the afternoon qualifying session. And the next day: Saturday. Women did not want to go to the racetrack, but I did. I went alone to the racetrack with the men. Beco went third place." – on July 10, 1987

I was already quite familiar with the environment; I knew where I could stay and what I could do there.

I followed the qualifying practices for the Great Britain Grand Prix and saw Beco in and out the pit, watching his every move. But I did not get close, as it was the first time I had accompanied him to training and I did not want to draw the attention of photographers or bother anyone. When training ended, Beco had improved his time and would start in third place on the race grid the following day. He came to the motorhome, took a shower and called his photographer, the Japanese Norio Noike, who was with him on all of our trips to take pictures of us, and he started making faces. He wanted to make me laugh and I saw that my shyness would be overcome by his irreverence when he stuck out his tongue. I started to laugh, and the photographer seized the moment for the clicks.

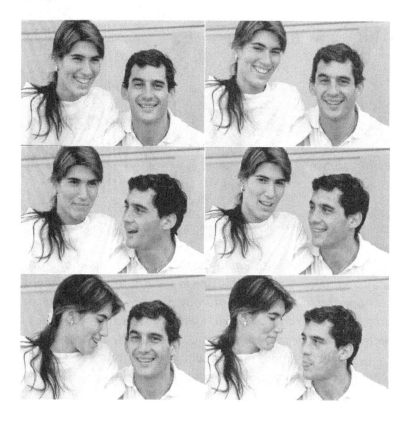

Photo caption:
"Hummm, Giggle at the photo, Dridrica!"
"Nope! No use trying to make me laugh, you will not make it!" I look at him, angry, and then he sticks out his tongue. Laughs...
"Oh, what a little beggar, Beco!"

Photo caption:
I said, fussy: "Ahhh Beco San, do not tickle me for the pictures! I want to look beautiful!"
"Ahhh, Drica San! I will think about it!"

Those moments added to the grandeur of our relationship. They were brief in time, but extremely significant in solidifying what we had in our relationship: Complicity, friendship, respect and love.

"Sunday, English GP. We went to the Silvestone racetrack by helicopter. Beco was tense, but he ended the race in third place. He started third and finished third. Beautiful win for Mansell, who kissed the ground." – on July 12, 1987

On Silverstone's race day, we went by helicopter to the racetrack, so as to not run the risk of being late due to possible traffic jams in accessing the site. Just before Ayrton entered the cockpit of Lotus, already in overalls, he took me into the motorhome:

"Dridrica, do you want to use the toilet? It is over there!"

"No, Beco, not now."

"When you want, you can go in and use the restroom here, which is cleaner than the chemical toilets outside."

"Thank you, but do not worry about that."

We sat around the table where there was a person waiting for him. We were introduced, quickly shook hands in a formal greeting, and they began to talk in English. Me, silent, trying to follow the conversation that my meager knowledge of the language allowed. I realized that they were reviewing the strategy for that race. When they finished, Ayrton got up, agitated, and I noticed he was totally energetic! We said goodbye and the man left the motorhome.

"Dridrica, now I have to go. Please root for me!"

"Of course, Beco San! Everything will be fine, then we will celebrate together. Take care and be safe."

We quickly kissed and he went for the race, while I joined the group who was watching the race on a TV monitor outside the motorhome. The group was made up by people who did not participate directly in the pits, but advised the drivers during the race. The monitor screen was small and the light was hampered by the reflection of the white color of a canvas used as a partition. This was making my eyes tired to the point of making me close my eyes. Chris, who was also there, when realized what was happening to me, started to nudge me so I would not embarrass myself. We had a few laughs about that. It was my second time in the paddock during a GP, and I recorded everything attentively. Lotus-Camel motorhome was an adapted bus and it had a small meeting table inside, as well as a room with sofas and a restroom. Outside, a tent jutted out from the structure, making a porch, with tables and chairs, where the staff stayed in the shade while the drivers were on the track. That Sunday, he started in third position and also finished in third.

On Monday, the 13th, the women returned to Kingstone and I stayed home, with Beco and Mr. Milton. We were visited by a McLaren representative. Their meeting lasted more than two hours. Then I learned that Ayrton was seriously considering leaving Lotus in 1988, and negotiations to change teams had already begun.

After the meeting, Mr. Milton went to get some rest and we quickly took the opportunity to make out. Without a word, Beco took my hand and pulled me into the office. This room in the house was very elegant, with off-white walls, a pale beige-leather armchair, a dark English-style wooden table, a sofa, and a small wooden bookcase. In the window behind the table, beautiful navy-blue velvet curtains. The entire house was really beautiful too. In the living room, there was a peach leather sofa. In the other corner of the residence, there was a TV room where Beco worked out. That was when I got to know cable TV and was amazed by the amount of channels we could have access to. A decoration detail in Beco's house was that the sofas in each room had a different color and the one in the TV room, in ecru fabric, made up of several modules with colored edges, was very similar to the sofa we had in the TV room of the farm. I had the impression that Beco took the style of our sofa to his own house, probably in an attempt to reproduce the cozy feeling he experienced with us in Porto Feliz.

On the left, Miltão, Júnior, Chris, Záza, Beco (their feet in a typical relaxing position) and Stella

But about what happened in that office: Beco, before locking the door and without I knowing, asked the maid to knock on the door when the women returned home. And so we were able to enjoy about fifty minutes of privacy.

"There, Drica, a little peace for both of us," he said as he closed the window curtains facing the front door of the house. "Come here!"

He sat in the office chair and I sat on his lap. We waited a lot for that moment, but the position did not help in the strokes.

"Drica, this chair is not helping us to enjoy ourselves, let's go to the sofa."

The loveseat had its back to the wall and was surrounded by wooden shelves between the table and the door.

"Beco, they will be arriving from the city and will catch us by surprise, with a locked door and drawn curtain," I warned.

"Relax! I asked the maid to give us a signal as soon as they were around."

There, that was all I wanted to hear from him. We kissed and caressed with all the intimacy acquired throughout our relationship. As we began to put ourselves together, we heard a knock at the door. Beco cautiously peeked through a crack:

"Dri, quick, they are coming."

We ran into the hall, between the front door, the stairs and the office door, and stopped there to welcome them. We tried to act as naturally as possible in the face of that nearly flagrant.

"Hi Mom, how was shopping? Do you need help unloading the car?" he asked, almost out the door.

"No, son. We have everything here. Where is your father?"

"He went for a nap," Beco said.

When the attention turned to me, with the biggest poker face, I immediately said:

"Wow, you took so long! We were chatting in the office and we thought about watching TV now."

I accompanied them to the kitchen to help with the groceries. Beco came too, soon after, but to check if everything was under control. We exchanged knowing looks and he headed to the TV room. Then I went to him and we agreed that we nearly did not escape.

"Tuesday. Beco went to Germany and we went to London by train. We spent all our time at Harrods (It was my shopping day). And the next day: Wednesday. We went to Esher. We went shopping. We packed our bags and met the men at the airport. We flew to Brazil." – on July 14, 1987

Meanwhile, we took the train to London and spent the day shopping at Harrods. The next day, the last day of our stay at Beco's house, we still walked around Esher before packing and heading to the airport. In the departure area, we met up with Beco, who had arrived from Germany in time to say goodbye, and we had a brief moment alone while my mother and Chris wandered around the stores.

I was sad, as I had thought I would be able to spend more time with him when in England, but there I also had to put up with his absences. Beco had gone to the Canary Islands in

France, and was now returning from Germany. He was not just mine all the time and neither did I want that. I just wanted him longer. However, the competition was very hard. What can I do? And so I had a fever. It was the sum of my frustration. Beco stayed with me, of course, but in the middle of all the other professional and sports activities already scheduled. He noticed the situation and asked, worriedly:

"Dridrica, what is wrong? Are you sad?"

I decided to speak up. With my gaze fixed on the floor, I spoke softly and slowly:

"Beco, I do not know if this will work. I came here to be with you, and you did not have enough time for us to be together. I am leaving with the same feeling of longing with which I came."

"Dri, I was busy deciding my future with another team, you know that! There are a lot of things happening at the same time and I have to handle everything, it is not easy for me either. But I am sorry. I wanted you to come, to spend these days here with me. You never came, you could never participate in this part of my life."

I enjoyed being part of Ayrton's life, having seen the races that I always followed on television, being so close to the drivers and feeling all the emotion behind the scenes of Formula 1. But I was distressed and did not know how to make our relationship work in the middle of it all.

"Look, you did have a few opportunities where you could have scheduled something for us to do together, just you and me, like what we do when you are in Brazil, but that did not happen. I dragged my family here so I could be with you. Beco, I love you. I loved being here. But I am leaving and I am sad because I do not know how to make it work. You have no room for me here."

In my heart, I felt: "I came to Europe to be alone." I noticed he was sad with my reaction. All I could think of was that, amazingly enough, in England we had seen each other less than in Brazil. If I married him, would I be alone most of

374

the time? That life awaited me and that scared me a lot. I tried, but I could not hold back the tears because my heart was so tight. He, visibly confused with what I had just said, remained silent, he did not know what to say. We said goodbye in this mood of uncertainty about the future of our relationship. I quickly collected myself by hearing my flight call. Mom and my sister approached, thanked Beco for the hospitality and we boarded the plane.

The good thing about my trip was that I met almost everyone who worked with Ayrton: The photographer, the masseuse, the receptionists, the mechanics, the team leader, among others. We spent a lot of time in the Lotus motorhome, where we ate and watched the races on TV. My family, his family and I together. Anyway, I was there for everybody to see me, and everyone found out about my presence in these two races, including the specialized press. On that occasion, I met Galvão Bueno and Reginaldo Leme, among many reporters, but nothing leaked in the media, at Ayrton's request. I had never been to a Brazilian GP at that time because the large volume of people in the paddock during training and in the race would make it more difficult to hold the information of my presence — definitely a sacrifice for not being able to be with him in my country! But that was the price to pay to ensure I could get on with my life without trouble. Thus, I had my adolescence preserved and, despite the difficult and somewhat painful choice I made when I got involved with Beco, I am grateful to him and my parents for taking such care of me.

I keep to this day many photos we took in the pits, including with Ayrton's friends and business partners, such as the president of Mercedes-Benz in Germany and Djino, Benetton's representative in Italy — photos taken by his photographer and Júnior, who loved to catch me off guard. We did not show intimacy, we were discreet, but during the fifteen days I was there, everyone knew about me in Ayrton's life.

Chapter XX

We landed in São Paulo before scheduled. After disembarking, no one was waiting for us at the airport, but shortly afterwards the driver arrived and we headed home almost just to leave the bags.

The next day, Friday, July 17th, we went to Campos do Jordão, where my parents had rented a house. Everybody went, including Lenise and her husband. That holiday season, both my father and Dadô only stayed with us for the weekend and returned to work on weekdays, each in their own company.

Some cousins, who were also on school holidays, like Patrícia Kaiser, stayed with us. A few days ahead of schedule for the end of this season in Campos, we were woken up early and asked to pack our bags without asking questions, because something serious had happened to uncle Ferdinando. We left Campos do Jordão in two cars.

Only when we arrived in São Paulo, they told us that my uncle Ferdinando Kaiser had been shot in a robbery, on his doorstep, when he was leaving for work. My cousin Fernando, who was with him, witnessed everything and tried to help his father, rushing him to the hospital, but time was not enough to save him. He was my mother's brother-in-law and my godfather in baptism.

Therefore, we were going to help the family at that very difficult moment. Uncle Ferdinando was a dentist, with German ancestry. At the end of World War II, his father was released from the concentration camp and migrated to Brazil to start life over.

At that time, I went through a very difficult phase without suspecting that it would get even worse during that second half of the year. I had come from Europe sad and was shocked by uncle Ferdinando's tragic death. I realized I could not count on the support of my absent boyfriend in difficult times either. Before the impermanence of life, I started to wish the freedom of living my own choices and to think more about myself.

"German GP, Hockenhein Circuit. He started second and finished third." – on July 26, 1987

In early August, Beco called me:

"Hi, Dridrica, how are you doing?"

"Fine."

"How are your parents and the others?"

"They are fine, thank God."

He noticed something in the tone of my voice and asked:

"Dridrica, what is wrong?"

"I do not know, Beco, I am not fine."

"Did anything else happen out there?"

"Aside from my uncle's tragic death, nothing else."

"What is it, Dridrica?"

After a brief silence, seeing that it did not convince him, I decided to open up:

"I am feeling a huge emptiness inside me."

"Drica, I will be there really soon!"

"I am missing feeling alive. I feel very lonely."

"Calm down, Drica, hang in there and I will be back as soon as possible, you know I wanted to be closer to you."

"I guess! Listen, I need to hang up, they are calling me."

"Okay, Dridrica, remember I love you, take care, kisses."

"Kisses."

"Hungarian GP, August 9, Hungaroring Circuit. He started in sixth, had a beautiful recovery, finished in second." On the 16th: Austrian GP – Zeltweg – Österreichring Circuit. He started in seventh, finished in fifth." – on August 9, 1987

I did not know when Ayrton would be able to return to Brazil, and after my trip to Europe I was sure I was just one part of his life, of leisure, support, affection, security, and — I believe — of love. But what part of my life was he? It seemed that somehow the love I felt for him was draining the life I had to live; so, I decided to allow myself living new experiences, just as he had his for a long time.

By then, I was seventeen and I needed to figure out if it was worth it to keep trying to overcome all the difficulties of our relationship or if I should move on to another one. That was when a boy, who was not part of my group and therefore did not know I was dating Ayrton Senna, approached me. He was a handsome young man, polite and kind, who was in college there at Mackenzie. After we met a few times during breaks, he asked me out, and I accepted to see what would happen. We went out, talked and kissed. It was a good kissing, but I did not feel butterflies in my stomach, like I felt with Beco. We always ran into each other at school, and he asked me out again. We went to a newly opened night club Limelight, we danced a little, kissed again and no butterflies in my stomach again. I then realized that I should not go any further and discreetly walked away. He asked me out other times, and I made some excuses until he understood and stepped back.

There was another boy, also at that time, who taught in the diving course I was taking since April, with uncles Zé Carlos and Zé Roberto and my cousin Kaco. The course was made up of practical classes in the diving school's pool, and theoretical classes, with the basics of the rules and previous calculations necessary for a safe dive due to the atmospheric pressure (ATM) of oxygen in our body when diving in deep water, in order to avoid the risk of embolism. Thus, I learned how to calculate the time of the air contained in the oxygen tank needed for the intent depth, what is the ideal time to reach and remain at that depth, and the pauses to be made when returning to the surface safely. I also learned how to read the diving equipment and the sign codes of communication between divers, the weight of ballast for each student, and dark diving tactics.

The course was much more complex and professional than I thought. My uncles, Kaco and I studied together for the written test and we were approved. Simultaneously, we had lessons in the pool, and the instructor was very handsome, with a breathtaking athletic build and princely face. I soon noticed his interest in me, but I stepped back because I was not open to anyone at that moment. However, the practical test for our graduation took place only in August, in the coast of São Paulo. It was a very nice and fun trip with my uncles, cousin and other classmates. Over the weekend, everything went professionally, but I knew I would not see our instructor again after that. And at that moment I really was looking for new possibilities, and when the handsome diving instructor discreetly and providentially asked for my phone number, I gave it to him. He called me a few times, he was a hardworking guy who worked to pay for his tuition, very polite and kind. We scheduled to go to McDonalds near my house and we went there on foot. At a certain point along the way, he kissed me, but again I did not feel the butterflies in my stomach. I never made another date with him because I understood I would not be able to feel the way I felt with Beco with anyone else.

I did not feel guilty for my fleeting encounters, after all, I knew Ayrton had sex with other women for a long time. Therefore, I felt it was my right to live those experiences that somehow were good for me. But I would never lie to Beco. When he came to Brazil, we talked in the car, in the garage, when we came back from a ride:

"Hey, Dri! Do you have anything to tell me?"

"Yeah… I hung out with other guys," I replied. "I decided to find out if it is really you who I want to be with and I did find out!" I said in a very low voice.

"And what happened?" he was interested.

"No biggie, what happens to everyone."

"How come? What happens? What did you do?"

"Basically what everyone else does!"

"Adriane, did you have sex with anyone?" he asked, almost desperate.

"What?! Who do you think I am? I kissed, damn it! Nobody touched me. If I were to have sex with someone, it would be with you, because you are the one I love. I am not like the women you hang out with!" I vociferated, totally shocked by that insinuation.

"Oh, good! That scared me! If it was just kissing..."

"What do you mean 'oh, good'? Is it okay for me to kiss other people then?"

"How many were they?"

"It does not matter! It does not make any difference if I just kissed, right?" I said indignantly.

"Okay, Drica! Let's not talk about it anymore. I hope you have already found what you were looking for. I am here in Brazil for you and it is for you that I try to fix my schedule to come here!"

"I did, yes. Beco, I was very upset and had to take a little risk, but it is you who I want for me, you are the one I love. What difference does it make if I kissed one, twenty or two thousand?" I tried to make him smell a rat, but he had more experience in life than I did, he realized my intention and was amused.

"Okay, Drica, you were curious and wanted to clear up your doubts. Let's not talk about it anymore!"

"Yeah, Beco, you are the one I love and who I want to be with! I have no more doubts."

"I know our situation is complicated, it is difficult for me too, but we have come so far, Dridrica! I also feel very lonely because of you when I am away, but we will get there. We will get through this phase together! Deal?"

"Deal, Beco San!"

And it was like all my doubts, questions, sadness, anguish and fear towards the two of us dissipated. He kissed me and

I felt butterflies in my stomach — it was like everything was right again.

On the weekend, my cousins Renata and Roberta, Chris and I decided to go to Campos do Jordão with Beco. Aunt Miriam, the owner of the house, was traveling and my parents agreed with the trip, because my uncle José Roberto would go too. But there was a catch. My aunt had already warned us that she did not want anyone to sleep there who was not family without her permission. But I did not have the heart to tell him that.

We stayed that late afternoon at aunt Muruca's house, which was very close to downtown. In the evening, Beco and I went to dinner at a small, cozy restaurant on the top floor of an imported goods store. The atmosphere was a little dark, perfect for a dinner for two! And miraculously, without being harassed by fans.

When we got back, I asked bed linen for my cousin and prepared one of the bedrooms for Ayrton to accommodate. When I went to sleep in my cousins' room, they questioned me for not complying with their mother's orders, but they understood my distress at not knowing under what justification to tell him to look for a hotel. Not even my uncle Zé Roberto, who was with us in the house, made any comments, once there were enough rooms in the house; also, that situation did not make any sense.

So we stayed there that weekend. We could barely leave the house at that time, and we had to avoid crowded places because of harassment. Beco left his Mercedes-Benz in the covered garage, which could only be seen by those passing in front of the house. It was more and more complicated to be with Ayrton without him being recognized, and that bothered me; we had to practically hide to be in peace, and that car only made it worse! Soon the rumors spread in the small town and the fans already identified him from a distance, because of the car.

Sometime later, when aunt Miriam found out Beco had been at her house in Campos without her authorization, I got the biggest scolding from her. She found out through her neighbors, who were her friends; they asked her why she had not told anyone that she knew Ayrton Senna da Silva, and she was furious with me!

Aunt Miriam recalls it: "When I traveled abroad, Adriane secretly went to Campos with him and my daughters. She did not ask me, because if she did, she knew I would say no. I found out when I returned to Campos do Jordão and the neighbors talked to me."

At the beginning of the relationship, everything was different. When Beco left, I did not know if he would come back to me. I also did not understand what was going on between us and imagined he could easily forget about me or replace me with someone else. But he always came back! He traveled again and came back. I did not understand why, but the thing is, he kept coming back to me. As time went by, anxiety and expectation of his return were softening, because I understood that he wanted to come back, by his own will. I received the letters he wrote, trying to make sure I knew he was thinking about me. I was happy when he returned and got sad when he left. It was a real relationship, with no other interest than the desire to be together, which was solidified with living together. That is why I was surprised when Ayrton wanted to talk to me about a decision made, according to him, by his father.

"Dri, there is something I need to talk to you and I do not think you will like it, but I have to tell you because I want your opinion on what I am going to propose. The thing is that this story of Júnior accompanying me to the races is giving me a lot of trouble, this story won't stop. But this is bothering my father too much! Júnior has already been invited to come back to Brazil because my father gave him an ultimatum, poor thing."

In complete silence, I listened attentively to him speak:

"I am not worried about it! No problem for me!" he said that because he did not want me to feel guilty, and went on: "But my father suggested that we hire a woman, a model, to appear by my side for some GPs to stop this fuss!"

How could I say no if it was partly because of me? He realized I was annoyed, but I could not find that ridiculous proposal cool. I was sorry about everything that was happening, but I understood he was asking for my consent. I did not want to upset his father and I washed my hands of it:

"Beco, what can I do? Do whatever you find best to try to resolve this slanderous situation! I am sorry about this!"

Ayrton returned to Europe to compete in the three Grand Prix in September.

"Italian GP, Monza Circuit. He started in fourth, Senna/Piquet dispute was exciting, and he came in second (strategy: do not change tires)." – on September 6, 198

My birthday was coming and Beco could not be here with me, but I was happy to receive the card below:

FOR YOUR BIRTHDAY
I WAS GOING TO SEND YOU
AN EXPENSIVE GIFT...

...BUT I WAS AFRAID
OF SETTING A
DANGEROUS PRECEDENT!

HAPPY BIRTHDAY!

"Drica,
With each passing day, I feel inside more and more what it is like to like a woman. Although we are far away and our time together is relatively low, I feel you strongly inside of me, and the pain in my heart is big for not having you closer to me. You are constantly in my mind and I have been feeling so lonely because I miss you. You know, this is not a love card or something totally romantic, it is the truth in my heart and mind that you are taking hold of!!! Only I know how much I wish I were with you 'today, yesterday, tomorrow,' but on your birthday I will think about you a little more, but there is one important thing about it all: It is to feel that we are together and that our time will tell; it is hard to control, but if you want me as much as I want you, then I am sure that this day will come. I miss you a lot,
    Love, Kisses Beco.
    09.15.1987 Portugal
    PS: Happy birthday!!!!"

384

On September 17th, I turned eighteen. Chris prepared a surprise party in our apartment in São Paulo, and invited my friends from Mackenzie and from the group of beach volleyball in Guarujá.

At that point, I could get my driver's license! I really wanted to drive and had already learned how to on the farm, using a cream Jeep we had there. Well, I was so happy with the possibility of driving that I took the course before reaching the age of majority, as allowed by legislation at the time, and a week after my birthday I was already qualified to drive. It was an important step towards my autonomy. I could come and go from Mackenzie every day and go out for lunch and dinner, of course all within the limits of the rules set by my parents.

Beco called on the day to congratulate me before the surprise party:

"Happy birthday, Drica San! "So it means you will be a good girl now?"

I laughed at his comment and said excitedly:

"Beco San, thank you, next week I will get my driver's license!"

"Wow, what a danger! You have to warn all the lampposts in the city that they will be in great danger with you around the streets," and he laughed his slow laugh.

"As if! I am great driver. Maybe one day I will teach you," and I laughed.

"Wow, Dridrica! What a back luck I have," he laughed and made a common joke back then: "Women at the wheel! Constant danger!" laughing at the end.

"Okay, you silly!"

"Look, Drica, take care driving around, okay?"

"Okay, I will be just a little good girl..."

"Look, Dridrica, you know I have spies everywhere out there to keep an eye on you!"

"Oh, I am scared! So I will be good!"

"Yes, you will, Dridrica! No going around to party."

"Look, I will not party if you swear you will not go either!"

He knew how to express himself through sounds very well, and made a sound expressing his disagreement before saying:

"So I will have to ask you not to party too much, is that better?" and laughed.

"It is perfect. It is fair and no one gets stuck at home."

"Okay, then! I have already bought you a gift. But you will have to wait for me to arrive to know what it is!"

"Well, well, well, congratulations, you managed to make me curious. Actually, that is why you mentioned about the gift, right? No problem! I can handle the curiosity."

He laughed at my comment, then said:

"Dridrica, I will be right there soon enough to grab you and shower you with kisses, get ready!"

"I am totally ready!"

Again, I heard his slow laugh on the phone and he said goodbye:

"I love you! Enjoy your day, Dridrica. I will be here thinking about you, wishing I were there. Hopefully, I will be there real soon!"

"Okay, Beco San, I miss you so much."

At that point, I could not even remember how disappointed I was when I traveled to Europe and I was left with the desire to be with him.

My parents gave me a brown Paraty, simple model, as a present. It was the car I wanted so I could take my dog Dumbo, a champagne cocker spaniel, to Ibirapuera Park with me on my daily runs. Not to mention that I could go to Mackenzie by myself, to my aunts' and friends' houses, among other places. I also started to receive a salary from my father's company, when I was hired as a regular employee and everything, as an allowance, to pay my personal expenses, including gasoline for the car. Some money so I could learn to manage my life as an adult. My father said:

"Pay attention! You will be able to buy your things and pay your daily expenses, but you also have to save a little for emergencies, you won't spend everything. You are grown up; it is time to learn how to manage your money. Do not even think about being indebted to the bank! Got it?"

I started to pay the gym's tuition, gasoline, some clothes, gifts and souvenirs I wanted to give to friends. Finally, I learned what I could and could not do within my budget. In case I had to buy something more expensive, I would talk to my mom, who would give me some money if she agreed with that. We did not have a consumerist upbringing and we were encouraged to value this behavior. But, in a way, these small changes made me feel I was taking the lead in my own life.

Portugal GP, Estoril Circuit. He started in fifth, came in seventh. Senna was disappointed with the team, which would not adjust the car. And on the 27th: Spanish GP — Jerez de La Frontera Circuit. He started in fifth, came in fifth. Loss of competitiveness in the championship. – on September 20, 1987

Now, I would not only have to deal with our distance and the constant goodbyes, I also had to deal with the situation of having my boyfriend appearing with a model in magazines and newspapers. Even though I knew it was all set up and had grudgingly agreed with that role play, I was being embarrassed in front of my family and friends who knew of my relationship with Mr. Ayrton Senna.

To make his situation more complicated, due to a coincidence, my parents traveled to Portugal that end of September. They accompanied their friends Vidal and Mariazinha, who were visiting their daughter in Portugal and stayed at the farm of the in-laws Maria José and José Maria, who had been with us so many times in Angra dos Reis. Gently, Beco invited them to Jerez GP in Spain, sent an airplane to pick them up, and provided them with the paddock access credentials. When they arrived at the circuit, my parents and their friends were greeted by the team's staff and directed to a special stand to watch the race.

Mr. Amilcar, my father, at the Jerez GP, Spain, on September 27th, 1987

The trip group with my parents, Marilene and Amilcar. On the right, my father, uncle Vidal, my mother, Melu, aunt Mariazinha, uncle José Maria, his wife Maria José and their son

After the GP, they met Ayrton in the paddock and returned that same day to Portugal, by plane. On that occasion, my parents and our friends met the model. I did not know details and did not know the model would be there in Spain. Precisely because I feel embarrassed by the situation, I tried not to know the details, to ignore it.

However, everyone seemed to know their own role in that Formula 1 circus. And at the end of the day, I am not exactly sure if people who were part of the Formula 1 environment understood the true dimension of the story. I thought it became even stranger. How did they tell Galvão Bueno and Reginaldo Leme, for example? They already knew me and my parents. I do not know how they explained to everyone who lived with Ayrton, mainly the Brazilians. And everyone who already knew about my visit there in July, now he was with someone else and having my parents over. That did not do any good. Just to get someone to pop photos in magazines? Wasn't it from the paddocks that the nasty rivals were on duty and the defamatory rumors were coming out? For me, that was totally nonsense.

The fact is, Ayrton was at the racetrack with his companion and, as we knew about the matter, he made a point of introducing her that day. When properly introduced to my mother, she asked politely:

"Nice to meet you, how is Adriane?"

"She is great, she could not come because it is her school period. But she is awaiting our return."

Beco was close and provoked his mother-in-law as usual, maybe to cut that strange atmosphere and make everything clear:

"Mrs. Marilene, I am going to arrive in Brazil before you and your Amilca!" he laughed, and added: "Do you want me to bring something for Dri?"

My mom, understanding what he was doing, smiled and said:

"Tell her to take good care of herself and be good! And that we miss her a lot."

Everyone burst out laughing and Beco brought a note that she wrote right there for him to hand to me.

"09/26

Drica, I miss my little darling girls a lot. I send you a hug (not very tight) through Beco, we will be together again soon. If you are happy, so am I. Hugs with affection, by mom.

Me."

One day before Beco arrived in Brazil, he called me. Christhiane and I were still at aunt Miriam's house and would not go home until my parents returned from their twelve-day trip to Portugal. When she answered the phone, my cousin asked him to call me later, because I was in the shower. Beco agreed and called later. But I, not knowing he had already called and would call again, decided to take a long shower.

"Dri, he has already called twice and is mad you did not answer!" aunt Muruca said.

"Huh? I am always waiting for him to call and I am always available. He could wait a little longer to call back. Didn't you tell him I was in the shower? It is not my problem if he is in a hurry!"

"Well, then you have to talk to him, I did my part. I am giving you the message and I realized he did not like not finding you," she finished her sentence laughing at him, like, "serves him right!"

"Yeah, Mu, it is once in a lifetime that he did not find me. Did he say if he will call again?"

"I think so. But he was pissed!" my aunt Miriam said, laughing.

"Well, so sorry!"

I joined the women who were watching TV in the TV room. The phone rang — it was the old-fashioned type that was glued to the wall, with a wooden body, just the mobile phone and the mouthpiece fixed to the body, so I had to answer it standing up and keeping my mouth close to the mouthpiece — and I got up knowing it could be him.

"Hello."

"Drica!" He already recognized my voice.

"Hi, Beco San! Everything okay out there?"

"Everything is great! Did they tell you I already called you there?"

"They did, but I was in the shower."

"Gosh! I have never seen such a long shower. I have called you twice! The first time you were in the shower. Half an hour later I called again, you were still in the shower! This is weird. Explain it right! I almost did not call you anymore thinking you would not get out of the shower today. And I stay here at the hotel lobby waiting for you to come out of the shower so we could talk, young lady."

I replied calmly because I had nothing to hide, although I did not like his tone for such a banal situation:

"Well, look, when someone says the person is in the shower, they do not always mean she really is taking a bath. People say this out of politeness, but she is actually in the bathroom doing something else. Got it? I cannot know where you are, when you intend to call or whether you want to call from a hotel lobby."

"Oh well, I get it now," and he laughed.

We went on with the conversation as if nothing had happened, him disguising the bloop and I pretending not to have noticed such rudeness. Only then did he say he would arrive in Brazil before my parents and that, when he did, he would pick me up at my aunt's house. He also said he would have a little more time this time and we would have two weekends together. We hung up and I kept thinking about that distrust of him, and I concluded that maybe it was insecurity because of the autonomy I had obtained with the driver's license and without the strict control of my parents.

As soon as he arrived, he picked me up at Muruca's house and we went out for a ride. Then he handed me the note my mother had sent. My parents arrived immediately after and on the weekend we all went to Porto Feliz.

"We watched Robocop at the cinema and went to McDonald's." - on October 13, 1987

We arrived at the farm at the end of the day, Beco called me and we sit on the sofa in the living room, because he wanted to give me a birthday present, which was inside a folded envelope, and it had considerable volume.

"Well, Dridrica, I know you are dying to see your present, but it will not be that easy! First you will have to find out what it is, before you can open the package."

And he handed me a box inside a white envelope. I looked at it, knew it would not fit a shoe in that box, but it was also too big to be a jewel. I guessed:

"It is a watch!"

"No, no you cannot get it right in the first guess. You are not even close! You will have to make other guesses."

I started to laugh, because he was surprised that I got it right in the first guess and tried to hide it by pretending I was wrong. I joined the game:

"A Watring?"

"Oh, stop it, Dridrica! For real?!"

"A Watlace? A Watcelet?" I said, laughing.

"Okay, then! Open it! It really is a watch. But how can you get it right in the first try? That is not funny."

"It is because I am very smart and you did not count on my cunning!" I said, opening the package.

"Gee, Beco San! I cannot believe it," I said when I saw it was a Rolex covered in gold, and I added, perplexed: "Are you crazy? It is so beautiful!"

I had already shown Beco the mixed Rolex I had gotten from my parents that year. Christhiane and I expected to get a gold one when we turned twenty-one, as it had been with Lenise. He knew that, just as he knew that I loved watches. I told him:

"Beco! My poor father. What will he give me when I turn twenty-one?"

"I know, Drica. But I wanted to anticipate it," he said, with a happy face.

I jumped on his neck and hugged him tight in thanks. That was the second watch he gave me. The first was an Yves Saint-Laurent he brought me in one of the surprise visits he made to me in Itanhaém, during the '86 Carnival, with a navy-blue background and very sophisticated, which I still have today.

The day before he left to the last GPs of that season, he picked me up at home to spend the day with his parents, a way to be with them but without giving up being with me. Now that we had acquired a little more autonomy, this was possible. Among the peculiarities of Beco's family that I became aware during the four years of our relationship, one of them particularly caught my attention due to the gesture of intrinsic affection. Mr. Milton's rice had to be fresh and made by Mrs. Neyde, even though they had a cook in the house to prepare the meals. In fact, Mrs. Neyde received from the cook the necessary condiments chopped and the boiling water when preparing rice; she sautéed the condiments in butter, poured the rice and boiling water, and covered the pan to wait for the rice to cook. I am sure that even today, whenever she can, she herself cooks rice for Mr. Milton.

Dinner was served and I felt quite comfortable. Mr. Milton was always trying to mess with me, in a loving and playful way. Mrs. Neyde was very kind and caring. Bili (as we affectionately called Leo), who went with us everywhere, had me in his house for the first time and he seemed happy. I had the impression that everyone was happy with my presence in Beco's life. He was very dear and loved by that family, but he was also the one who made them most worried because of the crazy life he had chosen. I thought I was experiencing what Beco probably felt when he was with my family: A sense of belonging, of being at home, in the nest. Surrounded by good people, no frills or affectations, well-educated, kind and playful. They were not perfect, just as my family was not! But for sure, a family to be proud of!

That day, I almost died in shame with the intimacies in front of his parents. Beco kissed me on the mouth, which, despite simple, as you know, was an intimacy that we could not have before my parents. And I, trained, felt like doing something disrespectful even in front of his parents; and he repeated the gesture more times during that day. Cheerful with my shyness, he got excited and at one point pulled me so I could sit on his lap, without giving me a chance to escape. He laughed at me and I pretended I was okay with that, but he knew I was not by the blush on my face, and was even more amused by the situation. His parents, knowing their son well, and knowing my discreet way, knew exactly what his intentions were and were amused by that scene too.

On our goodbyes to Ayrton's trip to the Mexico GP, we were talking in the hall at the front of the house. Knowing he would go to McLaren the next year and that the terms of the agreement were practically defined, he casually commented to me:

"Yeah, Dridrica, here in Brazil, when I go out with these women you know I do…"

I was speechless, perplexed. After a few minutes I managed to mumble:

"What do you mean here in Brazil?" He opened his eyes wide and replied:

"Hey Dridrica, you know I do. We agreed on that. You know I see other women. When I am traveling, working, I cannot think of women when I am there."

That made me sick. My hear spun a mile away. I did not know what to say and he asked me, scared:

"Dridrica, say it. What is it?"

I could not articulate any words. At that moment, my illusion was shattered. I thought he had other women, but far from me. But no, it was right here! How could he do this to me? How could he be with me, enjoy with me, and then have sex with another woman? After some time, I managed to speak in a breath:

"I thought you did not need other women when you were with me."

I could not even look at him, such was my disappointment, and I remembered once seeing a phone book in his car and asking:

"Can I look?"

He said yes and I saw he had a list of women's names along with the references: So-and-so (John Player), So-and-so (Marlboro), What's her name (Olivetti) and so on. I closed the notebook and thought no more about it at the time. But now it all made sense in my head. I could not imagine that after being with me, maybe even on the same day or in the same week, he would go out with someone else. After all, we were intimate enough, even though we did not go all the way. I was satisfied that way and naively believed he was too. I ended up saying:

"I thought you made out with those women when you were far from me. So, you mean I warm up the engine so you can get laid with someone else?"

He did not answer and left, crestfallen, but left a note at the building lodge:

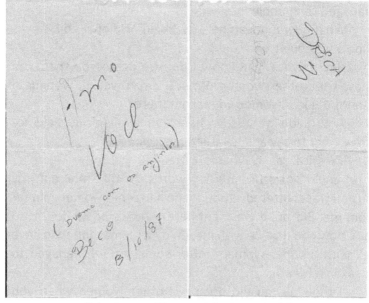

"I love you (Sleep with the angels)
Beco 10.13.87"

I was broken. To this day, the truth is, this memory saddens me. It was terrible to see the love I offered being treated like this. I spent days feeling confused, crying on my own so that no one could see, and even so, as I am naturally cheerful, people noticed I was sad and questioned, but I did not talk.

"Beco went away and left me alone." – on October 14, 1987

By coincidence, I received flowers with the card:

14. 10. 87

Adriane

AL. ITU

Drica,
Nestas Rosas vai um pouco de mim p/ você pensar um pouco em nós dois juntos. Você vive em meu pensamento "Beijos gostoso" em você Beco (14.10.87)

"Drica, I send with these roses a piece of me for you to think a little about the two of us together. You live in my mind.
'Delicious kisses' Love you Beco
10.14.87"

The Mexico GP took place on the 18th at the Hermano Rodrigues Circuit. Ayrton started in seventh place, but spun and hit hard on lap 54. He was taken to the hospital and spent two hours under observation before being released.

Before taking the plane to Japan, he called me:

"Dridrica, I do not know how many hours I will have to fly. I will have to stopover."

Beco would travel with Leo, but I realized that what he really wanted was to change the focus on the hard and cold revelation he had made, which showed I was not the only one in his routine in Brazil. However, he said nothing about it.

Shortly afterwards, when Beco called again:

"Hi, Dridrica, how are you doing?"

"Cool!"

"I am really upset, I had a bad discussion with Leo and now the mood is terrible to travel together..."

"Wow. That is bad! What happened?"

"Oh, we fought over nonsense, but it got ugly. Dridrica, I am very upset!"

"Well, Beco, I am sure this will pass. You are brothers, you love each other, and everything will be fine!"

"Hopefully, Dridrica, I miss you..."

"Glad you do! Have a good trip, take care."

"Okay, Dridrica, I have to go, take care, kisses."

"Kisses."

After a few days, I received the first postcard from Beco, from Tokyo:

"Drica,
We almost stayed on Wednesday night (10.14.87) in the
moment of the takeoff, one of the engines pretend to be
sentimental, but at the end it was okay. This time I have a
surprise for you and I bet you will not find out until I tell
you!!!
Kisses, Beco
10.15.87 (4:00 AM)"

Shortly afterwards, the second postcard

"Drica,
We just arrived in Tokyo. We traveled from Mexico City to Los Angeles by a commuter plane and then we took Jumbo from Japan Airlines. The weekend in Mexico should be cancelled, but it is okay, we just move on. Leo and I just talked to Junior; it was 5 AM in Brazil. Figure how happy Antifuro was to start the day that early!! Miss you a lot, kisses, Beco."

And then, I received the following letter:

① Tokio , 20/10/87   5:30 P.M. Tokio
                            5:30 A.M. Brasil

Hello Beto,
     Acabamos de chegar de Los Angeles
e estamos aqui no aeroporto a espera de
um vôo de conexão.

     Tenho vontade de ligar a você
mas com certeza nesse horário (5:30 a.m. Brasil)
o mínimo que ia acontecer é passar
um susto grande em seus pais com o
telefone ao pé da cama !!! Acho que
seria uma foca !

     Como já mencionei antes em meu
cartão postal, liguei p/ o Júnior p/ tratar
de business, imagine o bom humor dele
as 5 da A.M. ... pelo menos o Leo
conseguiu ~~~~~~~~~ acalma-lo. Por falar
em Leo, o Sacana tem bebido tudo o que →

tem direito no Avião, o cara não
perdeu um Drink sequer.

Sabe, tivemos que levantar as
5:30 a.m. no dia seguinte da prova
de México p/ fazer esta viagem por
isso no momento estou Trebado de
Sono.

Como é, Dna Marilene já colocou
ordem na casa e todo mundo na
linha? Ela melhorou ou não o sistema
de "classe de ferida" após a viagem de
Portugal !! Aliás, veja lá como é que
você vai se comportar agora com
carreta aí pelas ruas... os pedestres e
postes que se cuidem !!! HA, HA, HA, HA !!!

(3)

Quer dizer que você ficou sem graça na noite em que viajei quanto te dei uns beijinhos na frente de minha mãe, ou até mesmo quando te peguei no colo?

Você fez o favor de pegar o meu bicho de pelúcia e não devolveu mais, eu o vi dentro de um plástico ao lado de sua cama, não é verdade?

Deixa, estou preparando-me psicologicamente p/ este mês de Dezembro, vamos botar pra quebrar, OK!!!

Tenho mais 1 mês de viagens pela frente e minha única motivação é p/ quando voltar poder desligar totalmente por mais de 1 mês, pelo menos até janeiro!!

Veja se vai tomando sol aí por nós dois, e agora com o carro nas mãos não tem desculpa p/ não ir a ginastica, quero só ver quando voltar...

A japonesada aqui na sala VIP do aeroporto enxuga um uisque Bravo, e Lás rica só no controle, quero dizer, tambem esta perseverando entrar no vácuo deles.

Olha que a sua prenga deu ter sido das boas nessa ultima vinda minha, por falar nisso, de agora em diante vou está impossivel, fica a adivinhar todas as minhas surpresas, assim não dá!

DRICA, to desabando de vontade de te escutar.

O mês só faz é falar nas pequenas compras que o mesmo está a planejar aqui no Japão, imagina só o tamanho do contrabando!!! Ainda bem que a mãe volta no mesmo vôo, não quero nem imaginar a Alfândega em S.P.

Faz tanto tempo que não escrevo uma carta que a cada palavra tenho uma dúvida quanto a acentuação.

Veja se não faz como eu e vai fugir da escola, pelo menos até eu repetir você, tá ???

Beijos, por quanto tempo a gente vai ficar nessa? Não encontro uma resposta.

Daqui a pouco isso aqui vai
virar um livro, esta vendo só, e
vou nem liga p/ mim! Imagine
se ligasse!

Quando é que passou pela sua cabeça
que ia encontrar um cara tão bobita,
gente fina, simpático, dedicado, carinhoso,
bonzinho, chega mesmo a ficar sem pala-
vras, tantas as qualidades ...

Olhe menina, Vou ficando por aqui
com muita saudade, mesmo sabendo que você
não liga p/ mim ...

Um beijo bem gostoso,
daqueles bem ...... Você já sabe!

"Tokyo, 10.20.87

Hello doll, we have just arrived from Los Angeles and we are here at the airport waiting for a connection flight. I really feel like calling you, but definitely at this time (5:30 AM, Brazil), the least it would happen is to scare your parents with the phone near the bed!! I think it would be bad! As I mentioned before in my postcard, I called Junior to talk about business, imagine his mood at 5 AM. At least Leo managed to calm him down. By the way, Leo has been drinking everything he can at the airplane, the guy does not refuse a drink. You know, we had to get up at 5:30 AM the day after the race in Mexico for this trip, so now I am sleepy as hell. Tell me, has Mrs. Marilene put the house in order and made everyone behave? Has or hasn't she improved her "Screwdriver" system after traveling to Portugal?! BTW, be careful with your behavior in the streets now with your license... pedestrians and lampposts need to take care!!! hahaha!!

So it means you were embarrassed the night I traveled when I kissed you in front of my mother, or when I put you on my lap? You grabbed my teddy bear and did not give it back, I saw it inside a plastic bag next to your bed, isn't that truth?

Drica, I am preparing my mind for this December, we will rock it, okay?!! I have one more month ahead traveling and my only motivation is to when I get back, I can relax completely for more than a month, at least until January!! Please sunbath for both of us, and now with the cars you have no excuse for us to go the gym, I want to see it with my own eyes when I get back...

The Japanese people here in the VIP room at the airport drinks a lot of whisky, Leo controls everything – I mean, he is trying to follow their examples. Your curse on me was probably a strong one on this last trip; by the way, from now on it will be impossible to guess all my surprises!

Drica, I am dying wishing to listen to your voice. All Leo talks about is the things he is planning to buy here in Japan, imagine the smuggling!! I am glad I will not come back on the flight with him, I do not want to think about the customs clearance in SP. It has been so long that I do not write letters that at every word I am unsure about punctuation. Please do not do like me, do not run away from school, at least not until I kidnap you, okay??? Doll, how long will we stay like this? I cannot find an answer. This will soon become a book, you see, and you do not even care about me! Imagine if you did! When did you imagine you would find such a nice, friendly, dedicated, affectionate, good guy? I am even speechless, so many qualities...

Look girl, I will finish it here, missing you a lot, even though I know you do not care about me... Sending you delicious kisses... Those that are really... you know! Beco"

The letter made it clear for me that Beco was sad and wanted to redeem himself for having hurt me, although unintentionally. Perhaps, it had been a disappointment for both of us. After all, until that moment, he did not imagine I did not know that also happened in Brazil. The distance, somehow, helped us to get around the situation and move forward. I really did not know what to think. All I knew was that I loved him too much.

At that stage, my sister Christhiane and Otávio got back together firmly, they liked each other so much! Otávio remembers interesting situations of when we went out together: They, Beco and I, during that time: *"She was even jealous of him, she said: I think you come to the farm more to fly with Otavio and Dadô than to be with me. He liked everything related to speed. When he realized Amilcar liked model airplanes too, he brought him a plane, I think it was one of the first four-stroke engines that came out; he won the heart of his father-in-law with the plane. But he was a very nice guy. Dri has always been very beautiful, she was a very young girl. Ayrton was an extremely playful guy; we played all the time. They were boyfriend and girlfriend, but we were always together, we always hung out together; their relationship was super light, they never fought, although she was jealous of him because he was too harassed and too exposed. She let it show when he arrived in Brazil, getting a bit peeved, upset, but about half an hour later she was normal again. Anyone could see that it was an affectionate relationship, with real feelings. It was every weekend: We spent Saturday and Sunday flying. On Saturday and Sunday*

408

evenings we went out to dinner or to some party or club, but in the afternoons, forget it, we would not do anything other than flying in the farm, a part of the headquarters even turned into a model airplane runway. When they knew that Senna was coming to Brazil, to São Paulo, the farm employee would cut the grass very short, because he knew we would spend the weekend flying, it was sure.

The coolest thing is that we did not pay any bills, but he did not like to go out very much because we could not talk and have dinner properly, people came to ask for autographs and to take pictures. He really was very harassed, and I said: Dude, it is perfect when we go out with you, because we do not pay any bills. Because every time we went out together, when paying the bill, the restaurant did not charge him. The restaurant owner came to ask for a photo and get an autograph and said: Not at all, you do not need to pay the bill, we will not charge you. The fact that Ayrton Senna was having dinner there and having his picture on the wall were worth it. We went out once — there were Reginaldo, Galvão Bueno and some people, I cannot remember them all —, I think it was at the Esplanada Grill restaurant, but we had a funny night talking a lot of nonsense.

We went to the Gallery, I do not remember the restaurants. Once, I remember we went to Ibirapuera Park, where there was a boat that was a nightclub; half an hour later we had to leave because it was such a harassment, such a tumult, that we could not stay there. I remember we talked about Nigel Mansel, who is a gear breaker at the end of the championship. At the end of the year, the mechanics took all the gearshift parts and made a sculpture and gave it to him as a gift, saying: This one was the part you destroyed this season. So, we had many really cool chats about the backstage of Formula 1.

Ayrton talked a lot about having friends and said: Otávio, I have a lot of people around me, but to be honest, not so

409

many friends, because my presence brings so much interest and I can never tell who my real friends are. As we had absolutely no interest, we ended up becoming very good friends.

He always got along very well with Dri's family, after he won Mr. Amilcar's heart, it was very easy."

On November 1st, Ayrton competed in the Japanese GP at Suzuka Circuit. He started in seventh and finished in second, after a nice reaction during the race, but Piquet won the '87 Championship with that race.

Before the Australian GP, he went to Bali to rest for a few days and called from the reception, because there were no telephones in the rooms at that hotel.

"Hi Dridrica., I am in Bali, this place is wonderful! I am going to stay a few days to rest, Bili is on a roll!"

"I am glad you guys came to an agreement and things are going well."

"You are right, the stress left right away, as soon as we got in Japan and Leo got fed up with buying computers and all the electronic paraphernalia he likes," and he started to laugh.

"What is it? What are you laughing about?"

"Nothing, Dridrica, it is just that I am talking to you here at the reception and some girls have now entered the hotel with their boobs exposed!"

"Good, then. Now go enjoy your stay, we talk another day. Kisses."

He could not stop laughing, but managed to say:

"I was caught by surprise! Calm down, Dridrica."

I am calm, kisses."

"Okay! I will be in Brazil real soon. Kisses."

Ayrton's last race for Lotus was at the Australian GP at the Adelaide Circuit, on November 15th. He started in fourth and finished in 10th, but was disqualified for irregularity in

the size of the brake pads. He finished the Championship in
third place with 57 points.

When returning to Brazil, Ayrton brought from Bali beautiful straw bags as a gift for me and my sisters. We went out to dinner with Reginaldo and Galvão one evening, and Otávio, who was with us (and my sister Chris), tells us some details about that day: "I remember the dinner with Reginaldo Leme, I have always liked him! Reginaldo knew a lot about Formula 1, really, a lot! I was his fan. This dinner caught my attention, we talked about a lot of things. At the time, Ayrton was at Lotus. By the way, it was his last year in the team, and we talked about his last races in Lotus, when he even ripped the nose off the car. He said: *Dude! I will tell you something: I think this was the race I had the most fun in my entire life. Because I did what I really wanted to do: I drove the car to the limit! I went on the grass, I did everything with the car, I ran over the kerbs, I finished Lotus up! By the time I reached the end of the race, Lotus was in shambles. It was the race I had the most fun! I did not stop doing anything I wanted to,* and we laughed together."

When Beco returned to Brazil this time, he and I were trying to identify where we would go from then on. He followed the routine we had created over the years as if nothing had happened, but we were both wary of each other, unsure how to resolve the discomfort caused by knowing he saw other women near me. Actually, I thought he was the one who should find a solution to that situation, if he really wanted to continue this relationship with me. When he had the opportunity, he said:

"Drica, I felt really bad after that day we said goodbye. I realized I made you very upset, I did not mean to hurt you."

I just listened to him and he added:

"Look, Dridrica, the truth is that, for some time now, when I go out with others, it is not fun anymore. I do not even feel like kissing them anymore and when it is over, I feel like leaving right away and not even looking at their faces. It obviously satisfies me as a man, but it is incomplete," he said in a tired voice.

I felt honesty in Beco's words, eyes and body expression and was, in a way, relieved. He knew we could not be together anymore the way we were before this event, and by this point, I knew I had to take a stand.

A few days after this conversation, we agreed to have lunch together and then go to the movies. I had told my parents I would be back in about four hours. As soon as we left my house, Beco said:

"Dri, will you go somewhere with me? Just for us to have some time together and be able to enjoy ourselves properly."

"Let's go!"

I was a little apprehensive, but I had been waiting so long for that invitation! I had turned eighteen and we were already so close, but I was not sure how to act in that situation. He said:

"Nothing you do not want will happen."

We went silently to the love hotel named "Studio A Motel". At the entrance, Beco asked me:

"Drica, can I have you ID?"

I quickly opened my purse (yes, after getting my driver's license and opening a bank account of my own, I carried my purse with my documents whenever I went). The receptionist, of course, recognized Ayrton and was looking at him and me systematically in the meantime. On our way to our bedroom, I asked:

"Beco! That is dangerous! These people know who you are and have my name! What if it leaks?"

"Calm down, Dridrica, they cannot say anything about their customers, or they would close. No one else would use a motel."

"Oh yeah, and with this very discreet car, in front of a love hotel, I am super calm!"

"Calm down, Dridrica! It will be okay." Once inside the room, he offered:

"Dri, shall we have something to drink to relax?"

"Yes!"

He opened the fridge there and told me the options the place offered. Among them, we chose the peach Keep Cooler, a type of sparkling rosé wine. It was great for relieving tension. But I was still acting like I was in the TV room at home — not seductive, as I was embarrassed by being in a love hotel for the first time. We do not need to go all the way through today.

"Drica San, come next to me, look, let's take it easy, whenever you want me to stop, just say so."

"Okay, Beco San," I replied sweetly.

Beco started kissing me and I let myself be led. First, he started with the caresses that were already part of our moments, and then he slowly undressed me. It was with him that I learned about my sexuality in a quiet and loving way. My first kiss and the discovery of foreplay was with him, but always very tenderly. I trusted him completely, and he said:

"Drica, I will put a condom on as a precaution, if it starts to hurt, I stop."

At first, it hurt too much, I signaled and he receded, I took a breath, we kissed again and started again calmly. We spoke in whispers, in a loving and passionate way.

Though painful, it was a bearable pain and we moved on, coming to blows. The first time, it hurt a lot, especially in the beginning. Then we rested for a while and he wanted it again. With each new thrust, it was more pleasurable to me. When Beco dozed over my body, I stroked him and his hair. With my lack of references on the subject, I figured that performance was natural and did my best to try to keep up with him, with the intention of satisfying who was now also my man. However, on the fifth thrust, I exceeded my limit. He held on to pleasure me but then I asked him to let it happen, because it was hurting too much.

I was more than ready for that moment, but I did not expect it to hurt. When we stopped, we lay side by side, looking at each other in the mirror on the ceiling, when he concluded:

"Yeah, Drica, we got along well out of bed for so many years, and now it went well in bed too," he said in a serious voice, maybe thinking about how our relationship would be from then on.

"You know, Beco, I really do not understand! The act itself is very good, but we already had pleasure together. I mean, we already had so much intimacy. I thought the act itself was something out of this world, and it is actually not. Of course, it was amazing, an extra, different pleasure. But I do not get why so much trouble over a hymen."

I really came to a climax with the actions we conquered throughout my time with him and, after giving myself in to Beco, I began to consider society hypocritical. A step further, which would bring greater responsibility, of course, but nothing to justify the taboo. After all, pleasure is pleasure with or without a hymen! He was quiet with his thoughts and I with mine about what had happened. However, that step would imply a change in our lives. He was giving up on his complete freedom, but if he did not take that step, it could ruin everything between us.

"Drica, let's take a shower, we have to go."

"Okay, Beco San."

We went into the shower together, but the water splashed on my hair and I ran away, I did not want to get my hair wet. I waited my turn, but I was not even going to use a soap, due to the paranoia of getting caught. My father had the habit of sniffing us when we got home.

He disguised that gesture as affection, of course! But he smelled us and it made me terrified. How would I get home smelling as I had just taken a shower, after so many hours out? We cannot be too careful.

414

Anyway, I believe I had a healthy experience at the beginning of my sex life. I had learned everything little by little, as I grew older, which allowed me to enjoy the man I loved and admired, who never forced anything and, at the slightest sign, receded. I had time to fall in love with his kiss, his smell, his skin, his hair, his caresses, his hands, his feet, his voice, his way of walking, his gaze... I loved everything about him. However, I felt that Ayrton was always making my Beco far away from me. Ayrton Senna even put our relationship at risk with so much harassment and greed on my Beco San. I wanted Beco for myself so bad. Forever! But Ayrton was always on the lookout and always took him away. All I wanted was for him to be a guy with a normal life. But every day he became not only famous, but also a world idol.

Beco took me home and we said goodbye. I had the feeling that everything had fallen into place wonderfully between us, and I went to sleep sore but happy with our secret.

The next day I woke up expecting to receive flowers. I thought his kindness to me, so intense and frequent, would be even greater now, after what had happened between us. But it was not quite like that.

That morning, even though I was sore, I went to school as usual, but I did not want to go back home. I decided to stop by my aunt Miriam's house, because I was too anxious to talk to Beco. As I did not use to look for him, he was always the one looking for me, I waited until around three in the afternoon. Too anxious to wait, I called him. He answered coldly. I was dying to see him and really wanted his support, as I did not have anyone else's support in this lonely decision to give myself to him before marriage. My family could never know that. When I said I wanted to see him, he replied coldly:

"Why, come here. I am at home. You have a license and now you can come."

"But I do not know how to get there. I do not know the region," I said, embarrassed.

"Get paper and pencil to write down the coordinates."

I did what he said. I wrote down the guidelines, all the streets and tips, turn here and there. It was in Santana, on the north side, and I had to cross the city to get there. There was no GPS at that time and I had my driver's license for only two months. I barely knew the city, since until then I had only been going to school or to my aunts' house. But I faced the challenge, because I really needed his support. I was sore and fragile. I found the street and I got to his house. They were all sitting on the porch steps of the house, Júnior, Beco, Léo, Mrs. Neyde and, if I am not mistaken, Mr. Milton too. I greeted everyone. Beco was polite in his response but showed no special affection.

My head kept spinning a mile a minute. After all, the day before, what we had been longing for had happened. But he was there, in front of me, indifferent. I curled up next to him and instinctively leaned into his chest for a hug. He hugged me mechanically — a reaction in response to my action. Therefore, about forty minutes later, I felt an enormous urge to cry. I felt that I was actually very alone in that whole situation. I had several unanswered questions at the time. Hadn't it been good? Hadn't I been able to satisfy him? And so, to regain my remaining dignity, I stammered:

"Guys, I need to go because I have an appointment. I just came by to say hi."

I said goodbye to everyone quickly, holding back my tears, and without looking back I headed to the car parked in the house's garage. I tried to act normally until I opened the door, because I did not want to let it show, especially in front of his parents. But I think Beco noticed. And I do not know if on his own initiative or because someone had said something, he came after me and leaned against the side of the car already on, with the gear engaged, and asked me to open the window:

"Dri, why are you leaving?"

416

"I do not know what I was doing here," I said with watery eyes, looking at him through the window. I closed the window not wanting to hear anything else and left, crying. I got home worried about not meeting anyone, because my face was swollen; my parents and family could not see me crying because they would want to know why. I spent the next few days withdrawn, feeling a mixture of regret, shame, sadness and fear. I had made the decision to take that step because I believed I would have his support, but I was actually alone.

A few days passed, we did not speak until he called me, knowing I was going to the farm for the weekend. I answered politely but listlessly; he included himself in the schedule saying he would meet us there, not offering to pick me up so we could go together, and I did not feel like going with him either. I did not even feel like talking to him. I tried to act naturally, but the weight in my heart did not let me breathe. The lack of attention and support on Beco's part buried me deep in my soul and hurt me more than the pain caused by the rupture of the goddamn hymen. And, in the midst of this crisis, something happened that clarified things.

We, the younger ones, were talking during that weekend at the farm, he took the opportunity of some subject and said looking straight at me:

"Yeah, but they say women usually bleed when they lose their virginity."

When he said that, it hit me. I do not remember bleeding during intercourse. Afterwards, yes, there was some bleeding, but nothing that would make a stain on the sheet. I even thought that little bloodstain was some bruise caused by the excessive activity. I was so offended and furious that I left the place in a huff. I went to the bedroom, away from everyone's eyes, I walked back and forth, thinking: "Who does Beco think he is? Distrust me like that? What an asshole!".

After I calmed down, I took a deep breath and walked back to where everyone else was. I interacted socially, but in a cold way, especially with Beco. It seemed there was now an impassable wall between the two of us. We no longer played under the table, rubbing our feet or making hidden caresses, and we barely spoke.

I remembered magazines with content considered to be "feminine" we had on the farm, handy, that addressed these taboo subjects at that time. I searched the magazines and found an article that dealt with the subject: Bleeding in the first intercourse. It spoke of the various types of hymen, and the different ways in which they were broken, truths and taboos. I kept the magazine to go to Beco when he was alone. I put the copy on his lap, opened on the article page and commented harshly:

"Look, before you think anything, it would be nice to learn first. And I always thought this virginity thing was important to me! Not to you!" I turned away and left.

I was too offended. I had had one more disappointment. The third in a row, actually. The first, when he said he went out with other women when he was near me, here in Brazil. The second, his indifference after such a beautiful and desired moment of surrender in the relationship of a couple who intended to build a future together. And the third, now, because he doubted me. I felt he wanted physical proof of my fidelity, as if everything we had lived through up to that point was just a bunch of lies. But how could that be possible when, in fact, I chose to preserve myself and, for that, I tolerated him being with others for so long? Why did he react so suspiciously and rigorously to me, the only virgin girlfriend he had had? It became clear that no matter how much I was dedicated to him, loyal, faithful and honest, it was never enough. I then realized the trap I had gotten myself into.

This virginity thing was painful for both of us, but now as a grown woman, I know it was much worse for me. It was my choice, but also, since the beginning, as I wanted to be a good daughter and never shame my parents, there was hypocrisy in the name of morals and good customs: One person to love and dream with, all the others to enjoy without feeling guilty!

Chapter XXI

After this new phase in our relationship, only at the end of November did the discomfort between us dissipated. He, softly and subtly, was regaining his place in my life.

One day, still in the garage at home, Beco said in a strainer voice:

"Drica, we need to be careful. I spoke to a doctor and he indicated this contraceptive here, look. It is the newest in the market and with fewer side effects. You said your mother never took you to the gynecologist, right? So, I took the liberty of consulting one, because we cannot screw it up."

I opened the medicine box, surprised, because after his cold reaction after our trip to the love hotel and the subsequent dubious insinuation about my virginity, I had not thought about it, I did not even know if we were going to move on. He said:

"Drica, you need to take this medicine for a while before we can do things without worrying, so we will keep taking other precautions until we are safe, okay?"

"Of course! Let's do it!"

After reading the indications for use and other additional information in the patient package insert, I understood I should start taking it the day after the seventh day of menstruation, one medicine per day from the pack with twenty-eight tablets; then I had to stop it for seven days and restart on the following day. I said:

"My God! What if my mom goes through my stuff? I have not even written down the details in the diary for fear of her giving a look..."

"Well, Dri, you are going to be careful with you mom and take the pill properly, otherwise it will not work!"

"Okay, Beco, I will be careful. It was good that you took the initiative. If my mother never bothered to take me to a gynecologist, it will not be now that I am going to ask for it, right?"

In fact, after we started with our private moments, more and more I had to lie to my parents and that was not easy for me! As the youngest, I learned to speak the truth to defend myself from any "manipulation games" from the others, and I spoke the truth even though I knew I could pay dearly for my mistake, but in this way, I gained my parents' trust and they believed what I said, especially when there were contradictions in a conflicting situation. I knew I had credit with them; I did the same at school with teachers and in my social relationships. I even tried to do everything right so as not to give any opportunities for treacherous people and avoid problems.

Now, however, it was a personal choice my parents would never accept. So I was in this alone. Beco would not lie for me; at most, he would omit. And the consequences of some mistake of mine would trouble me, not him! That was the price I was willing to pay for giving myself to him. So I would act as cautiously as possible to protect myself and would have to lie to those who loved me so much.

Porto Aquarius Hotel seen from inside the Corona vessel. Miguel Abdelnur ahead and Alexandre Abdelnur sitting at the back

On the left, Eduardo, Alexandre, Júnior, Yuta, Leonardo and Miguel

On the right, Mr. Milton and, at the back, my father hugging Gino,
Beco's friend

We spent the Eve at my maternal grandparents' house,
as a tradition, and we spent this year's Christmas lunch in the
ballroom of my aunt Nadia's building. Beco, as usual, met us
there for both celebrations, after celebrating with his family,

as my cousin Fernando recalls: "We used to spend Christmas at my grandmother's apartment, in São Paulo, and I remember Ayrton always stopped by to say hello."

Shortly afterwards, we went to Angra for New Year's Eve.

Our families, Senna da Silva and Rocha Yamin, spent the 1988 New Year's Eve together, in Angra dos Reis, at Hotel Porto Aquarius. From Beco's family, it was his parents, Mrs. Neyde and Mr. Milton, his brother Leonardo, a couple of Italian friends, Gino and Yuta — representatives of the brands Benetton and Sisley, in Italy — and Júnior. From mine, my parents, my sisters, Chris' boyfriend, my brother-in-law Eduardo, with his brother Alexandre, who we affectionately call Queco, and his cousin Miguel, who we call Migue.

Although Yuta did not speak Portuguese, she made herself understood and made an effort to understand everyone. With straight blond hair and blue eyes, she was an elegant, reserved and kind woman. Her husband, Gino, a pleasant, relaxed and polite man, soon became friends with my father.

Mrs. Neyde, my mom and Yuta got along very well! Mr. Milton, on this trip, seemed happy with the company.

During the day, the younger couples practiced water sports with the single boys. But in the evening, they joined the elders, while the single ones disappeared after the girls at the hotel.

Beforehand, I remember an episode in which Queco and Migue were diving with a tank, but without the necessary precautions. Queco's oxygen ran out suddenly, at a considerable depth. The consequence was that he had to go up faster than he should have, and thus the oxygen decompression in his bloodstream did not normalize due to the sudden difference in pressure (ATM) over his body. Migue, on the other hand, when realized his cousin's situation in the water, went up at the right speed, slower than the speed of the oxygen bubbled that came out of the equipment.

As soon as they pulled Queco out of the water, he started vomiting and, if my memory serves me right, one side of his body went numb. As a precaution, he was given acetylsalicylic acid (aspirin), which is a vasodilator, for him to take, and the boys ran to take him to a hyperbaric chamber that, luckily, was nearby in Angra. Then he could perform decompression again, normalizing the oxygen in his bloodstream. It was a great danger! When they returned with Queco already out of danger, the vessel's commander, Mr. Amilcar, decreed pointing his index finger at the sky as usual:

"No one else leaves this boat to practice scuba diving. Enough of it! Understood? What a danger, guys!"

After calming down, the boys returned to the many other activities available.

That year, only uncle Vidal's boat with his family and guests accompanied us everywhere. We made itineraries to beaches with crystal clear and calm waters, suitable for practicing our sports, such as Gipoia and Macacos beaches (where my father and Ayrton met at the end of 1984). We made the biggest mess on the beach: We would bring tables, chairs, barbecue grill, cooler and utensils to eat under the shade of some tree. At the time, those beaches farther away from the hotels were deserted, because there were not as many boats as there are today. We felt like that natural paradise was ours alone. I even imagined that, when Brazil was discovered, some galleons could have been in that same landscape. It was all wonderful: The presence of loved ones, the fun, relaxed and harmonious atmosphere among everyone, in that isolated place without any trace of human interference. Leonardo filmed our trip.

On the left, me, dad, Chris, Beco, Hagop with his daughter on his lap and his wife Regina, in the stern of their boat

On Corona vessel, Beco, Hagopinho, Regina and me

On this trip, we also came across the Hagop family and we stayed with them on some tours around the islands of Angra, as you can see in the photos above. But only now did I hear

425

of a conversation between Mr. Hagop with Ayrton on that occasion.

Hagop tells us: *"I asked him: Are you going to McLaren? He said: I am going to McLaren, and I have Alain Prost there. Nobody knows, I am a second behind him. Nobody speaks, everybody is holding the information. Grandpa is going to suffer a lot this year. We both laughed, and he was world champion in his first year at McLaren."*

A nuisance on this trip was that Beco attracted the attention of the single women who were at the hotel. The single men, in turn, took advantage of Beco's presence to attract this attention. Right from the start, Jacoto invited two girls to have dinner at our table with my sisters and brothers-in-law. The mood became terrible and I was infuriated by his audacity. Especially because he was our guest. So, after dinner I said:

"Júnior, I will ask you a favor: Do not mix your disorder with our family place. Do whatever you want with these girls, but away from us. And if you want to invite them to dinner, take a seat at another table, because, as you and Beco usually say, 'they opened the door of hell and kicked them off of there.' And there is more: If they take any bold attitude with Beco or any other engaged boy in the group, things will be dirty!"

I spoke to him quite annoyed but away from everyone. Beco had also noticed the embarrassing situation at dinner. It was as if Júnior wanted to bring his friend to the disorder of a single boy life, as it had been in the past. I was very clear with him, but the girls did everything to stay close. And we, women, stared them at these times to contain any boldness, like saying "be careful, we are watching you"!

When the whole group gathered, we went to uncle Vidal's boat, where supper would be served and we would celebrate the New Year.

New Year's Eve on the Santa Maria boat. On the left, Mrs. Neyde, me, Beco trying to tease his mother-in-law

During supper, me, Mr. Milton, mom, Lenise and Yuta

On the right, Tata, mom, Miltão, me, Beco, Záza and Chris, everyone
happy to celebrate that 1988 New Year together

On the left, Yuta, us, Gino (from Benetton) and mom

Family joy and love: On the right, Yuta, my sister Lenise, mom, dad and I enjoying the moment

The two of us, celebrating the New Year: Ayrton already with streamers wrapped around his neck

Us, dressed in my father's company's new product campaign shirt (four seasons), in the traditional boat procession in Angra dos Reis: Dad, Gino, Leonardo, Chris with her boyfriend, me, Beco and mom sitting

At the vessel flybridge, the sailor Toninho in charge and the single ones in the group, Queco, Migue and Júnior

It is also worth mentioning that Beco and I were more relaxed with the family, now holding hands in front of everyone and allowing ourselves to have spontaneous expressions of affection between us. It was as if we had completely untied the knots that had held us back for so long; he was mine and I was his. Of course, in those days, I also managed to sneak out to his room, and we also made out in hidden places we found within that crystal clear sea, on remote beaches. I felt like the protagonist of *The Blue Lagoon* movie; that was wonderful.

Barbecue on the beach: In a bathing suit, Záza next to her son

Yuta showing a lobster, Gino, Neyde, Milton and Marilene

My father in charge of the barbecue, Miltão, me and Gino

Another night, we were alone on the deck waiting for the group to gather for dinner, and Beco told me:

"Look, Dri, we have to talk. It is very important and we need to deal with it. Now we are really together, I would like to tell you that in case you happen to get pregnant, we have three possibilities…"

I interrupted him, annoyed and afraid of hearing him say something that would hurt me:

"Look! You can have as many possibilities as you want! For me, there is only one, with or without you!"

I immediately got up and walked away from him. There were many possibilities on his part, I was sure one of them would be an abortion and I would not accept that. Therefore, I took a stand quite clearly and decisively. He never brought it up again, which confirmed my suspicion. He silently accepted my position and I was very upset with him for even considering such a possibility. After all, we had been talking about marriage for some time and I just had to finish another year of high school so we could define our future. I did not deserve that! It seemed like I did not know him anymore and felt that sometimes he treated me like I was a different person.

I was confused and did not get why Beco seemed to try to drive us away. I accepted him having sex with other women while I was not ready to take that step. I was the same person from the beginning of our relationship and I had always been by his side, despite all the difficulties. Why this attitude towards me now?

In fact, it was like he was feeling the weight of the commitment for being with me, the other side of the coin. He wanted so badly to be with me, but now he did not seem to want to give up his freedom. We were not scheduled to be married, and I tried not to have expectations about it, but he knew I was held hostage by the situation he had put me in — that is, in his hands. He started acting like I had done something wrong. I kept it all to myself, hoping he would be the person I loved so much again. I avoided thinking about the future to enjoy the good times, as if they were the last.

Ayrton returned to São Paulo with his parents one day before the group and left Júnior in Angra, in charge of pulling the speedboat in the trailer. When we were leaving, Júnior and I were sitting with some of our group at a table on the hotel's pier waiting for everyone to come back for us to gather, when he suddenly opened a note next to me to read. I saw it was for Beco.

"Júnior, what is this note?"

"No, it is nothing, Dridrica," he said, hurriedly bending the note.

"It is nothing? It is addressed to Beco, I saw it! And will you be the carrier pigeon? Whose note is this?"

"Oh, Drica, they told me to hand it to Becão, that is all!"

"Oh, that is all? So give it to me and I will give it to him, since it is no big deal!"

"Listen, they gave it to me to hand it to Beco himself and that is what I am going to do."

"Gosh! So much loyalty to the slut who gave you that note! Ah, excuse my indiscretion. After all, I am just Beco's girlfriend. And you, a fair-weather friend, will give this shit to him. From a whatshername? So loyal! She must be very important to you."

"No, Drica, it is no big deal..."

"All right then! Give me the note and I will see if it is no big deal!" I said, intimidatingly, holding out my hand.

"Okay, Drica!" and handed me the note.

I read it and I hit the bull's-eye! Last attempt by a slut to get close to my boyfriend. With a poem, phone number and everything. I tore up the paper right away, threw the pieces on him and said:

"Damn it! I did not expect that from you. What the fuck? I bet it is one of the little friends you took to dinner with us. Holy shit! So you are Beco's loyal friend, but you are not my friend? Because this is not something a friend does, man! All these years I thought we were friends!"

I lectured Júnior because I really did not like his attitude and I mentioned it to Beco as soon as I got to São Paulo.

"Listen, Beco, I did not like Júnior's attitude. I thought it weird that he opened a woman's note right next to me, it seemed he wanted me to see it. And more, does he want to tease you with women? Is that right?"

"Calm down, Dridrica! He was stupid, I agree."

"Look, I have my eye on him! It is like he wants to sabotage us. I did not forget he brought those girls to have dinner with us at our table. A lack of respect for me, my family and yours! Now that? I think it is time you had a little chat with him. He is single, but you are not! It is not easy for me to withstand the harassment when we are together, now Júnior makes it worse?"

"You are right."

"I am very upset, he has always been welcomed by everyone in my house, treated well. What the hell is he up to? Causing problems between us?"

434

"Let it go, Drica San! It was not that serious and it did not make any difference. I understand you and I will talk to Antifuro. Do not worry."

Obviously, as a result of Jacoto's regrettable behavior, Beco tried to avoid his contact with us and began to take better advantage of his friendship with his brothers-in-law.

Right after we got back from Angra dos Reis, Beco and I went to Chapadão farm with my whole family. We spent the January holidays together again, but at that time it was an uninterrupted fortnight on the farm. Of course, there, under the surveillance of so many people, it was a little more complicated to find a way for our escapes. But we did it.

The biggest problem that year was that, more than in previous years, I suffered in anticipation when thinking about the start of the F1 Championship. Beco and I were very attached. We saw each other every day, even after we got back from Porto Feliz. In São Paulo, if he wanted to spend the day with his family, he would take me with him, but we barely stopped in São Paulo until my classes started again. In Guarujá, São Carlos, Ilhabela, a lot of places to go.

When my father told me that his extensive cattle ranch, in the state of Pará, had the infrastructure finished for handling cattle, Beco, excited by the conversation, suggested that we went with his plane, to spend a few days there. They arranged everything between them, and then we went: Beco, I, obviously my father and my mother, plus Mr. Jarli, an uncle of my father's. We all had to vaccinate against yellow fever to go there, as a precaution, since the farm was almost Amazon Jungle.

Beco had planned this, to help defuse the discomfort of our recent mishaps. That is how things were worked out among us: With attitudes. That was good because it made discussions between us rare, however, there were already new situations that needed to be said and clarified, whether we liked it or not.

We flew from São Paulo to the airport in Marabá, the closest to the farm, to get off a jet plane (Learjet), and drove to our final destination for another two hours on paved road. We passed close by the famous Serra Pelada, a large gold deposit that was in full swing at the time, bringing some movement to the region. Nearby, along the road, we passed by the closest village to the farm and which provided some supplies for the miners, called Bafo da Onça. A very precarious and improvised place.

First, we went to the farm of friend and neighbor Maurício Fraga, who also helped supervise the work on my father's farm. We went there to drop off the English pilot of Ayrton's plane and uncle Jarli, because on that farmhouse there were not enough rooms for everyone.

Upon arrival, we were welcomed with joy by the Fraga family. My father was updated on the news with Maurício and arranged a meeting to see some installations around the farm. Meanwhile, his wife offered us some of the typical local treasure, which is exported all over the world — the well-known Brazil nut — as a gesture of kindness. She offered one by one to whoever was sitting inside her living room. We all accepted, and the only one who did not know it was the English pilot. Curious, he decided to try it and his face showed that he liked it a lot. That was it! Beco, realizing that, playful as he was, encouraged him to eat more and more for the time we stayed there. He knew that, although delicious, it was a nutrient-rich, high-calorie food and that, given the amount the pilot ate, he would definitely have a stomachache. Beco was amused by the Englishman innocence. We said goodbye and continued our trip to our destination, and throughout it, the Englishman and the nut were the joke, because we were already imagining the poor guy with a stomachache.

We arrived at my father's farm in the late afternoon, with a hot weather typical of regions closer to the equator. The house was made entirely of wood from the region, a stilt house that was close to the river that, during the rainy

"I know that, but do not take any chances with that kind of prank anymore, okay, Beco San?"

"Deal, Dridrica."

There was an arbor near the house, covered with thatch and a concrete structure on the floor and on the low walls that circled that hexagonal space, along with wooden-log columns scattered all around it, to give enough space for the hammocks between them. It was the perfect place to be at night with Beco under an amazing sea of stars, like those we only see in the planetaries. It was the perfect place to have a little fun, exchange caresses and chat. Those were rare moments of peace and quiet alone, when we did not want to talk about anything important that would ruin such a good moment for us, hugging each other in that hammock, contemplating the stars. I think that is what love is all about: Being with someone and doing absolutely nothing and still feeling incredibly happy. Too bad our time there was limited, we had to turn off the generators before bed, but we stayed there as long as possible.

Nearby, the houses of the employees who worked on the farm were neatly lined up and similar to ours, but smaller.

What impressed me was that, in the middle of the Amazon Forest, a place with jaguars, big monkeys, alligators and all the wild animals that exist in Brazil and live in our tropical forest, even the open grasses had a quote of natural preservation, of native jungle, proportional to the size of the pastures distributed by the farm, to preserve the local fauna and flora. I found it funny that, despite having frequented our farm my whole life, there, care and precaution were much higher. I was used to watch out for snakes and spiders, but with alligator in the river, on the side of the house... never! It tasted like adventure to me, wild life.

We rode a horse one day, to make a general reconnaissance of how the farm was — there were no access roads inside it, we had to go on horses —, Beco and I went because we were nosy. After a long walk, we came to clearing in the woods, where there was an unlit fire and the remains of a monkey on it — intruders did that. We had the company of the farm foreman and an armed guy, for our safety, because of the wild animals and because this was a lawless land. We were told that mainly because of the gold in Serra Pelada near there and far from everything, things were solved with guns. We decided to go back, afraid that the intruders were still holed up in the woods watching us. This was a matter my father would deal with the proper authorities, not with guns! We also came back, because Mr. Amilcar, averse to the practice of sports, who used to drive everywhere in Porto Feliz and would barely walk, could not wait to get off that horse. We took a different path on the way back, through the pastures.

We ate fresh fish every day — leather fish, as scaleless river fish are called. Its meat was wonderful, it was similar to chicken breast in consistency and flavor, all very well fried, rice, beans, fried manioc flour. Delicious. We were on vacation and it was not a place to worry about our diet, neither we had enough time to teach the cook how to prepare it differently; all I know is that she took great care to please us, with everything we were entitled to! Everything had to be fresh, because there was no energy to store the food in the fridge — we did not have electric energy twenty-four hours per day. In fact, I do not remember much about the kitchen, which was on the same side as the bathroom, with a side table, a sink and a stove, no appliances. A half-open place for ventilation.

The next day, we decided to go fishing, Beco and I. We waited for the sun to go down a little to relieve the heat. We got into a reasonably structured aluminum motor boat. An employee accompanied us as a guide, experienced in fishing, seated in the back, me in the middle and Beco in the front. He already had the appropriate rods and baits for our endeavor. I had not seen any alligators yet, so I asked, as we went down the river:

"Sir, is it true that there are alligators around here?"

"It is! But they do not attack us. Just do not mess with them."

"So there is no danger?"

Not at all! Just keep an eye out."

"But I have not seen any yet."

"They are out there!"

The river was about five meters wide, and as we ran along it, its length varied. There came a point where intertwined branches almost completely obstructed our passage to continue down the river; it was really beautiful. Beco and I were delighted to be in the middle of the jungle, as we saw in the movies, in such a remote place. Our guide, experienced, asked us to bend down and showed us where there was room for the canoe to pass through the branches. We managed to pass slowly, bending down to the height of the sides of our little boat, and then we came face to face with a wider stretch of river, like a naturally dammed area, and that was where we would fish.

The fisherman guided us in the tricks to catch the fish. When everyone was ready, we were silent and concentrated on the line. Unfortunately, we caught a small fish, but we did not give up. In that peace, that silence, just hearing the sound of the bird around us, Beco unintentionally farts. This happened very rarely, I had already seen it during a tennis match, but he managed to hide it and I pretended not to hear. Poor man, but that day, he himself did not even believe; as the boat was made of aluminum, the vibration of the sound reverberated throughout the boat, even forming small ripples in the calm water around us; as for volume, the boat also acted as a megaphone. I held myself for a few seconds, but this time I could not. What a situation! I burst out laughing unstoppably! In the beginning, Beco laughed too; the man who accompanied us tried not to laugh for as long as he could, pretending he was not there, out of respect for that important and famous man. I tried to stop laughing, I promise, but the scene came back to my mind and I could not control it and I started to cry again with laughter, even though I saw Beco was now embarrassed. Then he said:

"Enough, Adriane! You already laughed, had fun!"

"Sorry, Beco, I will stop..." I replied, trying to catch my breath.

I think it was the only time he called me by my name! That was it, all that was needed was that silence and concentration... the scene came back to my mind and I laughed again, and I said while laughing:

"Beco San... I am sorry! I do not mean bad. It was awesome! I think you scared off all the fish in the area."

He could not hold it back and laughed with me again:

"Well, I see we will not be able to fish anymore today," he laughed. "It is time to head home!" he said, giving up on our fishing and making fun of himself.

And I kept laughing about it all. I recently learned that this story is remembered in that region to this day. The life of famous people is hard!

When we got close to the disembarking place, it was already the end of the day, the sun was no longer visible on the horizon, hidden by the trees. We disembarked, and the man called us:

"Wait a minute!"

He picked up a powerful flashlight and pointed it to the opposite side of the river.

"Do you see some sparkles on the riverbank? Well, then! It is the alligator's eyes!"

He directed the beam of light everywhere, and you could see the reflection of light in the eyes of the alligators. Of course, he only showed me this at the end, so I would not get scared before fishing.

We enjoyed together our last night in peace under that amazing sky! The next day, we left for our trip back, right after breakfast. We picked up the pilot, who was already feeling better and properly uniformed. Although grateful for the care of those who hosted him, he was eager to get back to civilization.

I believe this trip was a once-in-a-lifetime opportunity and even today it makes me feel very privileged to have lived such an experience; I am grateful for that. I never again had the opportunity to return to that paradise, where my sisters, for example, had never been.

In my family, and I believe in most families we know, everything is more complicated to happen, but while I had Beco in my life, everything seemed possible and we had no whining: If we wanted something and we had means for it, this was enough to do anything or go anywhere. I miss him a lot in my life because of this too, for the thirst for life he had and which I have too.

During that January vacation, we also went to Guarujá. Some acquaintance of Dadô took his parachute — that type that is pulled by the handle of a speedboat — for us to play, and Beco had taken his to complete the adventure. It was midsummer, but it was not a sunny day, it was likely to rain, the beach was almost empty, which made it possible to circulate the speedboat near the beach without any danger, and there was space in the sand to put the parachute open and in position. It was teamwork: On land, to make the takeoff of one person possible, we needed the help of two more to open and hold the parachute in a takeoff position. The sea at Enseada beach, usually with calm waters, was atypically agitated. I believe only one of the guys managed to fly that day. I followed Beco on the speedboat, stopped where the cable would have enough reach to the takeoff site to pull the person out of the sand on the beach. This necessary distance placed us at the point where the waves break, and we shook inside the boat. A somewhat risky and tiring maneuver; Beco struggled to keep it in the proper place, until we were signaled from the beach that the adventurer was ready and in position, then we sped up the speedboat and got it off the ground.

And so it was a success. On the flight, we rode it for a while so that the person who was at the top could enjoy the view from above. But unfortunately, the game did not last long, because the speedboat was struggling to navigate at enough speed to keep them flying. When the game was over, we gave up on trying again in those weather conditions, leaving some of us frustrated, including me, who excitedly awaited my turn.

While on land, they collected the parachute, Beco moved away from the surf area as a safety measure and started the procedure to collect the cable. My father's yacht was parked at the far end of the beach, as usual, with all my family and within our reach. When all the arrangements had been completed, Beco jumped on me in a passionate kiss. I was sitting beside the driver's seat and I returned the so-welcome kiss with the same passion. On an impulse, he pulled me firmly to the floor, seeking protection from view by the edges of the speedboat and we made love right there. It was breathtaking! And even with our bodies still numb with ecstasy, we looked at each other with wide eyes, a little scared, afraid of being seen. Then, we took a deep breath and jumped up to take the speedboat to my father's boat. I admit that, before I got up, I looked out towards the yacht to see if anyone was watching us from a distance. Unable to see any suspicious movements, I got up and, along the way, I thought about what to say, in case anyone had noticed something. As soon as we approached, I quickly jumped into the sea because my body was dry and, if they said "we saw the boat but we did not see you," I would be wet and say: "We stopped to take a dip in the sea."

I was always alert and under pressure from both sides. I wanted to enjoy and help one, without getting into trouble with the other.

One day that summer, when we were at Beco family's house in a quiet dolce far niente, he decided to cut his hair. It

444

was a weekday, just before nightfall, and I went with him. The hairdresser worked on the top floor of a townhouse on the same avenue as his house. On the ground floor there was a business place. Beco told me that whenever he was in Brazil, he cut his hair there and he did not even instruct the hairdresser about the cut he wanted. By the way, I noticed by the lively conversation that they knew each other for a long time. When we left, in the car, I commented:

"Beco, don't you think it is time to go to a good hairdresser? One who knows how to shape your wavy hair? You are a public person; don't you think you should take better care of your appearance?"

I said without the slightest affectation, just meaning that Beco could improve a little his look, because I knew of his pragmatism in simplifying life.

"Okay, Dridrica, next time you take me to one you trust. I do not know about these things! I usually ask them to cut it really short so I do not have to worry about it when I am away."

I confess I was a little remorseful of "stealing" the former, illustrious customer from that hairdresser and I added:

"Beco, I can take you without problems, but if you do like the cut, you cut here with your friend again," I said, to relieve my conscience.

"Okay, Dridrica!"

Afterwards, I took him to the salon we used to go — my whole family, including aunts and cousins. It was one of the most famous in São Paulo at the time, and Beco's mother and sister also became customers at that salon. I chose the hairdresser who knew me since I was little and who always handled my mother's hair. My sisters and I would eventually go to the salon because we have straight hair that is easy to care for, but mom was always there! This hairdresser had recently prepared all my family's hair for my sister Lenise's wedding, including the bride. So, I bet she would be able to help with Beco's look. He approved the result and became her customer here in Brazil.

But it reminded me that, once in England, Beco was with hair and could not wait to get it cut. He went to the first salon that crossed his path and was attended by a woman. While cutting his hair, to start a conversation, he asks the hairdresser, noticing she had a very round belly.

"How many months are you pregnant?"

The woman stopped cutting his hair for a moment and replied:

"I am not pregnant."

He laughed his ass off telling this story. He said he spent the rest of the time afraid of what she would do to his hair after his faux pas and that he would never again ask a woman if she was pregnant.

Beco, from time to time, started to give his opinion about my outfit. He said "why don't you use this?" or "why don't you use that?". I tried to understand exactly what he wanted to know which style he liked the most.

I remember he said:

"Dridrica, I like those long skirts people wear, which do not leave your body so exposed but let my imagination run."

So one day I suggested:

"If you want me to dress differently, let's go to the mall with me so you can show me what you like!"

And so we went to Ibirapuera mall, in São Paulo.

Mrs. Valdivina, owner of the Colours by Valdac chain, remembers that day:

"They arrived in the morning, around 10 am. I walked into the store and one employee was attending to Adriane. When I walked into the dressing room and saw her, I thought: 'Wow, what a beautiful woman!'. Then the cashier called and said: She is Senna's girlfriend, Ayrton Senna!

Is she Ayrton Senna's girlfriend?!, I said incredulously.

She is!, the employee confirmed. That was when I saw Senna and said:

Hi Ayrton, nice to meet you! I am crazy for you! I love your elegance. A man with a good posture.

As the mall was still quite empty due to the time, shopkeepers started to come to my store to see Ayrton Senna, and so I did not let anyone bother. I said:

Nobody is going to bother the man. He is here with his girlfriend, leave him alone!

I pulled the curtains on one of the dressing rooms and invited him there. So he grabbed two linen coats and a pair of shorts and took them to Adriane to try them on.

Ayrton had said, when he entered the store, that he wanted to buy two or three pieces of clothing, but ended up buying ten because the clothes fit her very well. I told him I found Adriane very beautiful.

But he seemed shy to me, he did not speak much and spent most of his time fiddling with his car keys.

I asked him to give me an autograph and he promptly said:

Sure, now!

But I replied:

Calm down, let's solve your problem first.

When I talk about that day, I can see the image of Ayrton, cute, skinny and fiddling with his car keys. I could not believe Senna was right there in front of me. He found beautiful everything Adriane put on. I will never forget I gave her a pair of pants to try on and he asked her to put the shorts on, which were better to use in Angra, it was amazing on her.

In fact, when I called him to see Adriane, he said: It is beautiful, Drica.

So I put a lot of clothes for her to try on!

I realized that that couple had future, she was a serious person, I felt their relationship was serious, and that was also why I preserved him from harassment. I asked if he wanted to see anything else, and Ayrton replied he had seen everything,

447

that he had to go because he had to travel. Then he told me to calculate the price and I said:

This price. Your sister and mother are my customers at Center Norte Mall. They like the sewing at the store because everything is done right, well sewn.

I asked if he did not want to confirm with them, but he said he believed me. I added:

Ayrton, you are a knowledgeable man, you must like my clothes!"

He replied:

What I do not like is the prices! he laughed.

I then told him he would have ten percent off the purchase price, and he said:

Oh no, ten percent is too little!

But that is nothing compared to what you earn! You earn this value very easy!

But he insisted:

No, nobody is rich here! Everyone works hard.

I found him very humble, very cute! Later, when my children arrived at the store, I told them Ayrton Senna had been there and they did not believe me. I told them he was with a beautiful woman, with long hair, and I showed them his signed check. I also showed the autograph he gave me on the store card, written: To my friend Vina, thank you very much, Ayrton.

I could not believe it, I even put it in a frame. Due to fate, years later, my daughter Denísia became very good friends with Adriane and they are still friends today."

The thing is, the skirt he wanted me to wear was not available in that store collection. Still, he bought two lien suits and another piece of clothing, just because of how friendly the owner Vina was with us — today a dear lady, for whom I have great affection.

Chapter XXII

During our vacation on the farm, my parents suggested that Christhiane and I go to Switzerland to ski with my cousin Patrícia, who was very sad about her father's tragic death in July of the previous year. I arranged for the date of the trip to be a little before Beco returned to Europe, so, for the first time, I would leave before him and I hoped this would make me suffer less with our separation.

We traveled at the end of January and when I said Beco goodbye, I noticed he was a little sad. I knew well what he must be feeling with the emptiness of my departure. He came with us to the airport and saw me embarking to an incredible place, in which he was not included, feeling the pain of those who stay behind.

In the flight, we became friends with a boy named Riva whose destination was very close to our ski resort. We were lucky because when we landed in Switzerland, no one from our hotel was waiting for us at the airport.

Then our adventure began.

From the airport, we took a train. However, we had three giant suitcases and the car was old and narrow, thankfully it was empty. When we arrived at the indicated station, we got off with the suitcases that, at that time, did not have wheels. But Riva and a friend of his kindly helped us and offered us a ride to the place where we were supposed to take a tram-car to the ski resort.

Riva's car was compact and, I do not know how, the two boys managed to fit the bags and the three of us in the vehicle. In the next photo, my sister and I taking the suitcases out of the car:

Christhiane and I (on my back) and the suitcases next to the car, with the boys who gave us a ride

The three of us could not believe the mess he had gotten ourselves into in the middle of the European winter. The tram was for transporting skiers and had open sides with wooden benches. And we were almost freezing cold as the tram gained altitude. When disembarking, we had to step on soft snow to get to the hotel because there was no path, no trail. We laughed so as not to cry! I could not believe that my father, who had made a point of booking a five-star hotel even for security reasons, had forgotten to plan the logistics to get there. But when you are young, everything is an adventure.

The next day, we arranged the classes and rented skis. As Patu had never skied, we stayed with the teacher on the easiest slope and close to the hotel. But she quickly got the hang of it and, on the other days, we went skiing on other slopes. On that trip, Chris and I, with the instructor accompanying us full time, really learned to ski with parallel skis and really improved the technique. We did this all day long! We also met at the hotel a Brazilian guy who worked there as an intern in hotel management who gave us tips about the area.

However, I noticed something strange about me. When I felt like peeing, I had to run to the end of the slope where the hotel was, because it was really difficult to hold it. But when I got to the toilet, I realized that my bladder was not very full.

On the third day of my trip, Beco called me at the hotel:

"How are things there, Dridrica? Are you behaving well?"

"Look, now you are the one who must have cursed me!"

"Why?" he asked and laughed his slow laugh. I told him about our journey to get to the hotel and concluded:

"I am missing you so much! I wish you were here with me."

"Why, you did not tell me to go!"

"I know, but it is just that I thought that traveling to a place where I would have distractions, the pain of our separation would ease. It is no easy, after we have stuck together for so long."

"Oh, yeah!"

"But coming here did not solve the problem. I miss you a lot. Please, come!"

"Oh, well! I could go, before. But now, just like that, I need to see what I can do."

"Are you coming?" I asked in surprise.

"I will see what I can do! I already planned to go with my plane to Europe this time. So I leave the plane there all year round. And I invited Viviane and Lalli for this trip. I have to fix the logistics; I will try to anticipate."

"Bring them along! They will not think it is a bad idea coming here."

"Dridrica, you just get me in trouble!" I laughed and said:

"Come, Beco San! I am waiting for you, missing you."

"Okay, I will call you later to let you know. Kisses!" he said goodbye excited.

"Kisses, Beco San."

The next day he called again.

"Hi, Dridrica, are you ready? I am coming!" he said excitedly.

"Really? Did you manage to organize everything?"

"Of course, Dridrica! What can I not do for my needy one?"

"I cannot believe it. Come quickly!"

"I will, the day after tomorrow I will be there. Too bad, we could have enjoyed it more if you had called me before, right young lady? I will arrive, spend the whole day there and the next day I will have to leave because of the professional appointments I have scheduled."

"I cannot even believe it; come quickly, Beco San!"

"I am coming, Drica San. I will be there real soon!"

Two days later, Ayrton, his sister and brother-in-law Lalli arrived at the hotel in the afternoon, very tired from the trip. In the evening, I had dinner with Beco's family, in one of the hotel's restaurants, where they served fondue and raclette, accompanied by onions and boiled potatoes. Their fondue was made of meat, but in water, an unattractive thing, but we took it bravely.

It was the first time I spent some time with the only part of the family I hadn't had any contact with yet. Lalli was very friendly! With the conversation conducted by Viviane, with subjects I did not know about, I was a little apart, did not participate much, but the evening was very pleasant.

After dinner, we passed by an arcade machine, and Beco perked up because it was a car racing game. For a couple who had already played slot games together on the farm and Atari at aunt Nadia's house, that was perfect for us:

"Yay! Let's play it, Dridrica?"

"Let's go!"

And off we went after the tokens for that machine like two excited children:

"You go first, Dridrica"

452

In my turn, he was co-pilot:

"Go, Dridrica! Be careful! Overtake him! Now accelerate!"

After my turn, we both paid close attention to my result and he started to play. I just watched, because I would not dare give my opinion to the master of tracks.

"What a bloody game!" he complained, unhappy.

His score had been lower than mine.

"What a crap of a game! It has nothing to do with a car," he said.

"Beco, I have always played in arcades and I am more used to this kind of game. Of course, it has nothing to do with a real car," I said, unable to hold back my laugher.

He was annoyed. He was so competitive that even in an arcade game he wanted to win. We went to his suite together, but I would have to go back to my room soon. The girls had gone out to dinner with a new Brazilian friend and would be back soon.

The next day, Beco and I had breakfast with Chris and Patu. He had never skied and, by contract, was forbidden to do so. Still, he wanted to venture out. We rented the equipment while the girls headed to the ski slope:

"Dri! We are going, because the teacher is waiting for us near the ski lift."

"Go ahead, I will stay with Beco on the beginners' slope."

I then gave him some tips while the equipment guy defined the most suitable boot and type of ski for him:

"You will also need gloves, glasses and a hat to keep warm from the cold."

After Beco put on the boots and with the ski in hand, I guided him on the basics:

"Listen, before we go to the slope, put on your hat and leave your glasses on top; do not pick up the ski blades without gloves, there may be splinters, it is fiberglass and they are scratched from use; you'd better close the boots only when you fit the skis, when we are at the base of the slope; otherwise, it is harder to walk there, okay?"

"Okay, Dridrica, let's go. Positive and effective!"

Although he was talented in water skiing, snow skiing requires another kind of body balance, and Beco would have only that day to practice. So I tried to share what I knew and told him to watch me first. At the base of the slope with the equipment properly prepared, I kept a certain distance between the skis in parallel, flexed my knees and held the two poles in one hand to grab the poma pole (the ski lift seat) with the other to climb to the top of that slope, which would tug us to the top.

Beco took the poma and climbed the mountain right behind me. At one point along the way, we passed through some trees before reaching the top and we felt ripples in the snow, already compacted under our feet; it was a somewhat slippery place. After passing through that place, I observed him going. He fell. I let go of my poma before completing the journey to help him.

I helped him get into position to catch another poma that was passing and, as soon as he moved on, I did the same. When we reached the top of the slope, at the end of that poma, we went down. We stopped side by side for some more basic explanations:

"We are going to zigzag down, so we can control the speed on the way down. If you go straight, you will be too fast, you can fall and get hurt, so feel the movements little by little, but always keep your skis across the slope of the trail, feel the dynamics of the snow under your skis and use it to your advantage, avoid shiny icy-looking spots on the trail, because you can slip on them. If you cannot turn and start to be too fast on the way down, you wedge it like this so you can stop. But turn your shoulder to the underside and your skis into the snow, with an opposite force, to make resistance against the snow; if you leave the skis parallel, you will slip. Got it?" I made all the movements while explaining so that he

454

could visualize the dynamics between the ski, his body and the snow. He, as a good sportsman, would only have to re-educate his movements.

"Let's do it, Dridrica!" he said excitedly.

He came down cautiously and rather clumsy, trying to put into practice everything I said. He ended up tipping over a few times as he climbed, always in the same place on the path of the ski lift. I chuckled so he would not get mad at me, but the cool thing was to see his persistence. He went down a bit staggering, which was normal, because the balance required in snow skiing was different from what he knew in water skiing, and when he reached the base of the trail, he spoke excitedly:

"Dridrica, I will be soon mastering it! Let's do it again."

Seeing his reactions, looking like a child having fun, and loving him so much, I encouraged him, because I was sure he would learn very quickly:

"You just need to improve your technique. You go first now."

And off we went again at the poma. But he fell again on the same spot where he had fallen on the first time. He cleared the path, crawling through the snow so I could pass, and said a little irritated with himself:

"You go! I handle myself!"

And so it was several other times.

I no longer interfered with anything, only if asked, so that he would feel more comfortable. I noticed he was handling well and safely, so each one was at their own pace on that trail considered easy and suitable for beginners.

Beco and I had dinner together at the hotel, still in ski clothes, in a lively conversation about the day's adventures. His sister and brother-in-law preferred to eat in their room. I accompanied Beco to his room and we made love in that cold weather.

After that, I dressed up in an automatic attitude, but decided to lie a little longer next to him. He fell asleep.

Someone knocked on the door and I answered it. It was my sister, a little annoyed because she needed the key to our room that I had, and I had forgotten about that. I told her I would stay just a little longer there with Beco and then go back to our suite.

I snuggled back down carefully next to Beco, who continued in a deep sleep. I knew he needed to rest, but I did not want to leave, we were going to separate in a few hours and it would take some time for us to meet again. So I wanted to use that time to stay close to him a little longer. As I enjoyed the moment, I also thought about how much I would miss him and that I did not owe my sister an explanation! I stayed, stayed, and ended up napping. When it was already dawn, Beco woke up scared and, realizing I was there, he said, still dazed with sleep:

"Drica, wake up! Are you still here? What will your sister say?"

"Beco, I do not owe her an explanation!"

"But won't she tell your parents?"

"She would not dare!"

"Wow! If you had said before you would spend the night with me, we would have slept better together. But now I think you better go."

"I had no intention of staying. Holy crap! We always have to run out of places because of others, we never have the opportunity to spend the night together," I said weeping, "I was thinking about that tonight and I do not give a fuck about what Chris will think. I cannot take it anymore!"

A little confused by my unprecedented posture, Beco said sweetly:

"Dri you better get back to your room."

"Damn it!"

Even though I understood his reasons, I left frustrated with that whole situation. Both with the control we were subjected to and with the responsibility that rested on Beco's shoulders. After all, he was afraid of losing the trust he had gained with my parents. But I was even more irritated with myself, for not having decided to spend the night with him on that occasion, which would guarantee me to sleep close to him, after so long dreaming of the day that would happen. Instead, I ended up sleeping dressed and outside the blankets. That was the first opportunity we had to spend the night together.

Later that day, we had breakfast together and then Beco, Viviane and Lalli left.

My cousin Patu recalls some details of that trip: *"Aunt Marilene gifted me with that trip, to help me with the pain I felt due to my father's death. It was very cool. We were already there and Ayrton appeared with his sister and brother-in-law. We could not take pictures with him, as my uncles did not know he was there. The ski resort was called Villar, and the hotel was the only five stars in the place — I do not remember its name. We met Riva on the plane, who gave us a ride to the hotel's cable car. There, we met a Brazilian guy who was on an internship and became friends with Chris. We had a ski teacher, married to an Angolan who spoke Portuguese well, we became friends with them and one day we went for a snack at their house. I remember Ayrton trying to climb into the seats, he tripped, fell, and everyone laughed a lot, because he was learning how to ski. I also remember Chris being very angry looking for Dri, who had the room keys. She called Ayrton's room and nobody answered. Then she went to his room, knocked on the door and Adriane answered it, a little embarrassed by her sister's persistence. Adriane had urinary incontinence and answered a call in the phone booth, in the hotel lobby, and came out with wet pants, telling us: "Oh guys, you will not believe what happened. I do not remember who she was talking to or if she was very emotional, but I remember this episode."*

When we met again in São Paulo, at home, Beco and I, he said:

457

"Drica, we had better tell your parents I was in Switzerland with you."

"Well, if you think you should tell them, tell them!"

"I do, we cannot risk being caught in a lie."

"Ok!"

A while later, with my father in the TV room, Beco saw an opportunity and mentioned:

"Look, Mr. Amilca, I think I should tell you I was with Adriane and the girls there in Switzerland. My sister and my brother-in-law also went with me."

"Yeah, I heard, I was just waiting to see how you would act. I am glad you did not hide it," dad said.

"Dad, it was not planned. When I got there, I was missing Beco a lot, I asked him to go, he found a way to travel a little before scheduled, but he stayed just for a little while!"

"It is okay, little girl, you were honest, and I am glad."

The subject died there with my father.

Later, when were alone in the hall, saying goodbye, Beco said:

"See, Dridrica? Wasn't it better to tell the truth?"

"I do not know, Beco, my father is very smart and I doubt he knew it."

"Well, it was better not to take any chance, now we are clean!"

After talking about Beco going to the ski resort, he and my father also spoke about other matters. They always talked a lot! In fact, it was in one of those conversations that I first heard about electronic injection, intelligent suspension and a bumper made with a material with "memory", which made the car, when touching another one, not dent because this material returned to its original shape.

In addition to hearing about these innovations for the time, I remember a conversation in which my brother-in-law Dadô commented about an acquaintance from São Carlos who wanted an opportunity to show Beco a double-angle rearview mirror, to enlarge the rear field of view of the car.

Chapter XXIII

That year, Beco and I did not spend Carnival together — the holiday was on February 16th — because he was testing and adapting to the new car and his new team. Moreover, at that stage, he was also taking up residence in his new apartment in Monaco. Therefore, I went to play Carnival in São Carlos with the people there. My cousin Andrea and my sister Christhiane went with me. Dadô had many friends in the city. As usual, in the countryside cities of São Paulo, at least at that time, people drank until their eyes squinted! The three of us, slightly out of place but free of the usual watchmen, decided to bet who would get drunk first. We would go together to buy the famous cocktail at the bar and get into the middle of the dance floor, dancing. After a while, we would go again to the bar to fill the glass and counting. We had fun doing this, we loved dancing and samba, and it was not every year that we had the opportunity to "fall into the fun", as they say.

The previous year we had spent the holiday with Beco in Ilhabela and did not play Carnaval because of the harassment of the fans. In 1986, we were in Itanhaém and Beco showed up by surprise, the night we bought the invitations to dance at the Yacht Club, and I did not go! Thus, I was happy with that opportunity to "fall into the fun and tear up the costume" at the Carnival ball. Neither of us flirted with anyone, we were all in a relationship at the time, but coincidentally, without our respective boyfriends with us. We were actually waiting to party with each other. We jumped and sang along the traditional carnival songs and the best samba-songs of the samba schools that became famous and were played at that ball. We knew almost all of them by heart! But either we forgot to drink or alcohol did not work because of our sweating, jumping and dancing. I do not know, all I know is that I drank about five cocktails during the entire ball, without feeling, at any time, any change... I mean, we wanted to get drunk, but we could not! Maybe the cocktails had only water! Who knows?

Anyway, this was just a way to enjoy the moment and my youth. As soon as I had the chance, I told Beco everything that had happened, happy and excited. He seemed interested and asked a few questions, especially lately, to know who I had been with. But no further demands.

Piquet had been losing the attention of the Brazilian media to his younger compatriot and this may have motivated his attacks on Senna. For some time, since 1986, Piquet had been attacking Beco because he had engaged in a serious relationship with Katherine, with whom Ayrton had had a short affair in 1984. Piquet attacked, recklessly, and publicly raised questions about Beco's sexuality.

But as popular wisdom says: "What goes around, comes around." And he had to listen everywhere to a deserved and fair answer: "Tell Piquet to ask his girlfriend, because I have already seen her as a woman!".

Reginaldo Leme tells us this story from the beginning:

"There are two different things: Leaking in the media is one thing; the reason for the comment is another. I know exactly what happened because I saw everything. Piquet had a group of 'friends', and among them, some were suck asses. I was friends with both of them and when I occasionally heard one talking badly about the other, I did not let the other know, I poured oil on troubled waters. But these 'friends' of Piquet acted the other way round — for ethics, I will not say names.

The situation took an absurd proportion precisely because these 'friends' gossiped with Nelson: Look, the guy just said this about you.

What I can say is that I was with Ayrton the day he met Katherine, in Monaco, in the pits. I have always worked too hard and, therefore, I have spent less time with the drivers than Galvão. But the fact is that I never saw Ayrton with Katherine again and I only saw her again later, with Piquet.

However, Galvão told me that other people saw Ayrton with Katherine in Belgium too, and they threw it in Piquet's face. Honestly, when it was leaked in the media, I did not intervene, because I hate this kind of thing, and the first opportunity I had with Nelson, two of three days later, I said: That thing from Jacarepaguá did not look good for you. It was a sad episode and it will be engraved on the minds of both of your fans. You do not know what you have done!

And things got bad and it turned into war. After that, over the years, I managed to get the two of them together to talk once in Adelaide, Australia, inside Frank Williams' pit, who had not yet suffered the accident.

As for the worsening crisis between Ayrton and Nelson, I know some of these 'friends' of Piquet were at the racetrack, in Jacarepaguá, watching an interview with Ayrton, when Eloir Maciel, reporter for JB (former Jornal do Brasil) asked him: Why did you go missing?

And he taunted Piquet: Ah! I went missing to see if you paid attention to the champion, as you only pay attention to me. Piquet was the champion at the time.

When Eloir talked to Piquet, those 'friends' had already told him everything, but in their own way, and you know what happened. Armando Botelho wanted to go to court on the same day, which actually happened days later.

Talk about it with Piquet? Never! This was never the subject of my conversations with him and I think he did a big shit. Even though he did not seem sorry, I am sure he was. He went with the flow of those inciters and did not realize the harm he was causing. Maybe he did not even know about Adriane, because everything on that matter had nothing to do with her, just with Katherine. Some people helped to make Senna angry with Piquet and vice versa."

My uncle José Carlos also gives his opinion about this: "I met Reginaldo Leme and Galvão Bueno in a tire test at

Jacarepaguá racetrack, and then we went with Ayrton to dinner at a French restaurant in Rio de Janeiro. At the races, I used to see Reginaldo, and he would greet me normally; Galvão, on the other hand, was a bit far away. I have not seen Reginaldo for a while, the last time was at Café Journal, in Moema, and in my opinion, he is very honest. As for Piquet, he was a great driver who liked to be the spotlight and maybe that is why he tried to cause trouble with Ayrton, talking nonsense."

Unfortunately, Piquet's attacks only ceased after Ayrton filed a libel and defamation lawsuit against him.

That all bothered me immensely. In a way, I felt guilty for leaving Beco with his "hands tied" to defend himself. I simply wanted to be able to follow him on his travels, so that everyone could see me. However, that was out of question and I felt bad for it.

In addition to being lying insinuations, Beco knew they were nothing more than an attempt to disrupt his career. At this point, I think he got even braver because it messed with his pride. He was not concerned with giving explanations about his personal life; however, this situation did not fail to cause him problems.

In mid-March, I received a letter from Beco, written on the letterhead of Prince Hotel, from Akasaka, Japan:

"Drica, I am sorry if I have been a little distant these last days, you know how I feel about the problems... but you know well how much I like you. I will be back as soon as I can and I am definitely missing you a lot. I love you very much
Beco 03.15.1988"

One of the reasons that justify writing my memoirs is to be able to tell our context. There was no demerit in Beco's conduct, nor in mine. We were a couple who got along well. And the rest, we accepted so that we could be together. It was worth it. It was a soul affinity, we did not need to speak what we felt, because one could see the other. There was much more to attitudes than words between us.

I am grateful to my parents for the direction they have given to my life. Despite the obstacles Beco and I had to go through to be together, it was great. He knew that, although far, someone was waiting for him, missing him, watching the races and participating in his life, with all her heart.

My family knew Beco and ignored the insinuations. Nor did Mr. Milton had any kind of doubts, but this unnecessary disturbance of Piquet made everyone who loved Ayrton Senna very sad.

The Brazilian GP took place on April 3rd at the Jacarepaguá Circuit, in Rio de Janeiro. It was Ayrton's debut race at McLaren and he took pole position, but at the start the car had problems, and he had to use the spare car. However, during the race, commissioners deemed this change illegal, and he got a black flag. With the punishment, he had to go to the pits. He returned to São Paulo soon after.

Excerpt from Senna's TV interview with Leda Nagle — Training day in Jacarepaguá, Rio de Janeiro, 1988, for Rede Globo at CEU club: "(...) I have a very good life, I always did, thank God, and I enjoy everything that is part of it. Especially my family, as I said before, my friends... my girl... anyway, I have too many good things and unfortunately, little time to enjoy. I would need 36 or 48 hours per day to balance it, but I have nothing to complain about, my life is too good..."

*"Drica doll, it has been a while since the last time I sent you
a souvenir... not because I did not remember you, but as
everything in my life, a special motivation is always helpful!
Love you, Beco."*

Unexpected flowers, at an unexpected moment: This was
my boyfriend, my Beco, who went home at night to stay with
me and watch TV with my family.

On May 1st, before San Marino GP, in Imola, Italy, Beco
set a precedent previously unimaginable for me. Perhaps
because McLaren's motorhome was better equipped with
new technologies, but the fact is that I received his call
moments before the race started, on the other side of the
ocean:

"Hi, Drica San!"

"Hi, Beco! Has anything happened? The race is about to
begin!"

"Calm down, doll, it is okay, I just called to hear your voice.
But I do not have much time to talk because the race will not
wait for me," we laughed together.

"Beco, where are you calling from?" I asked, because I knew how hard it was to have a phone handy at a time like that.

"There is a phone I can use here inside the motorhome, cool, huh? And I am alone here, I just got ready and I am calling to hear your voice, Silly San."

"Wow, that is cool, Beco San! Everything will be fine, rest assured that God will protect you. I love you! I will be here watching you!"

"Okay, Dridrica, I am going now... I love you too, cheer hard there, huh?"

"Of course, if it depends on cheering, you will win all the races! Kisses."

"Kisses, Dridrica."

I confess I answered the call apprehensively, thinking something had happened, because that had never occurred before. I hung up the phone and walked quickly to the TV room, where everyone was waiting for the race to start and the live broadcast had already started. A few minutes later, the drivers began to line up on the starting grid with Ayrton in pole position.

I knew it was when he was with me that Beco expected to recompose himself, have fun, relax and recover his energy. The weight of responsibility on his shoulders, he tried to share with his family, but mostly with me, and I felt and was aware of that weight. But from that day on, he had added another expectation on me, by wanting to listen to me on the phone and making sure I would be there with him, in thoughts, on that race; by wanting to feel my trust in him and my peace of mind as to a positive result, in addition to my invocation of Divine protection. Therefore, I surrendered to his wills and needs, seeing nothing else. That was my conduct for our life together.

Ayrton won San Marino GP and had his first victory at McLaren.

In that year of 1988, our families were getting closer and, at Beco's suggestions, his parents invited me and my parents to have dinner at their house. On the day, he sent me flowers with the card below:

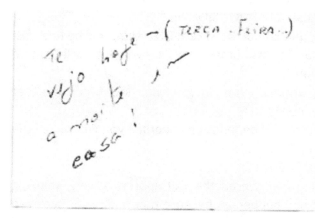

"See you tonight (Tuesday) at home!"

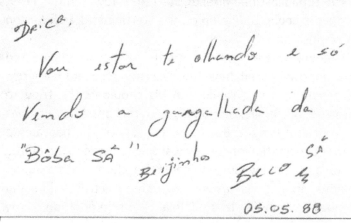

*"Drica, I will be watching you and seeing the laugh of my 'Silly San'. Kisses, Beco San
05.05.1988"*

We were welcomed at the Senna da Silva family's house with the greatest affection, for a dinner that was amazing in every detail. The night was very pleasant, everyone seemed happy with that reunion and glad with the direction my relationship with Beco was going, with the approval of our parents. He, in particular, was overjoyed with my and my parents' presence in his house. Families were gradually coming together for the expected outcome of our relationship.

Chapter XXIV

On May 15th, before the Monaco GP, someone at home called me:

"Dri, Beco is on the phone."

"Hi, Beco, another pole!"

"Hi, Dridrica. Yes, this year is promising!"

"Cool! Are you okay? Ready?"

"Super ready! I called you to send you kisses."

"Awesome! I love that you called me so I could wish you an amazing race. Go for it, Beco San! We are here cheering for you!"

"Thanks, Dridrica, miss you, I have to go."

"Miss you too! May God be with you, Silly San! Kisses."

Although less apprehensive knowing that his call did not mean problems with him, I was once again surprised by that phone call moments before the race. Such an attitude made my hurt feelings seem foolish and gave me a real sense of how important I was in his life.

Ayrton was leading the race when he got distracted and crashed alone on lap 66, and as the race was a street circuit, he was close to his apartment and went straight home, walking, leaving the entire F1 circus behind.

About this episode of the crash, I think it is important to contextualize what preceded the Grand Prix, which I myself only became aware when Beco returned to Brazil and came to my house. He was a bit anxious to clarify a news release about his departure for Monaco, because he imagined dad had read the article in the newspaper.

At the time, my father had not commented on what had been reported and I, therefore, only found out when Beco decided to clarify what had happened in front of me. He said:

"Look, Mr. Amilca, I know it was in the newspaper about me going on a trip with another woman, but actually this woman was traveling with Paulo, and he asked me to have him covered. So, I went on board with her, as if we were together, but it was just to get her off the hook. To make it worse, it seems that her mother told the press that her daughter was traveling with me. The thing is, when we got to the airport, at departure, the entire press was already there waiting for us. It was a very unpleasant situation, because none of this was supposed to be published. Leo, Armando and I did everything we could so they would not publish anything, but it did not work. I was being kind to an engaged friend, and he brought this big problem for me. I do not even want to hang out with him anytime soon, because he created this awkward situation for me, when I had nothing to do with it."

"I saw the news about it in the newspaper."

"Yes, Mr. Amilca, that is why I came here to clarify what happened."

I was there in the living room, mouth agape, because I knew nothing, as my father had not mentioned the subject to me and because Beco was caught in this situation. So, it is likely that he had been really concerned about the outcome and consequences of that fact, which led him to lose focus for a millisecond during the race and crash.

Reginaldo Leme tells us what happened:

"I learned that Armando Botelho hired people to go to the races and show up with Ayrton, so Ayrton started taking some 'girl friends' to the races. I told Armando that it disturbed his concentration, but Armando mentioned the example of Elio de Angelis, Ayrton's partner at Lotus. Elio had a great Argentine friend, Luís, really good person, who was always with him. Both were always surrounded by women. Then Elio started dating a wonderful Californian woman, the most beautiful woman in Formula 1 to date. But Elio and this Luís were always after women, and Armando used this example. I said: Armando, this is wrong, each person is one person.

I think bringing women like Marjorie, Carina and then Marcela Prado was not cool. They were nice, fun, but added nothing by being invited to the races."

The Mexico GP took place on May 29th, at the Hermanos Rodríguez racetrack, and Ayrton called me from the motorhome:

"Hi, Dridrica!"

"Well, well, well. I think I bring you luck when you talk to me before the races!" I laughed. "Hi, Beco San! How are things?"

"Dridrica, you have always brought me luck! Everything is fine around here, what about there? How is everyone?"

"Everyone is waiting for the race to start. Ready for another challenge?"

"Absolutely! Positive and effective, Dridrica!" he laughed.

"What about grandpa? Is he behaving around there?"

"Grandpa has not seen anything yet!" he laughed.

"So teach him how to drive. Take care, it will be okay."

"I will watch out for falling rocks, Silly San. Kisses."

"Remember we are here cheering for you, Silly San. Watch out for falling rocks. Kisses."

I thought it was incredible hanging up the phone and then seeing him on the TV, it could not be more in living color than that. It was real time!

Our relationship fluctuated between being the way we always were when we were together, and unexpected attitudes that were, for me, inexplicably hostile.

One day, we were on our way to the love hotel and he asked:

"Drica, are you taking the pill correctly?"

"Of course! I do not forget a day," I replied.

"But are you taking it according to the package insert?" he insisted.

"Of course!"

"Then explain to me when to stop, when to start over," testing me.

"I stop when the pill pack runs out, I menstruate, and I start again on the eighth day." I replied calmly.

"It is wrong! Can't you even do that right?" he said in a rather hostile tone.

"What?! I am doing it right! When it is over, you interrupt it for seven days and starts again on day eight!" I replied, shocked at the tone I had not known in that man until then.

"You are not! We read it together, dammit! It is on day seven!"

"Okay, so let's read it again and see who is wrong!" I took the medicine box from my purse. "Look, it says here: 'Interrupt for seven days and restart the new card the next day.' That is, on day eight, dammit!"

"No! It is not! he continued with that hostility, without even thinking straight.

"I will read again, pay attention: 'Interrupt for seven days and restart the new card the next day.' That is, the next day after seven days is day eight! I am not an imbecile! The day after seven days is day eight! It is the same thing! Maybe we are saying the same thing, but in a different way!"

He fell silent, resigned, and we went to the hotel, silent. I wanted to ask him to take me back home, but I did not know how to act towards that unexpected and stupid attitude. I froze!

We arrived at Studio A, we went in, I sat down on the chair at the dining table in the suite, my purse on my lap, not knowing what to do. Looking lost, not understanding any of it, I waited for him to resolve the situation he had created. He walked around the room as long as he could, buying time. I did not make it easy, I just stood there without looking at him, I think I was waiting for him to suggest we leave.

"Drica, come here!" he said, stretched out on the bed, still dressed. I did not answer for a while, I was not comfortable at all! Head down, trying not to cry...

"Dridrica, come here!"

"Look Beco, I am not in the mood," I said, without even looking at him.

"Stop it, Dridrica!"

Then I said, indignantly:

"Don't! You were stupid to me for no reason! You were wrong and did not even apologize! For me, we should leave now!"

He got up from the bed and came towards me, crouched down in front of me, lovingly sought my hands with his.

"Okay, Dridrica, I messed up, I am sorry!"

"Do not ever talk to me like that again, okay?"

"Deal!" he said, laughing, realizing he had broken the ice. He pulled out the purse from my lap, pulled me out of the chair and everything else happened... Finally, our stupidest argument ended in fun.

It was clear he was terrified with the possibility of me getting pregnant, to the point of causing such an embarrassment. But I believe that the greatest fear was mine! Imagine if there was any possibility of getting home telling my parents I was "slightly" pregnant? It would be like a 9-degree earthquake on the Richter scale, and I did not even accept the idea of having an abortion. At least in that event, it was clear that he should never again doubt my intelligence and responsibility.

And I continued playing a liar before my parents at home; when Beco arrived, he greeted my father and mother, and before we left, they asked:

"Where are you going?"

"We are going to the movies and then getting something to eat," I replied automatically.

Beco was silent, because he did not like lies. And did I like them? He only answered when they asked:

"What time do you come back?"

474

"Before ten o'clock," he replied in a rush, because it was the only truth of our schedule. Easy! Thirty minutes to go there, another four hours at the love hotel, and another thirty minutes to get home.

"Okay, have fun then. Be here at ten! Take care, be careful in the street with robberies," they said, and they would be waiting for us at ten.

And each time I became more and more expert in that lie, because they also asked about what movie we were going to watch, where we were going to eat etc. If I did not have to say anything on the way out, it would be fine, but I sure as hell would need to have an answer when I came back. We went back home deciding what to say, because he always came with me to drop me off, stayed for a while and then left. I was terrified of being caught, so I prepared in advance for the answer to be perfectly ready! I was not proud of lying to my parents...

Another conflict of mine: If I took a shower every time before I went out with my boyfriend, in the middle of the afternoon, could it arouse suspicion? Taking a full shower at the hotel before going back would make me get home smelling like soap? No way! My parents had the habit of sniffing us when we got home.

"Little girl, come and give me a kiss!" they disguised their intentions with affection.

At that time, it was very common to smoke indoors. In some of the more closed places, like nightclubs, a cloud of smoke was visible hanging over our heads. If we came home smelling like cigarettes, it was sure:

"Listen to me girl, you are smelling cigarettes! Are you smoking?"

"Noooo, mom (or dad)! We were in the middle of a cloud of smoke! How can we not smell like cigarettes?"

And that was true! I have never smoked, but imagine how terrified I was of coming home smelling like a fresh shower? They were terrible at control.

This all put me under stress and I had an inner conflict because I was lying to my parents. The thing is, I found no other solution; if I had decided to do what I thought was best for me, I had to lie so as not to cause more problems and unnecessary suffering. Anyway, I had to deal with the consequences of my choice. I took my life for myself, I stopped being a child and took my risks. Therefore, I stopped waiting for my parents' permission. Even though lying was not comfortable for me — it was and is totally against my principles — I am convinced I was very responsible, both before and after it happened.

In this Grand Prix, Ayrton had again taken pole position in training, but during the start, the car skidded and he took third place. At the end of the first lap, he regained second position and that was how he ended the race.

On June 12th, Ayrton competed in the Canadian GP in Montreal, and he called me before starting.

"Hi, Beco! Ready?" I said as soon as I got his call.

"Hi, Silly San. Ready!"

Wow, Silly San! The fifth consecutive pole?"

"Yeah Drica, you did not count on my cunning!"

"I really did not! I am starting to feel sorry for your opponents."

"Oh, no! That is too much. Let them suffer a little bit," he laughed. "I have to go, I just wanted to hear from you a little bit."

"Take care and be careful, okay? Kisses."

"Kisses, Dridrica."

At that point, I already knew these calls were an opportunity I had to help him relax a little of that absurd pressure, besides being able to tell him some words of support and confidence. He now counted on it. We spoke on the phone every week, at other times, but to talk about our personal stuff and talk calmly, plan what we would do together on his visit to Brazil; in short, keep up to date with the news in my life and his. But this call before the race was the time for him to let go of his problems, and I made him feel comfortable about it.

I had this skill. I have always been used to not asking my father questions about professional matters, but waiting for him to naturally share with us when he felt he needed to do so; we talked about it with some caution. Thus, I acted in the same way with Beco, no pressure, waiting for the best moment of his needs to deal with his professional affairs. So, as a rule, our conversations were light and caring.

Beco won that race, the fifth stage of the '88 Championship, accumulating 24 points in the World Championship.

The next race occurred a week later, on the 19th, in the United States, and Beco called me again:

"Hi!"

"Hi, congratulations! Another pole… Now I also just want you to win!" he laughed.

"Oh Dridrica, you are so demanding, what a mess I have gotten myself into!"

"Just kidding, Beco San! We are here cheering for you, but take it easy and come back as soon as possible, because I miss you very much."

"I miss you too, I will be there real soon! I call you again later. Kisses, Dridrica."

"Kisses, take care."

Ayrton won another first place on the podium in this Grand Prix. It was his third consecutive victory on the streets of Detroit.

As soon as Beco got a break from the Championship disputes, he came to Brazil, and on the weekend, we went to São Carlos.

On Sunday afternoon, Mig, Dadô and Fran decided to add some salt to the fun at Broa dam and planned a risky maneuver. Fran, in his ultralight plane, would try to approach Migue's ski, pulled by Dadô's speedboat. The objective was for Migue to reach the lower bar of the aircraft and climb aboard like in an adventure movie. And so it was!

Fran tells us: "At Dadô's house, we skied and did millions of crazy things; we were a group of united people and everyone was very skilled. So, we had this crazy idea, which is even recorded in footage and images taken by Ayrton, on the speedboat next to Dadô. Mig went skiing in slalom on the speedboat, and I had an ultralight airplane, so I piloted the equipment with a cable; he simply changed cables and we balanced the speeds. I piloted the ultralight plane alone, pulling a cable for the jet ski, and the speedboat pulled Mig on the ski, because the plane could not carry a person on the ski. We balanced the cables at the same speed, keeping a bow, and Mig would take the plane's cable and go skiing, as I took it in and out of the water, pulling with the aircraft. But not content, we decided to remove the cable, so that Mig would hold directly the ultralight airplane's landing gear. It was a very windy day and when he held the landing gear, which is an aluminum tube, he was scared, and when we started to go up a little, he dropped the ski into the water to get into the plane. He was wearing a life jacket that got caught in the main switch of the ultralight plane and the engine went off. We were about ten meters high, almost in the center of the dam, which was approximately twelve meters deep, when the engine turned off and we had to make a forced landing. Then it became a mess, because it was Sunday, and Senna was on the boat filming us at the time Dadô made a turn at high speed and he almost went into the water with the machine and everything. We have these images to prove how crazy it was."

Beco, Jacoto, Lenise, Dadô and I, on the speedboat, just followed the adventure with expectation. Someone on the speedboat filmed the scene, which we later watched over and over again in disbelief.

Along the length of that dam, they made some attempts and, as a safety measure, they had floating vests in case of any eventuality. It was very difficult to set the plane's height and speed for Migue to reach the bar and climb. At one point, almost at one end of the dam, he completed the feat. We saw him reach the bar, drop the skis, and start climbing the body of the plane. In the speedboat, we made comments, while Dadô turned around to get the skis left in the water. When we turned our attention to the horizon, where the ultralight plane would probably be, we saw nothing in the sky. The time lapse between seeing Migue going up, getting distracted, and the moment when we looked again was less than three minutes. We did not understand, until someone in the speedboat broke the silence:

"Look there! The tip of the ultralight plane's wing in the water."

Without blinking, Dadô quickly rode in that direction. In a matter of seconds, that wingtip submerged into the dam. As the boat headed to the location where we saw the wing, we were all silent and apprehensive about what could have happened. Close by, we saw Migue and Fran's heads out of the water.

"Dadô, give me the end of a cable so I can tie up the plane! Otherwise, we will lose sight of it!" Fran asked.

Immediately, the boys aboard rushed to provide the rope. Those who were in the water dropped their vests for us to collect them and dived in an attempt to find the aircraft, almost at the bottom of the dam, to tie it to the boat.

When they managed to tie the plane, they climbed aboard and told us what had happened.

"Gosh! How crazy we are, dude! When Migue climbed into the plane, he was inches from the propeller!" Fran said.

"But why did you fall?" someone asked what everyone wanted to know.

"My vest got caught in the ignition key and the engine went off. We immediately ran into the water!" Mig replied.

"Guys! When I put my face out of the water, the plane had already sunk almost completely; and where is Migue? So dangerous! I immediately dropped the vest and went after him. He was sinking, tangled up in the ultralight plane, so I helped him free himself, thank God!" Fran said, shocked at having agreed to that adventure.

As the oldest in the group, Fran felt responsible for the incident, but the truth is that none of them had foreseen all the risks of that adventure.

Migue, the protagonist, was a little silent, I believe he was embarrassed by the outcome or in shock. Moreover, he preferred that the other family members did not know about the risks he was subjected to.

The plane fell in an area close to the end of the dam, so they managed to catch it. If it had submerged in the center of the dam, at a greater depth, it would have been hard to recover it. The water in that dam is turbid, with a muddy bottom, and you cannot see anything beyond a meter deep.

Other friends' boats came to help us when they saw something was wrong and began to plan how to get the plane out of the dam to take it home. Once the plan was defined, Beco went to the other end of the dam to Dadô's house, hitching a ride with another friend, in search of ropes and the other materials needed for that rescue.

Fran tells us: *"Both Migue and I dived, we ended up at the bottom, but there was no impact, we had a forced landing. Then Ayrton went to my house, which was next door to Dadô; my father was on the beach super worried because it became and event and a crowd came close, but he could not go there because he had no boat. Ayrton stayed there talking to my father: Calm down, everything is fine! They are already taking out the plane, nothing happened!*

My father always says he was already an idol and he became even more after that."

When Beco returned with the cables, they secured the plane and began to bring it to the surface, slowly, with the power of the boats' engines, until it was almost completely out of the water. At that moment, smaller boats, like aluminum boats with outboard engines, approached to help, and the boys lifted the plane manually until they managed to use the boats to support it and tow it back home.

It was an operation that lasted most of the afternoon and became the subject of the rest of our stay. It is interesting to note that the collaboration and joint effort broke any barrier among the local people, thus becoming a cohesive group. I say this because there was a division between those who were fans of Ayrton Senna from Brazil and those who were not; but with him there, in flesh and bone, committed to make that endeavor successful, this became secondary and he began to be accepted as an equal to the others in the group.

Fran also tells us about Ayrton: *"He was a very distinct person. Dadô really liked model airplanes and Ayrton started to like it too, but he bought a small plane that was like a fighter jet, a Phantom of the time, I do not remember the model, but it was an extremely fast small plane, with an approximate speed of about 300 km/h. He began to get interested because Dadô did it, and he found model airplanes cool. In the beginning, the control radio was not so accurate, it was delicate, with a certain delay, a flaw. I remember one day I was beside Ayrton on the grass, in front of Broa's house, and he took off with the small plane. He flew with the plane normally, made a loop and came back upside down. Then, the control of this plane, the aileron, the elevator etc. was upside down. The small plane came very fast, at almost 300 km per hour. He targeted the plane at us, grazed on our heads, upside down, with frontal approach, which requires a lot of skill, because not anyone can do that. I got scared and dodged,* scared as hell. He did not even move, so sure of what he was doing.

He always told us he was taking a little risk, because with his contracts with Formula 1, he could not put himself in danger. Because, sometimes, we had a lot of ideas and he said he could not, because if he fell, he could suffer a sprain. But he also skied very well. As I wanted to try flying with the ultralight plane, he told me:

I have never flown with ultralight plane!

Well, there is a first time for everything, shall we? But worried, he warned me:

But nothing can happen to me. I have a contract, and if anyone finds out I flew an ultralight plane, I will lose contract!

No, we will not tell anyone.

So, for God's sake, do not even take a picture!

I took it! I have proof of him beside the plane, looking but not flying it. And then we went flying and he was the pilot; he was very skilled and learned fast. I think he and Adriane had a very nice relationship, so much that he went to São Carlos to be with her. Their relationship seemed to be light, they were always with other people, there should not be jealous; in the relationships, they do not share the other. He liked to listen more and did not expose himself very much — liking to listen is also a great skill; we have two ears and one mouth, after all."

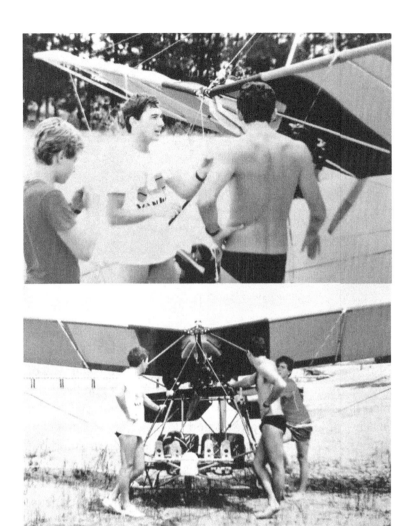

Beco and Fran with a relative, talking before the flight at Represa do Lobo, Broa

Ayrton on his first ultralight flight at Represa do Lobo, Broa. Photos courtesy of Francisco Pereira Lopes

I remember Beco was becoming more and more famous, richer and richer, and closer and closer to achieving his dream of being world champion — nothing could get in the way of this moment of him. When we started to date, he lived the nice life my family could provide him, he was still in the process of joining a top team and starting to earn significant money, he would become famous, and wanted to stand out among the best. Now he had almost all of that, he just needed to be champion, which would definitely consecrate him. The tension that year of 1988 had been tremendous; now at McLaren, knowing he could be the champion, he was determined to achieve this. As if he had to prove to himself that with the right car and the right team, he could make it and it had to be that year!

During that year, Beco started to demand attitudes that would only make sense if I was preparing for a married life with him. Except I was not! He had not taken any action on our engagement or the wedding date. Thus, we were in constant war with such demands. I remember a conversation:

"Dri, can you cook rice?"

"No! I never cooked rice, I always had someone to cook it for me."

"Can you even heat ready-made rice?"

"Dunno! In the oven?"

"No!"

"In a pan, with a little oil?"

"No!"

"It should not be too hard! So tell me how to heat rice."

"I will not tell you. I think this should be of interest to you to know!"

"I am asking now because I am interested to know! I know how to do other things, whenever my mother has no employee at home, I give her a hand! But she is the one who prepares the food, I do more of the boring work: Peeling potatoes, chopping onions, that sort of thing! But I can fry an egg, a steak; I am an expert in making pasta and sandwiches, as you know well! But I never cooked rice."

I answered him totally unworried because I was sure it would not be difficult to learn how to cook rice or beans. But he continued with those demands, and one day, while we were walking down the hallway of the rooms on the farm, he asked:

"Dri, are you taking any English courses?"

"No! I have untrained English, which I learned in high school since I was little, is it enough?"

"You need to prepare yourself, little girl..." he said, turning his back on me and going on his way.

Beco gave the impression that I was indebted for not preparing myself properly, and I asked myself: prepare for what? If he was not concerned with formalizing his intentions, I would not change anything in my life! That is how I reacted back then.

Anyway, I held back those unreasonable demands as long as I could, without creating any trouble until, one night, while we were returning to my house, I asked:

"So, Beco, I think it is time to talk about our future. As you know, I finish high school this year and I need to plan my life. We have been talking about marriage and stuff, but when do you think this is going to happen?"

"Long before you can think!"

"Well, first of all, we have to get engaged. We should say something to my family, and I will need time to prepare everything."

"Look, I have already been married and it would be ridiculous for me to get engaged. Furthermore, I am not getting married at church and I want no party!" he decreed.

"Well, but when do you think of getting married?"

"I told you, long before you can think!"

I fell silent, ending the subject. The day he decided to want something, he would have to ask me and find out what I wanted or not! But it was clear to me that he was not worried about my opinion at the moment. From then on, I programmed myself to move on with my life. I was too young and had to decide which course I wanted to take in college. If he ever wanted something else, he would have to discuss it with me. Therefore, nothing defined, but everything settled!

With our impasse of his demand to change my behavior, when he went to his newly acquired farm, I stayed on my own, I almost did not meet him there — it was a limitation due to my upbringing and my age, it was a space I would have to earn, but it would only be possible with full support! And one day, while we were watching television, I was kind of annoyed with him, with this demand without commitment, a children's program presenter appeared on the TV. I looked at the TV and said:

"Look, why don't you stay with a woman like that? A free woman, she does whatever she wants to, goes wherever she likes, does not need to tell anyone about her life. Is this the kind of woman you want? Why don't you go after her?"

One day after lunch, Beco arranged with Otávio and Dadô to go together from Porto Feliz, where we were, to his farm in Tatuí to fly with a small plane, when we would take the opportunity to take a look at how things were going there. And he called me:

"Let's go with us Dri?"

"Beco, you know my parents would not like it."

He turned his back, annoyed, loaded the car with Dadô and they left. Otávio stayed to meet them next. I just stood there, sad with the situation — I wanted to go! I still did not know the place and my boyfriend wanted to show me his new acquisition. And why not? I ran to tell Otávio to wait for me to go with him. I put on a quick outfit over my bikini, gathered my courage and went to "communicate" my parents I was leaving for Tatuí:

"Mom, I am going with Otávio to meet the boys in Tatuí, I will be back later with him."

"No, dear! You are not going there alone!"

"I will not be alone, I will be with Beco and the boys, what is the problem?"

"But you will be the only woman there?"

"Yes, just me! What do you think they will do to me there?" I challenged.

"Nothing, dear!"

"Well, then! There is no reason I should not go! Bye." I turned my back and left.

When I got there with Otávio, the boys had gone to get the small plane that had crashed. I stood there doing an area reconnaissance in the main house of the new farm, while Otávio ran to look for the boys, curious with the damage of the crashed plane. I asked him not to say anything about my presence, because I wanted to surprise my boyfriend.

The small and old house still did not have much structure and no furniture, the doors were locked, so I decided to get a towel from the car and lay down nearby, on the grass, among the trees, trying to find some sun.

When I heard their voices approaching, I held myself still, waiting to surprise him, and in a bikini... He approached with a wide smile as soon as he saw me.

"Dridrica, you came! What is that miracle?"

He leaned over to kiss me before I could answer him. I sat on the towel beside him and explained with a sweet voice:

"Beco San, I obviously wanted to come with you!"

"But how did you work out with your parents?" And I explained what happened.

"Wow, Drica San! I love it! You were very brave!"

"Ah Beco, you invited me and were upset that I did not come... I had to fix this! I cannot stand this control anymore! What is wrong with me being here?"

"But were they upset?"

"I do not know and I do not care, I made them accept the nonsense situation! So you bought a farm near ours so we can be close with your family around too and I cannot come here? Especially when we are not alone? Come on! They better get used to it!"

He answered with a happy smile, and pulled me by the neck affectionately for a sweet kiss, to show how happy he was. We got up, I got dressed and we joined the guys in a fun conversation about the recent plane crash. There was not much left of the small plane and they were having fun with it!

Toward the end of the afternoon, they decided to organize everything so we could go back. Beco quickly took me by the hand, saying:

"Guys! I will take a walk around the farm to show it to Dri, be right back. Meanwhile, you organize everything please!"

And we headed out to his silver truck, Ford. I loved the idea, wondering what path he was taking, looking back and around, to see I did not know what. He stopped at a private place, where no one would see us, got out and called me out of the car. He lowered the rear seats to further expand the trunk.

488

"Come here, Dridrica."

I jumped into the trunk without blinking.

After we had passionate love, we ran back so as not to let it show and soon returned to my parents' farm.

"I think I have been to his family's farm twice, in Tatuí, right when he bought it. We went there a few times, there was a big lake, a radio-controlled speedboat he brought, and we went there to have some fun. I talked to his family once or twice; in fact, when he was in Brazil, he stayed more with us than with his family," Otávio recalls.

My cousin Leonardo remembers about a trip to Ayrton's farm: *"It was me, Dadô and him by car to the farm in Tatuí, we went flying a model airplane. I have several memories of model airplanes at Chapadão farm, but this was an event on his farm. I was in the back seat, Beco and Dadô in the front, and the plane on top of me. And there was a bubble wrap around the plane that I sometimes squeezed and it made some noise. He got desperate thinking I was ruining the small plane. Dadô said: Hey, Leo! You are clicking... It is ruining the plane.*

Senna got a little angry and we stopped at the breakdown lane so they could see what I was doing and they found out it was just the bubbles in the bubble wrap. Then Beco was super embarrassed, and said: Gee, I was thinking you were breaking my plane, and you were actually not breaking anything!

Then we stopped at the gas station and that was where I realized how famous he was. People wanted autographs and many people were screaming: Senna! Senna! So we rushed to the road. It is funny, because I already loved cars, and from the back seat I saw the car was 200 km per hour. Gosh, but it did not look like it! And Dadô told him: You are 200 km per hour!

He replied: No, this is broken, and laughed.

Interestingly, he had a style of driving where he glued to the car in the front and overcame on the right, on the breakdown lane. And, even though I was young, I knew you should not overcome on the right.

Then we arrived at his farm; I was there only this time. I remember the place very well, the shed where he kept the planes. Then we went to fly with the small plane. He was there with the plane, I was watching that and the plane crashed, I thought: 'what a nice maneuver.' But the plane crashed to the ground and when I looked at him, he was pissed. I said: Gee, what the fuck, let's go get it!

And we talked, talked, went through the fence and we did not find the plane. We finally found it and it was shabby, each one brought a piece of it, I brought the gas tank. Then, he took another plane and flew."

Chapter XXV

After turning eighteen, as I mentioned earlier, I began to have more freedom. In fact, my parents started to allow me to travel on some weekends with the family of my closest friends; I even traveled with Mackenzie's people to Guarujá. They did not worry about me without Beco, they knew I was crazy about him! But they did not get off my back when he was around.

If, on the one hand, I was gaining more freedom in my routine in São Paulo, especially when Beco was not here, on the other hand, he had lost part of his freedom now that we had a complete relationship, especially with regard to women. Our situation was different and he was bothered by it, but we did not talk directly and objectively, everything was presumed:

"Hi, Dridrica. Have you been hanging out a lot?"

"Hi, Beco San. Just a little bit!"

"Are you behaving yourself, young lady?"

"Of course! You are always catting around the world and you are behaving yourself, so am I! Right?"

"Sure, Dridrica, I have always been a well-behaved boy!" he laughed his slow laugh and continued: "But it is different. I am working!"

"Well then, I also have things to do, I have my routine. But, like you, I have fun and leisure times. But you know I have always been a nice girl too!"

"Look, Dridrica... Watch out. I have a lot of spies watching you there."

"You could have millions of them, Beco San, but what I really wanted was to be able to hang out with you!"

"Deal! When I get there, we will go to the Gallery, it has been a while since we have been there."

"Deal, Beco San, come soon, okay?"

"I will be there real, real soon, Dridrica."

The lack of dialogue, of sharing his fears, his doubts and his sorrows made us distance ourselves, because some issues must be dealt with openly. Since the beginning of our relationship, we learned to understand each other in a silent and subtle way, but that was no longer effective. The issues that were not openly discussed accumulated and, in our new situation, the tension between us increased.

Also in 1988, I started working in a boutique near the famous Daslu store. That is because, on New Year's Eve, when I met Gino, Beco's friend and Benetton's representative in Italy, we talked about opening a brand representation in Brazil. Excited, I always brought up the subject with my dad, but he said:

"You will first work in a store to learn how it works, gain some experience, and then we talk about this."

And that is what I did!

The boutique was in the best neighborhood in São Paulo, and I worked there for two months, in the afternoon, after school. Unfortunately, I did not have access to the logistics and inventory control, entry and exit of goods, nothing that justified me to stay there. The store owner knew what my goal was, but she did not give me opportunities in my few attempts, and I, shy, did not want to be invasive or disrespectful. I ended up being part of the sales force during the short period I worked at the store. Of course, this experience was important for me to realize how unprepared I was to deal with situations outside my dome.

I was excited about the discoveries I had been making in this new phase of my life, but Beco had some strange reactions. For example, I wanted to be more and more attractive to him, to somehow receive a compliment from him. Thus, I took a risk one day when we went dancing:

"Beco, what do you think of me blushing my face?" I said, pointing to the spot.

"It is the same! You always use this."

"I never used it in my life! That is why I am asking. My face is angular, I know, but I never used it."

"Okay, Dridrica, but it is the same!" ending that conversation he did not like.

It seemed like he did not want me to change and thus devalued any attempt I made in that sense. When I was actually just trying to surprise him. I stopped seeking his approval and trying to earn a compliment, and he, proud as he was, did not give me any. At the same time, he began to be unreasonably jealous when I least expected it!

One day, when we were returning from the movies — we had seen The Woman in Red, which had a beautiful woman as a protagonist and I decided to ask:

"Beco, what about me caught your attention when we met?"

"Well, Dri, you are not the type to draw my attention on the street."

"Okay! But is there anything about me that caught your attention? What do you like the most?"

"Of course there is, Dridrica!" he replied, trying to string me along.

"Gosh! How hard it is to take a compliment out of this man," I thought. I need a good self-esteem! I had been raised to be distinct in relation to my behavior and my character, but I was also his girlfriend, not his best friend. I insisted, after all, he was the one who wanted to have a relationship with me at first. So, I had to have something about my appearance that caught his eye. I insisted:

"Well, Beco, can you tell me what you like most about me? Or is it too hard?" I asked, putting on the spot.

"I think I have always liked your eyes a lot, your gaze."

"Finally! It did not hurt to say that, did it? I have always liked your eyes a lot too. My mother always said a person's eyes are the mirror of the soul, so I pay close attention to people's eyes." I was pleased with his answer, I did not intend him to say it was my athletic body, I myself hated that about me, and he was not the type to catch my attention on the streets either, he had no profile to be a model, just like me! It was all very balanced between us, except for the growing harassment brought by fame.

Another day, in the car, the theme song for the movie The Woman in Red started playing on the radio. I teased him — I knew it was a song in which the male character, not handsome at all, drooled over that beautiful woman who was the protagonist:

"Beco, can you translate this song for me?"

"Of course! Wait, I will pay attention..." And he translated it:

"Lady in Red / is dancing with me / cheek to cheek / nobody here / just you and me / that's where I wanna be / but I hardly know / this beauty by my side."

"Thanks, Beco!" I said at that moment, interrupting him, but he went on.

"I'll never forget / the way you look tonight."

"Thanks," I said again. And he kept translating:

"I have never seen you looking so gorgeous as you did tonight."

"Wow! Thank you!" I exaggerated the teasing.

"Oh, Dri!" he said, annoyed by the prank.

"Oh, Beco! At least now I managed to get compliments from you," and I laughed.

And the more annoyed he was, more amused I was with what I had done. He just seemed to enjoy seeing me in sportswear, on the farm, with beachwear or casual clothes. Hair
messed up by the wind from motorbike rides or with my hair wet from the sea and pool water, or with my hair tied back to practice sports. Preferably sweaty. He did not like Adriane dressed up and was not about to encourage it. My behavior changed as I left puberty to enter adulthood, and it was more complicated for him to deal with the situation than for me, who was discovering myself.

494

Once, when Beco and I were getting ready to leave the Gallery, I met José Carlos Pileggi, aunt Regina Calil's nephew and son of one of the greatest cardiologists in Brazil, Dr. Fúlvio Pileggi.

We have known each other since we were kids, when we spent the summer season in Guarujá. Aunt Regina's apartment was next door to ours and, back then, the families were very close. My great-uncle, Roberto Zarif (from the extinct construction company Zarif Canton and my grandmother's brother, Catarina Zarif Yamin), aunt Regina's husband, got along very well with my father and they had some common business. My mother had also consolidated a strong friendship with Regina, and thus I spent a lot of time with her nephew and niece, Zé and his twin sister, Roberta, who were my age and were staying at their aunt's house.

That evening, when I crossed paths with Zé at the Gallery, I made a point of introducing Beco:

"Hi, Zé! How are you?"

"Hi, Dri!" We exchanged kisses on the cheek, as usual.

"Zé, this is Beco. Beco, this is Zé Pileggi."

The boys greeted each other quickly and soon Beco and I left. At the door of the club, while we waited for the car, he asked me:

"Dri, who was that guy you introduced me to?"

"Zé? He is aunt Regina's nephew!"

We got in the car and on our way to my house, Beco said:

"Dri, something is wrong there!"

"How come?" I asked, having no idea what could be wrong.

"Why doesn't this guy like me? Why did he greet me that way?"

"Huh? What way? What are you talking about?"

"The guy greeted me grudgingly. Why doesn't he like me? There's something there!"

"Beco, are you crazy? I have known him since I was little! He was always with us when he stayed at aunt Regina's house."

"Dri, something is wrong there!"

I started laughing at the nonsense situation to which I was being subjected and, annoyed, I said:

"Beco, you must have seen him a few times when he was with us in Guarujá. What do you want me to say? How am I supposed to know why he greeted you grudgingly? Maybe he was in a bad mood? Maybe he was jealous of you?

"I did not meet him! And why would he be jealous of me?"

"Dunno! Man thing? We have known each other since we were little. He liked my cousin Patrícia, but he was a kid for her at the time."

"This story is very strange!"

"Look, Beco, I dunno! As a boy, he imagined he would date those famous models, and now he sees me with you. How can I know his reasons? That is all I have to tell you!" I said, giving up on that unnecessary and unproductive conversation.

The subject ended there, but Beco left me at home and left frowning. For my part, I really had nothing to say about Zé's behavior. How should I know? It was not my problem; he would have to solve it himself. After all, as I learned since I was little, "if you have nothing to hide, you have nothing to fear", and I did not have to worry about proving something that never existed. What if the guy was a fan of another F1 driver? It is none of my business.

At one point that year, I was uncomfortable of going to the love hotel. I was terrified that our secret might leak, with our names on the documents presented at the reception and the images captured by the security camera in the hotel lobby. Also, I was bothered by the moans from the next suite and the pornographic movies we saw when we turned the TV on. It all brought some coldness to the situation that I did not like. I had the romantic dream of having a place just for ourselves, where I could surprise him with a candlelit dinner, where I could arrange everything with care, in advance, to please him, and where we could simply watch a movie together. Who knows, maybe, on special occasions, I could even find a good alibi for us to spend a few nights together, after all, I already had to lie to my parents! So why not? That atmosphere was very impersonal for me, I did not see any charm in being in a place where an unknown couple, half an hour before, had been in that same bed. A love hotel has its function, but I was not happy with that.

I had an idea and then decided to look for a flat to rent. I walked attentively through the streets where I passed, looking for a good place that was close to my house, dreaming of everything we could do in a place just for ourselves. I visited one that I liked, to get information, consult monthly prices, hoping that, who knows, Beco agreed to rent it! I knew the cost of it was nothing to him anymore. And it would be cheaper and more practical than renting a furnished apartment, however small. With all that in hand, I personally suggested it to Beco, but he did not even agree to think about my idea and said no. Even though I explained to him my reasons for it, his reaction was one of suspicion.

"Who gave you this idea? Who suggested you this flat?"

I once again was disappointed with his reaction and decided I would not take any further initiatives for us. So I reaffirmed to myself that I should take care of my life. When I wanted to do something, he did not like it; when I gave up on doing in, he demanded it from me?

After a while, Beco had a little health problem and asked me to go to the doctor to see how I was doing. I went, hidden from my parents, of course! My cousin Dea (Andrea), always a friend, went with me; I did not feel safe going alone. I told the doctor the problem, and after a routine examination, we all went into a room to talk. He said:

"Look, you show no signs of anything, let's see if anything shows up at the examination results."

"But how do you catch this?"

"It is a sexually transmitted disease, but it is only transmitted to the partner when it manifests itself, there is no danger outside this period. Many people have the virus, but spend their entire lives normally and it does not manifest. There is no cure for those who have it, you can just control the disease."

"When does it manifest?"

"Usually when the person's immunity drops."

"I do not quite understand it."

"For example, it is common for an individual who has gone through a long period of stress, when he enters a situation of relaxation, to have a drop in resistance in his health and then the virus can manifest itself. I will send you the result by mail and if you have any questions, please contact me."

I left the appointment, relieved to have finished that unpleasant clinical examination, and grateful for my cousin's consideration in accompanying me at that moment that, for me, was very difficult.

My cousin Andrea talks about my relationship with Beco: *"They had a deal, but at a certain point the person is so in love... He was too, and it was not fun anymore to go out with other women. If I like you, I want to stay with you, I am not kidding and I have already experienced that; then things happen normally, and she gave herself to him in a nice way — only after she was eighteen, due to our upbringing and the circumstances of their relationship, as he lived abroad. But in the end, he reassured her about it and it worked out.*

But once she called me, crying. They were intimates for a while now, he called her and said he had herpes, he told her to go to the doctor, very nervous, and she was pissed; she told me: I do not go out with anyone, just him, but I have to go to the doctor!

And I went with her because she was ashamed.
Then the doctor said: You have nothing, I think it is his."

When Beco returned to Brazil, he called me to ask where I would like to have dinner. I suggested La Tamboille, a restaurant indicated by Dea's boyfriend as the best restaurant in São Paulo and I was curious to get to know the place. On that very day, I had received the examination result and wanted to show it to him.

At that point, I was dressing up better and the intention was to look good. After all, I wanted Beco to be proud of being by my side, and I would always buy new clothes thinking about using with him.

When we were already seated at the restaurant table, I said:

"Hey, Beco, here are the examinations for you to see. I have nothing, but I am curious. Why did you think that I gave you this? If it is sexually transmitted and I have only been with you in my entire life! As for you, traveling the world for so long, having sex with a bunch of girls..."

"Dri, I had to ask you this to see if you were okay. I would be irresponsible if it did not do so, and in fact, I had never had it before. And it has manifested twice since we started getting together."

"Well, I think you should check with your doctor to help you understand why. But now you know that you did not get this shit from me! Even though you know you were and are the only man in my life," I said, quite upset with that situation he had subjected me to.

We ordered our dishes and, while they did not arrive Beco asked me in a suspicious tone:

"Dri, how did you know this place? When have you been here?"

"I have never been here before! Flavinho (who dated Dea) talked about this restaurant and I wanted to get to know it with you!" I replied calmly, thinking it was a trivial question, but I was wrong.

"But how did you know the location and everything?"

"I was in the car with Flávio and Dea, we passed by here and he spoke very highly of the place, I was interested in coming here," still calmy, but now suspicious.

"But how did you know it was here?"

"Beco, I already know how to walk around São Paulo, especially in the regions where I am used to going, and this is the way to Iguatemi mall. I waited for you to arrive from your trip, I called Flavinho to ask the name and address again so we could come today, he took some of my questions about how to get here and here we are! Why don't you ask him?" That was already becoming unbearable for me, and I added: "Look, I am tired of this attitude with me. I do not know who you have been with in your life and I do not care. But I am sure they were not my level. You have been mistaking me with those women, and I do not condone this kind of treatment. I did nothing to deserve it! If you believe in the possibility of me being a different kind of person, you should not be with me. You are being disrespectful. So I ask: Why are you still with me if you doubt me all the time?"

"I do not doubt you, Dri! But if I have doubts, I have to ask."

"And why do you think you have the right to question me like that? I did nothing wrong and I do not give you this right. You are offending me! That is not why I waited so long for the right time to become your woman! You have been extremely unfair to me and I will not accept it. I accept no doubts about my conduct. Maybe it is time to think about whether we should continue together. Feel free! I do not accept this kind of attitude anymore; you can ask whatever you want because I have nothing to hide. I think it is great to talk, it is good for our relationship. But not in the tone you have been doing! As if I were under suspicion. What the hell?"

"No, Dri, I love you and I do want to be with you!"

"I love you too much too. We have faced and overcome all the obstacles together, it was painful for both of us. But getting this far, without mutual trust, it is not worth moving forward."

I said that decisively and he listened silently. I let out everything that was hurting my heart, in a low voice that struggled to come out, as I held myself back from crying. I did not want to embarrass myself in front of the other customers in the restaurant, who had their attention focused on the Excellency Mr. Ayrton Senna. We were silent for most of dinner, a dense atmosphere between us, and I could not wait to leave. He took me home and left.

After that conversation, I left him free to decide what was best for him. He never talked about that again, nor did he speak to me suspiciously again. He made his decision aware of my conditions for us to continue dating and became Beco San I knew again.

Dea remembers this situation: *"She was really upset this time and wondered if she should break up or not. I went to the doctor with her and he said Dri had nothing. But that moved Adriane a lot, because how could she have anything if she did not date anyone else? The doctor explained that it was a sexually transmitted disease and that stress can lower a person's immunity, which enables the virus to manifest.*

Adriane told me: Come on, he says he was going to date only me and now he says I have herpes.

I knew they had a little fight over it. He called asking her to go to the doctor, this is offensive. But that was the only time I knew they had a disagreement and it created a rather boring atmosphere, but it was soon solved and they continued their relationship."

Once, when we were returning from Porto Feliz, we gave my cousin Patrícia Kaiser a ride to the bus station in São Paulo. It was night and he, with his usual good will, offered to drive her.

As soon as we arrived at the bus station, Beco parked on a very busy avenue, but only for Patrícia to get out of the car, when he saw a very dirty beggar about six meters away, sitting on ground, leaning against a wall. Moved by that scene, he took the highest bill of money and asked me:

"Dri, give this money to that beggar."

I looked around and analyzed our situation. I was afraid to get off the Mercedes-Benz at that place and I replied:

"No, Beco, I am not leaving the car."

"What does it cost you to do what I am asking you to do?"

"It costs me nothing! But I do not think it is safe."

"My God! I am asking you to go there and give him this money."

"If it is that simple, you go!"

"But they may recognize me and I do not want that!"

"So what if they recognize you? Do you think it will be in the papers? I think your intention is awesome, but I do not feel safe to leave the car in a place that I do not think is safe at all. You go!"

He was very annoyed and I, upset with his reaction, who, upon hearing a convinced and justifiable "no" on my part, frowned. The next day, he called me a little aloof with me and, for the first time, I went down my level, quite uneasy, maybe even enraged:

"Look, if you think you are right to play "offended and angry" with me, I will you tell you what! You did not worry about my safety there. What if I was not about to take a risk there, getting out of your super car that draws the attention of the entire planet? Why didn't you go there? Who are you to judge my attitude? I pass through several beggars on the street every day! I know it is a vision of a very and depressing life. I understand that maybe you are not so used to seeing it and you felt bad about that man, but that does not give you the right to decide for me what I should do or not do! Did you worry about the beggar's situation and not worry about my safety?"

502

"I just wanted to give money to help that man! It costed you nothing."

"Great! But your good intentions do not give you the right to decide for me. And it is not because I am not as good as you! I had good reasons for not wanting to get out of that car, and even if you did not, you should have respected me. I live in this country, I live with this misery in plain sight, with violence and the risk of robbery in the streets that we are subjected to every day, unfortunately! Who are you to judge me?"

He, somewhat disconcerted by my attitude, realized he had no arguments or reasons to continue this tantrum, and wanted to end the debate:

"Okay, Dridrica, I understand your position, I will call you later when you are calmer. Let's close this matter."

"Better that way. See you later," I replied hanging up the phone.

That year, something new happened in my life. I knew a prayer movement called IVI (*Invitation a la Vie*), created and led by a French woman called Yvonne Trubert. The women in my family already participated in the IVI house, in São Paulo, and in 1988, my cousins and I formed the group *Pérola* (Pearl, in Portuguese). We had weekly meetings, with two volunteers who had been participating in the IVI for some time and had experience in group dynamics, so they guided us. Basically, we learned how to use the tool given to all Christians, Lord's Prayer and the Hail Mary; we prayed the rosary at the beginning of the meeting and then listened to Yvonne's messages, recorded for the groups in France — we followed her voice with the content translated and printed in Portuguese. She did not preach what was right or wrong, who was good or bad, she just guided us to see the other as a human being who can fail, who is imperfect, just like us. A sweet and loving view of the world and its imperfections. She showed us that God is love, not punishment or rancor! That He is ready to help us as a good Father, as well as Saint Mary as a Mother. They gave us what they knew was good for us or what we really insisted on wanting, just to learn at the end of the journey that that was not the best path. Therefore, God, as a Loving and Educating Father, always respected each one's path and free will, because in the end only love "feeds", the rest is our ego. By the way, I remember a reflection by Yvonne on precisely this issue: "Love and ego."

The thing is that my sister Lenise started an IVI cell in São Carlos, where she moved to after she got married — that is how the movement spread, with people donating their time to start new groups with friends and acquaintances.

In addition to the weekly meetings, the group also made pilgrimages to places where Yvonne said to be energy points, chakras of our planet Earth. Everything was the vibration that reached the molecular level of our body through the energy of prayer, the intention of praying together, to help ourselves and something greater than us. At the seminar attended by Yvonne, participants learned to "harmonize" — they were guided and trained to use the technique developed by her, who also explained about the chakras of the human body, the location of each one, which organ of the body they are related and to which emotion it corresponds, to balance these energy points through hands. Thus, we learned how to be an antenna that captured the divine energy, channeled through the prayer that all of us, Catholics, know, to pass it on to others through our hands.

Beco was harmonized several times by my aunts and my sister Lenise — back then, the Pérola group had not yet participated in this seminar and, therefore, we did not know how to harmonize. He liked it a lot, said it brought calmness, peace and well-being. He was offered just once, kindly, as an affection to help him in that difficult phase of his life — it was the instrument we learned at IVI to help. In the following harmonizations, he asked them himself, when we were all at the farm.

504

The curious thing was that, just when I had sought this help, it seemed that the distance between us had widened. I prayed in moments of inner affliction, for me and for him. From Beco's side, he had already heard about the subject, in conversations with my aunts, and he liked that I participated in it. Sometimes he would ask me about the subjects we were discussing there and seemed to feel confident that I was taking part in that nice and inspiring movement.

Of course, we were not "saints" because we participated in these groups, but the intention of those who participate is to find help to understand and improve themselves as human beings. Changing yourself is a long and hard exercise! Only with perseverance, we can evolve. I remember a message that said: "We have defects, but if we do not recognize them, how can we heal? So we need to see ourselves; but it is not in guilt that you change — it is loving yourself. We need to love more in order to change," (Ivonne Trubert — *Aux responsables des vibrations*, Feb. 1998). Probably, because I was participating in this positive movement, he also wanted my presence in spiritual matters of his life.

My search for it was due to my demand. I was very young and felt overwhelmed. Being with Beco and thinking about having a life with him or not. Therefore, I wanted to find how to deal with that phase of my life, without fear of going out of my way or making the wrong choice. I was fighting against this fear and I needed to bring some extra strength to me, to believe and have faith; even though I have always felt divine protection, I tried to be my best self to deserve it! I wanted to deserve it, and this attitude towards myself made me like the person I chose to be. And even though I was having to lie to my parents, when I made my choice as a woman, they stopped deciding for me at that point. It takes courage to take your own risks and your own life! And I looked for help to be able to handle this new demand.

I felt sad when I thought about some situations we had experienced in the last year in our relationship. It was a

505

succession of attitudes I had not expected, like his lack of attention during my trip to England; the discovery that he was seeing other women in Brazil; his reaction the day after we consumed the act; his distrust and demands.

It was probably a combination of factors that affected me that year. I knew Beco wanted to be with me! But the impression of not seeing that joy stamped on him, when we were finally together, frustrated my expectation of "happily ever after." So I was investing in the relationship and, although I felt we were getting closer, more connected to each other, at the same time I did not see the joy in him that I had seen before, when were together. But when he saw me sad and upset — which happened several times —, he told me:

"Dri, if I do not marry you, I am not marrying anyone else!"

I think he also knew he could not be himself at that moment, and he tried to reassure me about his feelings and intentions. So this was all very confusing to me. Where had that joy gone, the happiness we felt when we were together? That one, before we turned into a man and a woman? It had worked while we were a man and a girl, but suddenly it felt like fear took over! And I did not understand that. That was why I joined this prayer group. To feed my soul, because I felt I had no more energy, nothing else to give from within me, from my heart to him, since my heart was hurt! So I went to look for light, for comfort, to find again that strength and to be able to help him, to be able to move forward. He noticed none of this, and I told him nothing. But this was very clear for those who knew me and my entire family. And yet I had a ghost in my mind, who wondered the possibility that I was not good enough for him in our private moments. Which was torture for me at the time, and I had no one to talk to about it.

Now I know I was wrong, I learned that nobody feels anything alone in this intimate moment and we both gave ourselves in completely. It flowed like everything else

506

between us, as if we were one. Perhaps, that had scared him. But things like that I only found out after a very long time: "If it makes you feel, it makes sense!"

During the meetings of the Pérola group, I was there to overcome my limitations, I was looking for more tools and more breath to move forward with that man I loved dearly, and who was worth fighting for, believing that, after the storm, the calm would come and we would feel happy together again, as we always were.

I was surrendered. I had no life baggage, no vision of human complexity. Everything, until then, had been easy and simple between us. Partners in everything!

Obviously, he must had been looking for the same thing: Support, both with his family and with me. I was part of his support, at that moment of extreme pressure from everywhere and every aspect; it was all too heavy for him too, I knew that, I saw that. I had my look for him, but he did not have his look for me, I did not know how to develop this with the weight I carried too. So, I kept self-developing, self-feeding with my spiritual quest.

His demands on me knowing how to cook rice, speak English and other things, which he simply thought "I had to", with an air of contempt, only reinforced my will power to take care of myself and of him too. I was only eighteen years old and he had been my first boyfriend and the first great love of my life. Because of the age difference, the dynamics of my life and his, I had to leave my childhood and take a leap to maturity, to be able to follow Beco and make that relationship possible with my family, somehow giving up of my adolescence, by my choice, in a difficult and very painful relationship. But how could I not love him? After everything he has done and accepted for us to be together? All the attention, care, affection... We had a natural affinity, we loved being together, we had the same energy, the same enjoyments and, in addition to having attraction and chemistry, we were great partners, our beliefs and way of seeing the world were aligned, it was the best of all worlds in terms of relationship. I did not have all that notion back then, but now I am even surprised by what we had naturally. I was in love with my best friend. And my best friend loved me. Plus, the chemistry, it was complete! And I would do and I did everything I could to make that relationship work and last for the rest of our lives — just like that! And I imagine it would be just like that for him too!

But that year, the relationship was changing, he was changing, it was like I was losing my Beco to Ayrton. I think he saw himself every day less like Beco, that simple boy, from a nice family, grateful for the life he had the privilege of living, good-natured, humble to the point of not thinking himself superior to anyone. His attitude was changing, even publicly.

Chapter XXVI

On July 10th, Ayrton competed in the Great Britain GP at the Silverstone circuit. Ayrton started in second place and won the race in the rain. It was his first victory in England in Formula 1.

A few days after the Grand Prix, we traveled to Europe at Ayrton's invitation. It was me, my father, my mother and my sister Cristhiane. We left Brazil on July 15th and landed at the airport of France the next day, where Beco was already waiting for us. He had left Monaco to meet us and go together to Pescara, Italy, to the house of friends Gino and Yuta.

In the middle of the European summer. Those were very pleasant days, the couple welcomed us with joy and affection, who thus returned our kindness during that New Year's Eve, spent in Angra.

Gino, I and Yuta in front of the beautiful landscape of their house in Pescara, Italy

View of the house where we stayed

The house was on top of a hill, on a large plot of land, overlooking the Adriatic Sea. We were surprised by its modern architecture and beautiful decoration. I remember it was the first time I saw genuine chairs by the great designer Mackintosh, the black ones, with the high and hollow back support, arranged at the ends of the dining table, and of course I wanted to sit on them, to test the feeling. Inside, the house was high-ceilinged, with an access walkway between the rooms on the second floor. I did not go upstairs, because the room I shared with sister was on the ground floor and Beco's too, a little further from our corridor, which was accessed by a few steps on a drop below our floor.

My parents were amazed when the owners of the house offered their own room to accommodate them. Then the discussion came up, trying to get this idea out of the house owners' minds, with Beco mediating the conversation in Italian, until he said to my father:

"Mr. Amilca, there is no point in discussing this matter with them, it is customary here to offer the best room in the house for a visitor. They will be offended if you do not accept it!"

That was not customary for us in Brazil, but my parents ended up respecting their custom without extending the subject further, even though embarrassed. As a matter of fact, I do not even know where the hosts slept, maybe there was another suite upstairs. They had two puppies inside the house, I do not know what breed, but from what I remember, they seemed to be one of the smaller types of Terrier.

We were all tired from the trip and went to bed early.

In the morning, when we woke up, we gathered at the table on the porch, where breakfast was served. In front of us was a large open garden overlooking the sea. Coffee was served with a round Italian bread, a giant persimmon tomato, with fresh cheese and fruit. Just thinking about it makes my mouth water: That crunchy, fresh bread with huge tomato slices, seasoned with salt and oil from the region; that was food fit for the gods, especially in that hot weather. We stayed there all morning, waiting for everyone to wake up — after all, this part of the trip was to rest, not rushing for anything. That was, for me, the best meal of the day! Then one day Beco complained:

"Oh, Dridrica! Take it easy! This way you will gain some weight," and laughed his slow laugh.

"Oh Beco, this is not normal! Later I run after the loss. Don't bother me, please!"

Gino, Yuta, my father Amilcar, Christhiane, me and Beco on the porch having breakfast

At the same moment, but now with my mother Marilene

On another day for breakfast, Gino (our host), me and Beco

View from the entrance of the house, Gino invites dad for a ride in his old car

I remember we only left the house a couple of times for a ride. In one day, at Gino's invitation, we visited his main office, where he commanded the Sisley and Benetton brands, which he was a representative in Italy, as I mentioned before. When we got there, he led us into a room full of products and asked my sister and me to look around to choose what we wanted, while he walked around with my father and Beco in other sectors. We stayed there looking at the pieces of clothes, we chose some that we liked, a little embarrassed, because we understood he was offering us. When they returned, he was surprised by the few pieces we had chosen and insisted that we took whatever we wanted. We looked at my father, waiting for a sign, after all, we did not want to abuse kindness.

"Dears, take whatever you like, I think he is thinking you did not like his clothes," dad said, putting a hand on Gino's shoulders comradely and thus taking any financial risk.

We took a few more pieces, they were relaxed and colorful clothes, very nice, but we chose the ones that caught our attention the most. They put everything in a small green cloth suitcase with the brand's logo and we left. Later, my father commented with us, amused:

"Girls, can you believe that Gino gave me the bill so I could pay for the clothes you took?" he laughed.

"Damn, dad! I cannot believe it!" I said, shocked and a little embarrassed for having helped Gino with that expense.

"But he hinted it was a present!" my sister added, for the same reason I did.

"That is okay, girls! It was not your fault, no problem!" He laughed before concluding: "I am telling you to let you know we have fallen for Gino's sweet talk." He laughed again. "Those Italians!"

He laughed because it was actually his friend's prank. He fell like a fool. But it was nothing serious. And he himself, my father, had encouraged us, aware of the risks. Gino was a very nice man! My father loved that Italian man and had taken a liking to him. Not to mention we were being very welcomed. My father always said, laughing: "Every streetwise is friendly."

Another day, we left in the afternoon and went to a fishing port. Gino had a big fishing boat that a fisherman friend used freely, the only commitment to him was that, whenever he asked, he would go out to bring fresh fish for his consumption, in addition to cleaning, preparing and serving his visitors. There was a small wooden house on the side of a cliff of reasonable height, the boat docked just below this little house that was sort of hanging there; it also had a small winch, so that you could hoist fish from the boat and other heavier objects. But this is all on the back side of where we were received. At the entrance where we were, there was a small wooden balcony with a simple table and chairs, and inside the house there was only fishing equipment, a sink and a stove, all very well taken care of and clean.

We stayed outside, having a relaxed chat, listening to how this arrangement worked and the logistics between the owner of the fishing boat and the fisherman, who, while preparing our meal, got in and out the house to participate in the conversation. By the way, my parents barely spoke English, and my sister and I understood more than spoke Italian. From Italian, we can understand some things because of the similarity with our language, so that was fun for all of us, and a banal subject took a long time to be fully understood.

Gino, "our fisherman and cook", Ayrton, Yuta and dad, on the small stilt on the cliff where the boat was anchored

Everything was very picturesque and showed us the wonderful quality of life they had in Pescara. Gino was a man who lived there, but participated in the Formula 1 circus, where he got to know Beco, for working with the sponsoring brand of the Benetton team. And obviously, after having spent a few days with us in Angra dos Reis, he realized that that schedule, although simple, would delight us. Needless to say, fresh fish with sides prepared by an authentic Italian could only have an amazing result.

On our third evening there, when everyone began to give signs that they would go to bed, Beco whispered to me:

"Drica, when the house is silent, go to my room so we can make out, I will wait for you."

I agreed with a discreet nod, we said our goodbyes, and each one went to their own room. I got ready for bed, my sister and I got into bed, and I laid there with all the lights off and my ears on standby until I was sure everyone was asleep. I got out of bed in that darkness, touching things to find the door. When I opened the door, I realized that the entire house was in complete darkness and I could barely see the path I would have to follow. Suddenly I saw a movement in that darkness. It was the dogs in the house that were right in the middle of my way, I stopped to think about what to do. I almost went back to my room, imagining they might attack me, but I could not even run into the room or defend myself from a possible bite because of the extreme darkness, and, at best, they could start barking and wake up everyone in the house. As they still had not reacted to my presence, I decided to tiptoe in their direction and with each step I took, I stopped waiting for some reaction. That corridor had one side made of glass, which opened onto a small internal flower bed, no more than one meter wide. And so I went until I managed to get past the dogs! Now my concern was the stairs in front of me, so I started groping with my feet until I found them. That corridor did not seem so big during the day, but now it looked huge. Of course, when I entered Beco's room, he had already fallen asleep. I took the risk, softly:

"Beco! Beco San!"

"Hi Dridrica, what happened? You took too long!" he said, a little confused, sleep-drunk.

"Beco, I am sorry, you were already asleep, I did not want to wake you up... So get some rest, I will go to my room." Bullshit.

"No, Drica! Come here! But what took you so long?"

"Beco, you cannot imagine the odyssey for me to get here! I waited for the house to be completely silent; when I left the room, I could not see anything at all, such was the darkness. I have been groping and, finally, the dogs are sleeping in the corridor, halfway here!" I tried to explain quickly because, once in his arms, even though he heard me, he was already kissing me all over.

"Glad you made it..."

We made love nicely to make up for lost time in this first opportunity. After that, we relaxed.

"Dridrica, you better go back to your room before we fall asleep."

"Oh, Beco! I think I'd better go back when day breaks so I can see the way!"

"I would love for you to stay too, but if you do, I will be worried we are oversight and get caught. And I have to rest because of the race this weekend."

"Dammit! Okay! Good night, Beco San."

"Good night, Dridrica." We kissed, I dressed, and when I got up from the bed, he added:

"Watch out for the dogs!" he laughed in a low voice.

"Holy shit! A house that big and the dogs had to sleep right there? My parents' Saint Patron are very strong!" I laughed. "Have a good rest, Beco San," I said, leaving the room.

There I went to face the same situation in which I came. I could barely believe when I finally found myself in my bed, ready to sleep happily.

On Thursday, the 21st, we said goodbye to our dearest hosts and thanked them for their attention. We were going to meet again soon on Sunday's race. We left Pescara toward Germany, where the GP would be held in Hockenheim. We flew to the airport in Germany, but Beco insisted on taking a trip along the highway to pass by the German factory of the Hugo Boss brand that sponsored him. So we did. We got to know part of its facilities, where there was a shed with a quadruple ceiling, with bars that crossed from end to end, in a zigzag pattern, with suits and jackets hanging, organized along the entire area. It was a garment rack on a gigantic and computerized scale. We, who knew the dynamics of an industry well, were fascinated by that cutting edge technology in large-scale inventory.

"Those Germans are amazing! This is another world!" my father said, taken aback by that.

"Yeah, Mr. Amilca, that is why I insisted on bringing you here. I knew you would go crazy by seeing this."

"Boy! Amazing!"

"We had access to the factory because I am sponsored by them and people already know me. Now, Mr. Amilca, we will have access to the clothes at cost prices too. Shall we?" he said, making a gesture with his hands for us to follow him.

We arrived at the room, a store where representatives and wholesale buyers were received to choose the garments, and we stood there, with everything at our disposal. My father and Beco went back and forth choosing the goods. Whenever Beco found a garment he liked, he picked it up in several colors — a typical practicality of men, my father was just the same! But they chose more relaxed clothes, for everyday life, taking advantage of the good price for garments of excellent fabric and cut, bringing quality to everyday clothes. No suits or other clothes they used little in their routines, including because they did not want to increase the volume of luggage for the rest of the trip. Beco, who had already planned that stop, took the opportunity to pack a suitcase with new clothes that he would wear in the following days. There were shorts, underwear, socks, T-shirts, polo shirts; in short, everything, and I only helped him choose the colors. Then one of the clerks showed us a black cold-weather jacket, basic to wear on all occasions, but made of pure cashmere and lined with a green fabric of pure silk. Dad went crazy with the touch of the fabric in that basic and elegant jacket, and wanted one right away! While the clerk went to get the ideal size for my father, I commented:

"Wow, dad! I want one of that too!"

"Daughter! That's men's clothes!"

"Wait, Mr. Amilca," Beco said, going after the clerk. They came back together, with various jackets of all sizes.

"Dridrica, I brought a small one of these for you to try, let's see how it looks!"

He handed me the jacket and took what would be his size too. Beco put it on, along with me, we looked at each other and then at the mirror and we immediately decided to take it. Meanwhile, the clerk offered my father other jackets of other sizes. Beco meant to gift me with that garment, for us to use together, but my father, proud, determined he should be the one to pay the bill and there was no argument. They were also offered to my mother and sister, but they thanked and refused.

We paid for our things and left happily with that precious shop.

We continued our journey to Heidelberg, an ancient city in the German countryside, close the Hockenheim racetrack. There, we found Beco's agent, Mr. Armando Botelho, waiting for us. Of course he had business to deal with Beco or give him some task. That evening and the following ones we had dinner together, but during the day Beco had business matters to deal with his agent.

In Germany, therefore, we no longer had Beco's company with us. He had his attention focused on the training days, but had already organized with his acquaintances to guide us, accompany us and even take us to the racetrack that weekend of race.

On training Friday, we did not go to the racetrack, to sightsee with Armando, discover the charms of that beautiful city. We learned that there was a castle at the top of a hill and there we could see far away from the city, and it had been very important in the medieval era. That region had a lot of historical content. I was dying to visit the castle, which was open to the public, and learn about its history, architecture etc., but it was near the closing time. I wanted to go there with no rush, so that I could enjoy the experience, so I decided to leave it for another day when we had time. Neither I nor my family knew the script set up by Beco, he had already made hotel reservations in advance, and we followed him here and there in Europe on his plane. Unfortunately, we did not have time to visit that castle and it was postponed until the next opportunity.

Mom, Dad, I and Chris walking around Heidelberg. Photo in motion, just like Mr. Amilca likes

I remember an interesting fact during our tour to Heidelberg, when we stopped at a place on our way, it was a room with a few small tables, which served coffee at a counter and ice cream at another. Everyone went for the coffee and I for the ice cream. Everyone was already sitting at one of the little tables and I, with my ice cream in hand, went after them. As soon as I turned away from the ice cream counter, a very white-skinned German woman with short, curly hair began to speak loudly and rudely. Hearing that, I stopped and looked back to see what was going on, then I realized it was with me. Without understanding anything, I went on my way and sat down with my family. The German woman started an impassioned speech in English, saying I could not sit there with the ice cream! Confused with the logic of that, I argued with gestures that we were all together and that everything was in the same environment. She roared again for me to get out of there and that infuriated me. I stood still! Then I said I was not going to leave and turned away. The German woman continued to roar and I stood there, ignoring her — that was an obviously absurd rule and totally nonsense. Armando, who did not know me very well, was wide-eyed and asked me if it would not be better for me to obey her.

"No, Armando, I am sorry, if the chairs were just for coffee and none of us were consuming coffee, okay! But you are sitting here, having some coffee, and I cannot join you? We are together! That is stupid; she, at the very least, should have asked gently, politely. That is not how you talk to people! She could have the rules she wanted to, here in this improvised little place, no problem! But she cannot think people will obey her to avoid embarrassment; let her put on her show! I am not leaving here!"

Armando stepped back in front of my justifiable conviction and insisted no more, but really that had all been absurd. They finished their coffee and decided to get out of there as soon as possible, to avoid any more problems. I made sure to get up and leave slowly, with my ice cream in hand, passing close to the counter of the crazy ice cream maker, looking into the German's eyes. She, even more enraged by my confrontation and disregard for her orders, started roaring again, saying I could not sit there because ice cream might fall on the floor, and that I had to eat it outside.

Mr. Armando, Beco's agent, and I, Germany

To my own surprise, I confronted her with fluent English, saying everything I wanted! No one who worked there, perhaps embarrassed, spoke up. I said, in English, pointing my finger explicitly at her:

"You are a stupid woman with stupid rules! That is not how you treat people, you crazy woman! If I drop ice cream, I clean it! You cannot treat a customer like this."

She fell silent, I do not think she was used to being confronted by tourists in her own citadel. It is very funny to experience the nuances of customs in other countries, imagining that discrepancies only happen in Brazil. We had seen an impressively efficient factory the day before, with cutting-edge technology, top-quality products, and there, now, we saw an attitude of ignorance and rudeness that was unimaginable for us Brazilians. If there is one thing I cannot stand, it is arrogance and impunity. We later told Beco the story and, laughing, I said:

"Beco San! I found out I can speak English! All I needed was a good stimulus."

Chapter XXVII

The next day, we took a ride to the racetrack with Paulo Casseb, who had been introduced to Ayrton by my brother-in-law, Dadô. Paulo was the guy who managed to bring heavy machinery for industries to Brazil at a time when imports were prohibited. He was the one who brought weaving machines to my brother-in-law's family's industry, Toalhas São Carlos, but he had legal means for this type of import. In fact, he was the one who brought the first Kawasaki jet skis for my father and he also helped Beco bring a few things. So Paulo was always around Beco to have access to F1 — an exchange of interests, let's say.

Paulo, who did not know the region but wanted to be efficient, did not accept help and followed the road map to reach the racetrack, which was about forty minutes away by car. We were me, my father, mother and sister in the car with him and we realized he was a little confused with the route.

"Paulo, do you want me to help you with the map while you drive?" my father asked, as he was in the front seat with him.

"No, Mr. Amilcar, I know how to get there, do not worry!"

We drove a little longer, and Paulo did not know if we were on the right way. We saw some uniformed personnel working on that local highway.

"Look, Paulo, let's stop and ask for directions," my father determined.

He parked the car, got out with the map in hand, asked one of the workers for help, who kindly assisted us. He supported the map on the hood of the car to exchange information, and by the delay, we knew we were not on the right way. From inside the car, we talked, laughing:

Damn it! Are we going to get there today?" I said.

"What a stubborn guy! It was obvious he did not know where he was going!" my father said, not amused.

"Dri, this scene deserves a photo!" my sister said, laughing.

"Good idea! Let's take one, quickly! Get the camera!" I agreed, laughing.

We did that to laugh at our situation, especially because we knew my father was not one of the calmest and most patient men in the world, so we tried to turn the situation into something light, punishing Paulo's stubbornness with our teasing.

Photo of the moment, mockery on our way to the racetrack

"Beco and Dadô will love this photo!" I said, laughing.

"I just want to hear what he is going to say when he gets in the car," my mother said.

We burst out laughing as we wondered what he would say.

"Enough, girls, he is coming back," my father warned.

Little did Paulo know what was going on in our minds after our side conversation in the car. He got in and started to say he had mistaken an entrance, which deviated us from the route, but we just had to go back and take the correct path. As he spoke, he showed the map to my father.

"Great, give me the map and I will help you," my father said impatiently, taking the map.

We finally made it to the racetrack, and Paulo headed for the exclusive parking lot, near the pits, with the credential previously provided by Beco to access the parking lot, in addition to the credentials for each one of us.

Following my father and Paulo, I allowed myself to walk around the cars in the pits, something I had not dared me to do on the previous trip because no one had told me I could, but now I knew… And I took pictures of his rivals, those I heard so much about.

Ricardo Patrese and the Williams team in action

Nigel Mansell, "the lion", Patrese's companion at Williams that year

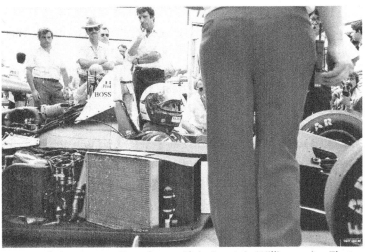

Ayrton's teammate, Frenchman Alain Prost, in Williams pits. That
day, he did not take pole at the German GP, 1988

Mr. Amilcar (on his back with his hands on the waist) attentive to everything he used to talk about at the farm about F1 cars, and Mrs. Marilene

When Beco was back with the car, in the pits, during the qualifying session, I stopped in front of him to take a picture of him inside the car, and to signalize we had already arrived. During the dispute for the best time for the start, he monitored the times of the other drivers from inside the car, thus receiving all the necessary information, including how many and which cars were on the track, who was leaving or entering the pits; in short, everything the driver needed to choose the best track conditions to get the best time. Sometimes it was enough to set the best time early in the day to get pole position, but all the drivers would go to the track as many times as necessary to beat him on training, all supervised from inside the car. Sometimes, he tried to beat his opponent's time at the end of the training period, because he knew he would make a better lap and would give them the opportunity to be beaten — a real chess game with them. We could say that on those days, the training "only ended when it was over". Well, when we crossed our eyes, with him inside the car, I could see, through his eyes, his wide smile behind the yellow helmet. It was the first time he saw me in the pits, he must have been surprised by my unexpected appearance, a nice surprise; I smiled back, took the picture, gave him a little wink and sent him a discreet kiss, a little secret of our own, in the midst of the rush and confusion around the car.

Just before he saw me in front of him

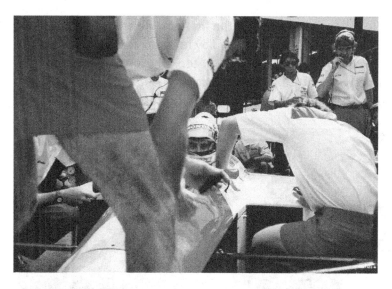

Photos taken by me in the paddocks on Saturday practice. The smiling look when he was surprised by my presence in the midst of that commotion

Day of another pole position of Mr. Ayrton Senna da Silva, my boyfriend Beco San

Happy with the result, after training and with us there to celebrate together the conquest of that day, after bath, we chatted in the motorhome tent. We met Gino again and got to know Galvão Bueno and his then wife Lúcia (in memoriam) better, who was also there at that GP, so we made a group. Then Beco called me to join him, and we went with Gino nearby to meet people he wanted to talk to. I remember one of them was the President of Mercedes-Benz, headquartered in Germany, a very important and influential man. Obviously, Beco introduced me to everyone who was standing. The conversation was in English and I understood everything they were saying, but I remained silent, as my communication was not so fluent. They congratulated Ayrton's pole, happy, and talked about another subject, which Beco quickly questioned, and then returned to their pleasantries. The President of Mercedes-Benz made a very sexist comment about women who keep surrounding the drivers, to tease me. I gave an embarrassed laugh as everyone looked at me, waiting for my reaction. And they laughed at my situation. But as I had not found the joke funny at all and I thought everyone's reaction was exaggerated, I then decided to ask Beco — maybe I had not understood what I thought was nonsense!

"Beco? What did he say?" I asked kind of discreetly, but I wanted the others to think the joke had not hit its target with my ignorance.

Beco, as if embarrassed by my expression of ignorance to the others, made a face of disappointment, did not answer me, wrinkled his nose and continued the conversation with the others.

Then, alone, I asked him again, because I did not understand why they were so amused. And he acted as if I was the one who had embarrassed him in front of his sexist friends. Yes, I was raised by a super sexist man, but he, my father, was never one to make malicious jokes, as if we women were a bunch of idiots. He thought that was a childish attitude! Those who do not respect, do not give themselves to respect! And I did not like the attitude of that "almighty" gentleman with me! And Beco, a bootlicker, found that rudeness funny! I would never imagine that the President of the best car factory, then, and at that age, would lend himself to do such a thing. But I am sure that man's attitude did not represent the serious business he ran. I was raised by a super businessman and I lived my whole life surrounded by important people here in Brazil, and I had never seen anyone make that kind of joke, that is why I know the proper conduct.

On July 24th, the German GP took place at the Hockenheim racetrack. We went to the track in a helicopter with Beco, the best option so that we do not run the risk of getting stuck in traffic jam. The narrow access roads to the racetrack were busy and full of cars.

Therefore, we went to the racetrack very early, spent some time there with Paulo Casseb searching for German culinary specialties. While Beco and team prepared for the race, we went where people were, in search of sauerkraut, sausages and everything that was typical of the country. Me, in a McLaren T-shirt I had won the day before. It was a cloudy day, with rain forecast!

Snack with a typical German menu, "guten appetit"

We saw Reginaldo Leme in the pits and he remembers our presence there:

"I only saw Adriane again long after the opening of the Bar Talento Jazz, in Germany, with her father and mother. Adriane and Ayrton were so alike! Even older than her, he was also very young at the time. He even committed several mistakes on his relationships to others because he was very young. I myself called him out several times along with other fellow drivers. Once we were on a Varig flight, when we met in Rio de Janeiro — this plane was coming from Buenos Aires and Michele Alboreto, Ricardo Patrese and Andrea De Cesaris were there, the group of Italians who were always together. He got on the plane, did not say hi to anyone, and we sat in the back. Then I told him: Dude, are you crazy? Those are the guys who race with you! You are always with them and did not even say hi?!

He got up, went over and chatted animatedly with them for around twenty minutes. He came back to the seat, patted my arm and said: Man, this is what I want from a friend: If you think I am doing something wrong, let me know! It would not be like that in the future.

Adriane is a good person, an example of posture, not shy but very discreet, for me she had nothing to hide. Maybe for others, because she was with him. She was there as his girlfriend, I always knew, and she was friendly all the time. Ayrton was like that; he always paid me a lot of attention before our discussion, and when he was in a hurry to get out of any situation, he did not pay much attention. I remember her calling him out once: Look, Reginaldo is talking to you!

And I never forgot that kind attitude towards me.

Brazilian fans at the ready

In McLaren pits, ready for another great day!

Just before starting the race, Galvão Bueno called me to watch the race from a place with the best view of the entire track. I followed him and when I realized it was the press stand, I asked:

"Galvão, you know I want to remain anonymous, right?"

"Do not worry, I will leave you with a friend of mine, a very nice guy who gave us this space when I said who you were, do not worry, you do not need to say anything!"

"Ok."

We went to the booth of that sports broadcaster, Oscar Ulisses, brother of Osmar Santos. It really was a great view! Right in front of the pits, from where you could see the entire start and it also overlooked the entire track. It fit just me and him there. Sitting next to each other, facing the track, there was a small television there so we could follow the live broadcast up close too. Galvão introduced us, we greeted each other, he invited me to sit in the chair beside him, I thanked Galvão for his kindness, I sat down, and Galvão Bueno left to start broadcasting the race.

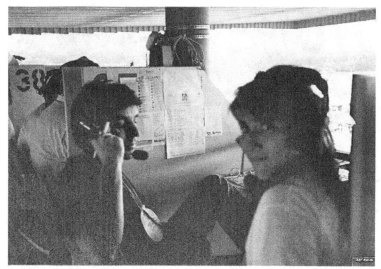
Me with broadcaster Oscar Ulisses in the Radio Globo booth

I also thanked Oscar for the opportunity and he kindly suggested that I put the headphones on, those big ones that cover the whole ear so I could follow his narration; I put the headphones on and they had a microphone attached. He adjusted the microphone to my mouth. But I said, already through our internal communication circuit:

"Look, I appreciate your kindness in having me here, but I do not want to say anything, okay? I hope you do not get me wrong, but I prefer to remain anonymous, I have been doing so for a while now and that is how I intend to continue."

"Of course! No problem."

"Thank you."

The sky was increasingly cloudy.

"Do you think it will rain?" he asked.

"I hope so!"

Then paratroopers appeared descending over the track, a sign that the show was about to begin. I was already excited. I saw the cars positioning on the track in their starting places. Oscar told me:

536

"I am going to start the broadcast."

He started the broadcast by greeting the listeners, giving an overview of the start that day, some information about the track, number of laps, possibility of rain, etc., then he said:

"Today, Ayrton Senna's girlfriend is here with us: Adriane Yamin. Good afternoon, Adriane, welcome to the radio, live from Germany at the Hungaroring racetrack. What do you think of this threat of rain for today's race?"

I remain silent for a few seconds looking at Oscar, in no hurry to decide if I would say something or not. I made an expression at him and shook my head, as if to say: "Right! Now what?" He stayed silent, leaving his listeners anxious. Then I decided to speak:

"Good afternoon, Oscar, I think it will be great if it rains, everyone knows Ayrton is an ace in the rain."

"So you think that if it rains, the race today will be for Brazil?"

"I hope and believe so, let's see!"

"Thank you, Adriane. She will be watching the entire race broadcast here today and will be cheering with us for her boyfriend, driver Ayrton Senna." And he went ahead with the broadcast.

Thank God, he did not ask any more questions during the race. Right after the start, a light rain began to fall. Of course, he won the race that day! Tam tam tam... tam tam tam... Tammmm... tam taram taram tammmm... Tararam... tam tam tam...(singing in humming way the theme known as Ayrton's Song - "Victory Theme" composed by Eduardo Souto Neto).

"Hey Adriane, what did you think of the race?"

"I found it was wonderful, and with the expected result under rain."

"That is it, listeners of the radio..."

I watched the podium from there. When he finished the broadcast, I thanked Oscar again and left to see my Beco San.

Starting time with my boyfriend in pole on a rainy day at the German GP, it could only be good!

Beco San in the background at the podium

Beco San ahead on the TV screen

Brazilian fans in front of the McLaren pit

When I got to the paddock, I found my family and Beco had went for a bath.

Shortly after the race, in McLaren's motorhome, Galvão Bueno, me, properly dressed in the team shirt, Chris, Lúcia (Galvão's wife at the time), Armando, Paulo and mom

In the background of the photo, to the left of Paulo, is the wife of the President of Mercedes-Benz of Germany; on the other side, my father Amilcar

We talked about the race, happy that he won from end to end right when we were there to celebrate. When Beco came, now fragrant, I ran to congratulate him and jumped into his arms.

"Congratulations, Beco San! I cannot believe I am here in person to congratulate you on your victory!"

"You bring luck, Dridrica!"

We smiled, looking at each other for a moment, in each other's arms, and he went on to receive the greetings of those who awaited him. That day, everyone was there: Gino, Paulo, Galvão's wife, even the wife of that President of Mercedes-Benz. People who were alone there found company in our group. Soon most of them left the covered area of the motorhome. With that humid weather, despite the summer, I was already feeling a little cold. Beco, noticing this, quickly got a Boss sweatshirt, which was commemorative. They made a different coat color for each race, with some imprint on it relating to the corresponding GP — of that GP was turquoise. I wore it, and as everyone loved it, he provided another one for my sister, who was also uncovered. Days later, Beco gave me one from another GP, that was in his suitcase, a yellow-canary one. Seeing there were now less people there, Beco said:

"Mr. Amilca, I have a fresh champagne here to celebrate!"

"Oh, boy! Cool! Let's have a toast!"

Beco got the bottle of champagne, with disposable plastic cups, which was all they had in that place. That was one more reason for fun. We all toasted, congratulating the winner of the day. And Beco said, laughing:

"And let the French not see us taking their champagne from these cups!" he laughed.

Dad, me, mother, Galvão, Beco, Lúcia, Chris and Paulo

At McLaren motorhome, celebration of end-to-end victory at the German GP

Our arrival in Sardinia with Ayrton's plane

With all the luggage in the car, we went to the airport that same day. Galvão and his wife accompanied us on this trip.

We headed to Sardinia, Italy, on Beco's plane. We landed at night and took a van to the hotel. Even without sunlight, but with the help of moonlight, I could see that the topography was totally different from anything I had ever seen before, very rocky, with low, sparse vegetation.

When we got at the Hotel Cala di Volpe, we learned that one of the 007 movies had been shot in that hotel (The Spy Who Loved Me, 1977). The hotel was very rustic, with the air of a den, a fox's cave — the walls and passages had light wavy volumes throughout, as if we were in a stone den. The literal translation of "Cala di Volpi" is fox's cave, but it looks more like a fox's den. It was in a privileged location on that very exclusive island, by the sea, but in a protected spot from the open sea agitation.

The room I would share with my sister had two charming beds, made of metal and with an ornate headboard, the walls had volumes, still looking like a stone den. And, on the wall, a painting of an English-style wooden desk, in real scale, with flower vase and other ornaments painted in perspective, giving the impression of reality, that is, trompe l'oeil — a work of art painted on the wall, adorning the room as if the furniture were really there. Other than that, just a built-in closet, with white shutters. It was simple and sophisticated at the same time, nice and brilliant!

We made other discoveries over the days about that hotel. It was frequented by the European elite, Arab sheiks, movie stars, top politicians. You could make reservations through well-known attendees and influential people. In our case, who got the reservation for our group was precisely our friend, President of Mercedes-Benz, and that was what Beco had talked to him in the paddocks days before. Over there, we saw some people walking around dressed in traditional Arab clothes.

On the first day, we were looking for information about what would be interesting to do and know. The hotel made speedboats available for rent, for sightseeing and reconnaissance around the island. So we decided to book one for the next day, and that day we would stay at the hotel pool.

My father on the sun lounger, with the famous Cala Di Volpi hotel in the background

Us, at the hotel pool

We solved it all in a bar, near the reception. We all returned to our rooms and got ready for the pool. After about five minutes, my father saw his reading glasses were missing,

545

a pair of gold-framed glasses, and went back to where he had left them, on the table where we were. But they were no longer there. We then went to inquire with the employees if they had seen the glasses and where they could have taken them — like a lost-and-found in the hotel. Everyone said they had not seen the glasses, so we went to the reception to check if maybe some guest found and left them there. Nope.

We were astonished as this type of situation could occur in a so selective hotel. My father said, in the pool:

"They must have thought my glasses were made of gold. Thank God I did not bring one of my best glasses for this trip, but whoever took them must have been very attentive to the theft, after all, it did not take me more than three minutes to get back to the table. Girls, be careful with your belongings in this hotel! Got it?"

We had a very peaceful day. Beco had to rest, recover his strength from the previous day's race. After showering, before dinner, we stayed in the hotel's bar, overlooking the entire length of the lawn, pool, and the sea in front of us — it was the group's meeting point until everyone was present for dinner. We watched the sunset there. It really felt like we were living a movie scene in that magical place.

At the hotel bar, the two of us waiting for everyone for dinner

After dinner, we went for a walk around the hotel, Beco and I, holding hands, we walked to the pier, from where, during the day, the speedboats departed. In that silence, with no one around, in a place also dimly lit, Beco finds a way for us to make out right there, under the starry sky. I actually did not like that kind of situation, I did not enjoy it, thinking someone might be watching us, but Beco did not ask. He put his plan into action, catching me off guard, and I could not say no to him. It was a conflict inside me, I was crazy about that man, I liked to feel wanted by him, but at the same time, that was not a proper place! In a way, that made me feel like a vulgar woman. And I did not feel well about that. But what would be our place to make out?

The next day, we all went out for a boat ride around the island. We passed a marina where the biggest boats were located. Among huge boats, we saw one that caught our attention: It was about 150 feet long and had a hull painting in the same colors as a jet we saw at the airport there when we landed. It was in a very light cream tone, not quite off-white, with thin stripes in guava, yellow and light green colors, from end to end. That way, we knew everything we came across there, in those days, with that painting, belonged to the same owner. The guide — and also the sailor of our speedboat — said that the big boats had their hulls checked daily by divers, fearing a terrorist attack. It was a place visited by billionaires from all over the world. We also saw berthed warships; that island was in a strategic location of the Italian defense for eventual attacks from the Mediterranean Sea.

The biggest boat in Sardinia, redoubt of millionaires from all over the globe

We continued our journey until we reached a beautiful area with calm waters for swimming. The sea color was very different from anything I had ever seen in my life: A crystalline turquoise, where you could almost perfectly see the rock bottom. We were dying to jump, but even in summer the water was pretty cold. So we threw ourselves into the sea in a single jump; us, the youngest ones, and Galvão, who was also very lively. In order not to be cowed by the temperature, it was either going at once or not going at all!

Beco taking up courage to dive in the crystalline and icy waters of the Mediterranean Sea

We also had brought a snack, some fruit, sandwiches and drinks. Obviously, the thinnest one would start the line: Beco! Nothing went unnoticed there and everything was a reason for mockery, so I took pictures of the sweet tooth on board. We only enjoyed the sun, the sea, the company and the stunning view for some time, as the tour was hired for four hours and we still had to go back.

Galvão, Lúcia (lying), Chris, Beco and, in the right corner, mom and dad (being funny)

At one point, Beco got a snack, and ate it on the boat making a mess; everyone was amused by it. Later, sitting with his back to everyone in the stern of the small boat, tired of his reputation as a glutton and so that we would not see the drip tray that came out of the fruit when he bit into it. Of course we did not ignore it. With the camera in hand, we called Beco, trying to catch him in the act, but as he was not a fool and was always attentive, he kept his back turned and waved his hands in response. We started to laugh and insisted that he looked back at us, until he decided to give up and accepted the mockery. And it was always like that, in a moment of rest, everyone messed with the other, mainly Galvão vs. Beco. It was a small boat and we were all very close, nobody could be off guard there, we were all pranksters. Galvão's wife was the only one to lie down in the bow of the boat; she wanted privacy to go topless, but her husband went there to mess with her! Later, when she was properly covered, Beco also went over to take pictures, just because she hated taking pictures.

The sweet tooth on board

At one point, I disconnected from everyone, quietly sunbathing. In a matter of minutes, Beco ran after a camera and surreptitiously loomed over me, casting a shadow. Realizing that, even with my eyes closed, I was surprised and opened them to see where that shadow came from, when I came face to face with Beco standing over me with the camera ready:

"Got you, Dridrica!" he laughed.

"How silly you are!" we laughed together.

We also took pictures for posterity.

His prank on the photo (casting a shadow)

Mom and I

Lúcia, mom, Chris, Beco, dad and me: relaxing day in Sardinia

On our way to the hotel: Beco and I

That same day, back at the hotel, around six in the afternoon, we decided to get dressed to visit one of the shopping centers in the local, with stores of the most luxurious brands in the world and good restaurants, located in Porto Cervo. Those were sunny days, with no clouds in the sky, and in the summer of Europe, the sun sets after nine at night. On our way, we crossed the road with a Jeep that also had the familiar colors: light cream and thin green and orange stripes. When we got there, it was still light, we walked around the place and its stores, all very expensive, with higher prices than in other places, with the same brands and products, so we bought nothing there; we would have other opportunities to consider buying something. But it was a very beautiful, Mediterranean-style place. We took pictures there to register our tour and went to dinner.

Marilene, Christhiane, Amilcar, me and Beco, in Porto Cervo

"Us" in Porto Cervo

Porto Cervo, Sardinia

Galvão and his wife, Lúcia, followed us for the rest of the trip, and little by little and were feeling more comfortable. We were more understated and conservative in style than they were. We learned she lived in Rio de Janeiro and was an interior decorator. We also learned that their children had stayed in Brazil. I remember she hated taking pictures and, realizing that, Beco insisted on taking pictures of her. We all died of laughter at her scolding, and she too, amused by that conspiracy. She was a polite and pleasant woman, but felt a little self-conscious with us, maybe because we had that aura of being conservative and serious; we made joke, but innocent ones, no one dared making dirty jokes. Or maybe she was just cautious, not to make mistakes. As said before, it was not easy to live with the Yamin family. We were and are people of simple spirit, but with a politeness that maintains our dignity in conduct and attitudes.

As for Galvão, he felt comfortable easily and was playful before his friend Becão. But he kept bugging his wife, who wore tiny bikinis, as usual on beaches of Rio de Janeiro, and wanted to follow the European custom of topless in the sun. Poor thing, maybe she felt inadequate because of her husband, not because of our actions. Discreet, she did not want to bother us with her topless. She moved away to feel free to do whatever she wanted, and it really was not that big of a deal, nothing that could shock us, but Galvão, just like Beco had done to me recently in the presence of the President of Mercedes-Benz, was more concerned about what we were going to think about his own image, and not in her right to do whatever she felt like. Around us, we saw a lot of topless people, but in a natural and discreet way, it did not shock anyone, it is a European habit. Therefore, we, the women, seeing the situation, were supportive and very kind to her.

When it got dark, we went for dinner right there at a restaurant in Porto Cervo.

Us in the restaurant, just after sunset, always cheerful

Dinner in Porto Cervo

I was so happy to be with my parents and boyfriend together on a wonderful trip! When I realized, however, that my sister felt a little out of place, I made a point of including her in the photos and in everything Beco and I did. He, in turn, also supportive, helped me to include her in conversations and everything else. We did what we could to bring her close to us.

On the way to the other side of the Island, in the background our hotel

Beco and I waving at the boat over the rocks

The next day, we repeated the schedule; we went for a speedboat trip, but now to the opposite side of the island. Another amazing day for us, but we came back earlier because it was too much sun on our skin. On the way back, uncomfortable with the sun and no shade to help me, even with the wind from the moving boat, I decided to wrap myself in the hotel towels, covering myself up from head to toe. Beco, by my side, did not resist the scene, discreetly signalized for someone to take a picture of me with him. He even made a horn on my back for the picture. I knew his intentions but pretended not to, just to give him a taste. I liked how he always kept an eye out for me, even if only to play tricks on me. In the other half of the day, when we were not on the speedboat, we were at the pool, and he said:

"Drica, you need to work out! Why don't you swim a little?"

He knew my body had changed a little because of the swelling caused by the pill. I did not mind swimming; I have always been a real fish! And I decided to comply with his request, to show I was not lazy to take care of myself. I made ten rounds of the pool extension swimming crawl, went back to his side and intended to go back into the pool and repeat the exercise, when he said:

"Only that, Dridrica? Ten times?"

"Listen, it is ten, then ten more, and then ten, I cannot monopolize the hotel pool. Is that okay for you?!"

"Oh, okay, Dridrica!" he replied, noticing I was annoyed with his insistence and control.

One day, when it was just the two of us from the group there in the pool area, we could be more comfortable. We kissed in the pool, I gently rubbed the sunscreen over him, and we laid down together a little entwined on the lounge chair. Gosh, how I wish I could have more peaceful moments like that with him! Just the two of us.

On another end of the day, we also visited Porto Rotondo, similar to Porto Cervo, but smaller. A tour that is also worth having.

The day before our departure for Monaco, we all went to get ready for dinner and have our bags ready for the next morning. Beco's room was next to ours, and farther away from my parents'. As I got ready, I called Beco from my room to go downstairs together, as usual.

"Hi Beco San, are you ready?"

"No, Dridrica, I am packing, how about you?"

"Completely ready!"

"So stop by my room, Drica San!"

"Okay, be right there!"

When I got there, all his clothes were spread around his bed.

"Gosh Beco, can I help you?"

"Of course! You fold them and I put them in the suitcase, is that okay?"

"Sure!" and I got my hands dirty, doing it with the greatest care.

Watching how he was packing the pieces in the suitcase, I saw I knew a better way. My aunt Miriam had taught me on a trip and they really were precious tips. I quickly finished folding the clothes that were lying around; those that had already been used and the others; the new ones from Hugo Boss were still folded individually inside the company's bags. I said:

"Beco San, can I give you a few tips to help you with your suitcase?"

"Help me how?" he asked, moving away from the bed where the bag was open, making room for me.

Confidently, I took everything out of the suitcase and showed him.

"See, you first put the pants like this, then the shorts, the shirts stacked like this, so as not to wrinkle the collar, and the T-shirts like this; that way you create piles at the same height.

561

And in these gaps, you put swim trunks. Here you put the socks and belts, skirting the clothes so as not to mark them. Can I see how many shoes you have? And how big is your toilet bag?"

He showed me and asked:

"Drica, won't your parents miss you?"

"Let them miss me! I tell them I am helping you pack your things!"

"Will they believe it?"

"They will have no choice; they will have to believe me! What outfit will you travel in tomorrow?"

He set out a new polo shirt and underwear.

"That is it! I am going with this pair of sneakers I am going to wear today, and shorts too."

"Okay, let's leave some space for your toilet bag, and you put it here tomorrow morning, put the pants stretched, around everything, and close it."

Before I finish the explanations, the phone in the suite rings, and he answers:

"Hello."

"Hello Beco, do you know where Adriane is?" It was my mother, the screwdriver.

"Hi, Mrs. Marilene!" he replied with wide eyes at me, not knowing what to say.

I went to him.

"Give me the phone here, let me talk!" and I took the device.

"Hi, mom!"

"Dear, what are you doing there? Everybody is down here and you sister told us you had been gone for a while, that you were only going to stop by Beco's room so you could go downstairs together. And you are not here yet! What the hell?"

"Mom, I am helping Beco fold his clothes and pack his things. Why?"

"Nothing, dear, you won't be long, will you? We are waiting for you and Galvão for dinner!"

We won't be long, we are almost finishing here, mom, we will be there soon enough!"

"Okay, dear!"

Beco, gaping at my courage, started laughing when I hung up the phone. And I added:

"Well, your bag is ready! If you get it off the bed, we still have some time to make out a little!"

Without blinking, he acted to clear the bed... When we met the group for dinner, I told them the truth, but exaggerating what could be said and omitting what could not.

The next day, during check-out, Beco was beside my father to help him with the language, when my father took out his credit card after checking the bill. He started to laugh when he saw the card and said:

"Wow, Mr. Amilca, it is the first time I see a Diamond card. It must only be for those who have a full account to be able to have a card like that!"

My father looked at Beco sideways without answering, but with an air of satisfaction. I laugh alone, just to remember. Then, at the first opportunity, dad commented with us:

"I said nothing at the time, and it is not a big deal — once in a lifetime it is fine! But what an expensive hotel! I was charged a thousand dollars a day per room! Do the math and find out how much this little game cost!"

Poor man! He got a scare! But if we think this was thirty years ago, those eight thousand dollars in four days were worth much more than they are today. So I said to comfort him:

Dad, Beco wanted to please you and chose the best place to bring us!"

Then he admitted:

"Wow! It pleased me a lot! But the bill did not!" And he laughed.

My father at the airport in Sardinia, photo for record of the commuter plane with the same colors as the huge yacht that we also registered

Beco and Drica San, photo for record of his plane, before departure to France

We took the flight to France and went from the airport to Monaco by helicopter. We stayed at Beco's apartment. I do not know where Galvão and his wife Lúcia stayed. Beco gave his room to my parents, Chris and I stayed in the guest room, and he slept in a small room at the back of the property, in a single bed. I recognized some furniture that was in his house in England, in Monaco apartment, which had a large balcony overlooking the sea.

The two of us on our way to Monaco

One day, we visited Nice, a city neighboring the Principality of Monaco. We walked along the shore and stopped for ice cream. We also found, in a corner of the rocky sand beach, some boys playing bocce ball outdoor. We immediately remembered my grandfather Rocha!

A tour around Monaco Marina; me, Beco, Chris and my mother Marilene

We returned to Monaco and went for a walk around the marina, on the outskirts of Beco's building. Two places that caught my attention and I wanted to take pictures with Beco: One of them, the tunnel that was part of the route of Formula 1 racing; the other, nearby, where Beco had crashed alone, when he was in the lead and with a few laps to go in the race. The tire tracks were still on the asphalt of when he braked hard trying to avoid collision. This curve, before the tunnel entrance, could be seen from the balcony of his apartment. Reluctantly, he agreed to take a picture there with me, with the tire tracks of his car on the floor and his apartment in the background.

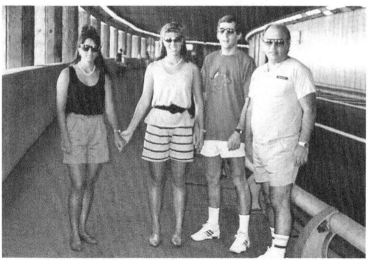

Inside the tunnel that is part of the Monaco GP circuit

Curve of the circuit before the tunnel, still with the tire tracks on the asphalt; brake before the crash that took Ayrton out of the lead in the GP that year. Just behind, Beco's apartment building

I also remember that, while we were waiting for someone to continue our journey, I decided to sit on the curb of a street without cars under the tree shade, trying to cool off in that European summer, a little away from the group. Beco, realizing that, went towards me and sat down next to me. With an Italian magazine I had in hand, he started flipping through the pages and had an idea.

Moment together, when Beco wanted to teach me to read in Italian

"Dridrica, I will teach you how to read in Italian, so you can get the hang of it."

While he spoke, he tracked the word in the magazine with his finger for me to read and repeat. I did not find it difficult and, as soon as he realized that I had gotten the hang of it, he asked:

"That is right! Read it to me, by yourself."

And I, without really understanding what I was reading, at least knew how to pronounce those words. I was enjoying the class, but soon they called us to continue on our way.

The other day, we went to Cannes, a city in the south of France, also close to the Principality of Monaco, but opposite Nice, where we took a tour with Galvão Bueno and his wife.

Marilene, Beco, me, Chris, Galvão and Lúcia (sitting)

To register the building where the famous film awards party takes place, Cannes Festival. And as usual, Mr. Ayrton tickling me at the moment of the photo. I had my hideous slippers to save my bruised feet from the walk

Ice cream time in Cannes. Galvão Bueno, dad, Chris, mom, Lúcia, me and Beco

Later, we went to place where you could rent parachute flights pulled by a speedboat and a banana boat. Of course, we all wanted to fly in the parachute to see Monaco from above. Then, we decided to take a risk on the banana boat, Chris in front, me, Beco, and finally, Galvão. The speedboat pulled us, we held ourselves not to fall, then the boat pilot, experienced, did some maneuvers to knock us down and succeeded! I remember it was an elbow in one's ear, a knee in another's nose, head in another's mouth, that is, it was painful for everyone, hitting each other during the fall, but there was no injury. We climbed up there from the middle of the sea and went on, but did not let ourselves fall again, out of pure fear of getting hurt.

Adventure time: Galvão, Beco, me and Christhiane

Coming back from the painful fall

End of banana boat adventure

Waiting for my turn for the parachute flight

Everything settled for my flight

Photo taken by Ayrton, who was amused by my distress when the speedboat slowed down so I "almost" landed in the middle of the sea until I regained speed to keep myself in flight. I have no doubt the prank was Beco's idea who, by the speedboat, watched in a ringside seat

When we arrived at his house, after his bath, Beco took two cotton rings and two ice cubes and placed them over his eyes, sitting in a reclining the chair near the balcony — what a memorable scene! He claimed he had his eyes burning, due to the fall into the sea in the prank that day. I did not hesitate, after all, revenge is a dish best served cold. I ran to get the camera, in silence so he would not notice, and took the picture. However, at the moment of the click, with the camera noise, he realized he had been caught! Everyone who watched the scene burst out laughing, and Beco did not know who had taken the photo to "give back" on another occasion. But after nagging at everyone during that trip, his time had come.

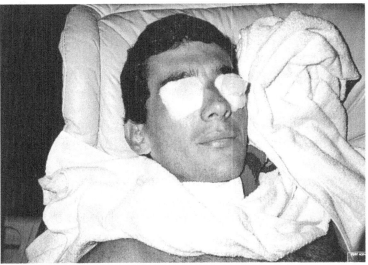

Mr. Ayrton Senna da Silva caught in the act: Care to rest his little eyes itchy by sea water. Revenge is a dish best served cold.

One evening, we all got dressed to visit the famous Monte Carlo Casino, which was in a very beautiful building; the F1 circuit passed right in front of its door. My dad gave us some money to play, around a hundred and fifty dollars.

Pose for the gala night at the Monaco Casino, in the entrance hall of the apartment, decorated in the same colors as his house in England (a peach tone that was fashionable at the time), chosen by Mrs. Neyde, obviously

"Look, today I will teach you how to play. Take the money: If you win anything, great; but if you lose, the game is over!" said my ever-controlling father.

We spread out through the Casino and I followed Beco and Galvão to a Black Jack table, to understand the rules. It was similar to Sette e Mezzo, a game we played at the farm, but the goal was to get twenty-one points to win. I started to play, but the dealer was taking everything on that table, so we gave up. We looked for another table that would bring us more luck. First, we watched the table's fortunes before venturing into it. When I realized my money was almost over, I decided to play on the machines, to extend the fun. I played a little bit, won a little bit and decided to stop. I went to meet Beco and stayed watching him and Galvão in a fierce dispute.

On the last day of our trip, we went to a beachside club where we could relax, sunbathe and swim. I had bought a sophisticated bikini, different from the girly bikinis I had taken on that trip. I decided to use it, it was strapless. There was a moment when I noticed Beco next to me, I was sunbathing on my back and I released my bikini clip, just to see his reaction. I pretended I did not know he was there, but when I noticed him very still, I decided to look at him, without leaving my position. Still, he looked at me, and we exchanged a hot look. But he did not resist and restrained me:

"Drica, close the back of your bikini..."

"Why? You cannot see anything! I am on my back; it is just to remove tan lines!"

"Dri, I am asking you to close it..."

I looked at him sharply and teasingly...

"Go playing with fire, doll! Then you cannot complain when I get you right."

I kept looking into his eyes, but now with the air of one who would love if he did what he had threatened.

"Oh Dridrica, poor me!" and laughed.

That night, of course, I was invited to sneak out to his little room, and I, as a good, obedient girl, went!

The next day, August 2nd, was the day we returned to Brazil. It had been a very different trip from the year before! Beco accompanied us to the airport when boarding. From then on, Beco was already preparing for the race in Hungary.

On August 7th, at the Hungarian GP, at the Hungaroring racetrack, Ayrton started in pole position and won the race. It was his first F1 victory in Hungary.

In the morning, Beco entered my room and, under protest, photographed me in my pajamas when I was packing my things. He did not miss an opportunity to mess with me

Selfie taken by Beco San (with those cameras with film rolls and everything), in the helicopter, on the way to the airport in France, from where my family and I would board for Brazil

When Beco and I met again in Brazil, after the Grand Prix and right after the trip we took together in Europe, talking alone, he told me:

"Dridrica, when we were at home, in Monaco, Galvão came to ask me if we were not having sex. I said no, and he asked me how I can stand to spend so many days by your side like that... I explained that your upbringing was different, when we started dating you were very young, and I asked him if he had not seen how your parents are always watching you. And I changed the subject."

I decided to express myself:

"Why did you lie?"

"Oh, Dri! I thought I should not say, that maybe you would be upset with it."

"Look, it is one thing for my parents not to know because they do not accept dialogue; lying to everyone is another thing! If I thought we were doing something wrong, I would not be doing it, got it? You can tell your friends! I decided to have an adult life, do not treat me like a child anymore in front of your friends. Why should you not tell them?"

He went silent and shut down in his thoughts with what I said. I did the same with that information. Why would he tell me that? Did he want my permission not to give the impression he was in a childish relationship? So I gave him!

The other days we just rested and enjoyed our routine in Brazil, but he was more tense and quiet than usual. I knew he was not managing to disconnect completely of the championship as before, his thoughts were running away from there all the time. Even though he was at a spectacular stage in his career, it was as if he would lose his pace if he disconnected or relaxed for a minute. Tension. I knew he was overwhelmed and could not think about other demands, like our future, for example. I resigned.

Beco returned to Europe, where he would dispute the Belgian GP, and on August 28th, before the race, he called me:

"Hi Drica San, here I come! Keep up with your lucky support!"

"Got it! I am here watching you, God and I!"

"Drica, just hang in there that this madness will be over real soon, and we will have a great time, okay?"

"Okay, so be careful! I want every piece of you just for me! Got it?"

"Yes, ma'am, Dridrica! I have to go."

"Take care, lots of kisses."

"Kisses."

Ayrton started in pole position at the Belgian GP, at the Spa-Francorchamps racetrack and won! It was his second win in Belgium, in Formula 1, and he was now leading the '88 Championship.

The day after the Belgian GP, Beco, now in Monaco, wrote the letter below that I received a few days later:

Drica,

Adivinhe quem tirou estas fotos?
Quando viram me mostrar, minha
reação imediata foi opa, quem é essa
boa...? Depois de alguns segundos
é que percebi do que e de quem
se tratava. Algum 'mafioso' fotografo lá na Sardenha pegou com uma
Tele objetiva na base da surpresa...
menos mau que é caso nada de
errado pegou, como por exemplo alguns de
seus beliscões em áreas meio proibidas.
A matéria em si também nada tem
de errado ou ruim, portanto a única
coisa que me deixou muito preocupado é
o que 'todas as outras' vão fazer agora.
→

que foi descoberto meu grande segredo !!!
AH, AH, AH !!!

Drica, vou dizer que a saudade é daquelas e só de pensar que antes de um mês não voltarei ao Brasil, fica meio difícil.

Bebe Sá,

Acho que estou muito perto de completar um grande sonho e sei que isso vai mudar muito as coisas p/ mim, agora devo mais do que nunca continuar nesse ritmo e não amolecer até acabar de vez esse campeonato.

Aguenta firme Drica, que agente vai se divertir muito quando isso aqui acabar, já estou movendo muos negócios p/ ter Dezembro e Janeiro livres e aproveitar muito, inclusive "fazer muita arte" !!!

Aqui em Monaco ainda continua
quente e vou esses próximos dias
dar uma volta na Austria e Italia
e depois finalmente vou a
Inglaterra p/ treinar, de lá
retorno por um dia aqui e então
vou p/ Monza.

Na última vez que viajei do Brasil
p/ cá demorou bem uns 3 a 4 dias
p/ dormir direito, esse fuso horário
nessa época do ano é muito grande,
no final do ano a diferença de horas
diminui de 5 p/ 3 ou 2 horas o que
já dá p/ enganar o corpo.

Beijão gostosão do seu ....   Bello 21.08.88
                                        Monaco

"Drica,
Guess who is it in these photos? When they came to show me, my immediate reaction was, hey, who is this [unintelligible]? After a few seconds I realized what and who it was. Some "mafia" photographer in Sardinia took us by a telephoto lens on the base by surprise... thankfully the guy did not see anything bad, like some of your tweaks in prohibited places. The report itself has nothing wrong or bad, therefore, the only thing that got me really worried is what "all the others" will do now that our great secret was discovered!!! ha ha ha Dridrica, I miss you so much that it gets hard just to think that I won't be back to Brazil before one month. Silly San, I think I am really close to accomplish a big dream and I know this will change things a lot for me, now I must more than ever keep up with this pace and not slow down until this championship is finally over. Hang in there Drica, and we will have a great time when this is over, I am already working on having December and January free to enjoy a lot, including, making "a great mess"!!!! Here in Monaco, it is still hot and I will go to Austria and Italy in the next days, then finally to England for practice. Then I return here for a day and head to Monza. The last time I went from Brazil to here, I took about 3 or 4 days to sleep well, the jet lag at this time of the year is huge; at the end of the year the time difference goes down from 5 to 3 or 2 hours, which helps the body a little.
Sending delicious kisses from your pervy...
Beco 08.29.88 Monaco"

586

ECCEZIONALE! IL «CHIACCHIERATO» BIG DELLA

SENNA: HO PRESO UNA SBANDATA

Il campione brasiliano, favorito numero
uno alla conquista del campionato del
mondo, è finalmente uscito allo scoperto,
cancellando le malignità di Piquet
che lo accusava di essere gay: lui ha
in realtà una bellissima ragazza
che nasconde perché tutti gli invidiano

PER ATTIRARE I FOTOGRAFI...

Portorotondo. Anche se fa una smorfia come se lo avesse
preso un crampo al polpaccio non è difficile
riconoscerlo: è Ayrton Senna (25 anni), il campione
brasiliano della McLaren che sta dominando il
campionato di Formula 1. Più sorprendente (e misteriosa) è
la sua compagna, che, con un simpatico gesto, attira
ancora di più l'attenzione del fotografo che li ha sorpresi.

... NON TEMIAMO PRIMI PIANI!

Ayrton e la sua compagna si avvicinano ancora di più per
scambiarsi un bacio. È la prima volta che Senna viene
fotografato insieme a una donna, sulla quale, comunque, è
riuscito a mantenere il segreto (di lei non si sa
neppure il nome). Fino ad ora il pilota l'aveva tenuta
nascosta per tenerla lontana dalle grinfie dei marpioni
dei box, specie del suo nemico Nelson Piquet, che tempo fa,
aveva addirittura insinuato che Ayrton fosse gay.

74

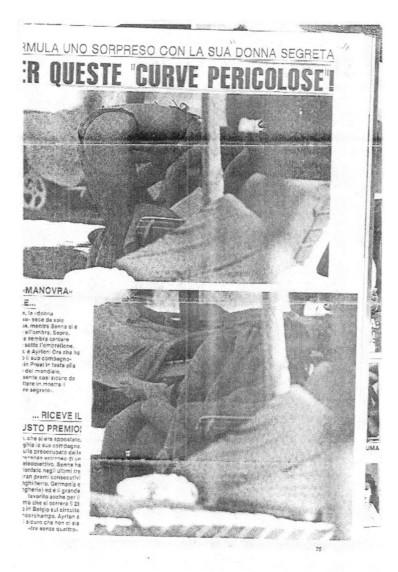

Xerox of an Italian report sent with the letter

In a television interview given by Ayrton to friend and sports narrator Galvão Bueno, from Rede Globo TV, in Monaco, in August 1988, right after our stay in Monaco, he said, moved:

588

"(...) There is Ayrton and there is Beco, and Beco does not live in Europe, he lives in Brazil and Ayrton lives in Europe. Beco is the one who is connected to the family, my father, my mother, my sister, my nephews, my brother, Leo, and my girl, my girlfriend Adriane, and it is a tremendous conflict! Between my profession and my personal life, and only with their help did I get where I am now, and with their support I had and have the strength to withstand this conflict between Ayrton and Beco (...)".

Chapter XXVIII

On September 11th, the Italian GP took place in Monza. Ayrton started in pole position — it was the tenth of the year. But he crashed on lap 49 and left the race.

Despite the result of the Grand Prix in Monza, this year Beco was winning a lot, and I, with that pressure inside me, suffering in anticipation of how my life would be the following year. I could no longer stand living in a long-distance relationship, having to schedule a time with him, enjoying ourselves in places I did not like during our intimate moments, always being with a lot of people around. I did not want that anymore and felt it was time to change the dynamics of our relationship. However, Beco's statement that "before you think" we would be making a commitment, left everything uncertain. Maybe he had said that because he felt pressured by me, because, after all, he had other priorities at that time, but I also had my priorities in life. Dream about what? What should I prepare for? To get married or to go to college? What course would I like to take? If I got married, what would I do during his travels? What would the marriage be like? What would my life be like with him? Where would we live? If I were to spend time in Brazil, would we have a house here? If not, where would my house be? Anyway, too many unanswered questions haunted me.

Moreover, such a difficult year for him made him transfer to me the conduct and attitude towards the life he imposed himself to win the '88 championship. He wanted to have total control over everything and to have everything on his own way, as he thought that in order to work, nothing could escape from his hands, so I was part of that scheme. The time had come when he was leading the championship, after a few troubles, it is true. For example, in Rio de Janeiro he did not score because he did not even finish the race and had to chase those points. The scoring dispute was very fierce, especially with Prost, who was now on his team. When I realized he was leading the championship, in a calmer moment in his career, I decided to ask for a break.

I knew Beco would take a while to return to Brazil, because of the F1 calendar that concentrated the European Grand Prix in the second half, and also because of the training scheduled in the interval between races. Therefore, I thought, I would have a lot of time to rethink my life. I felt that the year before, he had done everything he could to spend more time here; but in 1988, his job was the priority. I also felt that my transition from girl to woman was not well worked by him and we did not talk about it. When he talked about our future plans, he spoke in a demanding tone, expecting me to be carrying them out even though nothing had yet been settled between us. During a phone call, I asked:

"Look, Beco, that is good! Now you are leading the championship, and I am happy because you are closer to the title. I am sure everything will be fine, but I want to ask you one thing... I need some silence for me, I need some silence for Adriane, because I want to think about my life, what I want in life, what I am going to do, because, for you, we have nothing settled. I finish high school this year and I need to stop and think about my life, okay?"

"No, don't do that, Dri!" Beco said.

"There is no problem with what I am asking you, I just want some quiet time, a time when I am not worried about when you are going to call me, about how you are. Here, I am always expecting you to call me, so we can talk and I learn how things are. I do not want to worry about your championship and your life during this time. I do not want to worry about anything of yours, I want to worry about my life, just for a while, until you come back to Brazil. I love you! Nothing changed between us! What I feel for you has not changed at all, I just want some time for myself, I just want some silence. I need to breathe, because it has been a very difficult year for you and I have been supporting you as best as I can, but now I also need to stop and think about myself."

He insisted that I not do this. Then I said:

"Beco, don't do what? I just want some time for myself, I told you, nothing happened, and nothing will happen, there is no influence from others, this is just between you and me! I am still your girlfriend! I love you, I just need a moment of silence for me!"

We were each in a side of the world: He was there, focused on the good moment of his career, and I, here, just needing some time to focus on my life and organize my ideas. He repeatedly insisted for me not to ask for this break, and we stayed that way throughout the phone call until he gave up and turned off the phone.

I knew Beco had F1 training that week, in that year so essential for his career, but he canceled his appointments and came to São Paulo to talk to me. That made me feel incredibly important! Actually, I already knew of my importance in his life, but I did not imagine he would be so scared by my request! I had made it clear that it was not a break in our relationship, just a time in the relationship for me, I wanted to be quiet, it is not a crime for a person to want to be silent. Why such a fear of it? And he came, appeared here like that, I was scared. How come? What about training? He had really canceled training and, now in São Paulo, he came to pick me up at home, we went to the ice cream store, which was our usual spot to talk, and he began to say:

"Adriane, what are you up to? Are you trying to ruin my life? You cannot do such a thing!!"

"No, Beco! I do not want to ruin your life, it is not about you, it is not about our relationship, what I did was for me! I wanted to stop and think about myself. There is no other person in this story, I told you that in our phone call!"

"You can ruin my life this way! Got it?" he said, in tears.

"The story is still mine and yours! I still love you so much, I just wanted some time to think about myself. When I talk about our future, you change the subject, as if I were apart from your wishes! I finish high school this year, as well as I finish my duty to my parents. And what will my life be like from next year on? I will have to change my life; it is time to make choices! So, this is what I wanted. Because a lot of things were left behind and we did not talk about it, things got mixed up."

And he repeated crying, as if he did not hear anything I said:

"But Adriane, you will ruin my life! You will finish me off!"

And I smiled nervously, trying to calm him down. I said this was not what I wanted to do to him, I had waited for a calmer, safer moment for him, so that I could have this quiet time of mine, but he just cried and would not listen to me. That is, he was scared, because our entire relationship was focused at him. He was with me when he wanted to, invited me to travel when he wanted to, on my trips to Europe he programmed and acted as he wanted to. On the first trip, I was secondary; on the second, it was very good, but honestly? He really wanted to please my father. And why didn't he want to please me on the first trip? Or was it because he realized the mistake he had made in the first one and wanted to fix it in the second? And the successive distrust, as if we were two strangers! And the attitude of neglect to talk about "our future"? I was not the type of person that bothered all the time about a subject that the other "seems" not to want to deal with, but the clock was ticking and I am not one to fold my arms and wait for things to grow on trees. If, on the one hand, it would be of good judgement for me to solve my life and only then decide what I could do in 1989, on the other hand, I was already being demanded and reprimanded for lack of initiatives, as if he had a resolved future by my side — he resented that, but in fact, there was nothing really planned, no commitment made by him. That same dilemma that had been dragging on for some time.

He knew I was waiting for a position from him, but he always saw disadvantages in everything I did. Getting married sooner than I imagined, no engagement; he wanted to determine everything, without talking to me first? Those were sexist and authoritarian attitudes! He treated me as if I were a child, and in the first initiative I had as a woman, when looking for a place for us to hang out safely, he was pissed and suspicious.

Finally, we talked that evening and he stayed a few more days in Brazil because he had missed the training week, returning to Europe the following week. In the end, with his reaction, he ended up not letting me have this time to myself, time to think just about myself. I gave in because I loved that man too much, I knew of my importance in his life and would never take any action to harm him.

The Portuguese GP was on September 25th, in Estoril. Ayrton started in second place and finished the race in fifth place. He was in a bad mood.

Uncle José Carlos comments on the 1988 Grand Prix: "I went to seven Grand Prix: Rio de Janeiro, Phoenix in the United States, Portugal, Spain, France, Mexico and England. Ayrton would arrange credentials for me and he was very professional. However, in Portugal it was the only time he "scolded" me, when the car broke down and I went to talk to him: Leave me alone!, he roared and walked away angry.

It was McLaren's car, in 1988, that year he did not complete his race in Portugal."

Beco, who was also looking for spiritual strength to get to where he wanted to go, even with my and his family's support, asked his sister for help — I guess he mentioned I had asked for a break and he was feeling bad about it. As a graduated psychologist, she referred to a therapist, so that he could also begin to seek emotional help in therapy. From then on, he started acting with me as if I were someone dangerous and he was dealing with the enemy — a necessary enemy —, as if I had done something against him and put his professional life at risk, which was a very heavy burden for a girl to carry.

That year, when Beco was very close to achieve his goals in life, his dreams, it was not adequate for him to attach himself to someone. So, he did not see me, he did not realize my needs and he did not see why he was "dependent" on me. But he felt and enjoyed the quality of love I knew how to give! Of course, for my qualities, my values, my choices too, but suddenly it felt like I was his enemy and this is not how things work. I say that full of pride! By my inner strength, I always knew the right path and had no doubts which one to follow, it was never a matter of choice for me. I just did not know how to measure the consequences of following the path I chose, and, hoping to reap the rewards, I ended up exhausting myself. I was too young to face what I faced and paid dearly for it.

My family members, who loved me a lot, who warned me, who suffered from the risks I was taking and for the whole life I could be living but gave up because of that exhausting relationship, saw what I, for lack of life experience, did not see. Especially my mother…

When I did not live up to his expectations of "knowing how to cook rice," for example, he felt indignant! After all, he was on his way to Olympus, thanks to his effort and dedication, and I was not even learning the basics? This arrogant and extremely unfair attitude hurt me, but I forced myself to put my pains, doubts and demands inside a "drawer" until a more favorable moment for him. And it was not easy… I was everything to him and, at the same time, I was third or fourth on his scale of priorities. I had a fundamental role in something big, in which I participated directly and was very proud of it. What woman in the world would not want to be in my shoes? Now they know the truth, I do not know if all of them! But the fact is, I was not dating the idol, but from the beginning, I was dating the man I loved dearly and would love the same way in any other profession.

In fact, I would prefer! The relationship would not be so troubled and we would have a quieter life, spending more time together, but he, with his restless temper, had a lot to prove to himself.

That intuitive affinity of ours did not work anymore, and I did not know how to interpret what was going on with us. So I played my part with pleasure, trying my hardest to understand what was going on with him, but... however... nevertheless... I was waiting to solve our situation. After all, a relationship is made up of two people and I wanted my space in it, in case he wanted to share his life with me. He seemed to be close to some kind of trance that year. Everything was cold, calculated, controlled and demanded. Even in our intimacy. And that was not the relationship we had so far, because he did not relax like he used to. He could count on me to help him with his problems, but I had to handle the demands of my life alone!

"Beco San, everything will be all right, take care, may God bless and protect you. Love you." It was this kind of thing I was saying to him back then. I would hang up the phone and in ten minutes I would see him on the TV, in the car in his starting position. Sometimes, he would also call me after the race to celebrate the result. It is very crazy for me today to realize that, at the age of eighteen, I knew exactly what he needed and I could provide that. Maybe because I was raised by a man who was also a winner and as demanding, like my father, I knew their way of thinking, it was almost natural for me with my family experience. This was probably a crucial factor for Beco to feel so comfortable in my house, with my family, where things happened and worked with us as a focus.

I also remember the spiritual support Mrs. Neyde was looking for, to help strengthen her son's spirit. One day, at her home in São Paulo, they called a pastor, I do not know which congregation, but she was probably a member of the one Lalli's father was part of. She came to bring words of faith and courage from the Bible, and Beco wanted me to be there at the moment. We were about an hour listening to her advice, through the words of Jesus Christ, Our Lord, which I listened to carefully. Mrs. Neyde also heard, she was close, but at a distance so as not to interfere in that moment that had her son as a focus. And I was there in the middle, like a shield, a filter for Beco. When we were on our way home, he asked me:

"Drica San, what did you think of what she said today?"

"Well, I agree and believe in everything that has been said. But I thought it was said in an exaggerated way... a bit extreme."

"I felt that too!" Beco said.

Not that she said something I do not believe in, I think that was really the idea! But I found her statements a little extreme, and it was more than a conversation or advice, it was preaching. Maybe this was the role she had been called to play. I said:

"Great, I found it super valid to our faith!" I thought about that experience, like a typical Virgo that I was.

"That is right. Tomorrow another person is coming, also religious, but who can foresee something of what is to come..."

"Well, I hope they bring good news! Ask them about us too and then you tell me!"

"Deal, Dridrica!"

The other day, when we met again, I asked curiously:

"So? What did that other person who came to your house say about the future?"

"Ah... he told me to keep having faith, that I will get where I want."

"Um, that is great! But so far nothing new! Even I know that," I laughed, "And what did he say about us?"

He was a little embarrassed, not knowing what to say...

"So?" I insisted.

"I asked about you, and he told me to warn you to be careful with your lungs, something that could put you at risk. So take care!"

"Sorry? I have never had lung problems, that is weird!"

"Yeah, but you may have, and serious ones! According to him."

"What about us? What did he say?" I insisted again.

"Nothing much, he talked more about what I told you."

I had a distinct feeling that the guy had not said anything good about our future and Beco did not want to tell me. He probably did a disservice to our relationship, which already had some unresolved issues. It was in his mind now and I did not know what it was. All I know is that, to this day, I have never been stricken by any unusual lung disease or one that put me at greater risk. I wonder if that is what is going to happen when I am ninety-seven. Dangerous! But I am absolutely sure that it influenced the development of our story. That is why I never wanted to know about the future! If God wanted us, human beings, to see the future, then we would all see it naturally, but I believe it would influence in our journey. We are not here to know the future, but to build our journey today to get where we want to go — but with God's help! And believing that what we want can be taken away from us in a fraction of a second. Or even having to live a lifetime to discover that what we wanted was not part of our journey, of our destiny or whatever we prefer to call it.

I would say 1988 was a maddening year for Beco: The dispute was race after race, he could not make mistakes. But in the end, everything worked out... in his career!

I also remember one day when Beco and I went to dinner at the restaurant Rodeio, on Haddock Lobo Street. This street is sloping and, inside the restaurant, to alleviate this slope, the waiting line was divided into tables arranged on uneven floors, separated by thin wooden partitions above the waists, with steps for circulation between the uneven levels and, at the center, there were two rows of tables at each level.

Anyway, I am saying this because when we were entering the restaurant, heading for the table indicated by the maître, we did not have a broad view of the environment, but when we got to the room where our table was, we came face to face with a group of three or four ladies. I noticed an agitation from one of the girls sitting in front of the entrance and from Beco too. It was normal for him to draw attention wherever he was at that point in his career, but I found his reaction strange. We went to our table, right in front of them, I sat opposite and, before he sat down with his back to that girl, he greeted her with a gesture, which was replied with a certain sadness. I could not help noticing the attitude of that pretty girl, who looked embarrassed. After we placed our orders, I decided to ask:

"Beco, who is that girl you greeted?"

"It is a girl I met!"

"And why is she so sad to see you?"

He, not knowing how to avoid or evade the subject with my assertive question, decided to clarify.

"Look, we had something. But it is that complicated situation: There comes a time when it either becomes something else or it ends. When I realized she wanted this, we had to break up. That is it!"

"From the looks of it, you were the one who ended it, who did not want to go any further, is that right? She was literally shocked when she saw you!"

"Yes, Dri, it happens! It was the best thing to do. Get out as soon as possible, so as not to encourage what has no future. We do not hurt people intentionally, nor is it fair to keep them in the illusion, and knowing I wanted nothing else with her, I walked away."

We were silent for a few moments, each of us digesting the situation. For my part, I confess I was feeling extremely sorry for that girl, who visibly suffered with Beco's presence there, with another woman (me). There is a big difference between crossing with an ex of your boyfriend who has bold and provocative attitudes and realizing someone is suffering in front of you by seeing him again, even if discreetly. I was really upset by imagining myself in her shoes.

How do some men relate to women, even though they know it is not what they are looking for, and then easily dismiss them? In Beco's case, it could have been worse, because he did not fool or lie to anyone! Even so, there seems to be a typical male coldness, as if they were entitled to take advantage of whatever suits them, without getting involved.

With a tireless aching in my heart, I asked:

"Beco, will I ever be in this girl's position?"

"No, Drica! It is different with you!"

"Different how? I do not think I am better than anyone else! I may be different, but I am not better. I noticed her sadness."

"Drica, with you it is another story! It has nothing to do with that girl. Do not mix things up."

"What is the difference?"

"The difference is that what I feel about us is different from anything I have experienced so far, and I know that if I do not marry you, I will not marry anyone else!" he said decisively and with conviction.

"Okay, glad to hear that." Now calming my heart, especially at that phase.

The Spanish GP was on October 2th, in Jerez. Ayrton started in pole position and finished the race in fourth place.

He did not call me before the GP and I already realized that something had changed.

He returned to Brazil and we went out. We spent the day together at the love hotel and just before we left, he said:

"Dri, I do not think we should be so dependent on each other."

I was surprised by the comment, but if he felt dependent, so did I! And we would be in good hands. So I said:

"But what is wrong? Our dependence is so good! Isn't it? I take care of you, and you take care of me!"

600

"But that is not healthy for anyone. Dri, I was in a therapist referred by my sister Viviane and I realized this."

Not understanding why of that, after all, I was by his side, which was not easy at all, and now I had to hear that wanting each other too much was not good? So what would I have left? We were hardly ever together; when we were, it was always a complicated logistics to be able to enjoy ourselves. And now this? I did not know what to think or say. What did he mean, 'dependent'? Was he dependent on me? Why? Because I was all he needed?! Because I met all his requests and needs?! Because I supplied everything he needed in a woman?! Including giving him zero trouble and having zero desires?! Having zero space?! I had earned it all! It was not free! What was the problem with our dependence? So what? If it felt so good when we were together! It was not a problem being dependent, the problem was being dependent only when it was convenient. Love manifested according to one's own needs! Not love of wanting to be together under any circumstances, especially taking the burden of someone who wants to share their life with the other and all the responsibilities brought with forming a family. Meaning, he did not forgive me for the break I asked.

On the weekend at the farm, after lunch, I called Beco to accompany me on a bike ride around the area. He said he was going to play with the small planes a bit with his brothers-in-law and we would do that later. I agreed and, as usual, sat there near them to watch the fun; as always, I was there present and partner. At one point, I insisted on my invitation.

"Beco, let's go for a bike ride? Soon it will be dark and we cannot go anymore!"

"Just a little longer, Dridrica! Hold on!"

"Ok."

I stayed there for another half an hour and decided not to bother him anymore, I went for a bike ride by myself; after all, in his long absences I was always doing my things without him. I wanted to do it together, that is true, but he did not show interest in a simple request of mine, so there I went to do what I wanted!

I left with no rush, enjoying that late afternoon, with the wind in my face and the birds excited, as it was time for them to seek shelter. Nature has always fed my soul and that made me feel good. At one point, after about ten minutes of ride, I heard the sound of an engine behind me, I stopped and looked to see who was coming down the dirt road. It was Beco on the scooter, he was rushing on my direction. I thought it was strange, imagining something could have happened, because he was doing there to follow me on the bike, as he was on a motorcycle! Curious, I waited.

"Dridrica! What is it?" he said breathlessly as he came to stand beside me.

"Huh? How come? Nothing happened!"

"When I noticed your absence, I went to look for you and they told me you had left by bicycle. Is everything okay?"

"Yes! I wanted to ride a bike and decided to ride a bike!"

"But is everything really okay?"

"It is!"

"Well then, let's go back home together?"

"Okay! You go ahead I get there right after you."

"Okay, don't be long, Dridrica!"

"Go easy, I go at my pace," and he left.

What was that? I realized that, as I always accompanied him in everything he did, because I liked to do everything with him — even if it was to sit for hours watching his flights —, for the first time, I left him behind to do a simple will of mine, and he was scared by it. The funniest thing about it is that he was the one who warned me about "our dependence", and my attitude was exactly what he asked me to do!

I was only the only one who was confused.

The Japanese GP was on October 30th, in Suzuka. It was an exciting race in every way. Ayrton had problems at the start, dropped to 16th place, but then regained the third position on lap 10. And on lap 19, he was already behind

Prost, who was leading the race, but it started to rain on Suzuka. It was an amazing win! And so he was considered, in advance, because of the score, the champion of 1988. He got to where he had dreamed all his life: He got there! He thus reached the top of the world.

Once again, he did not call me before this GP.

This situation between us was strange until the day Ayrton won the championship. There, very moved, he again thanked the support of his family and also mine, in an interview with Reginaldo Leme, who recalls this moment:

Reginaldo Leme also tells what happened in those days. "It was also with Ayrton that I did one of the most important interviews of my career, and I'm also sure that one of the most important and most remarkable of his life - he said so himself. Right after '88 title in Japan, we did a long recording with him, in which I took the interview very personally. I asked some questions just like that about the human side and he got emotional, getting tears in his eyes the whole time. It was kind of a self-analysis he had never done. When I asked if he had left anything or anyone behind his way to the title, or if there was some kind of debt with someone, he said yes, but mentioned the family and especially "My Girl". He said exactly like that, in which in this case was his girlfriend, Adriane Yamin, with whom he was dating for four years and few people knew.

(Source: AutoMotor by Reginaldo Leme - Ayrton Senna's Story - Lendas Do Automobilismo EP10. Youtube).*

Excerpt from the TV interview given to Reginaldo Leme for Rede Globo, right after his win: "(...) Continue my life as it has always been, improve as a professional, learn more, much more, as I have a lot to learn, how to fix a car, how to take advantage of everything a car has to offer, improve as a person, especially as people, and live a little closer to my family, which I sacrificed somehow all these years that I dedicated myself a lot to my profession, to the people I like so much, my girl, anyway, all those who had been so close to me, close to me even with such a great distance, but always by my side, always supporting me, and I want to live a little longer to enjoy life a little more (...)."

This was said by Ayrton shortly after his win. He knew how important I was in his life, but it was not because I was there by

*

https://www.youtube.com/watch?v=8qmLANpT4Lo&t=791s

coincidence, it was because of everything I had been doing for us, to us, out of love — what held me to him was love. Nothing else! I did not need anything from him and was not dependent either, I just wanted him very much. I was more than a lucky and protective object in his life, I was a person who loved him deeply, and I was there all those years, for us, steadfast. However, when I needed his reciprocation, he was not there for me.

Reginaldo Leme also tells us what happened those days: *"In 1988, Ayrton was already the champion, we were together in Bali and we sat at the same table to have breakfast — we were not completely okay with each other; we talked, but still resentful.*

Days before, that great interview had taken place in Suzuka, when he won his first world title. Because we were not at a good moment in our relationship, I did not even enter straight into the motorhome. Japan was very complicated; at that time, the teams stayed inside containers used as motorhomes. I was not sure if he would give me the interview at the end of the race. I asked Betise Assumpção, who was his press advisor, to ask him if he would do the interview. If not, I would do my story in another way, talking about the race and interviewing the opponents.

I was in McLaren's pits when he showed up and pulled me by the arm. This image exists and was shown several times by Globo.

This was the famous interview, so often shown, in which he cried a lot. But he started to cry when I started asking very personal questions. For example, 'In this F1 dispute, did you leave behind someone who has been with you since the beginning?' From then on, he just cried. He knew very well what I was talking about, but he dodged the question. He talked about his family, those who had supported him, and 'his girl', who was Adriane Yamin.

The interview was long and when it ended, many reporters assured me that he was remembering me. But what was really curious was translating all that for the foreigners who watched in astonishment to the crying. I summed it up for them saying it was pure emotion after such an important achievement.

About four years after this interview, he was leaving from Cumbica to audition, and I went there just to interview him. Next to a Globo cameraman, I asked him: 'Of the great interviews you have done, is there one you like the most?' He replied: 'The best interview I did in my life was for you in Japan, in 1988.' It was the only time since our disagreements that I saw Ayrton refer to me like that!

In 1988, we came back from Australia together, he on one side and me on the other, sort of in parallel, and we were landing when I sat down next to him, and asked: Ayrton, why did you hesitate to give me that interview? I do not know if it is true, but I have been told that you hesitated! He said: I did not hesitate, I even sent word to you that I was coming. My only problem with you is that I always think you have more patience with Piquet than with me."

The Australian GP was on November 13th, in Adelaide. Ayrton again started in pole position and finished the race in second place. It was an amazing year, with thirteen poles and eight wins. But he also did not call me before this race...

At the end of 1988, he won in Suzuka, there was all that commotion, when Beco won his first Championship, once again he thanked those who were important for him to get there. He mentioned me with his family in the report after the race in Japan. At that point, even though he called me "my girl," he had already openly declared "my girlfriend Adriane", that same year, in the aforementioned interview he gave to Galvão Bueno, in his apartment in Monaco, for a television program.

As soon as he returned, everyone in Brazil was very euphoric with his victory; he was the subject in all kinds of media. But we all went to Tatuí farm to celebrate his victory together; we gathered my whole family and his whole family. They surprised him, with posters pasted on the living room walls, written by the family, for him, and Beco then asked them to fetch the champagne that was in the fridge, waiting for the appropriate moment — that same large bottle, which they traditionally burst in celebrations from the podium. He realized that was the right time to share it with us, in this celebration, but of course, without splashing its content at us. We all took pictures together, to remember that historic moment.

Front row, left corner, my mother Marilene and a lady; behind, Lalli (bearded) and Leo; in front of him, cousin Fábio with his parents and his wife crouched with their daughter; in the back, Dadô; in the center, Mrs. Neyde, Lenise, Beco, Mr. Milton and a couple of friends; my father Amilcar. Crouching on the right, Kaco, me with Bruno in my

606

arms, Chris with Paula in her arms, Bianca holding hands with her uncle, a boy and Viviane in a cap

Beco surrounded by siblings and family getting ready for a toast

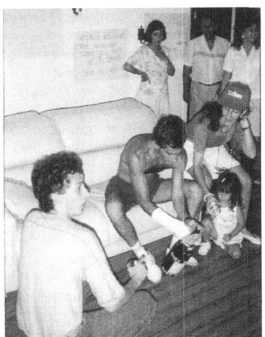

Paulinha crouched by her mother

At toast time, in the left corner, Leonardo, some family members, Beco, me, Mrs. Marilene (on her back), Mr. Amilcar and Viviane (right behind), Paula, Christhiane, Bianca and Otávio (striped T-shirt)

Beco was distant, totally disconnected, I cannot explain what it was, his mind was absent after the race. He was also annoyed with the cast that had been placed on his right wrist; he had injured it during a soccer game and they thought it best to immobilize, even for a short time, for his prompt and full recovery.

The only children present at this celebration were Ayrton's nephews, because my sister Lenise had recently discovered she was pregnant, and therefore, we did not have any children in my family yet. Once again, we took pictures of this gathering everyone together.

Back in São Paulo, Beco and I went to Milton Nascimento's concert, by his own personal invitation. It was the two of us alone! Our first public appearance and I was happy to, after so many family restrictions, gain autonomy with my boyfriend, without having to hide anymore. We entered through the side of Olympia, a well-known concert hall at the time, to avoid the commotion at the door. We were directed to a box with a privileged view of the stage, on the upper floor, in a corner that gave us some privacy. Beco continued that way with me, totally disconnected, as if we were practically unknown to each other. As if I were a simple escort, in a cold attitude, and that was an unpleasant surprise to me; I felt like I did not know what I was doing there with him. What had he invited me to? He had done so many things without me while dating, and now that I was there, he was acting like a stranger?

I was intimidated by so much news, after all, we were the target of many people's attention, and Beco was connected with the audience. At one point, the singer obviously commented and thanked the presence of the newest F1 Champion. Actually, he was there because of it; he already imagined that, being the newest sensation of the moment, that would happen, he was on this rhythm since Suzuka, where he became Champion. After the show, I was relieved, because I could not wait to go back home and end that night, but then someone came to lead us to Milton Nascimento's dressing room. He was very excited, while I curled up wanting to be invisible, I was very uncomfortable without my boyfriend's support. In fact, he did not care about my presence, the presence of his "escort."

We went into the dressing room and there was the singer of the night, a few other people and Paulo Handsome Ricardo — I confess I was encouraged to be there in the presence of that gorgeous man. So I stayed in a corner, watching, when I realized I would not even be introduced; I put myself in a position of invisible audience, enjoying being there, witnessing that encounter with those of whom I was a fan. After taking the pictures to record the meeting of the "famous ones", they said goodbye and we left.

Na estréia de Milton Nascimento, sexta-feira, no Olympia, o cantor com Airton Senna (dir.) e Paulo Ricardo (centro)

Beco, Paulo Ricardo and Milton Nascimento at "Estadão" of 12/06/1988

"At Milton Nascimento's premiere, Friday, at Olympia, the singer with Ayrton Senna (right) and Paulo Ricardo (center)"

I respected and understood Beco's moment of fascination, in his moment of glory; he deserved it all and, resigned, I believed he would soon be my Beco again. I did not comment on what happened, but I was very happy to go home.

Days later, Beco invited me to travel with him and his family to Europe, so that he could receive the 1988 Champion award. So I went to talk to my father, in the evening, at dinner with everyone at the table.

610

"Dad, Beco invited me to go to Europe with him, to receive this year's award. I have finals, but they are scheduled for after our return. Can I go?"

"Dear, you are grown up and you must choose what is best for your life!"

"Dad, I am not sure. Beco has been weird, and I really do not know if I should go."

As soon as we had Beco at home, when there were not many people around, my father put him on the spot:

"Listen, Ayrton! Adriane told me you invited her to go with you and receive the award... well then?"

Ayrton said emotionally, with his eyes full of tears:

"Mr. Amilca, Adriane has been absent from very important moments in my life until today, and I believe it is time for her to participate in my life!"

Everyone was moved by that emotional expression of affection and recognition of how important it was for me to be with him at such an important moment in his life. Then my father said:

"I agree! Listen, arrange the plane tickets along with yours, hotel reservation and whatever is necessary, and send me the bill so I can settle it with you."

"Got it, Mr. Amilca!"

I confess I was taken by surprise. I did not expect Beco was going to say such a thing, after all the distancing, nor the outcome of both parties. After that, all I remember is running out to have a party dress made. I bought a navy-blue velvet fabric and they had four days to make the dress. I also went after renewing the French visa. Between the day the trip was decided with my father and the departure date, I hardly remember anything: It was a rush between dress fitting, packing, deciding what to take and getting ready. I double-checked the dates of my exams and they would take ten days to start — I was still missing grades to pass and finish that school year. We were only going to spend four days in Europe, due to the awards ceremony. I traveled alone with

Beco first class; I do not remember where Mr. Milton and Mrs. Neyde were, if they had gone on another plane, but that is probably what happened. Beco and I boarded together, and in the departure area there was a jewelry store. He told me he needed to buy a gift for the newborn baby of his team leader, Ron Denis: It was a girl and he wanted to give her a gift. We went into the jewelry store and I suggested buying earrings, he let me choose. I chose a pair of earrings that contained a small sapphire stone, with adequate size for a child to use, and we boarded.

Although I noticed Beco was very angry and impatient, I was happy to travel with the man I loved so much, on our first opportunity to leave Brazil together. I had dreamed about it a lot! He was in a bad mood and noticing I had removed a necklace from a bag, whose somewhat rigid structure in the shape of a lap, with some diamonds, had bent in a corner, and that I tried to fix it right there, he asked sourly:

"Whose necklace is this?"

"It is mine! My father had it made for me to wear at Tatá's wedding, don't you remember seeing me with it?"

"I don't!" he replied with resentment.

When we arrived at our destination in England, I shared a room with Mrs. Neyde and her daughter, while Ayrton stayed in the men's room, with his father and brother.

The only day we shopped, Viviane asked her mother to buy her a fur coat. She had seen me with one, which was my mother's, and she wanted one too. They went shopping and I took the opportunity to choose some pairs of Reebok sneakers, which was new and did not exist in Brazil, to give as a Christmas present to some of my family members, since I knew more or less their shoe sizes. My father had given me some money before traveling and told Beco that, if I needed more, it was for him to give it to me and then he would pay it back. I bought it with great difficulty because the seller who served me was from I do not know which country in Africa and had a very heavy accent; I could not decide who spoke worst English: he or I. I talked to him, he did not understand; he replied, and I did not understand. I started to feel uneasy with that, he always brought the wrong shoes, and I said it was not what I wanted... it was a mess! And Beco nearby, calm, trying on a pair of sneakers for him, did not speak, while Mr. Milton waited for everyone, peacefully. But I was worried, because I did not want to delay the group with my purchase. At one point, trying to make things go faster, I asked Beco for help, who played deaf. I could have done it myself, but I did not want to make them wait any longer. So I took a pencil and paper to make myself understood, wrote down which number, model and color I wanted. I managed to put together all the pairs of sneakers. Beco simply pretended he was not listening to me, as if giving me a lesson because I had not bothered to take an advanced English class by then. The worst thing about this event was that, later, in Brazil, I noticed that my sister's pair of sneakers came with both right feet, but I could not change it anymore!

The next day, we went to Paris and stayed in a hotel next to FIA (International Automobile Federation) building, command of F1, and where the award dinner would be held.

I remember that, still at the airport in Brazil, I had bought an Asterix comic book, which I loved, to get entertained during the trip and, on the dinner day, we were in the hotel room and I was reading the comic when my sister-in-law at the time, who was placing her clothes in the closet, suddenly choked in a frightening way, coughed a lot and lost her breath. When I thought about getting up to help her, Mrs. Neyde already acted promptly to help her and everything worked out.

After the scare, we started to get ready for the awards ceremony. I wanted to tie my hair back, but I could not because I was agitated about having to say hello to important people, because I was following the night's star, Beco, and I was a little girl. So I went with my hair down and made up the way I knew how, that is, almost nothing. I got dressed, put on my fur coat and we all left the hotel together. Even in that cold Parisian winter, we were bundled up and walked there.

When we got there, all the attention was on Ayrton, obviously. I remember greeting Mr. Balestre and his wife, we were greeting everyone! Honda's Japanese guy was also there; the McLaren people, because they were the team that had scored the highest; and Prost, of course.

Beco and I, as soon as we arrived at the event hall. Photo courtesy of Neyde Senna da Silva

Beco and I with Jean Marrie Balestre (then president of FIA) and his wife. Photo courtesy of Neyde Senna da Silva

Viviane and Leonardo, right behind us in greetings. Images courtesy of Neyde Senna da Silva

Click time with "all the Japanese people" (as Beco said) from Honda.
Photo courtesy of Neyde Senna da Silva

After all the greetings, we were led to a table, Beco and I, where a countess and a count were. I do not know why they put us alone with the two of them, but I suppose they must be important people to sit with the champion. The countess was a very elegant lady, very well dressed, who wore flashy jewelry, and we started talking. Dinner was served and, when we were done, Beco left to say hello to the important people, talk, etc., after all, it was his night, and I stayed there with that lady, trying to talk. She had already come to Brazil and said she loved Brazilian clubs — I thought she was referring to night clubs, but it was really sports clubs. I found her observation interesting.

The two of us at the FIA awards dinner in Paris

Dessert was served in a pot, a small round box made of candied sugar with a lid and flower on top, all made of candied sugar. When I opened it, there was vanilla ice cream inside, to eat by breaking the cone; I got crazy about that and went to call Beco to eat it with me.

I looked for him around the hall and saw Viviane at Prost's table, speaking French, which she had learned, but I do not remember which table Mrs. Neyde and Mr. Milton were, until I finally found Beco, called him and we went back to our table. When we sat down, he asked:

"What is it, Dri?"

"Nothing! I just called you to eat dessert before it melts. Open it!"

"Did you call me because of that? I was talking to important people, important subject, and you called me because of it?!"

"Why did you think I had called you? What could be going on here for me to call you? As it was ice cream, I did not want it to melt so you could eat your dessert, that is all!" I said.

I was in an embarrassing situation with his attitude, as regardless of the language, the person could even be deaf that they would understand I was getting scolded there. I kept quiet, pretended it was not with me. He got up then, I went to the toilet to calm down with what had just happened and did not see him again until the end of the event. He was called to receive the award and the due tributes, and I was incredibly proud of my boyfriend, but quiet on my own after that blast.

After the ceremony, Beco said we were invited to dance and, of course, I accepted. It was Beco, me, his sister and brother and I only saw Prost when we arrived there. Afterwards, Beco explained that who invited us was the McLaren sponsor, an Arab man, married to an American woman. When we left, I put on my coat and we went together in a car; there were three cars, I know the car I got in was a Jaguar, very modern, I had never seen that type, metallic navy blue. When I opened the door, I found it very heavy, Beco said it was armored — it was also the first time I had rode in an armored car; this was in 1988, in Brazil, we had no idea what that was, especially in a passenger car. We had security guards with us too.

We went to a nightclub, a small place, quite boring, I do not know if it is a French thing, it was kind of empty, we all sat at a table and I was at the end, but the loud music did not let me participate in any conversation. I stayed there on my own, very chill, enjoying the moment and watching people, I was downloading everything and I was surprised that the Arab's wife, who was in a very beautiful paire, like bobbed hair swinging — she was a brunette with bushy hair neatly coiffed and wearing wide hoop earrings made of diamond, which you could see from a distance — stayed in a corner alone. It seemed like she excluded herself from the group and I asked myself "how come she did not want to participate?". Meanwhile, her husband was extremely excited and outgoing! A few seconds later, I saw he went dancing with a young, blond, thin girl, dressed a little sloppy, I do not know if she was drunk, because she was dancing really weird, almost alone on the floor. I noticed the Arab's wife was still there, sitting in a corner, almost facing the wall. So, seeing that, I told Beco to look at her and I said that it would not be like that with us. But what did I say that for? Whatever topic I brought up, he was not interested in talking to me. What was I doing there? I do not know. All I know is that there was something strange in the air and he seemed somewhat uncomfortable, but I know I was doing nothing.

We left, each one went to their own room and, the next day, we would have the day to walk around Paris. However, in the morning, we had breakfast, I got dressed, and where was Beco? He was still sleeping, so I called to his room. The phone rang and nobody answered. I went to knock on the suite door, which had a small room and two bedrooms. He was not in the mood to interact and stayed there, I think Leo did not go either. I was super upset and made a point of demonstrating it: The first trip with me and his family and he leaves me alone! He had to pay more attention to me, it was impolite of him. What was I there for? I remembered that episode Beco had told me some time ago about his ex-wife and the vacuum cleaner, at the end of their marriage. I felt that now I was the one in her position.

During our walk, Mrs. Neyde, seeing I was silent, a little isolated, approached me and told me not to be upset, to let him rest and that it was silly, it would pass. I replied that I did not agree, because I was there because of him and he just ignored me that morning, when he was supposed to be with me. I walked a little ahead of the group to calm down, when Viviane came and spoke in my ear:

"We do not like those who stick with us!" Shocked, I replied:

"Huh? We, who?"

I was even more annoyed. How can she talk to me like that? I was sticking with him? I spent four years waiting for my turn to come, and for the time when he would welcome me into his life. I was fifth in his life! How was that? Not to mention I had reached my limit; it was time to reap what I sowed. He sowed his whole life and he was reaping the rewards of the championship, and I sowed for all the four years with him and could not reap anything? I could not expect anything? I was very angry.

When we got back to the hotel, we met, but I did not say anything, I barely looked at Beco, indifferent to his presence. We traveled to Milan, Italy, left our things at the hotel and went straight to a TV studio, where he would receive an Oscar-like award. We went in a rented limo and we sat facing each other. Viviane was wearing a new coat she had bought at that same trip, but whenever she moved, white fur floated around the car, then she said, as if I were not there, listening:

"Mom, why does my coat's fur float and hers does not?" she said, pointing at my direction.

Mrs. Neyde was shocked with the comment, about the coat she herself had gifted her daughter, and said, embarrassed, shrugging:

"I do not know, dear!"

But Viviane was still looking at my coat, bothered: I could not resist that scene; trying to help Mrs. Neyde and putting an end to that uncomfortable situation, I said with a poker face:

"It is just that mine is a mink coat."

Mrs. Neyde did not know what to say, because her daughter had just got the coat she asked for and chose. Now she was demanding her mother? And, worse, in front of me? I felt sorry for that attitude towards me, I had always been extremely kind and polite to her in the few times we were together. But her posture only discredited her in front of her family, so I did not interpret it as my problem.

We entered the amphitheater, the audience was full of guests, and we sat all in the same row, except for Beco, who sat in a place with easy access to the stage where the ceremony was to take place. He still had his hand in a cast. When he went onstage to receive the award that TV night, they suddenly threw a light cannon at us, for the audience to welcome us as the family of the honoree, and some girls sitting next to me realized who we were and widened their eyes at us. Mrs. Neyde introduced me to everyone during the trip as "su novia, Adriane," so everyone knew my role there.

After the ceremony ended, when we got up to leave, as the theater was full and many people were leaving at the same time, we waited for our row to empty a little so as not to disturb even more. Then those girls who sat next to me started pushing me to force my way between the seats in the theater, and I elbowed the girl right behind me, like "do not squeeze me." She, giggling, mocking, squeezed me even more, and I almost fell on top of Mrs. Neyde. Then I stopped. I planted my feet firmly on the ground, looked back, and stared the girls showing my dislike. They were embarrassed, they were probably around fifteen, it seemed to me that they acted like that for fun. Anyway, we left, but I confess I was annoyed with those girls; it had been hostile, because they knew I was in the company of the honoree of the night.

From there, we went with someone else besides our group to the Vittorio Emanuele II Gallery and had dinner in the chic and elegant restaurant Biffi.

The next day, it was time to return to Brazil. Once in the van to the airport, Ayrton was very impolite with Mrs. Neyde, then I took the opportunity and said:

"Let him be, Mrs. Neyde, let it go, because he really is very rude to everyone! Leave him alone with his bad mood."

I gave him my message. We were in complete conflict, he and I, because he had no reason to act like that with anyone, he was acting like a spoiled boy.

We came back from Europe on Beco's plane, because he wanted to bring it for the holiday season in Brazil. I do not know if he had remodeled or changed aircraft, I know that two seats appeared to have been replaced by a small side bed. So there were five narrow places to sit, plus that bed. As soon as we took off, Beco lay down on the bed and "screw the rest". During the flight, I could see that his impatience was not only with me, but to his family as well. Rude answers for everyone, so I could not stand it and said:

"Beco, are you going to lie down without even offering your place to your mother? It is not for me, but for your family."

He replied with disdain, and I did not speak to him again until we arrived in Brazil. We stopped over the Canary Islands at night to refuel. I think we stopped over another place, in Brazil, also to refuel, then landed in São Paulo in the morning.

We barely said goodbye. I thanked him for the trip and left for my house, pissed off and with some questions on my mind: Why did I go there? What for? Being mistreated in front of his family?

And he went to his place, wherever it was.

During his absence, I received a Christmas card from him, which I did not understand at all, in which he said there were things about me that he did not like and did not accept:

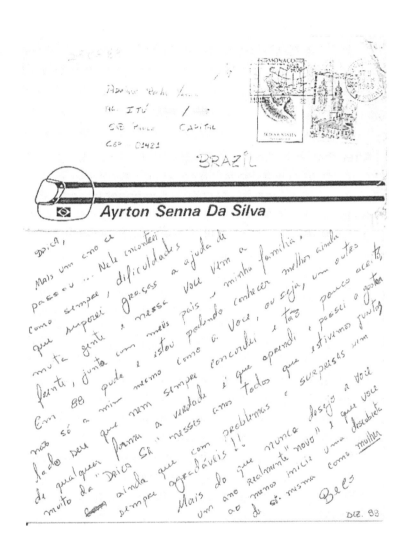

"Drica,
Another year goes by... In it, I found, as usual, difficulties which I overcame with the help of many people, and now you come ahead of it, along with my parents and my family. In 1988, I could and still can know myself better and also know you better, that is, another part of you that I sometimes did not agree on or accept. Anyway, the truth is that I learned and began to like 'Drica San' a lot during all these years we have

623

been together, even though with some problems and surprises not always pleasant!! More than ever, I wish you a really 'new' year and that you can at least start discovering yourself as a woman.
Beco
Dec. 88"

After that, he called me and was cold, he said he would spend a few days working in Rio de Janeiro, recording a Christmas special for a TV channel. When he returned to São Paulo, he called me again:

"Dri, are you at home? I will stop by, because we need to talk."

"Okay, will do."

He entered my house wearing dark glasses, continued with them, we went to the biggest living room to talk, and he said:

"Look, I am not very well, I have been a little confused, I am not happy with some things, I think you are not yet mature enough to get married."

"When did you realize I am immature? Is this now or since I was fifteen?" I said in a sarcastic tone.

"I do not know, Dri! But I want a break."

At that moment, I reached out to take the glasses off his face, taking them off gently, but holding the will not to destroy that pair of black-framed folding Carrera glasses. I added:

"You please take off your glasses to talk to me and look into my eyes."

"I knew you were going to do this!"

"So why didn't you take them off? I just turned nineteen, I do not understand what is new about it! Beco, it is not time for a break anymore. After everything? Now that you have exposed me to the whole world?"

My name and image had circulated in all the media at the time, television, newspapers, magazines, after four years in silence, putting up with everything I had put up with, all the struggle, the absence, the harassment on him I had to

624

endure, anyway, all those very complicated situations. Not to mention the demands of a teenager: Hormones, school, friends and everything that is part of adolescence, when you start to have your own life.

He repeated:

"Yeah, Dri, but I want a break!"

"So I think we better break up. There is no time a break anymore."

"Well, if you prefer it that way... I am very confused."

"I do! But why did you always tell me that if you did not marry me, you would not marry anyone else? Why are you doing this? Throwing it all away like that?"

He replied:

"Yeah, I will take that risk." I simply replied:

"Okay, so it is settled!"

He got up quickly to leave. In the hall, waiting for the elevator, I looked at him there, after everything, I could not believe it. I pulled him inside and said:

"Beco, what are you doing? I cannot understand, it does not make sense."

He replied shakily:

"Drica, leave me alone, I am confused, I need some time to think about my life."

I was devastated, days went by and he did not look for me, so I knew it was for real. Looking around me, in my room, he was everywhere: On the wall, a poster of ours, which he had made to present and tease my mother in 1987, when I was in England; I opened the closet and found a bunch of presents from him: teddy bears, photographs... Then I thought: Since he wants to get out of my life, I am going to get him out now! I grabbed a suitcase, collected everything within my reach in the bedroom: sneakers, T-shirt, sweatshirt, jewelry, poster, photo album — everything he had given me —, stuffed them into the suitcase as a rite of passage.

I asked our driver, Milton, to take the suitcase to the address I would tell him, at Ayrton's house, and said:

"Go give it to him, there is a note, and do not take that bag back, I do not want it back!"

Milton took the suitcase, handed over all the things with my note saying he had to find himself, because he could only be very lost, as it made no sense. But if he was not okay and wanted to get out of my life, then so be it and that he should not even think about giving me back that suitcase with his memories.

Otávio tells us what I only learned now, when writing this book: *"Senna was a bit closed, even though we were friends, he never told me exactly why they broke up, but what was pretty clear to me is that he was very fond of her. But he never opened up and said what happened; although we were very close, I also did not want to be intrusive and get into his intimacy to find out why they were not together anymore. In fact, we talked a few times after they broke up, but I still do not really understand why, because he liked her a lot and did not want to call her, so he called me. He called me four or five times from abroad: 'Tell me, how is she, is she okay?' And I said: 'Hey, man! I cannot say she is okay! She is a little upset!'."*

After a few days, everyone was confused, both my family and his, and I called his mother:

"Mrs. Neyde, I would like to talk to you, at any time when Beco is not there, because I cannot understand what is going on."

She replied:

"You can come now. I am here waiting for you."

I got in my car and headed to her house. When I got there, we talked:

"Mrs. Neyde, how can this be happening, what is that? I do not get it, what happened?"

She said:

"Look, Dri, what he told me was that he was really upset because you gave him back the things he gave you."

626

"How come? Mrs. Neyde, I went to Europe after four years of our relationship, I was everywhere in the media, showing my face to the world after these four years, and it was because he invited me, so after the trip he came over asking for a break; it is not time for a break, Mrs. Neyde! And now he is upset because I gave the things back? Is that why he is upset? But if after everything we have been through together, he wants to get out of my life, then I put him out of my life. My sister said she heard a rumor that he sent the plane for a children's TV presenter, I do not know where..."

"No, Adriane! Do not worry about that! That does not exist! I know my son and there is no such possibility!"

I closed this matter.

She comforted me:

"Look, Adri, go live your life in peace. I will tell you a story: I dated Milton for some time and there came a time when he decided to break up with me. I heard he was partying, I knew who he was going out with and everything he was up to, but I stayed quiet. After some time, when partying was over, he came looking for me and asked me to marry him and we got married. So, Adriane, be well and let the time go by, everything will settle down."

I got the message; I was grateful for what she told me with the heart of a mother. I thanked the affection, attention and I left. But I did not understand what was going on yet.

When the Christmas special show was displayed, which I knew had been taped before he asked me for a break — before the day Beco came home to talk to me wearing sunglasses —, I thought he and she had crossed the line and showed everyone what was "going on between them." Then I understood why he was wearing glasses inside my house: Those glasses were because he was ashamed of what he was doing to me!

The news about their relationship was like a bomb, it became news throughout Brazil. And we heard about it everywhere, especially later, in early 1989, when the presenter made a point of running and saying that they were dating, as if it were a fairy tale.

It all happened while I was taking finals at school, to end that school year. I had private classes to study the subjects and I had to hold back crying, trying to concentrate, because I had no choice! Sometimes, tears came down and I lost the focus of the books. But stoically, I focused again! I remember I used to walk to school to take the exams and, everywhere I went, I saw the covers of magazines with Ayrton and that presenter. This was right after appearing publicly with me in France. That is, who was I? A nobody who he had taken for a ride in Europe? That was probably the image that I was left with, and I did not need any of that. In fact, I avoided it during the four years of our relationship.

People who knew me heard about the news of the "fairy tale", that is, that exhibition was very vexatious, both for my family and for my closest friends, who lived with me and with him. We were all very ashamed for his attitude and what was happening; after all, I did not deserve to be going through this. It was the worst Christmas of my life, I did not feel the ground under my feet, and I felt physical pain, because I loved Beco too much. I learned to love his smell, his skin, his look, and I could not imagine how I would live without him in my life, without his kisses, without his voice! So, it was something I had to get over anyway.

Someone from the press even called my mother and asked:

"What do you have to say about Ayrton dating and traveling with your daughter and then being with the presenter?"

"Look, I think you better call him to ask!"

That was my mother's answer, short and to the point, as usual.

Chapter XXIX

My uncle José Carlos, who saw our entire relationship, gives his opinion about his relationship with the host: *"This thing about Ayrton dating the host, I was sure it would not last long, because they were two stars, one would start to overshadow the other and it would create trouble. They were two stars, he much more than she was, because she was only known here in Brazil. But I will tell you what: When he left Adriane for her, he thought it was one thing, but then he saw it was a road to nowhere."*

How Reginaldo Leme analyzes the breakup: *"Adriane and Ayrton's breakup, I saw as a clear dazzle on his part. On that Xuxa show, I am sorry to say, but for me, it was a disrespect to his history with Adriane, I did not like it at all. He was dazzled, and for her, he was somebody. So they created a relationship, not necessarily a loving one. I never thought he was happy at that time, I remember once we were together at Galvão's house and she came running and jumped on his back, like a horse, to me they looked like two children playing.*

That day, at Galvão's house, Dani (my oldest daughter, who was then eleven years old) was with us. She spoke to Dani, but in a cold way. Maybe Ayrton had already told her something about me. I have nothing to do with her life and did not even care if she was cold or not with me, but she could not have done that to a child. As soon as I could, I left.

About Adriane, little was said at the time. Later, when other models passed through his life, we saw it as something normal, a turnover. But for us, the real girlfriend was Adriane Yamin, period. Then she was the fiancée, period. For us, she was the girlfriend he was going to marry."

The world collapsed for me. I, who was worried about my life, divided between getting married that year or continuing my life with my boyfriend and going to college, never imagined reaping this "fruit", because that was not what I sowed. He reaped the fruits of the benefits of our relationship, but I did not. That hurt me a lot, I felt betrayed, and it was a tremendous betrayal and dirty trick, result of selfishness and stubbornness; that could not be happening.

My dad suggested:

"I want to give you a trip, to help you out of this sadness. Where do you want to go? Who do you want to take with you? Whatever you want... Whatever you think will make you feel better..."

I said:

"Well, dad, if it is to try to get me out of sadness, I am going to a place of joy: Disney."

"Great! Who do you want to take with you?"

"Well, I dunno! My sisters and Andrea..."

So the trip was arranged and we went to Orlando and Miami for twelve days, my sister was pregnant — she was probably about five months pregnant when we traveled.

I tried to move on, despite the inertia, because my life had fallen apart and I wondered how could he have done that to me. I had no words to explain how disloyal he was — I could not find a good justification for what he did.

I traveled to Florida feeling that it was not just my soul that hurt, but my body too, I cried myself to sleep and asked God: Why is that? I did not dream of any of this, I did not ask for such a man, a famous, rich man, I did not want it, I just accepted it when it happened. How could I not fall in love? How could I not like him with everything he did for me and to me? We were one! How come? With a woman so different from me? How come? He found a woman to share everything in his life, but hadn't he already found one? And he hurt me, even because it was a different type of woman, with a different upbringing and education, that is, I felt he had thrown all my virtues in the trash too! For a person who never cared about them.

I was very angry with life, because that was unfair, and I was angry with God. How could He allow that? I had done all my best and I had been my best self. I had been honest, loyal and sincere. I gave love and I did not deserve it at all, but God, how could You? Since we started dating, I had been careful not to kid myself, not to make a fool of myself, not to be silly, but at no time could I imagine such a thing happening... Why did he say I was childish? Was I the one who was childish? What was I so childish about? What being childish meant for him? Because I did not know how to cook rice?

Uncle José Carlos gives us his opinion: *"I thought Adriane and Ayrton's relationship was very cool for both of them. Because she, younger, was with a public person, and he was a gentleman, which he always was with her and the whole family. After they were together for a while, we started to see his problem with his job and the world demanding from him, I think this was decisive for the end of the relationship. So I realized that, if it worked, it would be very embarrassing for her, because whenever they went somewhere, everyone looked at him and not at her. If it worked, could you imagine the life Adriane would have? A lot of demands, too many people being nosy. Maybe she could even adapt to his world and he could not."*

Anyway, we went traveling and it was good, a distraction. But it did not solve the problem! My father had done that for me, because he was anxious to help me, to make me feel a little better, but actually he was also terrible with what has been done to his daughter and to him. After all, Beco did not just betray me, he betrayed the trust of my entire family.

During the trip, my mom provided a new decoration for my room that, in fact, had been set up for my older sister and was kept for me when she got married. She remodeled the entire room. All this effort to help me get better.

Meanwhile, I saw Ayrton in that little magazine love affair, but I noticed that when he appeared with the presenter at the racetrack, when she was with him there and a camera appeared in their direction, he pulled her, wanting to get away from the cameras. I knew he was ashamed because he knew it was not right, one cannot do such a thing. I thought: I wish he had not invited me to the awards ceremony! Why didn't he ask me for a break before taking me there? Why did he put me through such a public embarrassment? What was he thinking? That he was being loyal to me, taking me to receive the award? The award I also deserved to win with him? I did not want the F1 award! He was my award!

Among the support and the affection I received, there was a very dear family of my friend from Mackenzie, who welcomed me and hugged me, at a time when my family did not have much structure either, because they were also shaken. I remember I used to go to Rosângela's house to cry. Or I would go to my aunts' house, because I did not want to cry at home, so my parents would not be even more upset than they already were. But I did not feel good anywhere, I felt wherever I was, I would be carrying with me some sadness no one needed to participate.

My friend Rosângela tells us what happened: *"I remember that when they broke up, Adriane used to come to my house a lot. My father is a medium and he talked a lot to Adriane, especially because he felt they were very connected, he knew it was a sincere relationship. My father talked a lot to Adriane about their breakup, his will, what he felt about connections from another life, I have a vague memory of these things. After the breakup, Adriane thought about getting back together, but she was tough and did not want to confess, she had this position of not being like the others and throwing herself at his feet. Maybe she was right, he chose her precisely because she was different from the others. She has always been very strong. He even came to see her a few times after the breakup, and after a few years too. I do not know if he thought about getting back together when he came to see her, but I think he did. I remember he was very hurt because it was she, if I am not mistaken, who asked for a break before the breakup. He did not expect that from her, all he needed was to win the championship; I think that was also what he was mad about. When Adriane said she wanted a break, he could not believe it. How could Adriane want a break? He was hurt, I think that is what my father said to Adriane, how could she have done that to him? No woman would do that. He was at the peak of his career, and this must also have had a direct impact on the way he was of not resigning himself to losing anything, he just wanted to win, and that is what happened in his professional life."*

In a conversation with Rô's father, I remember him saying, because this marked me: "What I see is a thread of light that unites the two of you, and no one, neither you nor he can break thread that connects you, only God can do that!"

In fact, that is what I felt or knew in my heart. I cannot explain why, but that only caused me more pain and anger. Since he was liking someone else, I also wanted to move on with my life.

I even played Russian roulette, when driving my car through the closed headlights, through the streets of São Paulo, late at night, defying God, it was crazy! I confess I did not even think I could hurt other people. But if I was defying God, I felt that, since He was supposed to be in control of everything, He would have the chance to avoid the worst, but for me He did not! So let Him, from above, repair the damage down here, or take me at once! At that moment, I really would not care if the worst happened to me.

One day I was at Rosângela's, very sad, and I said:

"Rô, I cannot take it, why did he throw it all away? Why? What is the reason?"

"Adri, talk to him! Call him and tell him what you are feeling!"

So I asked her to call him. I do not know what story we made up, but he started to get annoyed because the story was poorly told and said:

"Listen, what do you want, huh?"

She was intimidated by his reaction and said who she was, said she was my friend and that I was by her side, giving me the phone. I said:

"Hi Beco, how are you? Beco, I cannot understand what you have done."

He spoke carelessly:

"That is life, unexpected things happen."

"Beco, you do not get it..." I said in a very low voice, afraid that someone might hear me, but I was telling the truth: "I have been thinking about dying..."

"Oh, that is normal, it will be gone soon," he replied.

I replied almost voicelessly:

"Do you think it is normal? In your world it may be, but in my world, it never existed."

And he said:

"Do you want to meet me at USP? I am running there with Nuno. Then we can talk better."

So I went to USP the next day, he was still running. I met Nuno, who did not understand anything about me being there. When he finished training, we sat on the lawn around the race track, and he asked:

"Speak up, Dri, what do you have to tell me?"

"The only thing I want to tell you is that I know people have a right to make their choices, whether or not they want to be in someone else's life, but to do it the way you did? And what I do not get either is, you are now with a person totally different from me! In fact, in addition to her story with Pelé, who is someone who has an agenda in the press about your sexuality."

"I know what I am doing," he snapped, annoyed at the glaring truth of what I was saying.

"I am glad you know what you are doing, but I have a question: You said you dream of having a child with her; didn't you dream of having a child with me? And is this the kind of woman you want to be the mother of your children? After all we have been through together, will it end up like this? Aren't you afraid to regret it? Afraid of having closed the doors behind you?"

"No, I am not afraid to regret it," he said haughtily.

"Good for you! That you are not afraid to regret it."

I got up, said goodbye and left without looking back. I had already said everything I had to say, and he was there, without arguments to justify his attitude towards me. I left because I realized this was not the man I fell in love with, he had nothing to do with him. This one really had nothing for me. Then I realized I should not have nothing more for him and that is what I imposed on myself, until the end of that year of '89 and I went on with my life.

But it was not easy, it required a very long process. There were moments that I remember clearly, because it consumed me from the inside, in which I thought I had nothing special to offer anymore, the virginity thing. I had decided to share this "very special thing" with the man I loved and who was going to be the man of my life, I was raised to believe in that. I felt I had nothing else to offer, nothing that was valuable to a man, so that was taking hold of me and it did me a lot of harm, I could not talk or share this subject with my parents. I sometimes felt like using it against Ayrton, I confess; just as he destroyed my life at that moment, I knew it would do good damage to his. But then I did not let it win, remembering that I was the one who made that choice. In times like these we have to be strong so that we are not destructive, as he had been to me; maintain a dignified attitude, so as not to erase all the good and right things that had been done — only character and self-esteem to keep us in the right path. We should not give reason to whoever was wrong, this can be used against you, giving the other room to justify himself, and I would not admit that at all! We must leave the weight of mistakes on the back of those who made the mistakes and not help alleviate with desperate attitudes. Using anger in our favor is a tool to face with inner strength and intelligence whatever is unfair. Over time, I accepted, but I ended up venturing on this subject with my aunt Nádia after a while:

"Auntie, there is something I need to say, because it is not doing me any good!"

And I told her I had lost my virginity to Ayrton. And she said:

"Oh, yeah? Really? Did you lose your virginity before you got married too? Welcome to the club! This is most often hypocrisy! I think your parents may have done that too! They were always rubbing each other around at home when they were dating."

My aunt spoke that way so I would not feel so bad, to take the burden of guilt off my shoulders. She wanted to comfort me, without judging me.

After nineteen years of thinking one way, with so many beliefs determined even at an early age, I was struggling to change my way of thinking and alleviate the feeling of guilt.

My aunt Muruca tells us how most of my family saw that situation: *"Adriane suffered with the breakup, and it is something that marks her life to this day. She was very young when she met Ayrton, and they spent a long time together. Then she came to love him a lot and vice versa. Maybe he did what he had to do. In my opinion, it was extremely selfish, because in his mind, he was a superstar, felt powerful and thought 'I will do whatever I want'. I know that when he went there to break up, he was wearing dark glasses and crying like crazy, his soul did not match what he wanted to do. He wanted total freedom to date a lot of women.*

But he respected Adriane, this is true! So much so that, during their relationship, they talked nasty things, because he was not seen with women, and they arranged a scheme for him to show up with models.

I did not care if this was painful for him, it was his problem, because the agreement was to keep their relationship anonymous. I have nothing against Ayrton Senna, the great guy who was an idol, I am talking about Beco who attended our family and dated our niece for four years, and I saw, day by day, and he seemed to be extremely proud and vain. I was super happy when they broke up, I am very devoted to a Higher Being, very full of faith and I know his sister is too, she believes in almost the same thing as we do. I always asked God for his and her happiness, for their light, because I was so worried about my niece. It was not a normal sixteen-year-old relationship, because he was very famous and everyone got involved, on her father's side and on his'. Wow, there was no peace in this relationship! And it was heading towards something more and more serious, Gosh! I was afraid she would not have structure, as she did not really."

I am just going to tell you two solidary attitudes towards me and my family, among many, of indignation from people who lived around us and indirectly participated in my relationship with Ayrton, in the four years of our relationship.

Once, I heard from my father, who went to Guarujá because he was super upset and needed to clear his mind, with the excuse of seeing how his boat was maintained and cared for, and there he had a conversation with our sailor, who had been the same since forever — a guy my father trusted a lot, and they both respected each other. He was also very responsible, competent and efficient, his name was Toninho. He knew the special affection my father had acquired for Ayrton in those years of living together, just like he showed for his son-in-law Eduardo, as if they were the son he had not had. He saw my father so sad, so disappointed! He also witnessed our relationship; as a sailor, he was always there and saw how it all started between us. He saw our families together, mine and Ayrton's. Then he saw Ayrton doing such a thing! So Toninho said to my father:

"Mr. Amilcar, I am here to serve you, whatever you ask me to do, I will do. Whatever it is!"

And my father, understanding the message, said:

"No, stop that, Toninho. We are not doing anything; we are letting God provide what belongs to each one of us."

I am telling this story to show how shocked it was for the people who knew my family and saw our relationship.

Another fact: When my spine was very tight, because of so much tension and nervousness, I went to Professor Adelino, the same one who put Ayrton's spine back in place on New Year's Eve of 1986/87, and he was with us a few times at Chapadão farm. He, with that somewhat shamanic thing, had done protective work with symbols that he drew on plain paper. Without speaking or explaining anything, he folded this paper several times until it was very tiny, and gave it to us to carry in our wallets, as a spiritual, karmic protection.

At a certain point in the appointment, after having put my back and shoulders in place, now sitting face to face at his work desk — for my part, I had not mentioned a single word about the recent events, I avoided talking about it not to fall into the crying, it was a way of keeping that within me, to move on with my life. He, who also witnessed our relationship and had known me for a long time, especially because that pain was clearly visible in my face, said:

"Wait, I will do one thing!"

He opened his desk drawer, took one of those pieces of paper, showed it to me and said:

"Do you see this? It was the protection work I did for Ayrton.   As you have that of the two of you, I made one for him without his asking me! I made it and kept it here," he pointed to the drawer, where he took out the paper.

He unfolded the paper and tore it into little pieces in front of me, saying:

"After what he did to you, he is on his own."

I also remember two situations as moments of great pain. One day, in my affliction and wanting to move on with my life — on the first quarter of 1989 —, I walked everywhere, going to the gym, to college, without finding peace. I could not stay home either; if I was watching television, I would get up and go to the bedroom. It was an endless internal restlessness. At home, there was a long hallway, which connected the social area to the intimate one. One day, I stopped in the middle of this hallway because I realized that the restlessness was the search for something I could not find to alleviate the pain. I collapsed to the ground and started crying compulsively. I tried everything to be strong, but that day I froze, my parents found me there; I wanted to hide this pain from them, but I could not.

I was always restless, running around (I could not stop), and at that time, I did gymnastics with Ala Szerman. I often crossed paths with the famous Angelica there, but no one knew my story there; but during exercise sometimes I would remember what had happened and tears would run down my face without my consent. The force that drove me forward was anger, a lot of anger, such an anger that I did not accept him to spoil my life in any way; he did not deserve for me to stop wanting to live and move on with my life; and that was what happened. I went to college, I took Industrial Design, I managed to get on the first list. It was a specter, but a specter that moved on.

I call this phase "Forrest Gump". Do you remember when in this movie Forrest (Tom Hanks) runs aimlessly and without stopping for a while right after being abandoned by his great love? Until his pain eased and he no longer felt the need to flee from it. Well, my moment was exactly like this, however, I could not flee from my house, which only made this stage more difficult.

On December 1989, about two months after they announced the end of the famous lovebirds' eight-month relationship on national television, he called. It was in the afternoon, I was at home, when I hear someone announcing:

"Adriane, Ayrton is on the phone..."

Surprised, I answered his call, cautious, and he was all excited:

"Hi, Drica, how are you? How are things? How is your father, mother, sisters? Did Lê and Dadô already have the baby?"

I replied we were fine and this kind of things, amenities. Then he asked me:

"Where are you guys going to spend Christmas?"

"On the farm," I replied.

"When are you going there?"

"I believe the 21st, Thursday, I will be there."

"Tell them I sent hugs and kisses to your family and that I wish all of you a Merry Christmas and a Happy New Year."

"Will do! Send kisses to everyone there too!"

I thought to myself: Umm... He waited sometime after the breakup with the other one to look for me, he wants to try to dilute the discomfort between us for the bad thing he did... Good strategy, now let's wait for the next events.

I went to the farm a day after scheduled, it was night when I got there. While we had a snack, my father commented:

"You will not guess who was here today..."

I immediately remembered my recent conversation with Ayrton and said:

"Ayrton. What was he doing here?"

"He came with his father, by helicopter, we talked a little on the porch, and when he asked for you, we said you would come later with your boyfriend. It was not easy for him to come here! Even with his father's support, even Dumbo, your dog, growled when he wanted to be funny."

As I listened to all of this, I felt an incredible pleasure, imagining his face. I was glad to know that he knew I was already with someone else. Caught by surprise and lost with what he had not foreseen in my life, he ran after that presenter in New York.

She was in a house in Hampton Bays, a stronghold of the New York elite, made up of small seaside villages. He headed there and, before knocking on the door, according to the story he gave to Braguinha, he dressed as Santa Claus. When the bell rang, the surprise was his. Ayrton then reported to friends, family and at least one of his future girls that "X". did not want him to enter.

"What are you doing here? I did not invite you. Please leave. You are not entering here."
(Source: Ayrton: *o herói revelado* by Ernesto Carneiro Rodrigues. Rio de Janeiro: Objetiva, 2004)

He who plays with fire gets burnt! So that Christmas 1989, for him, would be much worse than mine, since I was already starting my life over.

I no longer called him Beco, because to me Beco had died, but I called him Ayrton, who reminded me of Beco, but they were not the same person. I had lived through my grief these past few months, but I had survived.

I have to say that the arrival of my older sister's baby, my first niece, Bibi, helped me a lot in the process. A baby always renews the energies of the family. She and many others, who came later, filled our lives with joy, giving us back the lightness of innocence.

I know that, despite having done some silly things, I managed to start over, out of anger in not accepting that he interfered with my life. Gratitude for everything that surrounded me since my birth, which enabled me to have a great life, also helped a lot! And so I moved on.

In a rare statement by Ron Dennis about Ayrton's personal life, he said: *"Under normal circumstances, I would not comment on girlfriends, but so much fake things has been said that I feel urged to comment. The truth is: Ayrton was completely committed to Formula 1. It was the most important thing in his life and he made many, many sacrifices to be the best, at a level that no one has ever reached. He set standards for the future champions. And what made him suffer most was his private life.*

Trust was very important, and he did not put that requirement aside when it came to girlfriends. But he was somehow too kind, too thoughtful, too open. And virtually all

of his love relationships I have witnessed that were of any value to him have always ended in a painful way for him."
(Source: Ayrton: *o herói revelado* by Ernesto Carneiro Rodrigues. Rio de Janeiro: Objetiva, 2004).

Another thing that happened and is worth mentioning was that, one day in 1990, my mother and Mrs. Neyde happened to cross paths in an appliance store. My mother had gone to buy a wedding gift, and I am not sure what Ayrton's mom was doing there. Mom saw her from afar and pretended she did not see her, because she did not know what to say to Mrs. Neyde, even though she was very fond of her. I believe Mrs. Neyde thought the same thing. What would they say to each other, after all? By "chance", they ran into each other in the cashier and there was no way to escape that situation anymore, nor were there any reasons for that. Then Mrs. Neyde jumped into my mother's arms, hugging her, and began to cry. She said:

"I am sorry, Marilene! Sorry for what my son did to all of you, you did not deserve this!"

And my mother comforted her, saying:

"Neyde, Adriane is fine, everything is okay! The worst is over, and life goes on!"

But she kept crying and apologizing until they settled their business in that store and said their goodbyes.

My father and Mr. Milton also talked again, after he showed up with Beco in the farm, at Christmas 1989. They were breaking the ice and, in fact, they managed to keep the friendship.

Once, in 1990, I met Ayrton and Leonardo with two girls who, apparently, they had met that day. I say this because they were not dressed for the occasion. I was with my boyfriend, my sister and her boyfriend. We sat down near the dance floor, with Ayrton and his company close behind. My boyfriend decided to kiss me insistently, and at first, I did not repel him, after all, he was my boyfriend, too bad for Ayrton to be right behind us. When I realized his kisses were going beyond normal, I interrupted him and, discreetly, looked back and saw that Ayrton had positioned himself with his back to us. My companion protested, because perhaps he wanted to prove something in front of my ex. I justified it by saying that it was not our normal thing and he has known for a long time that I do not like showing off in front of strangers, and he stepped back.

It was a very uncomfortable night for me to be between them. I tried to keep my back to Ayrton in order not to have major problems and also because I did not want to know what he would be doing with his companions. I was afraid to see it and not like it, as I wanted to go on with my life in peace. But at the end of that night, on the way out, we said goodbye and when introduced, we were cordial with each other.

Ayrton dated Ferracciu in 1991, and their relationship ended by the end of that same year or in the beginning of 1992. Her mother had cancer, which is why the relationship came to an end, as she chose to return to Brazil and stay with her mother, and he did not accept that. I am not sure what happened exactly, but that is at least what she told me personally.

In January 1992, I went to a seminar in Rio de Janeiro, and again, by coincidence of fate, Ferracciu's mother also participated in the IVI groups in Rio, and they participated in the event. That was my first seminar, and we crossed paths. I had already been told she was there, but I had nothing to tell her, we did not know each other; however, just before we left, she ended up approaching me to talk, she said she knew what Beco did to me and explained the reasons for the end of their relationship. I said what I really felt:

My fateful encounter with Cris Ferracciu in Rio de Janeiro

"Listen, Cris, let me tell you something. You strike me as a nice girl, with a good education, a good family, I am sorry your mother is sick, and I hope she recovers soon. I will confess that when I saw your pictures with him, I was worried about you, because I know what he has to offer to a woman. I was sad because I knew he was going to hurt you. He has nothing to offer to anyone! He only thinks about himself. For people who are good to him, as long as they are useful, that is fine; if they are no longer useful for what he needs, then he discards them. I am so sorry for you, but it was the best thing that ever happened to you. For your sake, move on. Determination is one thing, which is quite alright. Stubbornness, however, is different; which destroys everything around him that may get in the way of his goals."

She, seeing me with that very tough attitude towards Ayrton, had an inexplicably noble response; she turned to me and said:

"Look, I think he is still going to look for you!"

I do not know what he had told her. I did not have the curiosity to ask, because I simply did not want to be having that conversation. I was sympathetic to her, because I knew

644

what Ayrton had to offer towards a decent person, and the risk she would be taking with him. And I think she felt my sympathy too. So, I told her:

"Cris, thank you, but I do not have anything else to give him either, I cannot imagine myself by his side anymore. Thank you for the kind words, and I hope your mother gets well soon!"

The conversation ended there. They called me, telling me that our group bus was waiting for me to leave, so we said goodbye.

In that same seminar, there was an episode that really impressed me, during Yvonne's lecture. She began to tell the well-known biblical story of the prodigal son who, as a young man, wanted his inheritance early and left his family, wandered across the world, spent all his money on traveling, luxuries and pleasures, until he lost everything. And, out of shame for what he did, he only returned home when he was already hungry, but his father welcomed him with great joy. Towards the end of our conversation, with all those people in that room, Yvonne looked right at me. I had never talked to her before and she probably did not know who I was, but she looked me in the eye and said the following sentence as the end of the story:

"Because you can be sure that wherever real love is found, even if it leaves, it comes back much stronger."

When she finished saying that, I looked around, and in surprise, realized she was talking about me! This was something that left a mark on me. At that moment, I just wanted to move my life forward and that was because of my plans for the future, which was to find someone else with whom I got along, who was fun to be with and who had fun with the same things I did.

I still deeply missed my Beco, and one day, already exhausted from struggling to start my life over, I walked into a church on the way home. I imagine that, for me, it was a more difficult process to turn the page because, like it or not,

I had the media rubbing Ayrton in my face at every moment. Besides, everyone always wanted to bring up the subject with me when they discovered I had dated him. When I was on the move, busy, I managed to be okay, but when I was idle, I fell into emptiness and sadness. Until that day, when I no longer knew where to go or what to look for, I stopped at the Nossa Senhora do Brasil church, and I went to pray to ask God to take away that pain inside me, to free me from that feeling of absence and that love that I could not replace. I prayed, asked, and cried. There were some other people inside the church because it was not mass time, but I cried silently, I cried a lot and prayed, thinking that no one would notice me there. Suddenly, I heard someone close by saying something. I opened my eyes, looked at the priest standing beside me and, realizing my distress, he asked:

"Hello, can I help you with something?"

I, still sobbing, shook my head. No, the priest could not help me, I was there to ask God to take that pain out of my chest.

Sometime later, my prayers were answered, and this pain had already diminished a little — or time itself was taking care of alleviating it — so I repeated this to myself, like a mantra: "There is no good that always lasts, and no bad that never ends."

What was good did not last forever, but it was really good, and the bad part would go away at some point, too. I read an article in a magazine talking about this, about grief. There are several types of grief, it is not just when a person dies; in a sudden separation, for example, grief is also experienced and that, depending on the way in which the breakup happens, one can feel the same pain as a death from sudden loss. That Is why I say: My pain was great. Certainly, as intense as the pain his family felt when he passed away; only that in my case, I did not allow myself to feel anymore, I had already had my share. In the magazine, it still said that the breakup could also lead to depression and, most likely, I suffered a deep depression, but no one at home knew how to deal with it and help me. It was the love I had for my family that held me back from making a mistake in the moment of greatest pain, because I did not want to cause more pain to others; they did not deserve it, so I put up with it. After I got over it alone, without the help of doctors or medication, I once tried to seek help from a psychologist. I talked to him a lot, to see if he would help me reach a conclusion, but I had to reach a conclusion myself, find out for myself what could have happened, so I gave up going to therapy. I used to go there to talk and cry a lot, I could not do it anymore.

After that, I was sure that nothing else would bring me down in life. After I got over all that, after facing what I faced, I was sure of my strength and my ability to withstand the difficulties. This discovery made me less afraid of taking some risks because, also, it would not allow myself to go deeper into a relationship the way I did with Beco. I should have protected myself more, or maybe not given myself so much, but what was the chance of not falling madly in love with him?

In 1992, Ayrton had some problem with having started the year without signing a contract, or at least the contract was not the way he wanted, or he did not sign a contract with any team that year and he was negotiating race by race, without a contract, and that bothered him a lot. I am not exactly sure. I only know that in the middle of the year, he called me:

"Hi, Drica, could we have lunch?"

I accepted the invitation.

He asked me to pick him up at his house because he had no car, and I went there. Then I learned where the apartment he had bought was, in Jardins, near my house, and we went to the Tatou restaurant, on Oscar Freire Street. Ayrton sat with his back to the room, wearing dark glasses, so people would not bother him, and I said:

"Can you please take off your glasses?"

"Ah, I knew you were going to ask me that."

Ayrton asked me how life was and I told him what I was doing, I updated him on my family and everyone he asked about. He said he had learned that my father was looking to buy a helicopter. By then, my father had already bought a plane and was studying how helicopters worked. Therefore, he used to charter one to go to the farm, near São Paulo, and evaluated the safety of the equipment; he was definitely interested in this little toy, too. Ayrton must have been told by his father or by the air force people, as everyone knows each other in that field. The fact is, he started to say:

"I am very dissatisfied with my profession. I do not race for the money, I race for the pleasure of it, and I lost my lust for it because it is a lot of dirt, it is a lot of interest, and I have lost the taste. Talk to your father, I would love to be his pilot, I already got my license, I know how to fly a jet, I know how to fly a helicopter, and I will become his pilot."

I heard that, shocked; he was serious, absolutely not kidding.

"What? Ah, Beco, this will pass, you will find a solution! Can you imagine stopping racing? No way!"

"I am serious!" he said.

"I know you! You will not stop racing, you will not be happy piloting a plane or a helicopter; I am not going to say any of this to my father because it will not happen, rest assured. Calm down, everything will work out!"

Did he come to me because he wanted to be my father's pilot? To get under my family's wings again? Huh? Do not count on me... I was not going to be anyone's crutches anymore.

When it was time to leave, we went to my parked car, I opened the driver's door that was next to the curbing, got in, and when I went to close the door, he was beside me, crouched down and stared at me with shining eyes. I looked into his eyes and asked:

"What is it?"

"Nothing," and he kept looking at me.

I, agitated, said:

"Come on, I will take you home, don't you want to go home?"

He smiled, let me close my door and got into the car. With this atmosphere, I already started putting my music tapes, the upbeat ones, and I told him that he was in a very low mood and needed to cheer up. When we were already near his house, he asked me to drop him off in the garage. I agreed. At the time of farewell, I took the Gipsy Kings tape off the sound system, plus another one and said:

"Look, I will lend you these two tapes to cheer you up, because you are in a very low mood. These are my favorites. But you have to return them, okay?"

I jumped out of the car, without turning off the engine, as if for a brief farewell, he also got out, and I amended:

"Well then! It was great to see you! I have to go, I have an appointment by the afternoon."

At the moment of saying goodbye, he approached me in a hug, I reciprocated the gesture and felt his trembling body... I patted him on the back, saying:

"Beco, everything will be fine, you will see, stay calm, everything will fall into place. Have faith and cheer up! Try to be happy, I loved seeing you!"

I dodged his arms and left. I would not accept his emotional blackmail; if he wanted me back in the first place, he would have to apologize to me, and he would have to find out if I still wanted him — not by leaning in. He almost destroyed me; I could not accept that! Go ask for help somewhere else. I left very upset. "How come?" He is so full of himself; I deserve more than that."

I remember that I traveled during next year's Carnival and went skiing in Aspen with Chris and friends, having also passed through New York, because I was seeing a guy who lived there. And during this period, I saw at TAG Heuer's a small-size watch whose all-steel bracelet made me crazy.

However, I wanted the medium-sized, but the store did not have it. As soon as I got back from this trip, Ayrton called me and asked how I was.

"Since you called me, I saw a watch … And since you are sponsored by TAG Heuer, can't you get this watch for me?"

I actually talked about the watch more as an excuse to tell him that I had gone away, that I had a great life, thank you, and to show how much I knew what I want. I really wanted to act cocky. Obviously, I did not think he would worry about it.

But Ayrton said he would look into it, I explained how the watch was, the model, and he said he would see if he found it. After some time, he called me and said:

"I got your watch, but you will have to come here to pick it up!"

"Okay, I'm going! It's the least I could do after all this trouble. When?"

"Tomorrow?"

"Only if it's around lunchtime, because I have to travel by the afternoon."

"Great, half past one, okay? I am at the same address you came to the other day; it is on the seventh floor" (if I'm not mistaken).

I was going to travel to Campos do Jordão; it was Easter holiday, so I had a great excuse to get away quickly. I went upstairs, and he received me shirtless, the rascal, and all satisfied, happy that he had gotten me the watch. We greeted each other, and I was already taking a look around the apartment — a bit cold, it did not feel like home. There was neon light under the step in the living room, I thought that was strange. It had a garçonnière air, it was not cozy like the other houses I have seen. We sat at the dinner table, he opened the box, showed me, and asked:

"Drica, was this what you wanted?"

"It was exactly that one, you nailed it, that is it." I put the watch on my wrist.

"Great! Because if it was the wrong one, I could change it for you! Wait a minute, let's try adjusting the size of the bracelet."

He left and came back with a few different tools in hand.

"How beautiful is this watch, I love it! Now I want to know how much I owe you, I ordered it because I could not find it, and I know it costs around 400 dollars, something like that." He didn't want to mention it.

Meanwhile, he was measuring the bracelet on my wrist and evaluating how many links he would have to take off.

"Let me see, Dri, give me your arm. No, no, it is a gift of mine, I liked it so much that I even bought one for myself, look!"

There I was, terrified of him touching me and, at the same time, I did not want him to let go of me anymore. I did not trust my resistance to that man, so I avoided any touch.

"Really, this is the most beautiful. You were right to get one for you."

Soon he was able to complete the adjustment.

"Okay, Drica, put it on to see if it is good!"

"Looking great! Thank you very much, I really loved it!" I tried it on quickly, I was more worried about leaving quickly than about adjusting the watch. It was not very conscious, more like a dread, a phobia, a situation in which I felt under threat. "Beco, as I told you, I cannot stay any longer because I am going to hit the road today. I am going to Campos do Jordão and driving, my friends are waiting for me, because we already have a hotel booked. Sorry, but I have to go."

"Too bad you have to leave so soon. We will talk soon. Travel safe."

"I really appreciate your kindness, see you."

I left, picked up my friends and went to Campos do Jordão. In our room, I showed the watch and what had happened that day, a little shaken. These friends of mine had a habit of opening the Bible, praying a little before opening a page at random and seeing a message in the Psalms. I did what they instructed me to do:

"Go, Dri, read a Psalm!"

When I opened the Psalm, it said something about no one being able to escape their fate. As soon as I started reading this, I closed the Bible and shouted:

"Oh, freaking hell!"

Throwing the Bible on the bed, I could not get rid of it, and my friends got scared:

"Oh, Dri! You cannot do this. Relax!"

"Sorry, guys, but what a pain! What the hell! I want my life to go on, I want to move on, and now what? If it is my fate, why did I have to go through what I went through? For what purpose? No! I want to start my life over with someone who can live by my side! Someone who takes care of me!"

My friend Denise Vasconcelos Farah also followed this post-dating phase closely and reminded me of how it was: *"We crossed paths with Ayrton once when we were together, at the Gallery, probably in the first months of 1990. Me, Adriane, André, Fábio and Chris. As soon as we entered, standing near the floor, was Ayrton Senna. Dri stopped to say hello, he greeted everyone, and she introduced me. It was like a little too much for everyone. He was very polite to us; I could see he was very considerate to her. He also looked surprised to see her. He observed who Adriane was with and was very polite to everyone. For us it was kind of complicated, because he was Dri's ex-boyfriend, but he was also an idol, so everyone was embarrassed.*

Dri has always been very authentic, very funny, very cool. We noticed that it was difficult for her to talk about the subject. Fábio, who was dating Chris before I met Adriane, had told me that she had dated a super famous guy and that she suffered a lot because of it, that he was exposed in the media, but he did not say who he was. Only then I found out who he was.

I remember that she did not talk about this subject with us and, the few times she did, she said very little and her eyes watered up. It was a very isolated situation; normally, with a friend you advise: 'look, this guy this, this guy that', but we could not say anything about him. What could we possibly say? 'He will regret it... One day he will come back...' The world pulled him to another side, a different situation, so we just listened!

People who knew about the case avoided mentioning his name in front of her; although she was always very cheerful, we avoided it. The times I talked a little about this subject with her, I could not tell if it was my curiosity about the idol or about him as Dri's ex-boyfriend. I remember that what happened between them hurt her a lot, she was caught overnight, so we avoided talking about it and tried to distract her from everything that involved his name. Because she would change from her spontaneous joy to a deep sadness. I even remember that, when we stayed at our house in Guarujá, everyone wanted to watch the race, but we were also aware that when she woke up we would have to run to turn off the television — I have this scene in my mind, we wanted to spare Dri.

Once, on a Saturday, we did not go out and at that time we used to do something at night! But we stayed at Dri's house. The house phone rang, there was no such thing as a cell phone, and it was him! I thought: 'It is not possible!' And she answered saying: 'Hi, Beco!' She used to call him Beco, right? She talked to him for a while and then hung up. Dri was no longer dating that mutual friend of ours, so she commented to me: 'Jeez, calling me on Saturday. He must be feeling lonely and decided to call me.'

He took her by surprise that day, she did not expect that! This was in late 1992 or early 1993. He really had a lot of regard for Dri."

This time we crossed paths at the Gallery, I was with my friend Denise, and Beco was accompanied by a famous model in Brazil, who was simply beautiful, inside a small white tube dress, with a huge opening in the back. She was so perfect that I could not even be jealous. A few years ago, we became friends, and she is a very dear person and still beautiful! Her name is Patrícia Machado.

Another story from 1992 happened when I was with my friend Priscila, and we passed Ayrton in traffic, at night. He was in a low car, small, I do not know if it was a Honda. At the time, imports into Brazil were starting out and many different cars appeared on the streets. I thought that Ayrton's car looked like an ant, it was black, and we crossed paths on República do Líbano Avenue. The city of São Paulo was empty; I stopped at the light and he stopped beside me, he was with a girl in the car, and he opened the window on her side, honked and started talking to me, shouting on the other side, all excited. When the headlights turned green, I went first with my car, teasing him, which I knew he would not resist. Then he came accepting the challenge! In this one, I drove in such a way so he could not pass me. Anyway, it was silly, but in the end, he could not pass me until after Avenida Ibirapuera, because right after, I went into one of the alleyways as we were going to drop someone off. He passed forward honking, and we parted.

My friend Priscila tells us what she witnessed at this stage: *"I remember the day when Dri and Ayrton raced at night, on the streets of São Paulo. I was in the car with her and I thought it was funny. We ran into him in traffic, and they sparred for about three blocks. He was in a low, black car.*

I also remember that she told me about returning the gold watch he had given her as a gift. And then her father gave her another one.

I still remember the motorcycle at the farm he gave her, but she took a while to show me...

I know that the relationship was very important for Dri and it was very difficult for her to talk about this subject. Sometimes she would tell a story of what had happened;

other times, she preferred not to speak. As we were very close friends, I respected her and avoided talking about it. She was very concerned about his family, was very fond of them, always wanted to know how they were; and her father, uncle Amilcar, when spoke of him, he spoke as if he was part of their family. Because they had a very good relationship for a long time. She also spoke of Ayrton with great affection. I myself thought that what he did at the end of their relationship was not very nice, but even so she was very fond of him."

At the end of 1992, Beco sought me out and invited me to go with him on a friend's birthday, it was already night and I explained that I was alone at home, I would have to get ready and there was no way I could tell my parents. I told us to leave it for another opportunity, but he insisted. I tried to get him to give up, claiming that I used to tell my parents when I went out by car at night, tell them where I was going, so they would not be worried, and he emphatically said:

"Then I will go get you. I am right next door, at the party, and I am going to pick you up!

"I am not dressed for a party!"

"It doesn't matter, come just the way you are! Leave a note warning your parents."

"Ok."

I ran out to put on a simple outfit, but something I knew he would like, like that long skirt, some mascara and lipstick. He arrived and we went to Massimo's Restaurant, in a private room. When we got there, I ran into his family, his parents and sister, they were tidier, but nothing too fancy, then Mrs. Neyde looked at me, widened her eyes and said:

"Ah, Beco... is this the surprise?!" She spoke with a smile, looking like she loved it!

I greeted them, feeling nostalgic, gave them a hug with great affection, also being very polite with Viviane. It was Bira's birthday, Ayrton's partner at Audi.

Faustão, Chico Anísio and Ronald were at that party, I looked at that and thought: "My God, am I in paradise? What is this place I came to?". My father, whenever he wanted to clown around, mimicked Ronald Golias, and I sat right at the table in front of him, I could not believe it, but I greeted him as I normally would. On the right side of the table was Beco, on the left side, Mrs. Neyde, and in front of me, Ronald — I was in the best of all worlds. Ronald Golias told funny stories from his real life and I stood there, delighted. He was a guy who did funny things in life and he was a different person. It was dinner and I had already eaten, but when they served dessert I accepted, just to tease Beco, because he was always attentive to what you eat or what you do not eat, making fun of everything. Then I accepted the dessert and nudged Mrs. Neyde to see the teasing, Beco was distracted at that moment, and when he turned his attention to me again and saw the ice cream in front of me, he said:

"Ah! Very well, miss, you mean you did not accept dinner, but you did accept dessert, huh?"

I started to laugh and said:

"Ah, Beco, I just ordered it to wind you up, I threw the bait to see if you could catch it, and I pulled the line. I did it just to see if you are still the same."

That day, I did not like the feeling. It was as if we had not spent a single day apart, we knew each other's reaction naturally, and that bothered me a lot.

When he took me home, still in the car in front of my house, on the street, I thought we were going to say goodbye soon and I would leave, but he started to talk:

"What about your parents? Did you mention you were going out with me?"

"No, I said I was going out, but I did not say it was you."

"You didn't? What did you say?"

"I said I was going out for a birthday nearby and would be back early. I do not need to say who I was with."

"And why didn't you say you were going out with me?"

"Because I did not want to worry my parents, they saw everything I went through, and I do not think it is fair to worry them. I went out with you, we went there, it was a super nice night, great, and when I get home now, I will say, yes, I went out with you, but they will see I am fine and everything will be fine. It is not a problem to say I will see you; the problem is making them worried after they have witnessed the state I was in."

His spirits were fading, I said that to make him feel really guilty! For all the mess he did, but in a polite way. During this conversation, my skirt, which was tied like an envelope, opened a flap and left my leg exposed; at that moment his eyes darted to my legs, and I quietly closed it, because I was not available. That was not intentional.

"Well, Beco, it is dangerous for us to be here on the street at this time."

"So, Dridrica, send my regards to your parents." He was kind of embarrassed after what I said, but I thought it was great, to keep him at a safe distance from me. He added: "We will talk to each other, you can call me, no, I will call you, no... We can talk." He did not know what to say and I just stood there, silently, looking at his face to see him unravel that knot.

When he saw that he did not know what else to say, I replied:

"It is okay, Beco. So, thanks for the night, it was delightful."

"Thanks."

I kissed him on the cheek, crookedly so I did not have a chance to be near his mouth, and walked away, annoyed, just as he seemed to be super annoyed too. That night moved us because we were both at peace. Finally, we found ourselves in peace, and I did not like the feeling of not having passed a day apart. This put me on alert for imminent danger.

"Years after his relationship with Adriane Yamin ended on Christmas 1988, Ayrton told his doctor and confidant Linamara Battistella that he was sure she would never adapt to his type of life, even though she represented everything he

wanted from a woman: A girl with the same structure and family habits as his, which included virginity: It was not shocking to Ayrton, at that time, that Adriane's mother said that she could not travel alone. For him, conservative that he was, that was right."

(Source: Ayrton: *o herói revelado*, Ernesto Carneiro Rodrigues. Rio de Janeiro: Objetiva, 2004)

I remember hearing that when Honda came to Brazil, they did not talk to Ayrton to offer representation in the country. He was very disappointed because he had been a partner with the Honda people for a long time. And he ended up bringing the representation from Audi. All this thanks to the change of rules and laws in our country, which opened up to import.

The following year, in 1993, after the Brazilian GP, a rumor began that he was seeing someone. I started to laugh; when I found out her name I was amused, because I dated three guys who had the initial "A" in their names, I just did not date another Ayrton because I did not find any other. All of them led me to an association, something that reminded me of Ayrton, whether by the first letter of the name, the star sign, the appearance, because I looked for Beco in other boys and, suddenly, he appeared with another Adriane. Apart from me, at that time, I did not know any other Adriane; it is not a common name, just like his is not, and he found another girl with my name. I thought: he is doing what I am doing, a transfer—I thought that was really interesting.

A while passed; I was dating the last boy with the A initial. We dated for about eight months and it was a half-assed, kind of off-kilter, with no connection relationship. Then I already wanted to finish and he did not. That was in 1993. And I learned that he was going out with someone else and leaving me as his second option; irritated with his conduct, I broke up for good! The couple who introduced us were going to a concert at the Palace and I knew he was going with this other girl he was already seeing. I was really pissed off; those friends were my best friends! And I knew that due to the financial position of my family and the fact that I had been Senna's girlfriend, I brought a certain prestige to whoever was with me. So I called Ayrton:

"Hi, Beco, how are you? Don't you want to go to a concert with me at the Palace tonight? I will be honest: I am sick of people wanting to approach me just to say they are with Ayrton Senna's ex. There is this guy who is going to be there and he made a big deal out of me, that is why I really wanted to show up with you. I am sick of it!"

"Fine for me, Drica, but wait, I need to call there, because there is a whole lot of logistics to get in, I cannot stay at the door around lots of people. Wait, I will check and I call you."

I then called Silvana, my friend, and said:

"Sil, he agreed. That A guy... he is going to have it!"

I was honest with Ayrton, I did not lie, I did not cheat, because that is my way of being. And he agreed. Half an hour before the show, he called and said:

"Dri, I cannot go, some problems got around that. I am fine, and she arrived here and did not like it, and I do not want to get in trouble, I do not want a fight, I am sorry, but I cannot go with you."

In other words, he did not go because his companion got in the way and messed up the situation, but he was definitely interested in going!

The next day, I was with my friend Sil in the car, coming back from somewhere, and I decided to call him — cell phones already existed by then. I knew he was with someone else and called anyway because I did not value that relationship of his but that did not give me the right to make trouble for him. It had not been the right thing to do and I was embarrassed. So I decided to call again to apologize.

"Hi Beco, how are you? I am just calling you to apologize for yesterday, I wanted you to help me solve my problems and not cause trouble for you."

"No, Dri, it was no problem for me!"

"Anyway, I felt compelled to call. If I have caused any discomfort in your life, I apologize."

"Nonsense, it did not cause any problem! And how are your father, your mother, Dadô, your sisters..." He really missed everyone, who had been his family too, for a while. He would always carry a piece of us with him and we would always carry a piece of him with us.

He wanted to know how everyone was doing. When the subject was over, I asked about his family as well, those I had grown fond of, and we ended the conversation. That was the last time I spoke to him in my life, in the second half of 1993.

After Christmas and New Year's Eve, the Formula 1 season started. After we broke up, I did not want to watch the races anymore and I did not want to know what was going on. I was a little curious when something different came up, but I did not watch the actual races, and if something like that appeared on television, I would leave and that was it. I ended it, took it out of my life.

Judging by the testimony of Cristine Ferracciu, Ayrton, during this period, also experienced moments of emotional conflict that led him to call her, in early March, in tears:

"He asked for forgiveness. He could not settle for the mistakes he had made and hurt the only two women he could have married: Adriane Yamin and me. And that he had hurt Yamin by doing to her what X. did to him.

Ayrton just cried, asked for forgiveness and, according to Cristine, tried to explain his relationship with Adriane G.: - *She doesn't disturb, doesn't ask questions and doesn't bother anyone."* (Source: O herói revelado, Ernesto Rodrigues. Rio de Janeiro. Objetiva: 2004)

Caras Magazine – Year 1, No. 25, April 29, 1994
By Mara Ziravello, São Paulo

"Shy as always and courageous like never before, the driver Ayrton Senna da Silva (34) says he has already forgotten what it feels like to be rejected by a woman. Maybe I'm a privileged

guy, he says. A privilege that began around the same time he started racing in the millionaire circuits of Formula 1 in 1984. Although he has been dating São Paulo model Adriane Galisteu (21) for a year – a new record in the life of the three-time world champion – the truth is that he remains divorced by conviction. Everything has its time, its moment, he responds, carefully choosing his words. For Senna, defining the woman of his dreams is easy. The hard part is being sure he has found her, as the constant travels required by his profession expose him to many different peoples and cultures. Still, his personal paradise is in Brazil, exactly 150 km from São Paulo, in Tatuí: the Dois Lagos farm, where he escapes with his girlfriend whenever he has a break in his hectic schedule. It was during one of these rare breaks that Ayrton Senna, one of the world's most popular idols, gave an exclusive interview to Caras magazine to talk about love, fidelity, and marriage.

*- **When the time comes for you to get married, how do you plan to adapt your family to your lifestyle?***

- First, I need to reach a point of maturity, security, and inner peace that will make it clear it's time for me to have someone by my side. When that moment comes and I am aware of the new path I need to take, there will be a need for me to adjust, to adapt to this new phase of my life. But I haven't reached that point yet, so I don't know how things will adjust. Some things you can plan, some things you have full or great control over, but others you only have partial control over.

*- **Which ones, for example?***

- You don't choose: I will love this woman, marry her, and have children. No one does that, and anyone who tries will surely fail. I've learned a little about this. I'm still young, but we live intensely.

*- **Is it hard to find the right person?***

- When you travel a lot, you end up living with different cultures, people completely different from what we consider standard in Brazil, from our own families, friendships, and social circles. All of this is baggage that teaches you. I hope

that with all this learning that I'm constantly having, I'll be able to choose wisely. Naturally, my expectations tend to grow, in a way. On the other hand, I think that due to the life experiences, and the situations we go through and the ones we witness. These teach us that certain things won't be exactly as we would like them to be, or as we dreamed.

- And how will they be?

- I think nothing is better than life itself, the situations, and the experiences, to form a database of information that allows you to understand, globally, what is really important in a relationship, what is 100% important, what is 90% important, what is 50% important. In the end, it's about what you can accept and what is unacceptable, and so on. It's an ongoing process.

- And still, only God knows when the time will come?

- Yes, only He knows.

- Would it be nice to be closer to this point?

-I wouldn't want to be any closer or farther away. I'm at peace exactly as I am. Because I have a lot of faith and certainty that everything comes in its own time. I feel that the time hasn't come yet.

- Do you usually set deadlines for achieving your goals?

- It's hard to generalize. I think that whatever is your goal, the important thing is to set it clearly. From there, the motivation to reach that point will give you the strength, and energy to use your dedication, commitment and creativity, whatever the distance or the difficulties you will deal with. You must be committed to that goal to find solutions to the problems related to the challenge. I think that commitment is everything. And it's not something that only I can do.

- Is that where your reputation for being a very demanding person comes from?

- I'm demanding of myself, not of the people I relate to or work with. At the same time, I'm fully aware of this elevated level of expectation, and I try to motivate everyone around

me in the same way. I'm not someone who is happy with middle ground.

- What satisfies you?

- I think that when you choose a direction, a goal, you really have to give your best, fight to reach that goal, within what is right, within what is fair, and what is deserved. That must be clear. But when it comes to dedication, commitment, and effort, there's no middle ground. Either you do something well or you don't do it at all.

- Where does that determination come from?

- It comes from my lifestyle, since I was a child, from the activities I did, and the responsibilities I had. I grew up, evolved, and at the same time some people, especially my parents, guided me. As I slipped, I don't know in what direction, they provided me with the necessary support to get back on track.

- Is that how you hope to be when you have children?

- Communication is the most important thing. That's how I learned. If I can keep this way of relating, living harmoniously with my family, I think I'll have great opportunities, along with my future wife, whoever she is, to create an extension of my current family, and of hers, logically.

- Despite all this reasoning, don't you think that when you get married, the decision will be made by the heart?

- It could normally be by the heart. But today I'm not sure of that. If it had been ten years ago, I would agree with you. Today, I wouldn't. Because I've learned that it's not just the heart that determines well-being and harmony between two people. The relationship between a man and a woman is the oldest thing in humanity, and there are still no formulas or parameters that, if followed, will ensure love, peace, the success of the relationship. Even though you know it's important, it's essential to love, to feel, and to be together.

- But deciding only with the heart can bring suffering.

- Exactly. That's why, at some point, you have to evaluate day-to-day, the real life. Not just the dream we all have, but the *reality. What is the reality of a relationship between a man and a woman, in a specific relationship? Because each person is unique, with their own character and personality. And even with a lot of experience, there's no point where you can say you know everything.*

- Is that where the rational side comes in?

- At that moment, we'll see. Everything will have to be directed toward that one person, or those two people who will have to find their formula, that's unique, to live in harmony, with love and peace. That's where the rational side will also come in. Because, unfortunately, the heart only works in the dream. In the world we live in, it doesn't work completely. Only partially. But you have to experience just the heart to learn that. Or experience a lot of the rational to also understand that it has nothing to do with it. And I think the combination of both should count.

- Have you been through both experiences?

- Yes, I have. That's why I've reached the point where I believe it's a little of each. It's a little of each ingredient that makes the ideal mix. And I haven't gotten there yet.

- Your heart, so admired by physical trainers, stays calm when you reunite with Adriane after a long trip?

- That's a secret.

- Do you usually stay faithful?

- I think that the truth, whatever it is, doesn't hurt because what is true is constant, it's not fleeting. I've been married, I've had serious relationships, even when I was a teenager, at 16 or 17. I've played, had fun, and had relationships that lasted for just one meeting. From all that, I think the temptation in a relationship with a woman is always very strong. But there's a difference between temptation and knowing how to admire beauty, whether it's in a woman's charm, her way of expressing herself, or her physical beauty.

- Even if you're well with someone?

- Even if you're stable, happy with your partner. You can't close yourself off and live only for your partner without

664

noticing what's going on around you. Above all, so you can feel truly confident, sure that the person beside you is the one you really want.

- So, you're not faithful?

- That doesn't mean you have to be unfaithful. Absolutely not. But at the same time, while I'm capable of being faithful, I'm also able to admire beauty. And when my relationship is no longer satisfying me, naturally the need to find something will grow. To the point where you might take the initiative and suddenly find someone else, whether it's for a single time, a few times, or even to completely change partners.

- What is harder for you: rejecting someone or being rejected? What hurts more?

. It's relative. It depends a lot on your involvement with the woman. I would say that there have been situations where it really hurt to say no, but it was necessary. Receiving a no... maybe I'm a privileged guy. That happened when I was younger, more like a child, during adolescence. So I know exactly what it means to hear a no today. But it hurts to say no. I think that what you don't want for yourself, you don't want for someone you admire or like. Suddenly love changes, but affection remains, and it hurts because there is no joy, no satisfaction, in knowing that someone is suffering because of you.

- How do you behave when you're suffering? Do you pray, do more exercise? How do you shake off the sadness?

- It depends. There are moments when the alternative is to focus on your work, or on some other activity within your reach, something that absorbs you. There are times when you absolutely have to deal with the problem, rationalize that part of your heart, and assimilate the reality, whatever it may be. It is a reality.

- Does this also apply to love?

- Even when you're with a woman you like, love, and conclude that she's not going to make you unhappy in the future, and you won't make her unhappy either, the best thing is to change direction. To come to that decision means that you, me in particular, really tried. I'm not someone who changes course easily. However, it has happened to the point where I've decided to stop. I won't insist anymore because everything has its limits, and even though I like her, I have to change.

- Would you name one or more names?

- Absolutely not. That wouldn't be right. But I had the strength to do it, and I think that the strength in these moments comes from clarity, from the combination of the rational and the heart. The heart I know is wonderful, it's amazing, but it has a very short duration, especially having to live in the world we live in. So, there must be the rational. And for that, many times you have to say no, even to yourself. You need the strength to change, to resist the temptation to go back to the pressure. That's tough. But you must be strong. If you're weak, you'll go nowhere.

- In Formula 1 cars, do you balance emotion and reason, or is it purely rational?

- There, it's a lot about the love I have for what I do.

- Which no woman has ever surpassed?

- No. It's something very strong that I've felt since I was 3 or 4 years old."

Hagop, his wife Regina and their son Hagopinho tell us what was happening in F1 in 1994. They were in Imola on the day of the GP: *"We went to watch it in Interlagos, I even told Hagopinho that Ayrton was too fast, he was outpacing the car, and what happened? He was very near his adversary from Benetton! In the second race of the championship, Portuguese racer Pedro Lamy beat him; and the third race was in Imola, where the accident happened. It was the following: Benetton was out of specification, racing with traction control and using the biggest gas inlet cylinder, out of regulation, so when it was time to stop in the pits to fill the tank, it took less time and Ayrton lost one or two seconds. The* active suspension had gone out and Ayrton was fixing the car, which was within the regulations, and he wanted to make the difference on the track. And Benetton's was not, because the Italian racer (Flavio Briatore)... Ever heard of flying too close to the sun? Ayrton flew very close to it, maybe even a little higher. What forced him to go very near his limit was that Benetton was out of regulation and they do not say that, but it was; and because of that, those behind had to work miracles. And he was head! In Interlagos, he was ahead, but he crashed.

When the third race started, in Imola, he was forced to outpace everyone! By the time we passed the pits, when I saw his airfoil, it was absolutely straight! Usually, the airfoil makes an angle to hold the car on the ground, I even took a picture of the airfoil, we saw the car. He went to Williams, which had been very strong in previous years with active suspension, but the FIA regulations changed, by pressure of Balestre! And the car was not set, he had to race more than the limit to keep ahead.

Regina and I went to Italy to watch the race. I got two invitations from another driver, and Regina and I went to the practice session, which was complicated: Barrichello crashed badly and a German died that day, Ratzenberger. Galvão and Reginaldo were also there, and Ayrton left a practice session and went straight ahead, just waved and left. And I thought he was not well and I asked Galvão: Galvão, isn't he okay?

He replied: He is not okay.

Practice ended and we left. The next day we went to the race. We arrived long before the race; when you have the credentials, you can walk around to see the cars. I have pictures, I could not take them, but I did. And Alain Prost was in the pits, we wondered: 'What is Alain Prost doing in Ayrton's pit lane?'.

I looked at his car, I got the impression he was not in the mood to race, but he was under very strong pressure from Benetton. And then, what happened? When the third race arrived, in Imola, wasn't he going to do his best? He was forced to do so!

And we went to the Marlboro paddock, our credentials worked, but I stayed upstairs — there is the ground floor, first floor and second floor — and they were upstairs warming up, which is where they gather, all the drivers were there. When he finished, Ayrton had his overalls tied around his waist and when he came down, he saw me, and came to greet me: Hagop, there you are! When he gave me his hand I felt a cold feeling, a strange thing, and he asked: Where's Regina?

She's downstairs.

And I managed to take a picture when he came to talk to me."

Hagopinho adds: "He was wearing the blue overalls and the Senninha shirt. He got out and went to the car and they went around; a guy crashed again at the start. A new start was made and another driver crashed on the first lap, they say the tire got cold, but the start was made and the guy crashed."

Hagop continues his report: "Then there was another start in the meantime, they say that the tire got cold and as he was on the limit, with the wing too smooth; the car could not possibly hold itself! On the first lap he passed Schumacher, on the second lap he went even further, and I was watching on the television there and suddenly he crashed."

Regina also narrates Ayrton's accident: "Apart from the strong emotions — when we lose a loved one in life, the death of a father, for example — that moment was very difficult. Hagop and I did not stop, we were agitated. The racetrack stopped; it was an absurd silence and nobody knew what had happened, and when it came to reporting, no one spoke. Then I looked at Hagop when they pulled him off the track and he was taken to the hospital, I asked: Hagop, are we going to stay here?

No, we are going to the hospital, he said.

We were not sure about anything; nor did we want to, to be frank. But there were some Italians saying: He is dead, he is dead!

We fought with them: But how can you say this? How? Then we went to the hospital. They opened a large auditorium that they had in the hospital to receive the people who were there."

Hagop continues: *"They broke the news bit by bit, not all at once. They gave the first one, that he was bad, and then came the second one."*

Regina: *"The second bulletin, then by the third time they talked about brain death. They did not talk right away that it was brain death. We went to the hotel and there was no mood to stay there."*

Hagop: *"It destroyed everyone's Sunday! When we learned that Ayrton had died, you had to see the Italians crying! And on Monday we went to the plastics fair, which is our branch, everyone in mourning, everyone! The Italians cried so much."*

Regina: *"When people noticed that we were Brazilians, it was crazy, the guys wanted to grab us! Look, that day at the fair we did not do anything, we did not work, we did not look at anything; every stand we entered, as it is a fair that we know and we have a commercial relationship, no one could talk about anything else, it was not just with us, but it was a shock for everyone."*

Hagop: *"Italy stopped, the Italians loved him, they were waiting to see him race in Ferrari, his dream was to race in Ferrari."*

My uncle José Carlos tells what he knows about the steering column: *"I have a magazine that has a drawn picture of the part of his car that broke down. I worked for many years with national steel material, steel plates, iron; I learned that for everything that is welded on a round shaft, to make something shaped liked a wheel, you have to leave the pipe joint; you cannot make it straight, it needs to bend a little bit.*

And this piece did not have this curve, it was welded on top of the iron, it must have been done quickly, so it must have damaged the material."

Chapter XXX

I was at the farm that GP weekend in Imola. My father and Dadô were watching the race. When I started to hear some background noise, I was curious and went to see what happened: He had crashed the car. I was in shock:

"What do you mean, he crashed the car?"

"It was a really hard hit, and he did not get out of the car," my dad said.

I left the room thinking: "No, nothing will happen to him." I was a little agitated waiting for the news, I did not want to watch, I did not want to see the scene, he could be hurt and I would not be able to see. So I stayed close to the hallway, going around and around to find out the news, until I was informed that they were already taking him to the hospital and there was no sign of him being conscious. I was already thinking about catching the plane and going to see him; if he was hospitalized, I would go there. I knew it was something serious and my impulse was to go to him, wherever he was; I did not say that to anyone, but that was what was going on in my mind, until the news of his death came.

That was a shock, for Brazil and for the world. Can you imagine the situation for those who lived, cheered, lived incredible moments with him? He had been part of our family for a while, so he was part of our life. Everyone was shocked and silent at the time, until it was clear in my mind: "Oh my God, that is why we did not stay together." There, it was the first time I understood. I was very sad, but it was enlightening: That was his fate.

My friend Priscila remembers what she spoke to me that day: *"On the day he died, I was very worried about her and called the farm to find out how Dri was. And she told me she was calm, that she now understood why they had broken up, because it really was not meant to be in this life, and that if they had married and raised a family together, it would have been much worse for her."*

Uncle José Carlos tells us what happened that day on the farm, when the news of the death came: *"I remember there was an accident with Ayrton, and Amilcar and Dadô went to his farm, near that region, to support Milton."*

My father's first action was to call Ayrton's family, to find out where Milton was, to help, and I learned that he was alone in Tatuí. My father and Dadô took the car and went together to see Milton, who had received that news alone. They quickly went to support him. They stayed there until Mrs. Neyde arrived; she went to meet her husband Milton, because they had to be together in that terrible moment. So, with nothing else to do there, with Ayrton's parents safe from the first moment of shock, they left them in their privacy in that moment of so much pain. Back at the farm, my father, shaken, did not tell me anything, just sadly said that Mr. Milton was devastated. I asked my brother-in-law:

"So, Dadô, what happened, what did you say? How was it?"

"Dri, I will tell you what Mr. Milton told us. He said they were already warning Ayrton that the girl he was with was not good for him, and he did not want to believe it. But they got material, proof of what she was up to with another guy; Leonardo went there last week to find his brother and take the evidence that she was deceiving him, with recordings and photos. She was waiting for him at the house in Portugal, they were going to receive some friends, after today's GP, but Ayrton told his father that he was already setting one up for her, he wanted to catch her on the act, alone. And he canceled the schedule with those friends. Dri, this is what was happening this weekend. Last night, Ayrton talked to Mr. Milton about this and what he intended to do; there was also the problem of danger on the racetrack, whether he should race or not. He still unburdened himself in that phone call with Mr. Milton: 'Dad, there is no way, the only honest woman I have been with in my life was Adriane Yamin."

I was totally confused after hearing that unexpected phrase after so many years apart. On the one hand, I was very happy because he talked about me, he remembered me and told his father, in their last conversation. My God! But that showed that we were getting very close to being together again! After so many years of silence, trying to understand. Knowing this was a gift to me and, at the same time, a huge sadness. I did not understand at that time his position regarding me, after all, I had many other qualities that held us together — was honesty the one that most affected him? Honesty is a duty of every decent human being, it is not a virtue, and if that was the virtue he was looking for in a woman, it was more than proven, even to him, that he was insisting on looking in the wrong places. I was kind of disappointed at that point. What about me as a woman? As a companion? And our affinity? That went unanswered for me for a while.

So I can say that my brother-in-law and my father were witnesses of Mr. Milton's last conversation with Beco, who told everything that was happening that last week, what was going on in his life. Many years later, this same episode ended up being reported in Ernesto Rodrigues' book, bringing to light the truth of those days.

"(...) She was getting ready to take a shower and answered, but he wanted to talk to Juracy first:

Juracy, I have a very serious matters to resolve with A (the other one, not me.) That is why nobody is going to Portugal with me tomorrow. No need to prepare that dinner we agreed. And do not pick me up at the airport either.

But who will pick you up, Ayrton?

You give her your car so she can pick me up.

The subject of that serious conversation for which Senna dictated such detailed instructions was known to very few people. According to Braguinha, they were recordings of conversations made on the telephone at Ayrton's apartment in São Paulo. Among the recorded conversations, one of them was between his current girlfriend and her old boyfriend. The contents of this recording were in Imola. It had been taken by Leonardo, who had received a copy and showed it to Ayrton early Saturday night.

Besides Ayrton and Leonardo, at least Braguinha and Galvão Bueno were aware of the tape." Source: *O herói revelado*. Ernesto Rodrigues. Rio de Janeiro: Objetiva, 2004)

I cannot complain, it was a gift to have been remembered by the man who was so important to me, in a decisive and conflicting moment like that, of great distress and yet another disappointment in his personal life. After all, it was not just me who was having trouble replacing him in my life — the reverse was also true.

My niece Isabela, Dadô's daughter, remembers, a few years after Ayrton's death, her father talking at home among his family: "I was little at the time, but I remember that we were at the family's house, in Broa, in São Paulo. Carlos and my father commented with us that Mr. Milton told him that shortly before he died, Ayrton was sad and said that my aunt had been the only woman who loved him for who he was and who really loved him, and he regretted having wronged her so much."

We returned to São Paulo, but I did not want to go to the funeral and I refused to go to the wake, because I thought I had already lived the Beco's mourning, my Beco, I did not want to experience Ayrton's mourning, I had already suffered too much. So I spared myself, I gave myself this right. I did not want to be irritated by the convenient widowhood of others, and I did not want to leave my state of mind; I was sad, but it was okay compared to what I had already faced alone. My worst moment with him had already happened and I did not want to sadden up again, so I tried to stay calm. I wanted to pay my condolences to Mrs. Neyde, to be with her; I was very worried, so my mother and I went to Viviane's house. Mrs.

Neyde asked her to welcome us and we went to pay our respects. The daughter was very shaken. I gave the Federal Police Chief's phone to her, told her that he was a friend of my family and that he had called me, making himself available to them for whatever they needed, to help ease the bureaucracy in whatever it took, to receive the coffin without any unnecessary inconvenience. I saw she was altered, but a little prostrate, it looked like she was taking a strong tranquilizer. Realizing this, my mother wanted to help her, called her homeopath, to get her a natural remedy, which would keep her calm without being prostrate. The doctor took a while to return. I was cold, I was not moved by her sadness. Then, when she said she was going to see a friend, she left and never came back (I only learned during the making of this book that the friend she was taking in her house was Ayrton's ex, the TV presenter); time went by and the doctor did not return about the medicine, so I told my mother to leave it. My worried mother wanted to wait for the doctor return, but I suggested that when he returned, we would provide the medicine and have it delivered or something. We left, I did not go to the funeral, they called us to ask about it, I said I was not going, we had already given our condolences. I watched from the television, cried, got emotional along with my family with all the commotion and expression of love from all Brazilians to that one Brazilian. It really was heartbreaking, and for me it was a finished story, a beautiful story that was now really finished.

A month went by and I got a phone call from a guy called Cristiano, whom I did not know and who I had never heard of, so I do not know how he got my phone number:

"Hi Adriane, how are you? Cristiano speaking. You do not know me, but I was a good friend of Beco's and I used to go to his house a lot, in Angra, in Tatuí, but we did not have the opportunity to get to know each other while you were with him."

I greeted him normally and he continued:

"I am calling you to tell you something I am sure Ayrton wanted to tell you and did not have time."

"Of course! What is it?"

"That the only thing he regretted in his life was doing what he did to you."

"Do you know how long I waited to hear it from him?"

"I can imagine that, that is why I am calling you, I am sure he wanted you to know that."

"Thank you, Cristiano, for your affection."

"Whatever you need. If I can help you with anything, you can call me."

I wrote down his number and name, because I did not know him, but he had brought me such an important message from Beco.

A month after this episode, I wanted news from Mrs. Neyde, but I did not want to call her. I figured there must be a lot of people after her and she must be suffering a lot, heartbroken. As I did not want to bother anyone and since this Cristiano had been so attentive by saying I could call him, I contacted him in search of news about Mrs. Neyde and Mr. Milton:

"Hi Cristiano, how are you? It is Adriane Yamin."

"Hey!"

"Cristiano, you called me a month ago saying I could seek your assistance, so I took the liberty of calling to have news about Mrs. Neyde and Mr. Milton."

"No, I did not call you!"

"Wait, you did call me, that is why I have your phone number."

"No, I did not call you!"

"Cristiano, I don't know you, and you called me introducing yourself, you gave me an important message from Ayrton and gave me your phone number."

"No, I did not call you, I do not remember calling you."

"Alright then. I am just calling you to ask you about Mrs. Neyde. Anyway, the fact is, I have your phone number and your name. I just wanted to hear some news."

I hung up the phone, stunned, and told my parents, I did not understand why a person would do that. I still do not have that answer.

I know that I only saw that same statement by Beco many years later in Ernesto Rodrigues' book, in an account by Cristine Ferracciu that was quoted in this book. And Cristiano called me, but I do not know why he does not remember or says he does not.

Then, on three different occasions that year, when I was on the farm, I scented Ayrton's perfume in the air — it was on three different weekends. The first time, I thought it was just an impression; the second, I had just come out of the shower and when I felt that strong perfume, I got scared; and the third, it was in the hallway of the farm, near the entrance door. Frightened by that, I called my mother, took her to the hallway and she said she also scented the perfume, but that it should be someone else's. I said it was Beco's smell. The following week, she had a mass in his name in a church in São Paulo, and after that I never smelled his scent in the air again.

Epilogue

Years after his death, Mrs. Neyde called me to ask if I would agree to look at a homemade footage taken by Leonardo. As it is a rare relaxed image of Ayrton in his intimacy. In this case, in the environment of my family with his', it would be necessary to authorize its use in the film about his life, which was being produced by Paramount Pictures.

I agreed and received the studio representative at my residence. I watched that unexpected scene of affection and explicit love between the two of us, caught 22 years ago. I immediately remembered what I whispered to him at that moment: *"Beco, you are giving me such goosebumps that I cannot concentrate on the conversation…"*. And he backed off.

That snapped me out of my comfort zone, a safe place I built to be immune to the memories of our love story, which made my soul ache. A poorly finished story, which at that moment, when watching the footage, brought with full force that pure, intense and complete feeling that we had.

I was newly separated at that time, with two children old enough to have an opinion on the matter; therefore, there was no obstacle in my life that prevented me from authorizing the use of that beautiful image! At this point, I also no longer had any illusions about my anonymity regarding the dissemination of the story of Ayrton Senna da Silva, which is undoubtedly linked to my life.

I then authorized the use of the requested image and later I was at the premiere of the film. By "coincidence," for those who believe in it, I found my friend Anna Osta there, who helped and encouraged me to write this book, as a friend who reaches out to help another in the process of healing a wound that remained open for so many years. And there, at that premiere, we decided to start collecting my memories together. I would not have the courage to face this process alone. As such, this is a very suitable time and opportunity to relive, free myself from the past, and start life all over again.

In this outburst of courage, I took advantage of my proximity with Mrs. Neyde and asked her, in case she had still kept the belongings I returned to Beco, such as photos, gifts, etc. at the moment of the breakup, that I would like to get them back for this journey of self-healing. Thanks to this material provided by her, it was possible to tell our love story, with so many details. She agreed and promptly sent them to me, with the following note:

Adriane

_Estou enviado tudo que eu
tinho guardado. Junto também
o relógio que o Beco lhe deu,
e que guardei estes anos todos.
Foi dado a você e só poderia
voltar p/ você. Creia é uma
peso que tira dos meus ombros.
Espero que possa sentir-se melhor.
Abraço_

Nyde

"Adriane,
I am sending you everything I have. I also send you the
watch Beco gave you, which I kept all these years. It was
given to you and could only be given back to you. Believe
me, it is a weight that you take off my shoulders. I hope you
can feel better.
Hugs, Neyde."

What defines our virtue: the intention or the act? Our actions are consequences of our goals. So why, in some situations, does the act become isolated from our desire? Is a well-meaning person virtuous, even if their actions cause pain to those around them? Or is the person who acts involuntarily, even against their interests, virtuous? Regardless of the answers, the fact is that any gesture always reflects what is in our heart and, perhaps, that is why we, human beings, with our idiosyncrasies, are so contradictory in our loving and personal relationships.

Bibliographical References and Image Credits

There were many clippings from newspapers, magazines, notes
in my personal diary and photos provided by:
Amilcar Farid Yamin, Marilene Rocha Yamin, Lenise Rocha
Yamin, Nadia Zarif Yamin, Catarina Zarif Yamin, Francisco
Pereira, Heloisa Abdelnur, Miguel Abdelnur, Marco Yamin,
Renata Belém, Rosangela Martinelli, Hagop Guerekmezian,
Fernando da Rocha Kaiser and Neyde Senna da Silva.

Book:
AYRTON "O herói revelado" by Ernesto Rodrigues. Rio de
Janeiro: Objetiva 2004

Internet:
Website: Instituto Ayrton Senna
https://www.ayrtonsenna.com.br/piloto/formula-
1/temporada-1985/
https://www.ayrtonsenna.com.br/piloto/formula-
1/temporada-1986/
https://www.ayrtonsenna.com.br/piloto/formula-
1/temporada-1987/
https://www.ayrtonsenna.com.br/piloto/formula-
1/temporada-1987/ area H
https://www.areah.com.br/cool/esportes/materia/7960/1/pa
gina_1/top- 10-os-melhores-carros-da-f1.aspx
https://www.youtube.com/watch?v=BleaAWwaiPs
https://youtu.be/8qmLANpT4Lo

Television Reports:
Interviews with Ayrton accessed via YouTube, carried out by
TV Globo.

Translation
Universo Traduções Ltda

Interviewees:

Stela Yamin Salmi, José Carlos Duarte, José Carlos Duarte Filho, Renata Belém, Fernando Kaiser, Rosangela Martinelli, Patrícia da Rocha Kaiser, Marco Yamin, Andrea Yamin Duarte, Nadia Zarif Yamin, Miriam Zarif Yamin, Amilcar Farid Yamin, Lenise Rocha Yamin, Leonardo Yamin Abdo, Marcelo Yamin Abdo, Marcio Yamin, Renata Yamin Queiroz Ferreira, Catarina Zarif Yamin, Monica Yamin, Regina Zarif, Francisco Pereira de Azevedo, Heloisa Abdelnur, Hagop Guerekmezian, Regina Nieto Motta Guerekmezian, Hagop Filho, Carlo Andrea Bauducco, Miguel Abdelnur, Layde Tuono, Isabela Yamin Abdelnur, Clovis Yamin, Reginaldo Leme, Valdevina Oliveira, Denise Farah Vasconcelos, Priscila Mara Seferian Cutrona, Ricardo Prado, Otávio Carrera Torres, Roberta Queiroz Ferreira Olsen.

Speed up, Brazil!

Death interrupts life, possibilities and plans for the future.

Death of a loved one (whoever they are: family, master, friend and/or idol) do not cease the love we feel for them — it often intensifies it.

Therefore, it is correct to say that death dignifies, expands and eternalizes the love we will nurture with the pain of loss and the emptiness of absence that the loved one will leave in our hearts.

But this painful experience can also be liberating, if we know how to channel it towards an ideal of life.

Made in the USA
Monee, IL
21 April 2025

16115569R00395